The GMAT® For Dummies®
4th Edition

P9-CRO-300

M A T H

Data Sufficiency Tips

✔ You won't find any multiple-choice answer choices in this section. The choices are A, if statement 1 alone is sufficient to answer the question; B, if statement 2 alone is sufficient to answer the question; C, if both statements are required; D, if either statement alone is sufficient; or E, if neither statement alone nor both statements together are sufficient. Think of the choices as AB-TEN (A, B, Together, Either, Neither).

✔ Don't work the problem through to the final solution. The goal is to decide whether you *could* solve the question.

✔ Try to predict what info you need; then look to see whether the statements give that info.

✔ Be super-careful to read each statement separately. Don't transfer information from one statement to another.

Problem-Solving Tips

✔ Pay special attention to what the question asks for: Perimeter? Area? And so on.

✔ Before you begin working on the problem, read the answer choices. You may be able to estimate an answer without working out the solution.

✔ When you don't know an answer, don't waste time. Guess quickly and go on.

✔ Plug answer choices into the question to see which one works. Do the easy choices first; you may not have to do the hard ones.

General Tips

✔ Lose the calculator, your own scratch paper, and testing aids. You can't use them on the GMAT.

✔ The GMAT tests algebra, geometry, arithmetic, and some basic statistics concepts. Calculus is not tested.

✔ Memorize formulas before you take the test. The GMAT doesn't provide them.

For Dummies™: Bestselling Book Series for Beginners

The GMAT® For Dummies, 4th Edition

Cheat Sheet

VERBAL

Critical Reasoning Tips

- Many questions ask whether a statement strengthens or weakens an argument, but be on the lookout for these other question styles: identifying a logical conclusion, identifying the assumption, and finding an inference.

- Remember that statements weaken an argument if they

  - destroy its premise
  - show an incorrect cause-and-effect argument
  - overgeneralize
  - argue in a circle
  - cite an inappropriate authority

Analytical Writing Tips

- Schools place different emphasis on this section; find out from your school how important this section is to your admission chances.

- You have 30 minutes to write an essay that analyzes an issue and 30 minutes to write an essay that analyzes an argument. Each essay is worth up to six points.

- Take a few minutes to write an outline before beginning the essay; the outline won't count, but it will organize your thoughts so that you can write more quickly.

- Remember your mission: Develop a position, support that position with well-argued statements, organize paragraphs and thoughts logically, and use proper grammar.

Sentence Correction Tips

- Identify any grammar, usage, diction, sentence construction, and ambiguous or awkward writing errors.

- If you find an error, skip choice A. It is the same as the original sentence.

- Predict a correction and look for it among the answer choices.

- Reread the entire sentence with your new choice inserted to see whether you've fallen for a trap.

Reading Comprehension Tips

- Biological/physical sciences passages are difficult to read. Skim them and do any relatively easy questions that follow them.

- Read social science passages slowly, because the questions ask for "between the lines" info.

- Business passages are very confusing because of their difficult vocabulary and sentence structure. You may want to guess quickly on these and go on.

- Questions are usually asked in the order of the passage: The answer to the first question is often in the first paragraph, and so on.

- Roman numeral and negative/exception questions are time-wasters. Guess quickly and go on.

- You don't have to read an entire passage to answer Detail or Fact questions quickly. Find a key word in the question and skim the passage for it.

IDG BOOKS WORLDWIDE

For Dummies™: Bestselling Book Series for Beginners

The GMAT® FOR DUMMIES®

4TH EDITION

The GMAT® FOR DUMMIES®
4TH EDITION

by Suzee Vlk

IDG
BOOKS
WORLDWIDE

IDG Books Worldwide, Inc.
An International Data Group Company

Foster City, CA ◆ Chicago, IL ◆ Indianapolis, IN ◆ New York, NY

The GMAT® For Dummies, 4th Edition

Published by
IDG Books Worldwide, Inc.
An International Data Group Company
919 E. Hillsdale Blvd.
Suite 400
Foster City, CA 94404
www.idgbooks.com (IDG Books Worldwide Web site)
www.dummies.com (Dummies Press Web site)

Library of Congress Control Number: 00-101151

ISBN: 0-7645-5251-1

Printed in the United States of America

10 9 8 7 6 5 4 3 2 1

4B/QT/QV/QQ/IN

Distributed in the United States by IDG Books Worldwide, Inc.

Distributed by CDG Books Canada Inc. for Canada; by Transworld Publishers Limited in the United Kingdom; by IDG Norge Books for Norway; by IDG Sweden Books for Sweden; by IDG Books Australia Publishing Corporation Pty. Ltd. for Australia and New Zealand; by TransQuest Publishers Pte Ltd. for Singapore, Malaysia, Thailand, Indonesia, and Hong Kong; by Gotop Information Inc. for Taiwan; by ICG Muse, Inc. for Japan; by Intersoft for South Africa; by Eyrolles for France; by International Thomson Publishing for Germany, Austria and Switzerland; by Distribuidora Cuspide for Argentina; by LR International for Brazil; by Galileo Libros for Chile; by Ediciones ZETA S.C.R. Ltda. for Peru; by WS Computer Publishing Corporation, Inc., for the Philippines; by Contemporanea de Ediciones for Venezuela; by Express Computer Distributors for the Caribbean and West Indies; by Micronesia Media Distributor, Inc. for Micronesia; by Chips Computadoras S.A. de C.V. for Mexico; by Editorial Norma de Panama S.A. for Panama; by American Bookshops for Finland.

For general information on IDG Books Worldwide's books in the U.S., please call our Consumer Customer Service department at 800-762-2974. For reseller information, including discounts and premium sales, please call our Reseller Customer Service department at 800-434-3422.

For information on where to purchase IDG Books Worldwide's books outside the U.S., please contact our International Sales department at 317-596-5530 or fax 317-572-4002.

For consumer information on foreign language translations, please contact our Customer Service department at 1-800-434-3422, fax 317-572-4002, or e-mail rights@idgbooks.com.

For information on licensing foreign or domestic rights, please phone +1-650-653-7098.

For sales inquiries and special prices for bulk quantities, please contact our Order Services department at 800-434-3422 or write to the address above.

For information on using IDG Books Worldwide's books in the classroom or for ordering examination copies, please contact our Educational Sales department at 800-434-2086 or fax 317-572-4005.

For press review copies, author interviews, or other publicity information, please contact our Public Relations department at 650-653-7000 or fax 650-653-7500.

For authorization to photocopy items for corporate, personal, or educational use, please contact Copyright Clearance Center, 222 Rosewood Drive, Danvers, MA 01923, or fax 978-750-4470.

is a registered trademark under exclusive license to IDG Books Worldwide, Inc. from International Data Group, Inc.

About the Author

Suzee Vlk

"I'm not a complete idiot. Parts of me are missing."

Although more likely to admit to being a mortician, used-car salesperson, or guinea pig for Army experiments, Suzee Vlk has been a test-prep specialist since 1975, working her way through graduate business school and law school by teaching courses in GMAT, GRE, LSAT, SAT, and ACT preparation. She found the paranoia and take-no-prisoners mind-set required for doing well on the GMAT a big help in developing cutthroat tactics to use in the boardroom or courtroom.

Today Suzee is president of Suzee Vlk Test Prep (no ego involved in *that* company name!) and has taught thousands of students in dozens of courses at universities and private corporations, including "mature" adults who have been out of school for a decade (or two or three) and international students from countries all over the world. (All victims have, so far, survived.) She has written material used in GMAT and SAT preparation software and videos (starring in one set of videos when she was younger and blonder). Her prep books for the GMAT and other standardized exams have been published worldwide.

Suzee currently specializes in one-on-one tutorials and teaches GMAT prep tricks and traps to all levels of students from those who are struggling to remember the basics ("Let's see: A triangle has three sides, or is it four?") to whiz kids who will probably be her boss one day. Her students have not only been accepted at graduate business progams in colleges and universities nationwide, including such dream schools as Harvard and Stanford, but also have done well enough on their GMATs to be awarded scholarships (to the unbounded joy of their parents, who can now spend what's left of their kids' college funds on sailboats, flashy sports cars, and other midlife crisis toys).

Suzee lives by the following motto, which she is delighted to share with you:

"Madness takes its toll. Please have exact change ready."

ABOUT IDG BOOKS WORLDWIDE

Welcome to the world of IDG Books Worldwide.

IDG Books Worldwide, Inc., is a subsidiary of International Data Group, the world's largest publisher of computer-related information and the leading global provider of information services on information technology. IDG was founded more than 30 years ago by Patrick J. McGovern and now employs more than 9,000 people worldwide. IDG publishes more than 290 computer publications in over 75 countries. More than 90 million people read one or more IDG publications each month.

Launched in 1990, IDG Books Worldwide is today the #1 publisher of best-selling computer books in the United States. We are proud to have received eight awards from the Computer Press Association in recognition of editorial excellence and three from Computer Currents' First Annual Readers' Choice Awards. Our best-selling ...For Dummies® series has more than 50 million copies in print with translations in 31 languages. IDG Books Worldwide, through a joint venture with IDG's Hi-Tech Beijing, became the first U.S. publisher to publish a computer book in the People's Republic of China. In record time, IDG Books Worldwide has become the first choice for millions of readers around the world who want to learn how to better manage their businesses.

Our mission is simple: Every one of our books is designed to bring extra value and skill-building instructions to the reader. Our books are written by experts who understand and care about our readers. The knowledge base of our editorial staff comes from years of experience in publishing, education, and journalism — experience we use to produce books to carry us into the new millennium. In short, we care about books, so we attract the best people. We devote special attention to details such as audience, interior design, use of icons, and illustrations. And because we use an efficient process of authoring, editing, and desktop publishing our books electronically, we can spend more time ensuring superior content and less time on the technicalities of making books.

You can count on our commitment to deliver high-quality books at competitive prices on topics you want to read about. At IDG Books Worldwide, we continue in the IDG tradition of delivering quality for more than 30 years. You'll find no better book on a subject than one from IDG Books Worldwide.

John J. Kilcullen

John Kilcullen
Chairman and CEO
IDG Books Worldwide, Inc.

*Eighth Annual
Computer Press
Awards ⪴1992*

*Ninth Annual
Computer Press
Awards ⪴1993*

*Tenth Annual
Computer Press
Awards ⪴1994*

*Eleventh Annual
Computer Press
Awards ⪴1995*

IDG is the world's leading IT media, research and exposition company. Founded in 1964, IDG had 1997 revenues of $2.05 billion and has more than 9,000 employees worldwide. IDG offers the widest range of media options that reach IT buyers in 75 countries representing 95% of worldwide IT spending. IDG's diverse product and services portfolio spans six key areas including print publishing, online publishing, expositions and conferences, market research, education and training, and global marketing services. More than 90 million people read one or more of IDG's 290 magazines and newspapers, including IDG's leading global brands — Computerworld, PC World, Network World, Macworld and the Channel World family of publications. IDG Books Worldwide is one of the fastest-growing computer book publishers in the world, with more than 700 titles in 36 languages. The "...For Dummies®" series alone has more than 50 million copies in print. IDG offers online users the largest network of technology-specific Web sites around the world through IDG.net (http://www.idg.net), which comprises more than 225 targeted Web sites in 55 countries worldwide. International Data Corporation (IDC) is the world's largest provider of information technology data, analysis and consulting, with research centers in over 41 countries and more than 400 research analysts worldwide. IDG World Expo is a leading producer of more than 168 globally branded conferences and expositions in 35 countries including E3 (Electronic Entertainment Expo), Macworld Expo, ComNet, Windows World Expo, ICE (Internet Commerce Expo), Agenda, DEMO, and Spotlight. IDG's training subsidiary, ExecuTrain, is the world's largest computer training company, with more than 230 locations worldwide and 785 training courses. IDG Marketing Services helps industry-leading IT companies build international brand recognition by developing global integrated marketing programs via IDG's print, online and exposition products worldwide. Further information about the company can be found at www.idg.com.   1/24/99

Dedication

This book is dedicated to all of the friends I have made on my travels, people who have dragged me through deserts and across ice floes. Thanks for not leaving me behind.

Liz O'Neill: Soviet Union/Poland

Helen and Roger Hurst: Antarctica

Larna Malone: Greece/Turkey

Donna Wender/Larry Jarchow: Nepal/India

Janie Marty: Bulgaria

Steve Wiley and Patricia Sandor: Peru

Tim Ballistros: Hong King/Singapore/Thailand

Betty and Lucky Henner (and of course, Edna): China

Deb Risching: Argentina

Mark Ridgeway: Australia/New Zealand

Michael Sanderson: Scotland/Ireland/Wales/England

Kelly Robbins: Romania

Judy Sullivan Folsom: Christ Church, Oxford

Author's Acknowledgments

After years of having California students groan at my puns, make rude hand gestures in response to my scintillatingly clever quips, and threaten to storm out of the classroom if I tell my geometry jokes one more time, it's wonderful to get the chance to inflict my dysfunctional sense of humor on a worldwide, unsuspecting audience. The decline of civilization begins here.

Thanks to my agents, Bill Gladstone and Matt Wagner, of Waterside Productions in Cardiff, California, for getting me this opportunity. A panegyric and paean for my project editor, Sherri Fugit, my acquisitions editor, Karen Hansen, my copy editor, Donna Frederick, and past editors as well, not only for their erudition but also for their effervescence and ebullience that didn't flag even under deadlines. Many thanks also go to Mark Butler, Kristin Cocks, Jennifer Ehrlich, and Linda Stark.

Thanks to independent college counselor Jill Q. Porter of La Jolla, California, for her up-to-the-minute insights about what college and university programs seek.

And thanks as always to my students over the years, those wonderful young and not-so-young adults who have had enough faith in me to use my tricks and tips and enough kindness to let me share their joy in the good scores that result. You all keep this fun.

Publisher's Acknowledgments

We're proud of this book; please register your comments through our IDG Books Worldwide Online Registration Form located at http://my2cents.dummies.com.

Some of the people who helped bring this book to market include the following:

Acquisitions and Editorial

Project Editor: Sherri Fugit
Previous Editions: Colleen Rainsberger, Barb Terry, Jennifer Ehrlich

Associate Acquisitions Editor: Karen Hansen
Previous Editions: Mark Butler

Copy Editor: Donna Frederick
Previous Edition: Linda Stark

Technical Editor: Marcy Denmark Manning

Editorial Managers: Jennifer Ehrlich, Kristin Cocks

Media Development Manager: Heather Heath Dismore

Editorial Assistant: Laura Jefferson

Production

Project Coordinator: Regina Snyder

Layout and Graphics: Mary Jo Richards, Janet Seib

Proofreaders: Corey Bowen, Paula Lowell, Marianne Santy, Charles Spencer

Indexer: Ty Koontz

Special Help

Melissa Bluhm, Laura Jefferson, Carol Strickland

General and Administrative

IDG Books Worldwide, Inc.: John Kilcullen, CEO

IDG Books Technology Publishing Group: Richard Swadley, Senior Vice President and Publisher; Walter R. Bruce III, Vice President and Publisher; Joseph Wikert, Vice President and Publisher; Mary Bednarek, Vice President and Director, Product Development; Andy Cummings, Publishing Director, General User Group; Mary C. Corder, Editorial Director; Barry Pruett, Publishing Director

IDG Books Consumer Publishing Group: Roland Elgey, Senior Vice President and Publisher; Kathleen A. Welton, Vice President and Publisher; Kevin Thornton, Acquisitions Manager; Kristin A. Cocks, Editorial Director

IDG Books Internet Publishing Group: Brenda McLaughlin, Senior Vice President and Publisher; Sofia Marchant, Online Marketing Manager

IDG Books Production for Dummies Press: Debbie Stailey, Director of Production; Cindy L. Phipps, Manager of Project Coordination, Production Proofreading, and Indexing; Tony Augsburger, Manager of Prepress, Reprints, and Systems; Laura Carpenter, Production Control Manager; Shelley Lea, Supervisor of Graphics and Design; Debbie J. Gates, Production Systems Specialist; Robert Springer, Supervisor of Proofreading; Kathie Schutte, Production Supervisor

Dummies Packaging and Book Design: Patty Page, Manager, Promotions Marketing

◆

The publisher would like to give special thanks to Patrick J. McGovern, without whom this book would not have been possible.

◆

Contents at a Glance

Table of Contents

. . . .

Introduction

Welcome to *The GMAT For Dummies,* 4th Edition. Don't take the title personally. You're no dummy; you're normal. Unfortunately, the GMAT is anything *but* normal. As I found out in more than two decades of fighting the GMAT wars, the GMAT has no connection to the Real World. When you were given the dire news that you had to take the GMAT to get into graduate business school, you probably flashed back to the SAT (lovingly known as Sadists Against Teenagers) that you had to take to get into college. While the exams have some similarities (both are the leading causes of ulcers, migraines, and decisions to become a Bora Bora beachcomber), you will find even more dissimilarities.

The first dissimilarity has to do with how familiar you are with the material. In high school, instructors often "teach to the test." They know that their students are going to take the SAT, know the kids themselves, and teach them what will be on the test and how to take the exam. In college, you're on your own. Your professors may not have any idea who you are ("The kid in the *I'm only here for the beer* T-shirt who sits in the upper row of the lecture hall? In my mind I call him Bud, but I don't know him at all.") and almost certainly is not going to take time away from class to discuss the tricks and traps on the GMAT. In addition, you have spent the last few years of college working on the courses specific to your major: invertebrate biology, lifestyles of the upper Botswana natives, or sociological and psychological implications of domestic dissonance. It's been a long, long time since you've taken basic algebra, geometry, and arithmetic (found in the math portions of the exam), or English and logic (found in the verbal portions of the exam). And what about those of you who are no longer in college? I, for one, entered college in the days of parchment and quills but didn't get around to taking the GMAT until the era of laptops and battery packs. No doubt about it: You need some help. And a specialist best provides the skills you need. Think of this book as a SWAT team that you can call in when the situation gets desperate.

Like a SWAT team, this book aims to deal with the crisis efficiently, do the job, save the day, and get you out as quickly as possible. I know that you have a life you'd like to get back to. The goal of this book is to help you learn what you need and can use on the GMAT — period. No extra garbage is thrown in to impress you with esoteric facts; no filler is added to make this book the fattest one on the market. If you need a doorstop, go pick up the New York City telephone directory. If you need a quick 'n' easy guide to surviving the GMAT, you're in the right place.

Why You Need This Book

It's Us versus Them. Who are They? The creators of the GMAT, those gnomes in green eyeshades. Imagine the effect you'd have at a cocktail party if you answered the typical question, "So, what do you do for a living?" with the response, "I create questions for the GMAT." What a conversation stopper! If you are a GMAT creator, just make sure that no one knows where you live. . . .

You can't avoid the GMAT torture if you intend to go to graduate business school. More and more graduate business schools are emphasizing GMAT scores to compensate for the grade inflation that skews GPAs (grade point averages). Because an *A* from Genius U is not the same as an *A* from Merely Mediocre College, schools need a standardized mode for comparing students. Believe it or not, that's good news for you. By doing well on this test, you can overcome years of goofing off in school. A dynamite GMAT score can get you into a graduate school that otherwise wouldn't look at you and your *C*+ GPA (or lower).

In *The GMAT For Dummies,* 4th Edition, I show you how to approach each type of question, recognize the traps that are built into the questions, and master the tricks that help you avoid those traps. The book is full of "Gotchas!" that I (a test prep tutor since the Dawn of Time) have seen students fall for repeatedly. In this book, you learn to think the GMAT way (don't worry; it's not permanent) to identify the point behind the various styles and types of questions and what each is trying to test. This book also gives you a review of the basics (math formulas, grammar rules, and essay-writing suggestions) along with a laugh or two to make learning the material as painless as possible.

Note to nontraditional students: As I mentioned before, I'm aware of the fact that some of you are not 21-year-old college seniors taking this exam to go into graduate business school right after college. You may have been out of college so long that your *children* are 21-year-old seniors! Maybe you've just decided to go to graduate business school now after a long career or after raising a family, and you need help getting back into math and verbal stuff that you had in what seems like another lifetime. I sympathize with you; it's tough to deal with nonagons, quadratic equations, and indefinite pronouns again. Don't despair; you can get outside help, especially in math, which is one of the first things to go for most people when they get away from school. Call a community college or even a high school to help you find a tutor or suggest a quick review course in your area. You can also call your local library for assistance. The math on this exam doesn't exceed what is taught in upper-division, high school math classes, depressing as that may seem to you as you sweat through it.

How to Get Your Money's Worth Out of This Book

If you use this book just to prop open a window or as a booster seat for a toddler, you won't get the best out of it. I suggest two alternatives:

- ✔ **Fine-tune your skills.** Turn to specific sections for specific information and help. The organization of the book makes it easy to find the type of math question you always have trouble with, suggestions for answering reading questions without having finished the passage, and tricks for guessing. If you are in college classes or in a career in which you use this jazz every day (maybe you're a math major at school or teach high school English classes) and need just a nudge in one or two areas, you can work through those sections only.

- ✔ **Start from scratch.** Read through the whole book. Actually, this is what I'd like you to do. No matter how well you do on a section, you can improve. It's a common mistake to believe that you should work on your weakest sections only. The 5 points you gain in your mediocre section by skimming through the suggestions in this book are just as worthwhile as the 5 points you get by grunting and groaning and sweating through the most difficult portions. If you have the time, do yourself a favor and read the book from cover to cover. Besides, you don't want to miss any of my jokes, now do you?

The GMAT For Dummies, 4th Edition, is simple and straightforward enough for first-time GMAT victims, er, students, so that they can understand the entire exam and do well right out of the starting gate. But it's also detailed and sophisticated enough so that veterans — those of you who have taken the exam once or twice before but aren't resting on your laurels (sounds painful, anyway) — can learn the more complicated information you need to get those truly excellent scores.

To help you to get through this book more quickly, I include some icons that flag the particularly important stuff. If you tend to fall for every trap, for example, flip through the book to find the trap icons. The icons look like the following:

The test makers throw in some nasty traps that may get you if you don't think about the questions carefully. Learn the tricks marked by this icon and you'll be amazed at how easily you can outsmart the GMAT.

This icon points out information pertaining to international students and suggestions that can make life easier for those of you for whom English is a second or third language.

This icon directs you to tips that should make taking the GMAT go much more smoothly. These tips alone are worth the price of this book. Trust me.

This icon marks sample problems that appear in the lectures.

Be wary of the important stuff that this icon points out to you. If you skip these sections, I claim no responsibility for what may happen to you.

Pardon Me for Having a Life: Who Has Time for This?

You have school or work, sports or other hobbies, family responsibilities, and, oh yes, a social life. How on earth are you going to fit in studying for the GMAT?

Time required to go through the GMAT lectures

Buying this book was brilliant. (Okay, so your roommate, your spouse, or some significant other bought it and tossed it at you with the snide comment that "Hey, you can sure use all the help you can get." Whatever.) How much time should you take to go through this book? I suggest 26 hours.

Each subject (Reading Comprehension, Critical Reasoning, Sentence Correction, Data Sufficiency, Problem Solving, and Analytical Writing) includes a lecture on the format, approach, and tricks and traps for that particular type of question. A quiz chapter featuring practice questions that test what you learned in the lecture follows each lecture. The detailed answer explanations point out the traps you may have fallen for and the tips you should have used to avoid the traps. You learn which questions to guess at quickly (as either too hard or too time-consuming) and which are worth investing more time in. It should take you about two hours per lecture, including the quiz. The book also includes a three-part math review; each section (geometry, algebra, and arithmetic) should take roughly one hour, for a total of three hours. A basic grammar review takes one hour.

Time required to go through the practice GMATs

At the end of the book are two full-length GMATs. Each exam takes three and a half hours to complete (not including the two ten-minute breaks you can give yourself) and about another hour to an hour and a half to review. My thinking that you should take an hour and a half to review the exam does not reflect a lack of confidence in you. (I have the utmost respect for anyone intelligent enough to purchase this book.) I'm not saying that you're going to miss a lot of questions. You need the time because I suggest that you review *all* the answer explanations, including those dealing with the questions that you answer correctly. You'll learn some good stuff there; you'll review formulas, find shortcuts, and see more tricks and traps. I'll exaggerate and say that the whole test and review should take you six hours. The following table gives you what I think is a reasonable timetable.

Activity	*Time*
6 lectures at 2 hours per lecture	12 hours
2 exams at 5 hours per exam (including review)	10 hours
3 math review chapters at 1 hour per chapter	3 hours
1 grammar review	1 hour
Time spent laughing hysterically at author's jokes	5 minutes
Time spent composing letter complaining about author's crummy jokes	5 minutes
TOTAL	26 hours, 10 minutes

No one expects you to read this book for 26 hours straight. Each unit is self-contained. The answer explanations may remind you of things from other units, because repetition aids learning and memorizing, but you can read through each unit separately from the others.

Are you ready? Stupid question. Are you resigned? Have you accepted your fate that you're going to take the GMAT no matter what and you may as well have fun studying for it? Take a deep breath, turn the page, and go for it. Here's hoping that for you, GMAT comes to stand for Genius Masters A Test!

Part I
An Aerial View: Putting the GMAT into Perspective

The 5th Wave   By Rich Tennant

"Ah, we're in luck - the Admissions Director is in."

In this part . . .

1 know, I know — the only aerial view you'd like to have of the GMAT is the one you see from 10,000 feet as a jet takes you far, far away from this exam. Use the info in this book correctly and you can ace the GMAT, go to a top grad school, get a great job — and then buy your own private jet and buzz the office of that college guidance counselor who told you your best chance at a good life would be to marry rich. Hey, it's something to aim for (the goal, not the college counselor!).

You're probably eager to get right into studying for the GMAT (or maybe not), but take a few minutes to go through this introductory material. It's good strategy to find out everything you can about your enemy before going into battle.

Chapter 1

The CAT Scan: What the GMAT Looks Like

●●●

In This Chapter

▶ Understanding the format: The number and types of questions

▶ Timing it right

▶ Doing the Backpack Boogie: What to take to the test with you

▶ Dealing with unusual circumstances

▶ Scoring the test

▶ Repeating the test

●●●

*P*ut down your pencils and grab your keyboards: The GMAT has gone high-tech. Since October 1, 1997, the GMAT is given on computer only. No more paper-and-pencil tests are available. Table 1-1 shows the breakdown of the computerized GMAT.

Table 1-1	An Overview of the GMAT Computer Adaptive Test	
Section	*Number of Questions*	*Time Allotted*
Analytical Writing Assessment	2	1 hour (30 minutes per topic)
Quantitative (math) questions	37	75 minutes
Verbal questions	41	75 minutes

The CAT has no separate *experimental* section of unscored questions, as the old paper-and-pencil test had. The CAT still has experimental questions, questions that don't count (the test-makers are fine-tuning questions that may show up on future exams; you're serving as the guinea pig), but the experimental questions are mixed in and are part of the 37 or 41 questions. You will not know which questions count and which don't. The number of unscored questions varies.

All Mixed Up: The Question Order

In the good old days of paper-and-pencil testing, every question type was in its own little niche. That is, you had one section that had all Problem Solving math questions, and two sections that had all Data Sufficiency questions (don't worry if you don't know what those names mean or those question styles are; excruciatingly detailed explanations are given later in this book). Now, the test has only one division for math and another division for verbal questions.

All the math questions are jumbled together in the quantitative section. That is, you may have two Problem Solving questions, then two Data Sufficiency questions, then three Problem Solving questions, then two Data Sufficiency questions, and so on.

All the verbal questions are jumbled together in the verbal section. You may whet your appetite by beginning with two Sentence Correction questions, then have two Critical Reasoning questions, and then a reading passage with several reading questions following it. While you will see only one Reading Comprehension question on-screen at a time, all the Reading Comprehension questions for a particular passage follow one another. In other words, you won't have three Reading Comprehension questions, then two Sentence Correction questions, and then two more Reading Comprehension questions based on the passage.

The Analytical Writing Assessment consists of two topics. You write a 30-minute essay on each. (Yes, you do write the essays on computer, not by hand, although you can use scratch paper to make an outline or jot down some notes to clear your fevered brain. More about these essays in Chapter 3.) Obviously, you don't select a multiple-choice answer in this portion, but you compose the essays right on your computer, as if you were doing a report for school or writing a letter to a friend.

Gimme a Break: The GMAT Intermission

You are entitled to take two breaks. One break of about five minutes comes after you have written the two essays. The other break — usually only one or two minutes — is between the quantitative and verbal sections. You don't have to take these breaks . . . but you may as well stand up, stretch, and get something to drink.

Bill Gates I'm Not: Help for the Computer Illiterate

What if you've never so much as touched a computer in your life? Not to fear. All you need are some basic typing skills — and even those can be of the hunt-and-peck, one-finger type. The computer screen shows a Help button that gets a lot of workout by students. That button will be available to you at any time during the entire test. When you push the Help button, most of your questions (about using the computer, not about the GMAT!) will be answered.

Before you begin taking the test, you will have a tutorial on the computer that takes you through the basic steps. The tutorial covers how to type a response, how to use a mouse, how to go on to the next question — all the basics you need to get by. You do not, I repeat, do *not* need to know anything about computers.

Incidentally, for those of you who are as spelling-challenged as I am, bad news: The software used for the essays is a very simple word processing program that has a cut-and-paste feature but no spell checker. If you're not sure how to spell a word, do yourself a favor and just choose another word.

Don't worry about being clumsy and accidentally marking the wrong answer by clicking the mouse at the wrong time. After you use the mouse to point to and click on the oval of your choice (the ovals are not marked A, B, C, D, E, but just left blank), you must point to and click on the Confirm button before you move on to the next question. Who says there are no second chances in life?

It's a Date: When Can I Take the Test?

Unlike the old paper-and-pencil test for which you had to register long in advance, the new computer adaptive test can be scheduled just a few days in advance. Students in the United States and Canada can register for the test by calling 1-800-GMATNOW. (Students in other countries should check with their colleges or universities for the number to call in their locations.) Of course, you want to be sure you call early enough to be able to meet the deadlines and to reserve a spot at your local testing center, but usually, scheduling isn't a problem.

The GMAT CAT is offered three weeks a month, six days a week. You can take it at one of about 400 computer-based testing centers. These centers are at schools (colleges and universities), offices of ETS (Educational Testing Service), and at private businesses (the Sylvan Technology Centers). Many computer centers are located overseas as well. In short, taking the CAT is relatively convenient; you are probably close to a testing center and can schedule the test for whenever you want. This flexibility is especially great for those people who are not "morning people," who would suffer if they had to take the test at the traditional 8:30 a.m. starting time. Now, if the center is open and available, night owls can take the test at midnight and get the maximum performance from their nocturnal brains.

You can call a test center and schedule an appointment for a practice CAT, an Official Computer GMAT that will not count. I strongly recommend you do so, just to make yourself comfortable with the format and to quiet your nerves. There's nothing like a dress rehearsal to make you less anxious during the actual performance.

I have even more good news. Because you probably will take the test in separated sections, like the carrels of a library, you will have a little more peace and privacy than you would in a regular classroom in which the desks are in rows.

Sign Me Up: How Do I Register for the GMAT CAT?

College counseling offices in your area probably have the GMAT information and application bulletin which gives the particulars of registering. If you can't get the bulletin, call 609-771-7330 to have one sent to you for free. You can register by calling 1-800-GMATNOW. Or if you want to get into the computer groove right away, you can register online by going to this site: www.gmat.org.

Appearances Count: What Does the CAT Look Like?

The computer shows you one question at a time. The first question is of medium difficulty. If you answer it correctly, your score goes up considerably, and you get a harder question. If you answer the first question incorrectly, your score goes down, and the computer reduces the difficulty level. This process (getting higher scores and more difficult questions after correct answers and the opposite for incorrect answers) continues throughout each section of the exam. The jumps in score and difficulty level are more dramatic at the beginning of each section. Toward the end of each section, you will probably be at a level at which you are answering about half of the questions correctly. At this stage, the computer will be making only minor adjustments in score and difficulty level.

You get a little more time per question than you would have on a paper-and-pencil test. Be sure to use this time wisely. You cannot go back and change your answers. Let me repeat that comment, because it is extremely important. You cannot go back and change an answer. After you have confirmed an answer, it's chiseled in stone.

It bears repeating that you sloppy typists need not panic about abusing and misusing the computer mouse. If you mark the wrong oval, you may change your answer before hitting the Confirm button.

Because the jumps in score are more dramatic at the beginning of each section, you must be extremely careful on the first five questions. Take as much time as you need on these questions; do everything you can to make sure that you are correct. If you answer the first five questions in a section correctly, the computer will have you well above the 700 level (of course, to achieve that score, you have to do comparably well on the other 75-minute section) and will give you hard questions for the rest of the exam. You should rejoice if you see hard questions even if you feel that you are answering many of them incorrectly. Your score is determined primarily by the level you reach, not by the number of correct answers.

Don't become obsessed with this information! You don't want to go overboard in monitoring your performance by trying to gauge the difficulty level of every question. Don't worry if you suddenly get what you think is an easy question. The question may actually be difficult for most normal people, but easy for a super-brain like yourself — especially after you've used this book for prepping for the test! Alternatively, you may think the question is easy because you are falling right into a trap. A third possibility is that the question may be one of the unscored or experimental ones and is there for the test-makers to measure exactly how difficult the question is. As you recall, the unscored questions — which you will not be able to identify — are scattered throughout the normal, scored questions.

If you slip up and miss one early question, you can still reel off a series of correct answers, show that your mistake was a fluke, and get to the harder questions. However, if you miss many of the first five questions, the computer will have you at around the 400 level or lower, and you will get easy questions for the rest of the exam. These later, easy questions will not be worth enough points to raise your score to a level that will make you competitive at the more prestigious business schools. You may answer all these easy questions correctly, but your test will be over by the time the computer raises the difficulty level to the high-score range.

Skipping

You may not skip a question. The computer will not budge until you put down an answer. Given that earlier questions contribute more toward your score than do later questions, you will typically want to keep working through a question early in the test until you come up with an answer that makes you happy (or at least content). However, you will be penalized if you do not make it to the end of the exam, so go ahead and guess if a question is serving as a brick wall and preventing you from making decent progress. (This strategy is the CAT equivalent of skipping.) Also, work through this book. You will have a better idea of which questions tend to drive you nuts and are candidates for a quick guess. When time is short, you may have to guess wildly on the remaining questions, regardless of the content, to ensure that you make it to the end.

Scoring

After you finish, you have the option of seeing your unofficial score (which, barring some complete computer malfunction, is very likely to be identical to your final, official score) or canceling it. You cannot, however, decide to cancel the score once you have seen it, so think carefully about how you feel you've done. You can also at this point select additional schools to which you would like your GMAT scores sent (you probably selected some when you first signed up for the exam).

Your official score will be mailed to you within about two weeks of the test. This score also arrives at the business schools in about two weeks, illustrating yet another advantage of the CAT over the traditional paper-and-pencil test: It's easier for you procrastinators to beat deadlines.

Your Brain: Don't Leave Home Without It (And Other Things to Take to the GMAT)

Take your brain down from the shelf, dust it off, and take it to the test with you. In addition, you may want to tote along a few more items, such as the following:

- ✔ **Map or Directions.** Be sure that you know how to get to the test center. Drive to the test site a few days in advance and check out how long the drive takes you, where to park, and so on. The last thing you need the morning of the test is more stress.

- ✔ **Photo ID.** You must take a photo ID with you. This photo cannot be one of you when you were young, blond, perky, and gorgeous, but instead must be a current, recognizable photograph (shoulders drooping, eyes glazed over from studying for this test). You may take, for example, a driver's license, a military ID, a passport, or an employee ID card with a photograph. A social security card, credit card, or library card won't cut it (even if the card does have your photo on it).

- ✔ **Pencils.** Take two, three, or a dozen sharpened number two pencils with you. Take a small pencil sharpener and a good eraser as well (for the *remote* chance that you're not perfect after all). Why do you need pencils for a computer exam? You are allowed to use scratch paper, which will be helpful for jotting down notes about your essays, making ovals for eliminating answers in math questions, and so on. These individual strategies are discussed in the lectures later in this book.

- ✔ **Clothes.** You signed up for the special Nude GMAT, you say? Well, everyone else should remember to take a few extra layers. Test centers are notorious for being either freezing cold or boiling hot. While you may have clammy hands and cold feet when you begin the test, by the time you get really cranking on it, you may work up a sweat. Be prepared for anything.

What Not to Take to the Test with You

Besides your dreams, hopes, goals, and aspirations, several things are not allowed in the GMAT testing room.

- ✔ **Books and notes.** Forget about last-minute studying. You aren't allowed to take books or notes into the room. If you don't know the material by then, you never will.

- ✔ **Scratch paper.** The proctor at the test center will provide you with scratch paper. It will obviously come in handy on the math, but you should also use it to summarize reading passages, jot down the key error on certain sentence correction items, and take note of the key logical connections on critical reasoning questions. When you are reading the general directions for each test section (before the clock starts), jot down several columns of the numbers 1 through 5. You should often use these columns to eliminate incorrect answers. For example, if you are sure that the first, third, and fourth choices (you won't have the letters A through E as you do on paper-and-pencil tests, just blank ovals, like Lil' Orphan Annie's eyes) are incorrect, cross them out on your scratch paper and then concentrate on the second and fifth choices. Use a fresh column for each question. While you are not allowed to bring in books or other study aids, feel free to use the test instruction time to write down key formulas, strategies, and mnemonic devices. In other words, perform a brain dump of all that last minute stuff you crammed into your cerebellum as you entered the test site.

✔ **Calculator.** You are not allowed to use a calculator on the exam. Those of you who grew up before calculators were common and learned your times tables have a definite advantage here over those young whippersnappers who can't add 2 + 2 without dragging out the calculator.

✔ **Watch.** The computer screen includes a clock, which may be turned on and off throughout the test except for the last five minutes of a section during which it will always stay on. Be sure to turn off the onscreen clock as you work through the first five questions of a section. As I will say again and again until you're so exasperated you're ready to cut off my air supply, the first five questions are key. You do not want a clock ticking down to force you (at least subconsciously) to rush through these questions.

Isn't That Special? Unusual Circumstances

Dare to be different. If you have a special circumstance, you can have a slight change in your GMAT. If you have a learning disability (no, that doesn't include being bored and frustrated), for example, you may be able to get additional testing time. Here is a brief list of special circumstances and what to do about them.

Learning disabilities

These can range from Attention Deficit Disorder to dyslexia and all sorts of other things. To find out whether you qualify for a disabilities waiver of any sort, read the incredibly fine print in the registration bulletin. Your college counselor may be able to help you fill out the appropriate form.

Physical disabilities

The GMAT tries hard to accommodate everyone. People can get Braille tests or large print tests, can have test readers or recorders, interpreters, and so on. You can get the information about what are considered disabilities and how they can change your taking the GMAT in the GMAT Information and Registration Bulletin.

Financial difficulties

The GMAT does *not* waive test fees. If you have difficulty paying fees, talk to your college counselor. Your university may have a program that can help you with the fees.

I wish it were all Greek to me: A welcome to international students*

Students the world over take the GMAT in order to attend American business schools. I've taught GMAT prep courses that had students from Brazil, Taiwan, the Ivory Coast, Egypt, Japan — all over the globe. When I got my own MBA, my courses were enriched by the contributions of students from Korea, Hong Kong, Saudi Arabia, the Netherlands, and Mexico. To all of you readers from other nations, welcome!

As international students, you have strengths and weaknesses that are different from those of American students; therefore, the focus of your study should be different as well. Here are my suggestions to help you get the most out of this book and to help you do your best on the actual GMAT:

✔ **Concentrate on Sentence Correction.** You probably have an advantage over American students on this style of question, believe it or not. You have learned the proper grammar, have been tested on the rules, and have used correct English in your speaking and writing. American students (myself included) not only use slang and substandard English, but also listen daily to others doing the same. Unfortunately, after we hear something often enough, it sounds correct. For example, in your English classes you probably have studied the subjunctive form and know that "I wish I were" is correct usage. Native speakers usually argue in favor of "I wish I was." Your superior knowledge of the technicalities of English grammar can help you score big points on the Sentence Correction style of question.

✔ **Chill Out about Reading Comprehension.** The GMAT's reading passages are long, hard, and b-o-r-i-n-g. They are difficult enough to understand for people who grew up speaking and reading English, and are totally demoralizing for people who didn't. My suggestion is that you not obsess over the Reading Comprehension. When you are taking the CAT, you have to answer every single question; you can't leave any blank. However, if you encounter a reading passage that is absolutely bewildering to you, fill in the answers quickly so that you can go on to the next questions. Remember that different question types are scattered throughout a section. After the Reading Comp questions, you'll get some Sentence Correction or Critical Reasoning questions, which may be easier for you. While you, of course, want to get as much of the reading right as you can, you don't want to spend so much time on one passage that you don't get to the other types of questions.

✔ **Concentrate on the math, especially geometry.** While you do get separate verbal and math scores, many business schools concentrate on your overall or combined score. Doing extremely well on math can compensate for weaker verbal skills. I suggest that you pay particular attention to the geometry problems. They rarely are "word problems" — questions that require a lot of reading. Geometry problems usually feature figures that you can easily understand and you can use to answer the questions even if English is not your strongest suit.

* **NOTE:** A paper-and-pencil test may be offered at overseas locations that have not yet developed computer-testing facilities. Check with your local university to find out whether you have the option of taking a paper-and-pencil test. (These locations are rare.)

Everyone Wants to Score High

You don't have the Ferrari yet (if you do, and you are a single, eligible male, please write to me care of the publisher). You don't have the six-digit paycheck yet (please see parenthetical comment supra). It's rough being 21 (or 25 or 30). You need something to boast about. How about your GMAT scores? GMAT scores are to would-be graduate students what salaries are to those people out there in the Real World. Students brag about them, exaggerate them, or try to impress others with them. How are your scores figured?

How scores are determined

The GMAT has four separate scores: verbal, quantitative (math), total, and analytical writing. The verbal and the math scores range from 0 to 60; very few people get scores below 10 or above 46. The total score, which is based on both verbal and math, ranges from 200 to 800. The analytical writing score goes from 0 (lowest) to 6 (highest). The writing score is the average of four evaluators' reviews of your two writing samples. (More detailed info on the writing score is given in the Analytical Writing Assessment Lecture.)

Before you spend a great deal of time studying one particular section (panicking over the grammar, for example), find out from the universities to which you are applying just which scores are emphasized. You may be pleasantly surprised to find that a school cares more about the math score, less about the verbal score, not at all about the analytical writing score, and so on. Some schools look only at the total score, which would allow you to do very well in some sections and completely blow off the others. *Find out your school's focus before beginning your study program!*

How you win — and lose — points

When you answer a question correctly, your score goes up, and you get a harder question. When you answer incorrectly, your score goes down, and you get an easier question. Your score is determined by the difficulty level that you reach.

Scores change dramatically at first as the computer finds the test-taker's general level. Because of the big jumps that occur at the beginning, be as careful as possible on the first five questions. By the end of the exam, most test-takers (except those scoring at the 200 or 800 extremes) will find themselves answering about half of the questions correctly, going up or down about ten points with each question.

Does a good GMAT score make me a nerd?

No. It makes you an applicant for a great graduate school, a success in a high-profile career, and ultimately a gazillionaire with the best car and hottest spouse at your 20th college reunion. Plan ahead.

What is a good score?

On recent exams, approximately 50 percent of the people got a score of 32 or better on the verbal and quantitative portions (remember the verbal and quantitative scores range from 0 to 60). The total score averaged 500. That is, half of the people got a 500 or better, and half of the people got below 500. Your individual goals should depend on which grad schools you are applying to and what GPA *(grade point average)* you have. There's no such thing as a passing or failing score — only what you need to get accepted by the college you have your heart set on.

Number of correct answers needed for specific scores

The first question is worth approximately 100 points. Answer it correctly, and your score is around 600. Miss that first question, and your score is around 400. The second question is worth 70 points or so.

- ✔ If you answer the first two questions correctly, your score is approximately 670.
- ✔ Answer the first correctly and the second incorrectly, and you'll be looking at a score of 530.

✔ Answer the first question incorrectly and the second correctly, and you'll have a score of 470.

✔ Miss both of the first two questions and your score starts at 330.

The scoring possibilities become far more numerous as you start factoring in subsequent questions, but you can see that you are well above 700 after answering the first five questions correctly and well below 300 if you answer the first five incorrectly. The rest of the test simply fine-tunes your score. Because the first five questions do a good job of determining test-takers' general ability, most test-takers will find themselves producing a pattern such as this: miss a question, get an easier question and answer it correctly, get a harder question and answer it incorrectly, and so on.

Guess for success: Intelligent guessing strategy

You must be certain to get to every question on the GMAT CAT. You are penalized for questions you don't reach, so if you have to guess, even guess wildly, to get to the end, do so. You can use these basic, guessing guidelines:

✔ If you have 6 to 10 questions to go with less than 5 minutes left, stop trying to figure everything out. Quickly eliminate what you can and make an educated guess.

✔ If you have 11 or more questions to go with under 5 minutes left, start making wild guesses until you get to the final question.

✔ Use all your remaining time on the final question. While you may hit the Confirm button after time runs out, you may not change your selected oval after time runs out.

Of course, even before the end of the exam, you may want to make a few guesses. If a question is making you crazy and eating up time, guess so that you can get to the next question. Keep in mind that the computer doesn't move on until you give an answer.

Déjà vu all over again: Repeating the test

Should you repeat the test? Before you decide, ask yourself the following questions:

✔ **Am I repeating the test to get a certain minimum qualifying score or just to satisfy my ego?** If you have your heart set on a particular graduate school that requires a minimum GMAT score, you may want to take the test again and again and again until you get that score. If you're taking the test only because your ego was demolished by your not scoring as well as your friends, you should probably think twice before putting yourself through all of the trauma again.

✔ **Am I willing to study twice as hard, or am I already burned out?** If you put your heart and soul into studying for the exam the first time, you may be too pooped to pop for the second exam. Scores don't magically go up by themselves; you have to put in a lot of effort.

✔ **What types of mistakes did I make on the first test?** If you made mistakes due to a lack of familiarity with either the test format (you didn't understand what to do when faced with a Data Sufficiency question) or content (you didn't know the grammar concepts or were baffled by the geometry problems), you're a good candidate for repeating the test. If you know what you did wrong, you can fix it and improve your score.

If your mistakes were due to carelessness or to a lack of concentration, however, you are very likely to make those same types of mistakes again. If you truly, honestly, and sincerely feel that you can sit in the test room and stay focused this time and not make the same stupid mistakes, go for it. But chances are, if you're the type who either always makes a lot of careless mistakes or rarely makes them, you're not going to change your whole test-taking style overnight.

✔ **Were there extenuating circumstances beyond my control?** Maybe your nerves were acting up on the first exam, you were feeling ill, or you didn't get enough sleep the night before. In that case, by all means, repeat the exam. You're bound to feel better the next time. If you absolutely know that the low score you got is an anomaly because of such circumstances, call right away and make an appointment to take the test again. You may take the test once every calendar month. In theory, provided that each date falls on one of the weeks that the CAT is offered, you could take the test on both October 31 and November 1. If you got your low score toward the end of a month, you can improve on that score in just a week or two.

✔ **Did I guess randomly?** Did you fail to get to the last question? If you lost track of time and found yourself well short of the last question when time ran out, you may have scored lower than desired because of the penalty for not answering questions. Take the test again and make sure you get to the end, even if it means guessing randomly on the last few questions. A few guesses may be correct and bump your score up at least a little. You'll never have that chance if you don't guess.

Can repeating the exam hurt you? Not really. Most schools look only at your highest score. Find out whether the individual schools you are interested in have this policy; not all schools do so. If you are borderline or several students are vying for one spot, sometimes having taken the exam repeatedly can hurt you (especially if your most recent score took a nosedive!). On the other hand, an admissions counselor who sees several exams with ascending scores may be impressed that you stuck with it and kept trying even if your score went up only a little bit. In general, if you're willing to take the time and take the repeat seriously, go for it.

You *cannot* choose to have only specific scores sent. That is, if you bombed the exam in 1995, aced it in 1996, and are taking it again now, you cannot opt to have your 1995 scores deleted from your record.

Can you use older scores?

What if you took the GMAT years and years ago when you thought you were going to go to graduate school and then elected to take a job or start a family instead? You can specifically request that the GMAT send your scores for exams you took between October of 1974 and June of 1989 along with your score report. However, the GMAT washes its hands of you by sending along a statement saying that the old exam scores may not be interpreted in the same manner as the current GMAT scores. The university determines how to use those old scores. But the good news is, if you liked your scores from as long ago as two decades, you may be able to get away with sending those and not taking the exam again at all. If that's so and you're waving good-bye to me at this point, *adiós,* and good luck to you. For the rest of you who can't escape my company so quickly, read on.

Seven things you'd rather do than study for the GMAT

1. Have baked beans with your grandpa.

2. Actually wear the underwear your mother got you for Valentine's Day.

3. Listen to Michael Bolton music.

4. Take your little sister to the big Homecoming dance.

5. See your new romantic interest and your former romantic interest sitting together, pointing at you and laughing.

6. Be voted first runner-up in a foot odor contest.

7. Hear yourself described as having "a nice personality."

Part II

A Word to the Wise: Verbal Questions

The 5th Wave   By Rich Tennant

"C'mon Fogelman-talk! And I don't want to hear any of your non-parallel sentence structures, incomplete sentences or dangling participles!"

In this part . . .

Those of you who live by the maxim "quality, not quantity" are gonna love this section. The GMAT contains 41 qualitative (often called Verbal or English) questions in three styles: Sentence Correction, Reading Comprehension, and Critical Reasoning. The Sentence Correction questions test grammar and writing skills; the Reading Comprehension and Critical Reasoning questions test — you guessed it! — reading and reasoning skills (and you thought this was going to be hard!).

The GMAT also features the somewhat stuffily named "Analytical Writing Assessment." To us mere mortals, that means two essay questions. Because you are obviously judged on your grammar and writing skills when composing an essay, the information given in the grammar review will be helpful for the Writing Assessment as well as for the Sentence Correction questions.

As I mention in the Introduction, the GMAT CAT mixes the qualitative questions together. That is, you may have a Sentence Correction question first, then a Critical Reasoning question, then a passage followed by several Reading Comprehension questions, then another Critical Reasoning question, and so on. While the questions are all mixed up, there's no reason for you to be. Study each section separately, because each question type has a definite approach and a separate bag of tricks that you can use to answer it correctly.

Chapter 2

Write On: GMAT Grammar Review

In This Chapter

▶ Making subjects and verbs agree

▶ Deciding which pronoun to use

▶ Placing adjectives and adverbs in the correct spots

▶ Using correct sentence structures

▶ Tackling parallelism

▶ Keeping the -er and -est forms straight

▶ Watching your diction

▶ Conquering miscellaneous mistakes

The entire verbal or qualitative portion of the GMAT has only 41 questions. Approximately 40 percent (the number may change; no absolute guarantees here) of those questions test your grammar skills. For many people, doing well on the grammar portion of the test is the easiest way to improve a score. Let's face it: Your reading ability is not going to double overnight or change dramatically in a few hours (although your ability to recognize and avoid the traps built into standardized Reading Comprehension questions just may). A few hours of grammar study, however, can refresh your knowledge of those rules you learned in seventh and eighth grades (and then promptly forgot).

The following is a very brief grammar review covering the most important (which in GMAT-ese means the most frequently tested) concepts. You should memorize all these rules. Burn them in your brain, carve them in your heart, and imprint them on the very molecules of your fiber. Study them until they are second nature to you because during the actual GMAT, you won't have time to stop and think, "Now, wait a minute. Wasn't there some special rule for *neither/nor?*" You have to know and go.

 Some of these rules may seem almost insultingly easy to you. Bear with me. Every rule discussed is there for a reason. If you fall for a trap in the practice exams because you didn't plod through the boringly simple grammar review, you can't say I didn't warn you.

Subject-Verb Agreement

1. **A singular subject takes a singular verb.**

   My <u>pencil</u> *is* (not *are*) dull.

2. **A plural subject takes a plural verb.**

   My brain <u>cells</u> *are* (not *is*) dull.

3. **A compound subject — two or more subjects often connected by the word *and* — takes a plural verb.**

   My <u>pencil</u> and my brain <u>cells</u> *are* (not *is*) dull.

4. **The following words are always plural and therefore require plural verbs:**

few: Few people *score* (not *scores*) 800 on the GMAT.

both: Both the GMAT and the GRE *are* (not *is*) entrance exams to graduate school.

several: Several of my friends *have* (not *has*) taken the GMAT and the GRE.

many: Many of my friends *wish* (not *wishes*) they had never heard of the GMAT and the GRE.

5. **The following words are always singular and require singular verbs:**

each: Each question on the GMAT *has* (not *have*) the potential to be a trick question.

every: Every question *is* (not *are*) to be approached with trepidation and paranoia.

The *every* words — *every*one, *every*body, *every*thing, *every*where — are always singular.

6. **The following words may be singular or plural, depending on what follows them: *some, any, most, all, none.***

some, plural: Some of the jokes in this book *are* (not *is*) beyond hope and should be given a decent burial.

some, singular: Some of the humor in this book *is* (not *are*) inexcusable.

You can remember these words with the acronym S.A.M.A.N., the first letters of the words. Think of the sentence, "S.A.M.A.N. (Say, man), can you tell me which words are sometimes singular and sometimes plural?"

7. **The following collective nouns look plural but are singular and require a singular verb: *group, public, club, government, union, organization, collection.***

The group *is* (not *are*) interested in hearing how my studying is coming along; the club *is* (not *are*) going to hire me to give a speech on preparing for the GMAT.

8. **A prepositional phrase does not affect subject-verb agreement.**

When you have a prepositional phrase, mentally draw a line through it, and simply read the noun (subject) next to the verb.

That irate group ~~of test takers~~ *is* (not *are*) bombarding the proctor with tomatoes.

(Did you remember from Rule #7 that *group* is singular even though it may look plural?)

Five words are exceptions to Rule #8: the S.A.M.A.N. words. Do not ignore prepositional phrases with the S.A.M.A.N. words.

All of my friends *are* (not *is*) working overtime tonight; all of their time *is* (not *are*) spent complaining about work.

9. **Some nouns have irregular singular and plural forms.**

Singular	Plural
criterion	criteria
curriculum	curricula
bacterium	bacteria
phenomenon	phenomena
medium	media
datum	data

A solar eclipse is an interesting <u>phenomenon</u>; meteor showers are interesting <u>phenomena</u>.

When in doubt about whether a word is singular or plural, remember that, in general (but not always), the plural form of the word ends in a vowel (data, criteria) while the singular form of the word ends in a consonant (datum, criterion).

10. **The second subject in an *either/or* and *neither/nor* construction determines whether the verb is singular or plural.**

Neither Kimberly nor her <u>parents</u> *are* (not *is*) on the cruise.

Neither her parents nor <u>Kimberly</u> *is* (not *are*) able to afford cruise tickets.

Neither Kimberly's friends nor her <u>parents</u> *are* (not *is*) going on a cruise vacation this year.

Many people are so concerned with the subject-verb agreement of *neither/nor* that they forget that *neither* and *nor* belong together and that *either* and *or* belong together. In other words, the constructions *neither/or* and *either/nor* are wrong. Double-check whenever you see these words.

Pronouns

1. **A pronoun (a word that takes the place of the noun) must have the same number (singular or plural) as the noun it is replacing.**

<u>Everybody</u> is on *his* best behavior during a college interview.

You would probably be wealthy if you had a dollar for each time you had heard someone say, "Yeah, everybody is trying *their* best." Because the construction *everybody/their* is so commonly used, it sounds correct. Make this expression a red flag one. Whenever you see the word *everybody*, triple-check the pronoun to make sure that it is singular.

2. **A pronoun must have the same gender (feminine, masculine, neuter) as the noun it is replacing.**

<u>Mrs. Velez</u> is notorious for *her* difficult accounting projects.

3. **A pronoun must have clarity (that is, you must be able to tell what noun the pronoun is replacing).**

Matthew asked Franklin to pick up *his* laundry off the floor.

Did Matthew want Matthew's laundry picked up, or did Matthew want Franklin's laundry picked up? This reference is unclear — and thus a wrong sentence.

An unclear pronoun reference often requires major reconstructive surgery. In this example, the entire sentence must be rewritten. Here's one possibility:

Matthew, disgusted at seeing Franklin's laundry on the floor, asked him to pick *it* up.

(Now you know perfectly well that the pronoun *it* is referring to Franklin's heap of clothes, not Matthew's.)

4. **A pronoun must be in the proper case: subjective (I, you, he, she, it, we, they); objective (me, you, him, her, it, us, them); or possessive (my, mine, your, yours, his, her, hers, its, our, ours, their, theirs).**

A pronoun following any form of the verb *to be*, such as *is, are, was,* and *were,* is going to be in the subjective form. This form often sounds pretentious and bizarre (a sure clue it's probably correct on the GMAT!). Following are common constructions:

It is I.   It was she who . . .

It was he.   This is he.

It could be they.   It was they.

I confess it is *I* who insisted on including the lame jokes in this book.

Adjectives and Adverbs

1. **Place an adjective (which modifies a noun or pronoun) or an adverb (which modi-fies a verb, adjective, or adverb) as close as possible to the noun or pronoun it is modifying.**

   That rule is *not* followed in this sentence:

   Wrong: Nancy and Frank left the neighborhood they had lived in for ten years *reluctantly*.

   This sentence sounds as if Nancy and Frank had been reluctant to live in the neighbor-hood, when in fact they were reluctant to leave. Change the sentence so that *reluctantly* comes just before *left:*

   Right: Nancy and Frank *reluctantly* left the neighborhood they had lived in for ten years.

2. **An adverb (which modifies a verb, adverb, or adjective) often answers the question "How?" and may end in *-ly*.**

   <u>How</u> do I study? I study *reluctantly*. *Reluctantly* is an adverb.

3. **Place *not only* and *but also* in parallel positions within a sentence.**

   People often place *not only* and *but also* in the wrong positions. Following is an example of a wrong way to use these expressions:

   Wrong: Angelique *not only* was exasperated *but also* frightened when she locked her-self out of the house.

   See the problem? In this wrong example, the phrase *not only* comes before the verb *was,* but the phrase *but also* comes before the adjective *frightened.*

   Right: Angelique was *not only* exasperated *but also* frightened when she locked herself out of the house.

   Not only and *but also* precede the adjectives *exasperated* and *frightened,* respectively.

Sentence Structure

1. **A run-on sentence (two or more independent clauses incorrectly joined) must be changed.**

   The following is a run-on:

   Wrong: Jessimena was furious when she went to the party on the wrong day, she went home and yelled at her boyfriend who had given her the wrong information.

   You can choose from five ways to correct a run-on.

   • **Make two separate sentences.**

     Jessimena was furious when she went to the party on the wrong day. *She* went home and yelled at her boyfriend, who had given her the wrong information.

- **Use a semicolon to separate independent clauses.**

  Jessimena was furious when she went to the party on the wrong day; she went home and yelled at her boyfriend, who had given her the wrong information.

- **Use a semicolon, conjunctive adverb, and comma (as in this construction: ; *therefore*,) to separate the clauses.**

  Jessimena was furious when she went to the party on the wrong day; *therefore,* she went home and yelled at her boyfriend, who had given her the wrong information.

- **Use a subordinating conjunction (such as *because* or *since*) with one of the clauses.**

  Because Jessimena was furious when she went to the party on the wrong day, she went home and yelled at her boyfriend, who had given her the wrong information.

- **Use a comma and a coordinating conjunction (as in this construction: , *and*) between the two clauses.**

  Jessimena was furious when she went to the party on the wrong day, *and* she went home and yelled at her boyfriend, who had given her the wrong information.

2. **A sentence fragment (an incomplete sentence) must be changed to reflect a completed thought.**

   Wrong: Wendy, singing merrily to herself as she walked to class, unaware that the professor was at that very moment preparing a pop quiz.

   Right: Wendy, singing merrily to herself as she walked to class, *was* unaware that the professor was at that very moment preparing a pop quiz.

Parallelism

Parallelism (also called *parallel structure*) means that objects in a series must be in similar form.

Wrong: I spent my weekend *shopping, doing* chores around the house, and finally *got* out on Sunday evening to play a set of tennis.

Rewrite the sentence so that the verbs are in the same form:

Right: On the weekend, I *shopped, did* chores around the house, and finally *got* out on Sunday evening to play a set of tennis.

or

Right: I spent my weekend *shopping* and *doing* chores around the house, finally *getting* out on Sunday evening to play a set of tennis.

Items in a series may be nouns, verbs, adjectives, or entire clauses. However, nonparallel verbs are the items that most commonly have errors. When a clause has more than one verb, watch out for this particular error.

Comparisons

1. **Use the *-er* form (called the *comparative* form) to compare exactly two items; use the *-est* form (called the *superlative* form) to compare more than two items.**

   I am *taller* than my brother <u>Beau</u>, but <u>Darren</u> is the *tallest* member of our family.

   A particularly difficult comparison uses the words *latter* and *last*.

   My boyfriend asked whether I would like to go to Chicago where the temperature was –5 degrees or Los Angeles where the temperature was 80 degrees; I told him I preferred to visit the *latter* (not *last*).

   Comparisons may trap you when you refer to twins. Remember that *twins* indicates two people. The following is a good trick question:

   Wrong: <u>Myron</u> and <u>Mayor</u> Thibadeau are identical twins, but Myron is the *oldest* by five minutes, a fact he never lets Mayor forget.

   The error is in the comparison because there are only two twins.

   Right: Myron is the *older* by five minutes.

2. **Compare only similar objects or concepts.**

   Wrong: The motor skills of a toddler are more advanced than a baby.

   The problem with the preceding sentence is that it is comparing *motor skills* to a *baby*. Its intention is to compare a toddler's motor skills to a baby's motor skills. Following are two ways to correct the error:

   Right: The motor skills of a toddler are more advanced than those of a baby.

   or

   Right: A toddler's motor skills are more advanced than a baby's.

Diction

I like to refer to diction errors as *twosomes* because they are errors that you make when you swap two (or sometimes three) commonly confused words. Following is a list of the most commonly confused words, along with short-and-sweet definitions and examples.

it's . . . its: *It's* (notice the apostrophe) means *it is*. *It's* good to know the distinction between these two words. *Its* (without an apostrophe) is possessive. The GMAT is ruthless in *its* insistence that *it's* important to know the difference between these two words.

assure . . . ensure: To *assure* means to convince. Quentin talked fast, trying to *assure* his girlfriend that the black negligee in his closet was in fact a belated birthday present for her. To *ensure* is to make certain. To *ensure* that his girlfriend believed him, Quentin called a friend, who pretended she was the salesgirl who had sold the item to Quentin.

lie . . . lay: To *lie* is to recline. I *lie* down in the afternoon for a nap to reduce stress. To *lay* is to place. I *lay* a cold washcloth on my head every time I get a headache from studying for the GMAT.

Do you often get *lie* and *lay* confused? I have an easy way to remember them. To *lie* is to recline. Listen for the long *i* sound in l<u>ie</u> and the long *i* sound in rec<u>line</u>. When I lie down, I recline. To *lay* is to place. Listen for the long *a* sound in l<u>ay</u> and the long *a* sound in pl<u>ace</u>. Now I lay me down to sleep. Now I place me down to sleep.

Few of us know how to conjugate these words correctly. <u>Memorize</u> the following:

✔ *lie, lay, have lain* — Today I *lie* down, yesterday I *lay* down, every day I *have lain* down.

✔ *lay, laid, have laid* — Today I *lay* my keys on the table, yesterday I *laid* my keys on the table, every day this week I *have laid* my keys on the table.

Note how confusing the past tense of *lie* is because it is the same as the present tense of *lay*. Do not use the past tense of *lie* as *lied*. The sentence "I *lied* down yesterday" is egregiously incorrect.

affect . . . effect: To *affect* is to influence or concern. A good GMAT score will positively *affect* your chances of admission to graduate school (it will positively *influence* your chances). *Effect* means cause or result. A good GMAT score will have a positive *effect* on your chances for admission (a positive *result*). A good score will *effect* (or *cause*) a change in which schools you consider.

Affect has another, little-known meaning. To *affect* also means to pretend. When I want to get out of meeting with my friends to study for the GMAT, I often *affect* a headache.

imply . . . infer: To *imply* means to suggest. I didn't mean to *imply* that your dress is ugly when I asked you whether you bought it at an upholstery store. To *infer* is to conclude or deduce, to read a meaning *into* something. Did you *infer* that I think the dress looks like a sofa covering?

who . . . whom: Who is a subject and does the action. *Who* wants to study on a weekend? *Whom* is an object and receives the action. I don't know *whom* to ask for help in deciding on the topic for my thesis.

eminent . . . immanent . . . imminent: Eminent is outstanding, distinguished. Dr. Regis Weiss is an *eminent* oncologist, well-respected by his peers. *Immanent* is inherent, innate. I think that compassion probably is an *immanent* trait in a good physician; it doesn't seem possible that someone could take a course to learn how to be caring. *Imminent* means about to happen. When I saw Dr. Weiss shaking his head at me as I stood on the scale, I knew a lecture about weight management was *imminent*. *Hint:* Think of imminent as in-a-minute. Something imminent is about to happen in a minute.

less . . . fewer: Less modifies a singular noun. I have *less* <u>patience</u> with problems than I should have. *Fewer* modifies a plural noun. I would make *fewer* careless <u>mistakes</u> in math if only I had the patience to finish each problem completely.

amount . . . number: Amount modifies a singular noun. I have a large *amount* of <u>respect</u> for the poetry of Dorothy Parker. *Number* modifies a plural noun. A *number* of <u>times</u> I have read her poem that contains the lines, "The lads I've met in Cupid's deadlock / were, shall we say, born out of wedlock?"

farther . . . further: Farther refers to measurable distance. I made a mistake on the test when I said that Morocco is *farther* from Egypt than it is from New York. *Further* refers to a figurative degree or quantity that can't be measured. Obviously, I need to study my geography *further*.

between . . . among: Between compares exactly two things. I have difficulty choosing *between* rocky road and fudge ripple ice cream. *Among* compares more than two. I go crazy when I have to choose *among* the desserts in a smorgasbord.

The word *between* is often followed by *and:* I have difficulty choosing between this *and* that. A trap answer may have a sentence asking you to choose between this *or* that; the *or* is wrong.

stationary . . . stationery: Stationary means unmoving. The little girl tried to remain *stationary,* hoping that the birds would come up to her and eat out of her hand. ***Stationery*** is writing paper. The little girl used her new *stationery* to write a letter telling her grandmother about the birds.

Stationary means something that *stays* and *stays*. Note the letter *a* in st*a*y and the letter *a* in station*a*ry. *Stationery* is something you write a letter on. Note the letter *e* in station*e*ry and the letter *e* in l*e*tter.

if . . . whether: If introduces a condition. *If* the teacher allows an open-book exam, I will be ecstatic. ***Whether*** compares alternatives. I don't know *whether* I could pass a normal, closed-book exam.

If usually sounds correct even when it is wrong. Personally, even though I know better, I hear myself saying, "I don't know *if* I can make it tonight," when I know I should say, "I don't know *whether* I can make it tonight." Try *whether* first. If it sounds right, it probably is right.

rise . . . raze . . . raise: To ***rise*** means to ascend. It is time to *rise* when your significant other yanks the covers off the bed. To ***raze*** means to tear down. When she threatens to *raze* the bedroom around your head, you know she means business. To ***raise*** means to lift. You wearily *raise* your body, ready to face another day.

anxious . . . eager: Anxious means worried or doubtful. Meg was *anxious* about the call from her mechanic, knowing that her car probably needed some repairs. ***Eager*** means joyously anticipating. The mechanic was *eager* to work on Meg's car, as he needed cash.

principle . . . principal: Principle means rule. The *principles* of justice upon which our country is founded apply to all. ***Principal*** means first in authority or importance. The *principal* reason democracy works, in my opinion, is that it gives everyone an equal opportunity to succeed.

Principle means ru**le**. Note that they both end in *-le*. If the word does not appear to mean rule, it can't be principle; choose *principal*. The English language has many uses of the word *principal,* including (for example) investment principal, the principal reason I telephoned you, and the principal of a high school.

good . . . well: Good is an adjective that modifies a noun. You're doing a *good* job learning these rules. ***Well*** is an adverb that modifies verbs, adverbs, and adjectives and usually answers the question *how.* How do you study? You study very *well.*

Well also refers to physical condition. By the time you leave the GMAT, huffing, puffing, sweating, and fretting, you may not be feeling very *well.*

complement . . . compliment: Complement means to complete. The buzz haircut *complemented* the image Chan wanted to project as a no-nonsense guy. ***Compliment*** means to praise. Chan's girlfriend was eager to *compliment* him on his hot new look.

flaunt . . . flout: To ***flaunt*** means to show off. Brittany was thrilled to get her engagement ring and couldn't wait to *flaunt* it to her friends at work. To ***flout*** means to show scorn or contempt. Her fiancé was furious that Brittany had *flouted* their agreement to keep their engagement a secret for the next few months.

founder . . . flounder: To ***founder*** is to sink, fail, or collapse. Reports estimate that one of every two new businesses *founders* within the first three years. To ***flounder*** is to thrash about. A new business owner, desperate for advice, will *flounder* wildly, running from government bureau to government bureau attempting to get help.

phase . . . faze: Phase means a stage or a time period. College years are just one *phase* of your life. To *faze* means to upset, bother, or disconcert. Do not let the pressure of the GMAT *faze* you.

Many students look at the word *faze* and immediately assume it is misspelled. The GMAT has *no* misspelled words. If you think a word is misspelled, you are in error. I have another example. Do you know the distinction between the words *prescribe* and *proscribe*? To **prescribe** is to recommend. I *prescribe* you learn these two words. To **proscribe** is to outlaw or forbid. I *proscribe* your believing that the GMAT has typographical errors. (My favorite is *judgment*. Most people misspell the word as *judgement* but there is no *judge* in *judgment* in American English.)

everyday . . . every day: As one word, **everyday** means usual or customary. I wore my *everyday* clothes for a quick trip to the grocery store, little realizing that I'd run into Brad Pitt next to the kumquats. **Every day** as two words means each 24-hour period. From now on, I'm going to go to the store *every day* to get fresh fruit. After all, everyone needs fruit, kumquat may. . . .

Miscellaneous Mistakes

Following are some of the miscellaneous grammar mistakes that many of us make every day. In the real world, we can live with these mistakes; on the GMAT, they are deadly.

In regards to . . . in regard to: The English language has no such expression as *in regards to*. Dump the *s;* the proper expression is **in regard to**. We need to have a heart-to-heart talk *in regard to* your making this mistake.

Hopefully: Use **hopefully** only where you could plug in the words *full of hope*. Hearing the telephone ring, Alice looked up *hopefully,* thinking that Steve might be calling her to apologize for sending her flowers on his ex-wife's birthday. Many of us use the word *hopefully* incorrectly as a substitute for "I hope." The sentence "*Hopefully* my GMAT score will improve" is completely wrong. Your score won't improve unless you learn to say, "I hope that my GMAT score will improve."

If . . . would: Do not place **if** and **would** in the same clause. A common error is to say, "*If* I *would* have studied more, I would have done better." The correct version is, "*If* I *had* studied more, I would have done better," or "*Had* I studied more, I would have done better."

Where . . . that: Do not confuse **where** with **that**. **Where** refers to physical location only. Saying "Did you hear *where* Professor Denges ran off to Tahiti with his secretary?" is wrong. The correct structure is, "Did you hear *that* Professor Denges ran off to Tahiti with his secretary?"

Hardly: **Hardly** is negative and often shows up in a trap double-negative question. Do not say, "Ms. Hawker has *hardly nothing* to do this weekend after she's finished the GMAT and is looking forward to vegging out in front of the TV." The correct version is, "Ms. Hawker has *hardly anything* to do this weekend after she's finished the GMAT and is looking forward to vegging out in front of the TV."

You get double value for your efforts in learning these rules. You use the rules, of course, in the sentence correction section, but they are also invaluable in the analytical writing assessment — the essay portion of the GMAT. I chose most of the rules I've listed in this chapter for two reasons: First, the GMAT tests you on these rules, and second, most people make many errors when they use these rules. In other words, not only will you find a question testing *affect* versus *effect* in the sentence correction section, you are likely to use —

misuse, rather — those words in an essay. If there's one thing that ticks off the evaluators of the essays, it's a grammatical mistake. A glaring mistake colors an evaluator's thinking about the entire essay. If you keep nodding to yourself as you go through this grammar review, saying, "Yeah, I always wondered about that rule," or "I remember every teacher since fifth grade yelling at me for that mistake," then pay special attention to your essay if you use these troublesome constructions (especially the twosomes — the commonly confused words).

Chapter 3

If You're Illiterate, Read This: Sentence Correction

In This Chapter

▶ Appearances count: What sentence correction questions look like

▶ It's not whom you know, it's what you know: What sentence correction questions test

▶ A journey of a thousand miles: Where to begin

▶ Grammar gotchas! Tips and traps

Sentence Correction questions are the Yogi Berra-isms of the GMAT — brilliantly garbled sentences that seem to make sense until you examine them more closely. Fortunately, the grammar questions are (in my not-so-humble opinion) the easiest questions to rack up the points on because the rules are finite. After you know the rules for using the words *among* and *between,* for example, they never change. Grammar questions aren't like math questions, in which all sorts of tricks and traps can ruin your life, or like Reading Comprehension questions with those long and booooooring passages. If I had to choose one type of question to use for improving my score, Sentence Correction would be it.

I've Seen the Error of My Ways: What Sentence Correction Questions Look Like

A Sentence Correction question features a sentence with an underlined part. The underlined part can be a word, a phrase, a clause, or the entire sentence. Choice A is exactly the same as the underlined portion. Think of Choice A as "it doesn't get any better than this." If you think the original sentence is perfect and you wouldn't change a thing, then choose A. Choices B, C, D, and E are alternate ways of writing the underlined portion. Choose the one that best fits the sentence.

When a student's essay defined *monotony* as being married to just one wife, the student's teacher <u>had to choose among correcting the mistake or</u> photocopying the essay and circulating it in the teachers' lounge.

(A) had to choose among correcting the mistake or

(B) had to choose between correcting the mistake or

(C) had to choose between correcting the mistake and

(D) chose, instead of correcting the mistake, to be

(E) was choosing between correcting the mistake and

Among is used with more than two options. *Between* is used with only two options or possibilities and is always followed by the word *and,* not *or. Correct Answer:* C.

What Do They Want Outta Me? What Sentence Correction Questions Test

After reading the preceding heading, you're probably thinking, "What does she mean? A Sentence Correction question tests grammar, right?" Well, right, but things get a little more complicated than that (this *is* the GMAT, after all).

Effective writing

One area that the GMAT tests is effective writing (now there's a vague phrase if ever I heard one). Writing effectively means using words that are accurate and well chosen; they aren't slang or substandard English, and they are appropriate to the writing level. A good sentence is clear and unambiguous. It expresses ideas concisely and makes the relationships between concepts clear and understandable. Here's an example of an ambiguous sentence, one that does *not* express a clear relationship.

Hal told Ty to get his golf clubs out of the closet.

(A) Hal told Ty to get his golf clubs out of the closet.

(B) Hal told Ty to get his golf clubs, which were in the closet, out.

(C) Ty was told by Hal to get his clubs out of the closet.

(D) Hal told Ty to get out of the closet and get his clubs.

(E) Hal said, "Ty, get my golf clubs out of my closet."

Whose golf clubs are you referring to? Did Hal want to go golfing and hoped that Ty would get Hal's clubs out of the closet and hand them over? Or was Hal, sick and tired of storing Ty's clubs, demanding that they be removed from the closet in order to give Hal more room to store his golfing trophies? The sentence does not make clear to whom the pronoun "his" refers.

The best answer is E. It corrects the error (the ambiguity in the original sentence) without creating another error. Choice B is vague; after reading it, you still don't know whose golf clubs were in the closet. Choice C is both vague and in the passive voice ("Ty was told by Hal" is passive; "Hal told Ty" is active). Active voice is usually preferable to passive voice. Choice D is totally bizarre: Why was Ty in the closet? Was Hal trying to expose some secret about Ty by asking him to come out of the closet? And besides, you still don't know whose golf clubs were in the closet with Ty. *Correct Answer:* E.

Sentence construction

A sentence may have two fundamental problems: It may be a fragment (an incomplete sentence, one that doesn't finish the thought), or it may be a run-on (two independent clauses incorrectly joined). Here's an example; identify what's wrong, and choose the best alternative.

When Ms. Mosher told me she was going to sue me for deformation of <u>character, she couldn't understand why I started laughing, she became even</u> more upset with me.

(A) character, she couldn't understand why I started laughing, she became even

(B) character; she couldn't understand why I started laughing, she became even

(C) character and she couldn't understand why I started laughing, because she became even

(D) character, she couldn't understand why I started laughing; she became even

(E) character, she couldn't understand why I started laughing, as a result, she became even

The original sentence is a run-on. There are two independent clauses that are incorrectly joined by a comma. A comma is too weak to hold together two such strong entities; a semicolon is needed. Choice D corrects the error. Notice that choice B has a semicolon, too, but in the wrong place. The semicolon goes between the two independent clauses — between the two separate sentences. *Correct Answer:* D.

Diction

A diction error is a wrong word choice. I call these errors "twosomes" because usually they occur when two words are confused, misused, and abused. Common twosomes are *lie/lay, affect/effect, between/among,* and so on. (You can find a long list of twosomes in Chapter 2.)

The crime beat reporter pointed out that due to budget constraints and personnel cutbacks, the police would be trying <u>to run down less jaywalkers</u>.

(A) to run down less jaywalkers

(B) running down less jaywalkers

(C) to prosecute fewer jaywalkers

(D) prosecuting fewer jaywalkers

(E) and prosecuting, in fact, less jaywalkers

Oh, those poor jaywalkers! This sentence sounds as if the police are aiming right at them! Eliminate choices A and B. The primary grammar error in the sentence, however, lies in the misuse of *less* for *fewer.* As you saw in the grammar review, *less* precedes a singular noun, as in less mayhem; *fewer* precedes a plural noun, as in fewer injuries. Choice C is correct here because jaywalkers is plural. Some questions test diction errors, which are among the easiest to detect and correct. All you have to do is memorize the common twosomes and be on the lookout for them. *Correct Answer:* C.

Grammar

Grammar covers a multitude of sins. Grammar mistakes can include problems with subject/verb agreement, pronoun reference, redundancy/verbosity, parallel structure, comparisons, and a variety of other plagues and pestilence. Here's an example of a common grammatical mistake.

The humor of the headlines in the golf magazines <u>never fail to amuse me; last month</u> the magazine pointed out how a mother of five made a hole in one!

(A) never fail to amuse me; last month

(B) never fail to amusing me; last month

(C) never fails to amuse me; last month

(D) never fail at amusing me; last month

(E) is failing almost never at amusing me; last month

Can't you just picture this poor, perforated progeny? Somewhere, it seems, there's a child running around with a hole in him! However, because the portion of the sentence that ventilates the child is not underlined, you can't change it. All you can do is change the underlined parts. The question tests your skill at handling subject/verb agreement. The subject of the sentence is *humor,* a singular subject. It requires a singular verb, *fails.* It's easy to make the mistake of thinking that the subject is *headlines,* which is plural, or *magazines,* which is also plural, and which would require the plural verb, *fail.* (Subject/verb agreement is covered in Chapter 2.) *Correct Answer:* C.

Awkwardness

This concept is my favorite. A sentence can fail because it is awkward — the equivalent of a clumsy kid failing in gym class. Nothing that you can put your finger on is wrong, but things just don't work somehow.

<u>I am often asked where I dig up my jokes, which are not to be laughed at, because my friends want to stay away from that contaminated site.</u>

(A) I am often asked where I dig up my jokes, which are not to be laughed at, because my friends want to stay away from that contaminated site.

(B) My friends want to stay away from the contaminated site where I dig up my jokes, which are not to be laughed at.

(C) My jokes are so poor that my friends ask where I get my material; they want to stay away from that contaminated site.

(D) Not laughing at my jokes, my friends want to know where they come from so they can stay away from that contaminated site.

(E) When I dig up my jokes, what my friends want to know is, where I get jokes that are not to be laughed at, and they'll stay away from that contaminated site.

What a mess! One sentence is worse than the other. This sentence doesn't test one specific point, but just the overall sentence. I'd choose C here, not so much because it is good but because it stinks less than all the other answer choices. You don't get to create your own answer choice, so you have to choose one of the above. *Correct Answer:* C.

Smart from the Start: Where to Begin

Take a three-step approach to a Sentence Correction question:

1. **Identify any errors.** Read the sentence quickly and pinpoint any blatant mistakes. These are usually mistakes in basic grammar usage, such as subject/verb agreement, or in diction problems, like confusing *rise* and *raise*.

2. **Predict a correction and look for it among the answer choices.** If you know that the sentence should say, "the media are" rather than "the media is," look for choices with that construction.

3. **Reread the entire sentence with your new choice inserted.** This last step is critical and traps many lazy or rushed students. If you don't read your sentence again, you won't know whether the new and improved version actually works.

These three steps sound pretty simple, right? Well, the approach is easy, but wait until you see all the traps that are lurking to catch the careless and unwary.

Grammar Gotchas! Tips and Traps

The following techniques can help you to recognize and avoid the built-in traps for which the GMAT is notorious:

1. Check for multiple errors.

Just because you recognize and correct one mistake does not mean your task is finished. Questions often feature more than one error. It's easy to be in a rush, find an obvious mistake (for example, using *its* instead of *it's* in place of *it is*), choose an answer featuring the correction, and zip off to the next problem. If you're in too much of a rush, you could miss a second or even a third underlined error in the same sentence.

Its not hard to find a good joke to tell, but it's nearly impossible to predict the affect it will have on an audience of strangers.

  (A) Its not hard to find a good joke to tell, but it's nearly impossible to predict the affect it will have on an audience of strangers.

  (B) It's not hard to find a good joke to tell, but it's nearly impossible to predict the affect it will have on an audience of strangers.

  (C) Its not hard to find a good joke, but telling it could have a nearly impossible-to-predict affect on an audience of strangers.

  (D) Finding a good joke is not hard, but it's nearly impossible to predict the affect telling it will have on an audience of strangers.

  (E) It's not hard to find a good joke to tell, but it's nearly impossible to predict the effect it will have on an audience of strangers.

If you chose B, you fell right into the trap. You probably deduced that *it's* was required, saw *it's* in choice B, and thought you'd done your duty for the day. Alas, the original has a second error: *affect* instead of *effect*. To *affect* means to touch or concern. To *effect* (as a verb) means to cause or (as a noun) a result. In this case, the joke has an unpredictable result, meaning the word must be *effect*. Choice E has both corrections. *Correct Answer:* E.

2. Don't correct one error only to introduce a second error.

This trap is even more vile than the previous one. Suppose that you read a sentence carefully and note that it has one and only one error. You predict how that error is to be corrected, skim the answer choices, find one that corrects the error, and choose it. You are completely oblivious to the fact that you have inadvertently introduced a new error! That's right. The answer you choose brings in an error that wasn't in the original question.

The sportscaster inferred to his audience that the Miami Dolphins' 17–0 season was a phenomenon that will never be matched.

  (A) The sportscaster inferred to his audience that the Miami Dolphins' 17–0 season was a phenomenon that will never be matched.

  (B) The sportscaster's inference to his audience that the Miami Dolphins' 17–0 season was that it was a phenomenon that would never be matched.

  (C) The sportscaster implied to his audience that the Miami Dolphins' 17–0 season was a phenomena that will never be matched.

  (D) Phenomenally, the sportscaster inferred, the Miami Dolphins' 17–0 season will never be matched.

  (E) The sportscaster implied that the Miami Dolphins' 17–0 season was a phenomenon that will never be matched.

The question mistakes *infers* (meaning deduces, concludes) with *implies* (meaning suggests). The sportscaster cannot infer something to someone; he implies something to someone. Choice C changes *inferred* to *implied* — but it also changes the correct word *phenomenon* (one singular event) to the wrong word *phenomena* (several events). Careless readers don't notice that a new mistake has joined the club, and they can easily miss this question. The right answer is choice E, which corrects the error without introducing a new error. *Correct Answer:* E.

3. Don't change the meaning of the sentence.

This trap is rare, but it has in the past reared its ugly head, or shown its ugly face (I have a two-for-one special on clichés today). Be very careful when you correct a grammar, diction, or sentence construction mistake so you don't change the meaning of the original sentence.

The teacher is recuperating in the hospital and doing better, he was hit in the head by a book tossed by a disgusted student.

(A) The teacher is recuperating in the hospital and doing better, he was hit in the head by a book tossed by a disgusted student.

(B) The teacher is recuperating in the hospital and doing better after being hit in the head by a book tossed by a disgusted student.

(C) The teacher is better after being hit in the head by a book tossed by a disgusted student; he's recuperating in the hospital.

(D) Recuperating in the hospital, the teacher is better after being hit in the head by a book tossed by a disgusted student.

(E) After a disgusted student's book hit him in the head, the teacher is better and is recuperating in the hospital.

Choices C, D, and E all make it sound as if the teacher were improved by being hit in the head! Choice C sounds as if the student is recuperating in the hospital. The best answer here — although none of the sentences are too hot — is choice B. *Correct Answer:* B.

4. Don't leave the question without rereading the entire sentence with your answer choice inserted.

I can't emphasize this point highly enough. An answer choice on its own may look perfectly logical. But when you reinsert it into the sentence, it causes chaos and consternation. It's common for students in a rush to think that they can save a few seconds by choosing an answer and going on without reinserting that answer into the sentence; doing so may save you a nanosecond or two but can cost you a lot of points. Invest the extra time.

The experts estimate that breast cancer kills ten times as many women <u>because it kills fewer men</u>.

(A) because it kills fewer men

(B) as men

(C) because men are less likely to be killed by it

(D) and not nearly as many men

(E) than men

Did you fall for the trap answer, choice B? Choice B makes the sentence sound as if women are killed ten times as often by breast cancer as they are killed by men! If you read choice B by itself, it seems to make sense. It's not until you insert it into the sentence and then reread the entire sentence that you find the problem. *Correct Answer:* E.

5. Don't choose good enough; insist on the best.

Be a discriminating test taker. Don't settle for an answer that is just okay; hold out for the best you can get. Sentence correction is not a test of right versus wrong, but a test of good versus better versus best. All five answers could possibly be correct. Your job is to choose the one that is the best, the one that seems to flow the most smoothly, the one that expresses the thought completely but concisely.

When Larry told me that because the elevator was broken, I would be unbearable, <u>I groaned at his pun and told him to go away</u>.

(A) I groaned at his pun and told him to go away

(B) I said that his pun made me groan and then I told him to go away

(C) I groaned (his pun was awful) and told him to go away

(D) I told him to go away after I groaned at his pun

(E) I groaned at his pun and then I told him to go away

Every one of these answers is grammatically correct. No choice has an error in diction, sentence construction, whatever. How do you choose? You use your ear to sound out the sentences and listen for which one just plain sounds best. Choice A is the best answer here. Choices B and E have unnecessary words. Keep the answer short and sweet; if a word isn't vital to the sentence, dump it. Choice C breaks up the sentence with a parenthetical aside that isn't necessary. And choice D is a bit vague: Did I groan at Larry's pun and then tell him to go away, or did I want him to wait to leave until after I had groaned at his pun? *Correct Answer:* A.

If English is not your first language, this type of question may be very difficult for you. You probably would do well to guess quickly at this sort of question and focus on questions that have more obvious problems, questions in which you can detect and correct an error. A sentence in which you change a *good* to a *well* or a *principal* to a *principle* is custom-made for you. (Don't panic if you don't know the difference between these words; twosomes are covered in detail in the grammar review in Chapter 2.)

6. Don't automatically, unconsciously correct an error.

In everyday life, you read memos, reports, and books with grammar misteaks (sic . . . sick . . .). Unless you're as obsessive as I am, you don't blue-pencil the material and hand it back for revisions (I, on the other hand, have been known to correct my boyfriend's love letters!). Chances are, you automatically supply the missing words, make the necessary changes, and read the material the way it was meant to be read. Doing so is great for the real world, but inappropriate for the GMAT. When you unconsciously correct each sentence, you end up choosing Choice A for every single Sentence Correction question . . . and it's highly improbable that every single question will have no error in it.

Miguel and José <u>never have and never will be world class soccer players, but</u> they love the sport and continue to improve at it.

(A) never have and never will be world class soccer players, but

(B) never having been, and probably never becoming world class soccer players,

(C) never have been and never will be world class soccer players, but

(D) have never been world class soccer players and will never be, but

(E) without being and probably never becoming world class soccer players still

The original is missing the word *been* after never have: Miguel and José never have *been* and never will be world class soccer players. It's very, very easy to supply this missing word without thinking. Careless students who don't read all the answer choices select choice A and lose easy points. Students who at least eyeball the answers probably wonder what the difference is between choices C and A, and take a few moments to find the problem. The moral of the story: If you think the sentence is correct as written, double-check to make sure that you have read what is actually written, not what you wanted to see. *Correct Answer:* C.

I Don't Have Time to Serve This Sentence: Timesaving Suggestions

Question: Why was the ink blot crying?

Answer: His father was in the pen and he didn't know how long the sentence would be!

The Sentence Correction questions can require a lot of time, especially if English is not your native tongue or your best subject. Some of the sentences are quite long and must be read and reread a number of times to make sense. Some of the answer choices are confusing and tortuous and have to be read and reread and reread. (*Tortuous* means twisting, winding, serpentine. Don't confuse it with *torturous,* which means tormenting, or excruciating, although you may think that both words apply here.) And of course, I've already warned you that you have to plug your answer choice back into the original sentence. What can you do to speed things up a bit?

- **Correct an error and eliminate answer choices without that correction.** This suggestion works especially well for twosome errors. Suppose that the sentence refers to someone who feels good. You know that a person feels well, not good. Eliminate answers with the word *good* in them. This tip also helps in sentences with basic grammar errors, such as pronoun reference. If a sentence implies that everyone is doing *their* best, you know that everyone is doing *his* or *her* best. Eliminate answers with *their;* look for answers with *his* or *her.*

- **Read the answer choices from the bottom to the top, ignoring choice A**. Choice A is the same as the original. (Remember: On the computer, the choices are not lettered. What is Choice A in this book will simply be the first answer choice on the computer.) You read it just a moment ago when you read the question, so why bother to reread it? If you start at the top, you can't help but go over choice A. But if you start at the bottom with choice E and then read choices D, C, and B, you can ignore A. The few seconds you save may not seem like much, but they do add up over the course of the test.

- **Predict a rewrite and look for it.** Some of the sentences don't have simple one-word errors such as verbs or pronouns. They may be awkward, redundant, or verbose. In this case, you must rewrite the entire sentence. Do so before you look at the answer choices. Let's face it — often every answer choice looks good. If you have already predicted what you think would be a good sentence, then that sentence will leap off the page at you.

Course Corrections Complete, Captain: A Final Review

A Sentence Correction question is one sentence with an underlined portion. Your job is to choose the best way to state that underlined portion. Here's a three-step approach:

1. **Identify any errors.** Sentence Correction questions test effective writing, sentence construction, diction, grammar, and awkwardness.

2. **Predict a correction and look for it among the answer choices.**

3. **Reread the entire sentence with your new choice inserted.**

You can avoid traps built into the Sentence Correction questions if you do the following:

✔ Check the underlined portion for multiple errors.

✔ Don't correct an error only to introduce a second error.

✔ Don't change the meaning of the sentence.

✔ Don't leave the question without rereading the entire sentence with your answer choice inserted.

✔ Don't choose a sentence that is good enough; insist on the best.

✔ Don't automatically, unconsciously correct an error.

The following tips can help you make the most efficient use of your time:

✔ Correct an error and eliminate answer choices without that correction.

✔ Read the answer choices from the bottom to the top, ignoring the first choice.

✔ Predict a rewrite and look for it.

Chapter 4

Cheesier by the Dozen: Sentence Correction Practice Questions

It's that time again — time to use it or lose it. Remember that the actual CAT GMAT could have from about 10 to 15 sentence corrections; however, answering the following dozen questions should reinforce what you learned in the preceding chapter about sentence corrections. Heads up, though! No way is the actual GMAT going to be as much fun as the following questions. I've written these questions to be silly and stupid enough for you to *remember* them and the points they teach. The real GMAT will, of course, have dull and boring questions. Both theirs and mine, however, require the same approach and test the same concepts. During the actual GMAT, you'll use everything you use on these practice questions — except your sense of humor.

1. Dismayed by the symptoms of Dunlap's Disease (his belly done lapped over his belt), <u>Santa, going to Weight Watchers</u>.

   (A) Santa, going to Weight Watchers

   (B) Santa went to Weight Watchers

   (C) Santa, having gone to Weight Watchers

   (D) was Santa, at Weight Watchers

   (E) Weight Watchers got Santa

When a sentence begins with a subordinate clause (a clause that can't stand alone), it must be followed by a noun (or pronoun) doing the action of that clause. Santa is the one who went to Weight Watchers. Therefore, Santa must follow the subordinate clause, eliminating choice E. (Choice E makes it sound as if Weight Watchers was dismayed by Dunlap's Disease.) Choices A and C are fragments, or incomplete sentences. They don't complete the thought but instead leave you dangling, wondering "What *about* Santa?" Choice D is unnecessarily awkward and changes the meaning of the sentence slightly by making it seem as if Santa were already at Weight Watchers instead of going there. *Correct Answer:* B.

Be sure to reinsert the underlined portion into the original sentence and reread the whole shebang.

2. "I thought I was a man but I'm just a mouse!" cried Mickey in terror as he tried to escape from the farmer's wife <u>who was wielding a knife that was big in size</u>.

   (A) who was wielding a knife that was big in size

   (B) whose wielded knife was big in size

   (C) who wielded a big in size knife

   (D) who was wielding a big knife

   (E) who had been wielding a big knife

First, eliminate the redundancy *big in size.* Something big is necessarily big in size; you don't need to use both terms. Eliminating the redundancy rules out choices A, B, and C. Go ahead and guess; 50-50 odds are pretty good. Choice E slightly changes the meaning of the sentence by changing the tense. Change as little as possible in Sentence Correction questions. Identify the crisis, resolve it, and move on. *Correct Answer:* D.

3. <u>Unphased by the piteous screams coming from their victim,</u> the torturers continued to show reruns of *The Partridge Family,* determined to make the spy crack and reveal her secrets.

 (A) Unphased by the piteous screams coming from their victim

 (B) Unphased, and with the victim's piteous screams coming

 (C) Unfazed by their victim's screams which were coming from

 (D) Unphased by their victim's piteous screams

 (E) Unfazed by their victim's piteous screams

To phase is to carry out in planned installments. This sentence requires the verb *faze,* meaning to upset or bother. Eliminate choices A, B, and D. Choice C, when reinserted into the sentence, makes it sound as if the screams were coming from the torturers (and the rest of the sentence makes no sense). *Correct Answer:* E.

4. Melissa dumped a bucket of water on her dog Karl's <u>head, however, he continued to attempt</u> to develop an intimate relationship with the leg of the sofa.

 (A) head, however, he continued to attempt

 (B) head; however, he continued to attempt

 (C) head: however; he continued to attempt

 (D) head; however, he was continuing attempting

 (E) head, however, he continued attempting

The proper punctuation/construction for two independent clauses (sentences) that are connected with a conjunctive adverb (words like *however, moreover, nonetheless, therefore*) is a semicolon, then the adverb, and finally the comma (this is discussed in the grammar review in Chapter 2). Eliminate answers A, C, and E. Choice D unnecessarily changes the form of *to continue* to *continuing,* making the sentence awkward. Change as little as possible from the original. As many divorced people have found, change for the sake of change can really mess things up. *Correct Answer:* B.

5. <u>Looking at Olana as she lay giggling in a crumpled heap</u> on the ice, her pairs partner told her that the next time she did the jump he'd be sure to catch her.

 (A) Looking at Olana as she lay giggling in a crumpled heap

 (B) Looking at Olana as she laid giggling in a crumpled heap

 (C) Olana, giggling and looking like a crumpled heap

 (D) Laying in a giggling crumpled heap and being looked at

 (E) Looking at Olana as she was laying giggling in a crumpled heap

If the use of *lay* sounds odd to you, it's because 99 percent of us misuse *lie* and *lay.* To *lie* is to recline, to plop down and stretch out and demand that Beulah peel you a grape. The conjugation of *lie* is bizarre: Today I lie down, yesterday I lay down, every day this week I have lain down. That's right; the past tense of *lie* is *lay* (do you think English could possibly be any more confusing?). Knowing that some form of *lie* is correct allows you to eliminate choices B, D, and E. Choice C maligns poor Olana by making her look like a crumpled heap rather than having her lying in a crumpled heap. *Correct Answer:* A.

6. <u>Finding hairs in the sink, his brush, and the drain was clogged</u>, Mr. Vader knew his days as a shampoo model were coming to an end.

   (A) Finding hairs in the sink, his brush, and the drain was clogged

   (B) Finding hairs in the sink and his brush and clogging the drain

   (C) Hairs in the sink, his brush and the clogged drain

   (D) Finding hairs in the sink, his brush, and the clogged drain

   (E) Clogging the drain, his sink and his brush

The original sentence lacks parallel structure: Items in a series must be in the same form. Mr. Vader found hairs in the sink, the brush, and the drain. Choice C has parallel structure but doesn't fit when reinserted into the sentence. Choice E makes it sound as if Mr. Vader himself were clogging the sink! *Correct Answer:* D.

You often can predict the correct form of the underlined part and look for that answer. But be very, very careful not to make an automatic correction. That is, don't correct the sentence as you read it and then shrug and say to yourself, "Nope, nothin's wrong here; I'll choose A." Of course, nothing's wrong; you've just corrected it in your head! Any time you select choice A, double- and triple-check it to make sure that you didn't rewrite the sentence to fit your own demanding standards.

7. <u>The pitching ability of Ms. Wender is very similar to Mr. Jarchow, in that each</u> can hurl a water balloon through a window and hit the other at 60 paces.

   (A) The pitching ability of Ms. Wender is very similar to Mr. Jarchow, in that each can

   (B) The pitching ability of Ms. Wender, very similar to Mr. Jarchow: each can

   (C) The pitching ability of Ms. Wender is very similar to that of Mr. Jarchow; each can

   (D) Ms. Wender's pitching ability, very similar to Mr. Jarchow, is that each can

   (E) Ms. Wender's and Mr. Jarchow's pitching ability each can

This question is an exception to the rule that shorter is better. Rarely, very rarely, is the longest answer the right answer. (I put this question in just to keep you from getting complacent.) The original sentence, along with choices B and D, incorrectly compares the pitching ability of Ms. Wender to Mr. Jarchow himself rather than comparing the pitching ability of Ms. Wender to the pitching ability of Mr. Jarchow. As I discuss in Chapter 2, comparisons must be made between similar objects: person to person, thing to thing. Inserting the simple phrase *that of* (referring to Mr. Jarchow's pitching ability) solves the problem. Choice E makes no sense when reinserted into the sentence. It is not the pitching ability that can pitch the water balloon, but Ms. Wender and Mr. Jarchow themselves. *Correct Answer:* C.

8. <u>Its rare to find agreement among the twins, who are</u> both pig-headed fools who refuse to compromise.

   (A) Its rare to find agreement among the twins, who are

   (B) It's rare to find agreement among the twins, who are

   (C) It's rare to find agreement between the twins, who are

   (D) It's rare to find agreement between the twins, whom are

   (E) Its rare to find agreement among the twins, whom are

This question tests three concepts: *it's/its*, *between/among*, and *who/whom*. (I did warn you in the lecture, if you remember, that a question may test multiple points.) *It's* with an apostrophe means it is, as in "it is rare to find. . . ." Because the *it's* form is correct, you can eliminate choices A and E.

The *among* form compares more than two items; the *between* form compares exactly two items. Because "twins" means two people, the word *between* is needed. Eliminate answer B. *Who* is subjective, serving as the subject, doing the action. *Whom* is objective, serving as an object, receiving the action. Because *who* is doing the action here (being pig-headed), it is correct. Eliminate answer D. *Correct Answer:* C.

Don't make the assumption that after you find an error, you're home free. Don't be in such a rush that you correct one error and forget about the others (or worse yet, correct one error and create another, as choice D does here).

9. When it comes to spitting for distance, <u>Jim is as talented, if not more talented than,</u> anyone else in the class.

   (A) Jim is as talented, if not more talented than,

   (B) Jim is as talented as, if not more talented than,

   (C) Jim, more talented than

   (D) Jim, who is at least as talented, if not more talented than,

   (E) as talented as, if not more talented than, Jim

The correct expressions are "as . . . as/more . . . than." In the original sentence, the second *as* is missing.

If you chose A, you probably automatically supplied this missing *as*, correcting the sentence unconsciously. Anytime you choose A, you must double-check to make sure that you haven't accidentally added, deleted, or changed something in your mind to make the sentence correct.

Choice E contains the second *as* but completely messes up the sentence. If you plug that choice back into the sentence, you'll see that it doesn't work. Be sure to take this last step of reinserting your answer into the sentence; saving a few seconds by neglecting to do so can cost you more than a few points. *Correct Answer:* B.

10. When asked who painted the sign reading, "Open 365 days a year except Christmas, other holidays, and weekends!" Mr. McKee <u>had to admit it was he</u>.

   (A) had to admit it was he

   (B) had to admit he was it

   (C) had to admit it was him

   (D) admitted it was him

   (E) admitted because he had to that it was he

Aha! I bet you chose D, right? In common speech, most of us say "it was him" because that form seems to sound better. It's a vicious cycle: We usually say something wrong because it sounds better, and the wrong way sounds better because we usually say it like that. What can you do? You could memorize a big, boring rule about predicate nominatives, but I wouldn't ask that of you. Here's an easier way to remember the rule: A pronoun after any form of the verb *to be* (is, are, was, were, had been, and so on) is in the subjective, or subject form. In other words, when you say, "It is . . ." the verb *is* tells you to use a subject pronoun, such as I, you, he, she, it, we, or they. Think of how you answer a telephone. "May I speak with Michael, please?" "This is he." Using the *he* form narrows the answers down to A or E. Choice E is unnecessarily wordy. *Correct Answer:* A.

11. The principal objection Larna has to this sofa's being advertised as suitable for a lady with large legs and thick cushions is that it is overpriced.

   (A) The principal objection Larna has to this sofa's being advertised as suitable for a lady with large legs and thick cushions is that it is overpriced.

   (B) The principle objection Larna has to this sofa, which has large legs and thick cushions for a lady, is that it is overpriced.

   (C) The principal objection Larna has is to the overpriced lady's sofa with large legs and thick cushions.

   (D) The principal objection Larna has is that the sofa, which has large legs and thick cushions and is suitable for a lady, is overpriced.

   (E) The overpriced lady's sofa with large legs and thick cushions is objected to principley by Larna.

Wow — talk about a rude sentence! The original and choice B sound as if the lady has large legs and thick cushions! Choices C and E sound as if the lady is overpriced. Choice E has a second mistake in that it uses *principle,* meaning rule, rather than *principal,* meaning main or primary (there's not even such a word as "principley"). *Correct Answer:* D.

You should know a list of "red flag" words — words and expressions that are commonly misused and frequently tested such as principle/principal in the preceding sentence. When you see one of these words, double-check it. Do not automatically assume that it is misused; just look it over to see what's happening. These red flag words may contain diction errors, covered in the grammar review in Chapter 2.

12. When Janet forgot her husband Marshall's name while renewing their wedding vows on their twenty-fifth anniversary, he laughed and teased her about doing it for the next ten years.

   (A) about doing it for the next ten years

   (B) for the next ten years about doing it

   (C) for the next ten years about having done so

   (D) and did so for the next ten years

   (E) about it for the next ten years

It and *so* are two words that are often confused. *It* refers to one specific thing or item. *So* refers to an action or situation. Usually, the verb *to do* (and its forms such as *doing* or *done*) is followed by *so:* The photographer asked me to smile, but I refused to do so. Understanding this rule eliminates choices A, B, and E. Make a guess and go. Choice D looks good on its own, but it is definitely awkward when reinserted into the sentence, making it unnecessarily wordy and also changing the meaning of the sentence. Don't forget to take the final step of rereading the entire sentence with your answer choice inserted. *Correct Answer:* C.

Part III
Everyone's a Critic

The 5th Wave   By Rich Tennant

MITCH HAD TROUBLE CONCENTRATING ON THE "PHYSICAL SCIENCE PASSAGE OF THE GMAT, TITLED: "VIOLENT MUTANTS LIVE AMONG US RECOGNIZABLE ONLY BY THEIR HUNCHED SHOULDERS AND BLAND EXPRESSIONS"

©RICHTENNANT

In this part . . .

Do you love to debate with your friends, picking holes in their arguments, rubbing their noses in the flaws in their reasoning? Well, good news: All those years of harassing people are about to pay off for you. You may have lost friends, but hey, you developed skills that enable you to ace the Critical Reasoning section!

In Critical Reasoning, the test makers evaluate how well you make an argument and develop a plan of action. The section counts as part of the verbal score. (The verbal score includes questions in Reading Comprehension, Sentence Correction, and Critical Reasoning.) The questions in the Critical Reasoning section follow short (usually one paragraph) passages. Sometimes a few questions are based on the same passage.

The GMAT Critical Reasoning has traditionally been approximately 25 percent of the overall verbal score. On the new CAT, expect 8 to 13 questions. Always keep in mind that the number of questions varies, depending on your skill in the section. If you nail all the CR questions quickly, the computer figures you're so good it doesn't need to pester you any more on this topic and gives you more questions in your weaker areas, such as Sentence Correction or Reading Comprehension questions. That's just the price you pay for success.

Chapter 5

Readings That Can Affect Your Future: Blood Pressure, Astrology, and GMAT

• •

In This Chapter

▶ Three commonly tested reading passages

▶ Questions to focus on

▶ Tricks for making life a little easier

• •

*F*eared by more students than Monday's mystery meat in the college cafeteria, Reading Comprehension (RC) questions comprise about 10 to 15 (the number can vary; students get different exams) out of 41 verbal questions. Usually, about 40 percent of the questions test Reading Comprehension. Remember that this number definitely can change from student to student. If you get every single RC question correct but miss a lot of Sentence Correction questions, the computer adapts to you and gives you fewer Reading Comprehension questions and more Sentence Correction questions.

Your verbal exam will have at least one, probably two, and possibly even three reading passages. They may be from 200 to 400 words. After each passage, the GMAT gives you four questions, one at a time. That is, the screen doesn't feature all four questions together. You answer question one, then question two, and so on. Like all the questions in the CAT, you must answer a question before the computer allows you to go on to the next question (in other words, you may not skip a question) and you may not go back and change an answer you have given previously.

Don't panic and think that you have to memorize the passage. The reading passage itself stays on the screen; you can go back and look at it as much as you like for each question.

Why Do They Call It Reading Comprehension If I Don't Understand a Thing I've Read?

The origin of the misnomer "Reading Comprehension" is a great topic for a *deipnosophist*. (A deipnosophist is one who converses eruditely at the dinner table. Don't worry; you don't have to know the word for the GMAT; I just threw it in so you could sound smart to your friends.) For now, you don't care so much what the section is called; you just want to get through it. The following information presents an overview of the types of passages you will encounter, the best approach to each distinct type of passage, and tips and traps for answering the questions based on those passages. Let's start by seeing what a Reading Comprehension question looks like.

Which of the following best describes the tone of the passage?

(A) sarcastic

(B) excited

(C) objective

(D) saddened

(E) pessimistic

All questions may be answered from information stated or implied in the passage. You aren't expected to answer questions based on your own knowledge, and you don't need to know anything special about science or business to answer these questions.

The Three Commonly Tested Reading Passages

In their torture chambers over the years (would someone please call Amnesty International?), the test makers have decided to write passages based on biological or physical sciences, social sciences, and business-related fields (economics, human-resources management, marketing, and so on). The following sections offer a preview of the passages to help you separate the devastating from the merely intolerable.

If you are an international student, you may find that you take a long time to read and at least partially understand a Reading Comprehension passage. That's normal. Unfortunately, on the GMAT CAT, you don't have the option of previewing all the passages (as you would do on a paper-and-pencil test) and deciding which one to focus on. You have to answer every question in order before the computer lets you go on to the next question. That's the bad news. However, I have some good news. If you are totally lost in the passage, you can always just guess wildly on the questions. You may not get too many correct, which is a signal to the computer that you need an easier passage. The next reading passage you see on the screen should be significantly simpler. Note that "significantly simpler" doesn't mean it's a piece of cake (very easy), just that it's easier than the first passage.

Beam me up, Scotty! Biological and physical science passages

A science passage is straightforward, giving you information on how laser beams work, how to build a suspension bridge, how molecular theory is applied, and so on. Although the passage itself is often very booooooooooring to read (because it is full of just facts, facts, and more facts), this type of passage often results in the most correct answers because it has so few tricks and traps.

Reading tip

Let's talk reality here: You're not going to remember — and maybe not even understand — most of what you read in a science passage. It's all just statistics and dry details. No matter how carefully and slowly you read through it the first time, you're almost certain to need to go back through the passage a second time to find specific facts. You end up reading the passage twice. Why waste time? Zip through the passage, just to get a general idea of what it's about and where the information is. (Paragraph one tells how molecules combine; paragraph two tells how scientists are working to split the atom; paragraph three tells. . . .)

Question tip

Science questions can often be answered directly from the facts provided in the passage itself. They are rarely the "inference" type that require you to read between the lines and really think about what the author is saying, what point he or she is trying to make, how he or she feels about the subject, and so on. Here's an example:

The author would most likely agree that which of the following is true of a species whose members are widely scattered?

    I. It has a high tolerance for limiting factors.

    II. It has few natural enemies.

    III. It is resistant to environmental change.

    IV. It is capable of surviving in both marine and freshwater environments.

(A) I only

(B) III only

(C) I and III only

(D) I, II, and III only

(E) I, II, III, and IV

The answers to this very straightforward type of question are given, usually pretty directly, in the passage. They're worth taking the time to go back and find.

It's not a disease: The social science passage

The GMAT usually includes one social science passage. It may be about a person, history, psychology, or a variety of other topics. The term *social science* is broad enough, in other words, to include whatever the test makers want it to include. The social science passage is often the most interesting of the passages you'll encounter. It may give you a perspective on history that you didn't know or tell you tidbits about a person of whom you've never heard.

Reading tip

In many ways, social science passages are nearly the opposite of science passages. The questions here deal more with inferences and less with explicitly stated facts. You must read the passages slowly and carefully, trying to understand not only what is said but also what is implied. Take your time.

Question tip

The questions that follow social science passages may not be as straightforward as those for a biological or physical science passage. You may not be able to go back to a specific line and pick out a specific fact. Instead, you are asked to understand the big picture, to comprehend what the author meant but didn't come right out and say. You may be asked why an author included a particular example or explanation. In other words, you're expected to be a mind reader. For example:

The author's primary motive in listing Dr. Buttinski's accomplishments was to

(A) impress the reader with Dr. Buttinski's importance.

(B) show that Dr. Buttinski overcame great odds to become a physician.

(C) ridicule Dr. Buttinski's adversaries, who were unable to accomplish as much as she did.

(D) predict great things for Dr. Buttinski's future.

(E) evaluate the effect Dr. Buttinski's work has had on our everyday lives.

Determining the author's motive involves as much reasoning as reading. No sentence specifically says, "Okay, listen up, troops. I'm going to tell you something, and my motive for doing so is blah, blah, blah." You need to read the passage slowly enough to develop an idea of why the author is telling you something and what exactly he wants you to take from this passage. Going back and rereading the passage doesn't do you much good; thinking about what you read does.

In the sample question provided here, every answer given probably would be true in the context of the passage itself. That is, the author probably thought Dr. Buttinski was important, probably believed that Dr. Buttinski had to overcome great odds to become a physician, and so on. Keep in mind, however, what the question is asking; *Why* did the author mention this specific thing? You must probe the author's mind.

What business is it of yours? The business passages

The business passages combine the worst features of the biological and physical science passages with the worst features of the social science passages. These passages are often very difficult to read, full of dry and boring statistics like the biological and physical sciences passages. Yet the questions expect you to understand the whole passage, to comprehend the reasoning behind statements, to read the author's mind and understand his or her implications, like questions about social science passages. In my mind, this type of passage is far and away the hardest of the three to read, understand, and (what's most important) answer questions on correctly. This may surprise you. Chances are you're interested in business (why else would you be trying to get into an MBA program?) and think that the business passages would be the most interesting. Wrong. While "interesting" is subjective, virtually all my students over the years have told me that the business passages were boring, incomprehensible, and frustrating. A business passage can make you go back again and again and again searching for an answer that in fact is not given specifically in the passage but which you have to infer. If you don't truly comprehend everything in the passage, making inferences is extremely difficult.

Reading tip

Of all the types of passages, this type is the one I think may frustrate you the most. If you are unlucky enough to encounter it early on, don't feel guilty about making wild guesses and hoping the next reading passage will be more tolerable.

Question tip

As I mentioned, the questions following a business passage often require you to understand the whole passage thoroughly. They may ask for inferences. They also tend to be "comprehensive" questions. That is, you get questions that you can answer only if you read the whole passage rather than bits and pieces of it. Here's an example of one such comprehensive question.

Which of the following tactics mentioned in the passage would be most appropriate for the pricing strategy advocated by the author?

  (A) gathering information directly from target market groups

  (B) using long-term economic forecasts

  (C) incorporating historical information and trend analysis

  (D) evaluating the competition

  (E) using a linear mathematical formula

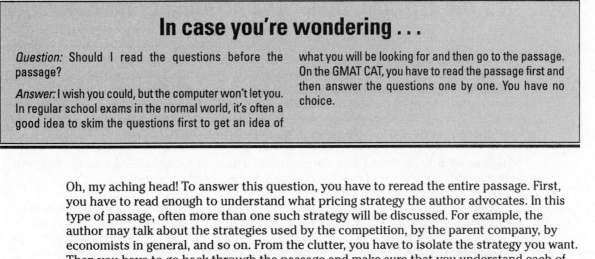

In case you're wondering . . .

Question: Should I read the questions before the passage?

Answer: I wish you could, but the computer won't let you. In regular school exams in the normal world, it's often a good idea to skim the questions first to get an idea of

what you will be looking for and then go to the passage. On the GMAT CAT, you have to read the passage first and then answer the questions one by one. You have no choice.

Oh, my aching head! To answer this question, you have to reread the entire passage. First, you have to read enough to understand what pricing strategy the author advocates. In this type of passage, often more than one such strategy will be discussed. For example, the author may talk about the strategies used by the competition, by the parent company, by economists in general, and so on. From the clutter, you have to isolate the strategy you want. Then you have to go back through the passage and make sure that you understand each of the types of strategies mentioned in the answer choices. Probably one strategy would be discussed in each paragraph. For five strategies, you'd have to go back and read five paragraphs — the whole stupid passage.

Do you get the idea that I don't think too much of this passage style? You're right. While I, of course, hope you do well on all the passages, my goal is to make you aware of which passage gives you the best chance at answering correctly the greatest number of questions. It sure isn't this passage.

International students, take note. I find that the business passages often feature quite difficult vocabulary. Some of the expressions used can be confusing: intuitive versus empirical, problematic cycles, cognitive processes, or multioccupational jurisdiction. If English is not your first language, you want to be extra wary of these terms. (And to my American readers who are feeling a little woozy right now: Don't worry; many of us don't understand that jargon either.)

Focus Your Fire: Questions to Do Quickly; Questions to Do Carefully

Knowing how to approach the Reading Comprehension passages on your GMAT is extremely important. Even more important than the passages themselves, however, are the questions following each passage. After all, the admissions officer at Harvard is not going to say to you, "Hey, tell me about that GMAT passage you read about the curative properties of heavy metal music." The admissions officer is far more likely to ask, "How many reading comprehension questions did you answer correctly?" No matter how carefully you read the passage, no matter how well you understand it, you must be able to put that knowledge to work to answer the questions that follow those passages.

So just what kind of questions are you most likely to encounter in the Reading Comprehension portions of the test? The following sections describe the several basic question types you may face in the dark alleys of the GMAT.

It's the attitude, dude: The attitude or tone question

✔ The author's attitude may be described as . . .

✔ The tone of the passage is . . .

These two types of questions are variations on a single theme: What is the tone of the passage or the attitude of the author? Nothing in the passage answers this type of question directly. You can't find any one line reading: "In my opinion, which, by the way, is sardonic, the importance of. . . ." You simply must reason this one out.

The tone or attitude (found after the type of each passage in the following paragraphs) usually depends on the type of passage that the question is asking about.

International students, take note. The answer choices to an attitude or tone question often use quite difficult vocabulary. If you knew from reading the passage that the author was delighted with something, which of the following would you choose to describe his attitude: phlegmatic, dogmatic, ebullient, cantankerous, lethargic? The right answer is ebullient, which means bubbling over with enthusiasm or excitement — but how many people know that word? I mean, it's not as if your best friend asks you, "So, how are you today?" and your immediate response is, "Well, I'm ebullient, thanks; and you?" If you don't know the vocabulary, guess quickly and go on. After all, sitting there and agonizing over the words won't suddenly make the definitions pop into your brain (especially if they're totally bizarre words you've never seen before). Remember: The GMAT has no penalty for guessing except the one you create for yourself: the penalty of wasting time by not guessing quickly.

Table 5-1 lists the tone or attitude likely found in each type of reading passage.

Table 5-1   Predominant Tones or Attitudes Found in GMAT Reading Passages

Passage Type	Tone or Attitude	Explanation
Physical or biological sciences	Neutral or positive	A physical or biological science passage gives you just the facts. The author rarely evaluates the facts one way or the other and rarely expresses an opinion. After all, how opinionated can someone be about a color spectrum?
Social science	Positive or neutral	A social science passage may be about how some event unfolded or some theory was developed. For example, a passage may talk about history, presenting the good events and downplaying the bad ones. Think positive, or at the very worst, neutral.
Business	Positive or neutral	Most of the business passages discuss a business philosophy or trend or evaluate how a business is run (the intuitive style of management versus the empirical style, for example).

I have said repeatedly that reading passages are usually positive or neutral; they are very, very rarely negative. If you are going to encounter a negative passage, it will probably be a business passage. Occasionally, a business passage criticizes a particular management decision, points out the flaws used in developing a policy, or explains why a particular product failed.

Because so many of the tones or attitudes of the Reading Comprehension passages are positive or neutral, certain words are often good to choose as answers to attitude or tone questions. The following list offers several positive words that you may want to consider choosing should any appear as potential answers to this kind of question:

Common Positive-Attitude Word	More Difficult Word with the Same Meaning
Optimistic	Sanguine
Praising	Laudatory
Admiring	Reverential

You get the idea. Wrong answers — that is, negative answers — may include the words in the following list. **Remember:** These are words that you usually *don't* want to choose.

Common Negative-Attitude Word	More Difficult Word with the Same Meaning
Ridiculing	Lampooning
Sarcastic	Sardonic
Belittling	Denigrating

Because so many passages are neutral, the term *objective,* which means neutral, not taking one side or the other, not subjective or opinionated, is often a correct answer. Don't simply turn off your own brain and choose *objective* automatically, but it's a good guess if you're stumped for an answer. Think of it as guilty until proven innocent.

What's the big idea: Main idea or best title

You can bet the farm (but, of course, only in states with legalized gambling) that you'll see a few main idea or best title questions; each Reading Comprehension passage usually has one. This type of question can assume any of the following forms:

- ✔ The main idea of the passage is . . .
- ✔ The primary purpose of the author is . . .

The best place to find the main idea of the passage is in its topic sentence, which is usually the first or second sentence of the first paragraph. The topic sentence may be the last sentence of the passage, but such a structure is rare. Your game plan upon encountering one of these questions should be to head right back to the first sentence to locate a main idea.

Suppose that the passage begins as follows:

> The uses to which latex has been applied have exceeded the wildest fantasies of its creators.

What is the main idea of the passage: The uses of latex? The applications of latex? The many products made of latex?

After you read the entire passage, all the darn answers in the main idea question may look pretty good. That's because all of them usually consist of facts stated in the passage. Just because something is true and is discussed in the passage doesn't mean it's necessarily the main idea.

Don't pester me with details: The detail or fact question

Unlike main idea questions, the detail or fact questions focus on particular parts of the passage. These questions require you to go to one section or a few sections of the passage and use the information found there to answer the question. Sometimes the test maker provides you with a line reference, making the location job extremely easy.

Be sure to read more than just the line or lines mentioned. If you read just the line or lines stated in the question, you may get an incomplete understanding of the detail. (After all, the test makers are not testing your ability to look up a fact the way you look up a name in the phone book!)

If you are not given a line reference, identify a few key words in the question and try to find those words in the passage. The answer is usually within a few sentences of those words. If you are having trouble finding the key words, find the part of the passage that discusses the general notion mentioned in the question and then read that part of the passage carefully to find the answer to the question.

Several detail or fact questions begin with "According to the passage. . . ." Such wording should be your cue to search the passage and look for something explicitly stated. Keep in mind, though, that "explicitly stated" does not mean that the correct answer choice will repeat the text verbatim. The answer choice typically paraphrases what is in the text. To answer the questions more quickly, try to paraphrase the text yourself after you read the answer in the text. By doing so, you're more likely to recognize the correct answer quickly; you can simply skim through the wrong answers rather than having to read them carefully before you toss them out.

Here are a few common detail or fact question stems:

- ✔ The passage (or author) states . . .
- ✔ Why did the attempt fail?
- ✔ What was the most important advantage of the plan?

If you're stuck, remember that even a question that deals with the most minuscule detail has to be consistent with the main idea. The purpose of details is to develop or support the main idea. Therefore, be sure to eliminate answer choices that go against the grain of the passage or the author's overall opinion.

Get the hint? Inference questions

Inference questions are common on the GMAT. Most questions of this type are similar to detail questions in that they focus on a particular part of the passage. (Some, however, cover more territory.) Inference questions differ from detail questions in that they require you to come up with an answer that is not *explicitly* stated in the passage. In order to answer the question, you have to put a couple of the presented thoughts together and come up with your own idea. You do a bit more than simply summarize what is in the passage. You must use your logical thinking processes to determine what point the author is trying to make. If one sentence says that Americans had hoped to be the first to launch an artificial satellite and a second says that Americans were disappointed, for example, you may infer that another nation beat out the Americans.

Don't go overboard with your inference; it must fit into the passage. A common wrong choice on inference questions will disagree with the author's main idea. Another wrong choice may distort something mentioned in the passage. For example, the author may disagree with the notion that Americans have always been fair to minorities. This does not mean, however, that Americans have always been unfair. A wrong answer choice may deal with an issue that is outside the realm of the particular topic under discussion. Suppose that a passage defends tax shelters because they stimulate investment and economic growth. A choice that talks about overhauling the entire tax structure is wrong because it is too broad to match what the author is discussing.

Here are a few common inference question stems:

- ✔ The passage (or author) suggests . . .
- ✔ It can be inferred from the passage that . . .
- ✔ The author implies . . .

Use it or lose it: Application questions

Application questions require you to take an idea presented in the passage (typically a major, if not *the* major, point) and use it to answer a question that concerns a concept not directly addressed in the passage. In other words, you must apply some knowledge you gained from reading and thinking about the passage to a different context.

Suppose that you read a passage about how hard Congressional proponents of the 1964 Civil Rights Act had to work to get the legislation passed. The passage mentions the filibuster imposed by Senate opponents, who were in the minority, and what prevented the measure from getting to the Senate floor for a vote. The passage emphasizes how supporters had to invoke some rarely used measures to overcome the filibuster. An application question on this passage may be:

With which of the following statements would the author most likely agree?

(A) Civil rights legislation has always been unpopular.

(B) Filibusters are common for many types of legislation.

(C) The Senate should pass legislation that would outlaw filibusters.

(D) Proposed legislation can sometimes be blocked even when most Senators favor it.

(E) Legislation is more frequently blocked by the Senate than by the House of Representatives.

The passage talks about how the filibuster blocked the proposed civil rights legislation for quite some time. The filibuster did not ultimately succeed only because supporters were able to conjure up some rarely used measures. Because everything had to go just right to overcome the filibuster mentioned in the passage, the author could easily see that filibusters could completely kill some legislation, thereby allowing a minority of Senators to block proposed legislation.

The passage gives no indication about how often filibusters are used, so choice B is out. Neither does the passage discuss the history of civil rights legislation, so dump choice A. The House may not have filibusters, but perhaps a lot of proposed legislation gets stalled there for other reasons. Eliminate choice E. Choice C is the most tempting choice, given that the author approved of the Civil Rights Act and clearly did not appreciate attempts to block it. However, what would the author say about filibusters used to block proposed legislation that she didn't like? She would probably be very grateful for the filibuster. *Correct Answer:* D.

Here are a few other question stems common to this type of question:

- ✔ The argument made in the final paragraph would be most strengthened by . . .
- ✔ Which of the following is analogous to the situation described . . .

Sense and nonsense: Logic questions

Logic questions are similar to Critical Reasoning questions. Your job is to follow the way the author presents his point. Many logic questions require you to determine how a certain part of the passage fits into the author's overall argument.

Suppose that you read a passage arguing that undocumented workers from other nations provide a valuable service by performing tasks that American citizens are unwilling to do because of the low pay. The author quotes a famous economist, who says, "Minimum wage laws have made Americans think that they have an inherent right to wealth."

The logic question for this passage might be:

The author quotes the economist in order to . . .

The correct answer will reflect that the author quoted the economist to support the point he was making about undocumented workers taking jobs that would not be filled otherwise. (Keep in mind that a good writer will mention a detail to develop or support a major idea.) Classic wrong answers will deal too much with the quote itself (in other words, stating that minimum wage laws have spoiled American citizens) or lead to a point the author is clearly not trying to emphasize (saying that American citizens make more money than undocumented workers from other countries).

When a question asks why the author included a certain part of the passage, be careful to focus on the *why* of the detail rather than the *what*. The *what* may be true and a fine answer to a detail question or even an inference question, but it won't work here.

Some logic questions require you to analyze the structure of part or all of the passage. A question may ask, "Which of the following describes the organization of the first paragraph?" A correct answer might be, "A theory is presented, counterexamples are given, and a new theory is proposed."

A slight variation of the purpose of detail question ("The author mentions . . . in order to. . . .") is a question in which you must identify what the author used in the passage to support a point.

The power of positive thinking: Negative or exception questions

One type of question is a trained killer that can strike you down in an instant: the negative or exception question. Here are a few ways this question may be worded:

- ✔ Which of the following is *not* true?
- ✔ The *least* likely situation is . . .
- ✔ With which of the following would the author *disagree?*
- ✔ All of the following are true *except* . . .

These questions are phrased in the negative, which make them very tricky. You are actually looking for four correct answers, and then by the process of elimination choosing the one that is not correct. It's easy to get confused, and even easier to waste a lot of time, only to miss the question anyway. If you're feeling rushed for time or the question is totally bewildering you, don't waste a lot of time. Punch a button and get outta there.

Toga! Toga! Toga! The Roman numeral question

A Roman numeral question looks like this:

The author mentions which of the following as support for her argument against unilateral intervention?

   I. economic considerations

   II. moral obligations

   III. popular opinion

  (A) I only

  (B) II only

  (C) III only

  (D) I and II only

  (E) I, II, and III

Roman numeral questions are usually time-wasters. In effect, you have to go back and reread almost the whole passage to find whether I, II, or III was mentioned anywhere. A common trap is to have I and II mentioned close together and then have III mentioned far down the passage. Most people will find I and II and then, when III doesn't appear to be hanging around, choose I and II only, going down the tubes. (Hey, maybe the test makers get bonus points for every student they snare with a trick, rather like a cop writing speeding tickets to meet his quota in a speed trap. Just a thought.) With a Roman numeral question, you have to make a commitment (did I just lose half of my male readers?). You have to commit to rereading most of the passage just in case one of the concepts is floating around where you least expect it. If you are not willing or able to commit the time, guess quickly and go on.

Something up My Sleeve: Tricks for Making Life a Little Easier

After you know about the types of passages and primary types of questions, it's time for the fun stuff — the tricks.

Be positive or neutral, not negative

I will say this over and over and over until you are exasperated enough to cut off my air supply: Because most of the passages are going to be positive or neutral, many of the correct answers are going to be positive or neutral. The test makers don't want to get sued for saying mean and vicious things about anyone.

Choose answers containing key words

The key words, often found in the topic sentence, are what the whole passage is about. The right answers usually feature those words. If the passage is about Chicano history, the right answer will often have the words Chicano history in it. Don't immediately choose an answer *only* because it has the key words in it, but if you can narrow the answers down to two, choose the one with the key words.

Correct answers are usually a little above or a little below the key words or indicated line numbers

This can get nasty. The question will ask you about something and send you to a particular line number. When you go back there, either you won't find an answer, or you'll find the trap answer. Expand your horizons. Read a few sentences above and a few sentences below. The right answer will usually be found in the vicinity. If you just keep looking where they sent you, it'll be like looking for your car keys where they normally are and where you've searched a thousand times already, to no avail. You have to branch out.

One More Time: A Final Review

I've thrown a lot of information at you. You've learned about the types of passages, the types of questions, and the tricks and traps built into both. Are you having trouble keeping everything straight? Here's a short 'n' sweet summary.

An overview of the types of passages and reading suggestions for each one

You are likely to encounter three basic types of reading passages, as described in the following sections.

Biological or physical sciences

- ✔ The passages may be hard, but their questions are easy and straightforward.
- ✔ Read science passages quickly, just to get an overview of what they cover; don't try to understand everything you read.

Social science

- ✔ These passages are often about history.
- ✔ Read the passages slowly and carefully; questions usually require an understanding of between-the-lines concepts and cannot be answered merely by going back and skimming for a fact.

Business passages

- ✔ Of the three types of passages, this type may be the one you want to make random guesses on and trust that the next passage you get will be more user-friendly. Remember, you can't preview the passages as you could with a paper-and-pencil test, but if you miss a lot in one type of passage, chances are the computer will give you a different type of passage the next time.

✔ These passages combine the worst elements of the reading passages (difficult and/or boring to read) with the worst elements of the questions (inference rather than straightforward detail questions).

✔ Questions on these passages are particularly difficult to get right for international students whose first language is not English, as the terminology is unusual and confusing.

An overview of the types of questions and the traps hidden in each one

As you take the GMAT, you'll encounter the following types of questions. When you do, remember the traps and tricks for handling them.

Main idea/best title

The following is true of a main idea or best title question:

✔ You can frequently find the answer in the topic sentence, which is usually in the first paragraph of the passage.

✔ The correct answer often contains key words that usually come from the beginning of the passage.

Detail or fact

A detail or fact question has these characteristics:

✔ You can skim the passage to locate a specific answer.

✔ Correct answers are usually found in a line that's either a little above or a little below the line containing the key word or indicated line number in the question; you need to expand your search until you find it.

✔ This type is a quick question to get right even without reading the entire passage.

Negative or exception

Remember the following about a negative or exception question:

✔ This question is phrased negatively (Which is *not* true) or as an exception (All are true *except . . .*).

✔ This type of question is often very tricky or time-consuming.

✔ Unless you've read *and understood* the entire passage, you may want to make a quick random guess at this type of question.

Roman numeral

Here's what you should remember about Roman numeral questions:

✔ They are often very tricky or time-consuming.

✔ These are very good questions to guess at quickly if you're short on time.

Reading passages you'll never see on the GMAT

✔ **Biological science:** Cannibalism and You: The Science of Pigging Out at a Barbecue.

✔ **Social science (humanities):** The End of Political Correctness: An Analysis of Howard Stern and Rush Limbaugh.

✔ **Social science (behaviorism):** An excerpt from Confessions from the Funny Farm, Chapter 2: "How the GMAT Pushed Me over the Edge."

✔ **Business:** Difficult Managerial Decisions: Lobotomy or GMAT — Which Messes up Your Employees Less? The Insider's View.

✔ **Business:** The Art of Continuing Education for Your Decision-Makers: A Debate between National Lampoon and National Enquirer.

Chapter 6

Practice What I Preach: Reading Comprehension Practice Questions

• •

This section gives you a dozen questions based on two full-length passages and one passage that is abbreviated. For now, don't worry about timing yourself. Try to identify each selection as one of the types of reading passages that I describe in Chapter 5 (biological and physical sciences, social science, and business) and use the tips I give you for reading that type of passage. When you answer the questions, try to identify which type each question is (attitude/tone, main idea/best title, Roman numeral, and so on) and to recall any traps inherent to that type of question.

Passage 1

Line Microbiological activity clearly affects the mechanical strength of leaves. Although it cannot be denied that with most species the loss of mechanical strength is the result of both invertebrate feeding and microbiological breakdown, the example of *Fagus sylvatica* illustrates loss without any sign of invertebrate attack being evident. *Fagus* shows little sign
(05) of invertebrate attack even after being exposed for eight months in either a lake or stream environment, but results of the rolling fragmentation experiment show that loss of mechanical strength, even in this apparently resistant species, is considerable.

Most species appear to exhibit a higher rate of degradation in the stream environment than in the lake. This is perhaps most clearly shown in the case of *Alnus*. Examination of the
(10) type of destruction suggests that the cause for the greater loss of material in the stream-processed leaves is a combination of both biological and mechanical degradation. The leaves exhibit an angular fragmentation, which is characteristic of mechanical damage rather than the rounded holes typical of the attack by large particle feeders or the skeletal vein pattern produced by microbial degradation and small particle feeders. As the leaves
(15) become less strong, the fluid forces acting on the stream nylon cages cause successively greater fragmentation.

Mechanical fragmentation, like biological breakdown, is to some extent influenced by leaf structure and form. In some leaves with a strong midrib, the lamina break up, but the pieces remain attached by means of the midrib. One type of leaf may break clean while
(20) another tears off and is easily destroyed when the tissues are weakened by microbial attack.

In most species, the mechanical breakdown will take the form of gradual attrition at the margins. If the energy of the environment is sufficiently high, brittle species may be broken across the midrib, something that rarely happens with more pliable leaves. The result of attrition is that, where the areas of the whole leaves follow a normal distribution, a bimodal
(25) distribution is produced, one peak composed mainly of the fragmented pieces, the other of the larger remains.

To test the theory that a thin leaf has only half the chance of a thick one for entering the fossil record, all other things being equal, Ferguson (1971) cut discs of fresh leaves from 11 species of different leaf thicknesses and rotated them with sand and water in a revolving

(30) drum. Each run lasted 100 hours and was repeated three times, but even after this treatment, all species showed little sign of wear. It therefore seems unlikely that leaf thickness alone, without substantial microbial preconditioning, contributes much to the probability that a leaf will enter a depositional environment in a recognizable form. The results of experiments with whole fresh leaves show that they are more resistant to fragmentation

(35) than leaves exposed to microbiological attack. Unless the leaf is exceptionally large or small, leaf size and thickness are not likely to be as critical in determining the preservation potential of a leaf type as the rate of microbiological degradation.

1. The primary motive of the author is to

   (A) explain why leaf disintegration is an important event in maintaining ecological balance.

   (B) analyze the leaf structure and composition of various plant species.

   (C) compare lakes and streams in regard to leaf degradation.

   (D) outline the process involved in the mechanical breakdown of leaves.

   (E) discuss how microbiological activity interacts with other factors to affect leaf mechanical strength.

The author presents microbiological activity and mechanical strength of leaves in the first sentence of the passage. He then explores other factors but keeps coming back to the importance of microbiological attack. This repeated mention in the midst of a discussion of key elements in leaf breakdown reflects the author's motive. Choice E fits nicely.

Choice A is out. The author mentions the environment, but he hardly provides a thorough explanation about leaf disintegration and ecological balance. If he had, he would have provided a lot more information about topics such as how the organisms that feed on leaves allow other species to flourish.

The author analyzed certain physical properties of leaves but did not include information about many different species. More importantly, choice B is inappropriate because the author did not analyze structure and composition throughout the passage. Choice C is even worse than choice B because it refers to something mentioned only briefly in the passage (in the first paragraph). Finally, choice D is wrong because the author is concerned with what acts on leaves rather than what the leaves go through. If choice D were correct, the author would have included a more systematic explanation of the various steps of leaf degradation. *Correct Answer:* E.

2. Which of the following is mentioned as a reason for leaf degradation in streams?

   I. mechanical damage

   II. biological degradation

   III. large particle feeders

   (A) II only

   (B) I and II only

   (C) I and III only

   (D) II and III only

   (E) I, II, and III

Paragraph two of the passage tells you that ". . . loss of material in stream-processed leaves is a combination of biological and mechanical degradation." Statement III is incorrect because lines 12 and 13 specifically state that the pattern of holes is contrary to that of large particle feeders. *Correct Answer:* B.

3. The conclusion the author reached from Ferguson's revolving drum experiment was that

   (A) leaf thickness is, at best, only a contributing factor to leaf fragmentation.

   (B) leaves submersed in water degrade more rapidly than leaves deposited in mud or silt.

   (C) leaves with a strong midrib deteriorate less than leaves without such a midrib.

   (D) microbial attack is exacerbated by high temperatures.

   (E) bimodal distribution reduces leaf attrition.

Lines 30–32 tell you that it is unlikely that leaf thickness *alone* affects the final form of the leaf. You probably need to reread that sentence a few times to understand it, but this is the type of question worth investing your time in: a detail or fact question. The last sentence of the passage, which says that leaf size and thickness is only rarely a key factor, reinforces choice A as the answer. Choice B introduces facts that are not discussed in the passage; there was no talk of leaves in mud or silt. Choice C is mentioned in the passage but not in Ferguson's experiments. Be careful to answer *only* what the question is asking; the mere fact that a statement is true or is mentioned in the passage means nothing if the question isn't asking about that point. Nothing appears in the passage about high temperatures, which eliminates choice D. (Did you recognize the word *exacerbated?* It means made worse — as in, this reading passage probably exacerbated your headache.) Choice E sounds pretentious and pompous — and nice and scientific — but again has nothing to do with Ferguson. To answer this question correctly, you need to return to the passage to look up Ferguson specifically, not merely rely on your memory of the passage as a whole. *Correct Answer:* A.

4. The author's attitude toward those who claim that invertebrate feeding is necessary for the mechanical breakdown of leaves is one of

   (A) mild approval.

   (B) derisive scorn.

   (C) reserved disagreement.

   (D) ambivalent skepticism.

   (E) complete indifference.

In the first paragraph, the author presents evidence that shows loss of mechanical strength without evidence of invertebrate attack. Therefore, the author would disagree with anyone who claimed that invertebrate feeding was necessary for mechanical breakdown. This allows you to eliminate choices A and E right away; these choices indicate that the author would be neutral toward or agree with those who claim the necessity of invertebrate feeding.

Choice B is far too strong for any GMAT passage. *Derisive* means extremely disrespectful, and scorn is a feeling of complete ridicule for someone. Such strong feelings are especially inappropriate for science passages, which are almost always objective in tone. Choice D doesn't make a lot of sense. Skepticism, meaning doubt, may work, but what makes you think the author is ambivalent, or has mixed feelings? To reinforce choice C, note that the author does not say in the first paragraph that beyond a shadow of a doubt, there was no invertebrate activity. Choice C expresses the author's differences without going overboard, typical for the GMAT. *Correct Answer:* C.

5. The author most likely is addressing this passage to

   (A) gardeners.

   (B) botanists.

   (C) hikers.

   (D) mechanical engineers.

   (E) Adam and Eve.

The passage is talking about the microbiological activity affecting the strength of leaves. (You know this because you already answered a primary motive question on the topic — question number one.) Although choosing D is tempting, given the topic of the passage, mechanical engineers are usually interested more in machines than in leaves. Botanists are the ones who would most likely read this passage. The advice is probably too technical for gardeners — choice A — and is waaaay too specific for hikers — choice C. Choice E was added for comic relief. (If anyone needed to know how and why leaves disintegrate, especially fig leaves, it would be Adam and Eve. . . .) *Correct Answer:* B.

Passage II

Line   Multinational corporations frequently encounter impediments in their attempts to explain to politicians, human rights groups, and (perhaps most importantly) their consumer base why they do business with, even seek closer business ties to, countries whose human rights records are considered heinous by United States standards. The CEOs pro-

(05)   pound that in the business trenches, the issue of human rights must effectively be detached from the wider spectrum of free trade. Discussion of the uneasy alliance between trade and human rights has trickled down from the boardrooms of large multinational corporations to the consumer on the street who, given the wide variety of products available to him, is eager to show support for human rights by boycotting the products of a company he feels

(10)   does not do enough to help its overseas workers. International human rights organizations also are pressuring the multinationals to push for more humane working conditions in other countries and to in effect develop a code of business conduct that must be adhered to if the American company is to continue working with the overseas partner.

The president, in drawing up a plan for what he calls the "economic architecture of our

(15)   times," wants economists, business leaders, and human rights groups to work together to develop a set of principles that the foreign partners of United States corporations will voluntarily embrace. Human rights activists, incensed at the nebulous plans for implementing such rules, charge that the State Department is giving their agenda low priority. The president vociferously denies their charges, arguing that each situation is approached on its

(20)   merits without prejudice, and hopes that all the groups can work together to develop principles based on empirical research rather than political fiat, emphasizing that the businesses with experience in the field must initiate the process of developing such guidelines. Business leaders, while paying lip service to the concept of these principles, fight stealthily against their formal endorsement as they fear such "voluntary" concepts may someday be

(25)   given the force of law. Few business leaders have forgotten the Sullivan Principles, in which a set of voluntary rules regarding business conduct with South Africa (giving benefits to workers and banning apartheid in the companies that worked with U.S. partners) became legislation.

Q 6. Which of the following best states the central idea of the passage?

   (A) Politicians are quixotic in their assessment of the priorities of the State Department.

   (B) Multinational corporations have little if any influence on the domestic policies of their overseas partners.

   (C) Voluntary principles that are turned into law are unconstitutional.

   (D) Disagreement exists between the desires of human rights activists to improve the working conditions of overseas workers and the pragmatic approach taken by the corporations.

   (E) It is inappropriate to expect foreign corporations to adhere to American standards.

The main idea of the passage is usually stated in the first sentence or two. The first sentence of this passage discusses the difficulties that corporations have explaining their business ties to certain countries to politicians, human rights groups, and consumers. From this statement, you may infer that those groups disagree with the policies of the corporations.

In choice A, do you know the word *quixotic?* It means idealistic, impractical (think of the fictional character Don Quixote tilting at windmills). While the president referred to in this passage may not be realistic in his assessment of State Department policies, his belief was not the main idea of the passage.

Just because a statement is (or may be) true does not necessarily mean that it is the correct answer to a question. The answer choices to a main idea question in particular often are true or at least look plausible.

To answer a main idea question, I like to pretend that a friend of mine just came up behind me and said, "Hey, what 'cha reading there?" My first response is the main idea: "Oh, I read this passage about how corporations are getting grief from politicians and other groups because they do business with certain countries." *Before* you look at the answer choices, predict in your own words what the main idea is. You'll be pleasantly surprised how close your prediction is to the correct answer (and you won't be confused by all the other plausible-looking answer choices).

Choice E is a moral value, a judgment call. An answer that passes judgment, one that says something is morally right or morally wrong, is almost never the correct answer. *Correct Answer:* D.

7. According to the passage, the president wants the voluntary principles to be initiated by businesses rather than by politicians or human rights activists because

   (A) businesses have empirical experience in the field and thus know what the conditions are and how they may/should be remedied.

   (B) businesses make profits from the labor of the workers and thus have a moral obligation to improve their employees' working conditions.

   (C) workers will not accept principles drawn up by politicians whom they distrust but may agree to principles created by the corporations that pay them.

   (D) foreign nations are distrustful of political intervention by the United States and are more likely to accept suggestions from multinational corporations.

   (E) political activist groups have concerns that are too dramatically different from those of the corporations for the groups to be able to work together.

When a question begins with the words "according to the passage," you should go back to the passage and find the exact answer. In lines 21–22, you are told that ". . . businesses with experience in the field must initiate the process of developing such guidelines." Great — but what if you don't know the word *empirical,* which means based on experiment or experience rather than on theory? You keep on reading. The rest of the sentence divulges the right answer. Don't tune out as soon as you encounter a difficult word.

Choices B, C, D, and E are all judgment calls. You are assuming facts not in evidence, as the lawyers say. While you personally may believe the statements in these answer choices to be true, they don't answer the specific question. *Correct Answer:* A.

8. Which of the following best describes the reason the author mentions the boycott of a corporation's products by its customers?

   (A) to show the difficulties that arise when corporations attempt to become involved in politics

   (B) to predict the inevitability of failure of any plan that does not involve customer input

   (C) to disagree with the president's contention that big business is the best qualified to draw up the voluntary principles of work place conduct

   (D) to indicate the pressures that are on the multinational corporations

   (E) to ridicule the consumers for believing that their small boycott would significantly affect the sales of a multinational corporation

This question is one of those mind-reading questions I warned you about. You are expected to get into the author's mind and understand why he or she said what he or she did. The concept of the consumer boycott follows closely the main idea of the passage, which is that the corporations have difficulty trying to explain themselves and their actions to all sorts of groups, including their customers. From this, you may infer that the point of the statement is to indicate the pressures placed on the corporations.

The next line in the passage states that human rights organizations *also* are pressuring multi-national corporations, allowing you to infer that the consumers are applying pressure. Remember that one of your tips was to expand your horizons. Read until you find what you think is the right answer . . . and then read a little further.

Choices C and E begin with negative words, *disagree* and *ridicule*. Negative answer choices are rarely correct. Be careful, however, not to take this tip as a hard and fast rule. If you go back to the correct answer to question number six, you see that you might interpret that answer as negative.

Choice B seems logical; common sense tells you that a company that ignores its customers will probably fail. However, a strong, dramatic word such as *inevitably* is rarely correct. Few things in life are inevitable, as I've said before: just death, taxes, and the GMAT. *Correct Answer:* D.

9. Which of the following statements about the Sullivan Principles can best be inferred from the passage?

   (A) They had a detrimental effect on the profits of those corporations doing business with South Africa.

   (B) They represented an improper alliance between political and business groups.

   (C) They placed the needs of the foreign workers over those of the domestic workers whose jobs would therefore be in jeopardy.

   (D) They will be used as a model to create future voluntary business guidelines.

   (E) They will have a chilling effect on future adoption of voluntary guidelines.

Choice A is the major trap here. Perhaps you assumed that because the companies seem to dislike the Sullivan Principles, they hurt company profits. Nothing was said in the passage about profits, however. Maybe the companies still made good profits but objected to the Sullivan Principles, well, on principle. The companies just may not have wanted such governmental intervention even if profits weren't decreased. If you chose A, you read too much into the question and probably didn't read the rest of the answer choices.

In choice E, the words *chilling effect* mean negative effect, discouraging effect. Think of something with a chilling effect as leaving you cold. If your friend asks you to taste his soup, saying the dog loved it when he lapped up a few swallows, the statement about canine cuisine will have a chilling effect on your desire to taste the soup. Because few corporations have forgotten the Sullivan Principles, you may infer that these principles will discourage the companies from agreeing to voluntary principles in the future. *Correct Answer:* E.

In order to get this question correct, you really need to understand the whole passage. If you didn't know what was going on here, you would be better off making a quick guess and going on. You don't want to waste a lot of time on a question that most people are likely to miss anyway. An inference question usually means you have to read between the lines; you can't just go back to one specific portion of the passage and get the answer quickly.

Q 10. The author's primary objective in the passage is to

   (A) discuss the conflict between political, business, and human rights interests.

   (B) predict less multinational involvement in overseas employee workplace rules in the future.

   (C) argue against political involvement in multinational business.

   (D) analyze the strengths and weaknesses of current voluntary principles.

   (E) refute the idea that the State Department is involved in setting goals for multi-national corporations.

Did you panic when you thought about choosing A, believing that the answer was too close to what you chose for number six? I put this question here just to instigate such a reaction — and then to tell you not to worry. Questions often seem to be repeating themselves. Two or three questions may test the same basic concept. The reason for this is rather interesting, actually. A test maker sometimes asks the same question in two or three slightly different ways in order to test the validity of the question. For example, if 90 percent of the people answer the question right one time but only 40 percent answer it correctly the next time, something is probably wrong with the question. As far as you're concerned, you couldn't care less why the variations on a theme are there (in fact, one of the questions may be experimental. Remember that the experimental questions are scattered throughout the test.) Just relax and accept the fact that if two questions are asking you basically the same thing (what's the main idea, what's the primary purpose), your answer choices will be basically the same as well. *Correct Answer:* A.

Passage III

Line   Gustave Eisen was a cosmopolitan, world-traveling, many-sided scientist who was drawn in the spring of 1898 to a study of ancient civilizations and turquoise mining in a far corner of San Bernardino County.

(05)   He was born in Stockholm, Sweden, on August 2, 1847. He came to America in October 1872, after taking a Ph.D. degree at Upsala University earlier that same year. He apparently headed straight for California, settling in Fresno, then a pioneer community. There he became interested in horticulture. By pamphleteering and by lecturing, he urged the introduction into California of the Symrna fig and the avocado. He joined the California Academy of Sciences in 1871, serving as curator from 1892 to 1900. Eisen helped to create the Sequoia

(10)   National Park; as a result, Mount Eisen, elevation 12,000 feet, was named in his honor. He led academy expeditions to Baja, California in 1892, 1893, and 1894. In these years, Eisen's interests broadened to include geology, archaeology, and helminthology.

Therefore, when in March of 1898 the San Francisco *Call,* as a circulation stunt, decided to send an expedition into the deserts of San Bernardino County to verify the prospectors'

(15)   tales of long-lost Aztec turquoise mines, the newspaper asked Dr. Eisen, as perhaps California's leading scientist, to accompany its expedition. In early March 1898, the *Call's* party left for the desert.

The expedition began in comfortable luxury aboard a Santa Fe train, which it rode to Blake, a small station 25 miles west of Needles. From Blake, a spur line led to Manvel, a

(20)   supply point in the eastern California mountains. It had taken 44 hours to get that far from San Francisco. From there, the group proceeded by wagon and team over a rough trail of 60 miles to the site of the rumored mines, under the guidance of veteran desert traveler J.W. Stine.

When the expedition reached the mines in northeastern San Bernardino county, it found

(25)   them in the center of an extinct volcanic crater. This spot was "almost" where Arizona, California, and Nevada met just west of the Colorado River. The principal turquoise mines in the area were fifteen miles long by three or four miles wide. Delighted with the find, Eisen argued that he believed a Paiute legend that some Mayas had taught the Mojaves to mine. Then, out of jealousy, the Paiutes had killed most of the Mojaves and had driven out the rest.

11. It can be inferred from the passage that the San Francisco *Call*

  (A) did not expect the expedition it sent to the desert to find turquoise there.

  (B) desired to include qualified individuals on its expedition.

  (C) was concerned about the expense of the expedition.

  (D) boosted its circulation when it reported on the expedition.

  (E) reported that the Paiutes had driven out the Mojaves after the Mojaves mined the turquoise.

The newspaper asked Dr. Eisen to accompany the expedition because he was a leading scientist. In addition, J.W. Stine, a veteran desert traveler, was on the expedition. It can be inferred that the *Call* did what it could to increase the probability that the expedition could locate any supposed turquoise. Choice B says something more modest than this, so it is a very safe answer for this Inference question.

The passage does mention that the *Call* put together the expedition as a circulation stunt, but this does not mean that the expedition was engaged in a complete fantasy. The *Call* would not have been so interested in sending Dr. Eisen if the expedition were a lark. Eliminate choice A. Just because the expedition was put together as a circulation stunt does not mean that the stunt worked. The passage provides no information about whether more people bought the newspaper. So much for choice D. Choice C is contradicted by the fourth paragraph. The descriptions there imply that the paper spent quite a bit of money on the expedition. Choice E was mentioned in the last sentence of the passage but only as Eisen's hypothesis. You cannot tell whether the paper published this hypothesis. Eliminate choice E. *Correct Answer:* B.

12. Which of the following question(s) is/are *not* answered by the passage?

  I. Why was Dr. Eisen asked to participate in the search for turquoise mines?

  II. Why were turquoise mines located in a volcanic crater?

  III. Why did Dr. Eisen believe the Paiute legend of killing the Mojaves that the Mayans had taught to mine?

  (A) I only

  (B) I and II only

  (C) III only

  (D) II and III only

  (E) I, II, and III

The first question is answered in lines 15 and 16, which tell you that Dr. Eisen was asked to go along "as perhaps California's leading scientist." Eliminate all answer choices with I in them. Hey! The answer must be C or D. When you eliminate answers as you go, you are often rewarded by not having to do so much work. Answer II is tricky. You are told in line 24 that the mines were *in* a volcanic crater, but not *why* they were there. Because the question was not answered, II is correct. (If all this double negative jazz is confusing to you, make a quick guess and go on.) As for III, line 28 only tells you that "out of jealousy" the Paiutes killed the Mojaves; it doesn't explain why Dr. Eisen believed the legend. *Correct Answer:* D.

Chapter 7

Even the GMAT Can Be Unreasonable: Critical Reasoning

No, Critical Reasoning is not what physicians in the Intensive Care Unit (ICU) use. Critical Reasoning is the logic portion of the GMAT. Here, the test makers evaluate how well you create or assess an argument and develop a plan of action. Come to think of it, these are skills that a good emergency room or ICU physician would have to use every day, after all.

The RC Wanna-Be: The Format

Many of my students call Critical Reasoning "mini Reading Comprehension" because the questions follow short (usually one paragraph) passages. It's as if Critical Reasoning passages want to be Reading Comprehension passages when they grow up. Here's an example:

Two generations ago, women outlived men by as much as twenty years. A generation ago, women outlived men by about ten years. In this generation, many women are outliving men by only a year or two. This proves that women's lives have become more stressful, negatively impacting their health.

The author fails to consider which of the following in reaching his conclusion?

(A) Men's health may be improving rather than women's health worsening.

(B) Men used to marry younger women; now the trend is women marrying younger men.

(C) Stress can be positive if channeled properly.

(D) Women in general receive better health care than men do because they are more conscientious about doctor's visits and routine medical appointments.

(E) Men have developed better coping mechanisms to deal with stress than women.

For Better or for Worse: Strengthening and Weakening Arguments

I spend a good deal of this chapter on strengthening and weakening questions because they (especially weakening) are often the most common types of questions found in the Critical Reasoning section. The good news is that — with practice — they are also the easiest to answer correctly. Strengthening and weakening questions may be phrased in several different ways. Here are a few examples:

- ✔ Which of the following, if true, would most strengthen the author's reasoning?
- ✔ Which of the following indicates a flaw in the conclusion in the preceding?
- ✔ Which of the following true statements would most support the preceding claims?
- ✔ If true, which of the following would most seriously weaken the argument made by the speaker in the preceding?

Notice how the questions use different terms to refer to the main idea of the author: *argument, reasoning, claims,* and *conclusion.* To strengthen or weaken the conclusion (argument, reasoning, or claims), you must first *identify* the conclusion. As soon as you see this type of question, go back and paraphrase the conclusion, or the main idea, in your own words. If you can't restate the argument clearly, you probably don't understand the question well enough to identify something that would strengthen or weaken it.

Don't assume that the conclusion is at the end of the passage. Often, the first sentence of the paragraph contains the conclusion (which may just be the main idea), and the rest of the paragraph provides information that supports the conclusion.

Try to predict an answer. If the author argues that one company produces the best widget on the market, for example, predict what would weaken that argument: Statistics showing that the safety record of a rival widget is better, a consumer magazine's rating a rival widget superior to this widget, and so on. You may find an answer you predicted just waiting for you to claim it from among the answer choices.

Look out for what I call "yeah, so what?" answers. These answers are statements that are true or informative but utterly irrelevant to what the specific question (called the question *stem*) is asking you. Suppose that you are asked to find something to strengthen the claim that the widget is the best widget on the market. A statement that says, "Widget X is the most expensive widget produced" is a trap answer. More expensive does not necessarily mean better. Don't overgeneralize the reasoning.

Most of the time the question tells you that you are to assume the following answer choices to be true. Do not, therefore, waste any of your valuable time trying to rebut the answer choices. If choice D says something like, "A law degree is worth more than an MBA," you must take that as the gospel truth. You are not allowed to challenge the veracity of the statements, whether you personally agree with them or not.

Mentally circle the word in the question that tells you whether you are trying to support or refute the original information. Many students get confused on whether they are arguing for or against a statement and consequently fall for a trap. If a question asks you which would most seriously undermine the author's conclusion, make a mental note that you are looking for something to *weaken* the argument. This tip sounds simplistic, but during the pressure of the GMAT, you can make the mistake of misreading or misinterpreting what should be an easy question.

Search and Destroy: Ways to Weaken an Argument

Because so many questions ask you how to weaken the argument, I'm devoting this entire section to showing you ways to weaken arguments.

Reverse these tips in your mind as you go along, and you will learn how to strengthen arguments and receive two tips for the pain and indignity of one.

1. **Destroy the argument's foundation.** Identify the assumptions the author makes and then show that those assumptions are without merit. For example, if the author says, "Milk is a perfect food because it provides protein and calcium," the underlying assumption is that any food that provides protein and calcium is a perfect food. If you can show that another food, such as chocolate, provides protein and calcium yet is not a perfect food, you destroy the argument. (Who *says* chocolate is not a perfect food?)

2. **Show an incorrect cause and effect argument.** You weaken an argument when you show that the author assumes two events are connected when in fact they are not. Look at this example:

   Every time I hear the radio play Our Song, I smile at my girlfriend. Therefore, smiling at my girlfriend must make the radio play Our Song.

   The reasoning is true only if your braces pick up radio transmissions of the tune! There is an invalid cause-and-effect relationship.

3. **Search for overgeneralizations.** Some passages give you a small sample of events — or even one event — and then generalize from that.

   All four of the psychology professors I have had for my classes have beards. Therefore, all psychology professors have beards.

   I wonder what a female psychology professor would think of such logic?

4. **Look for reasoning that uses the argument to make the argument.** You may have heard this called *circular reasoning.*

   The GMAT is the hardest exam because it has the hardest questions. The exam with the hardest questions is the hardest exam.

   Getting dizzy from going around in circles? The conclusion is that the GMAT is the hardest exam, but absolutely no support is given for this conclusion. The author of the statement simply says that the hardest questions make the hardest exams, and these are the hardest questions. She gives no proof or information to support either statement — first that this is the hardest exam, and second that these are the hardest questions.

5. **Cite inappropriate or irrelevant experts or authority.** Weaken a statement by proving that a so-called expert is unknowledgeable in the field or has a bias. Suppose that the argument is this:

   You should stop children from watching more than two hours of television a day. Bob Ludwig, my CPA, says that watching too much television can hurt children's development.

Unless CPA Ludwig also has a degree in child psychology, I wouldn't put too much stock into what he says about child development. Here's one that's even worse because of an implied bias:

> As a dentist, I can tell you it's impossible to stop children from eating candy, so you may as well let them eat as much as they like.

That dentist is out to make his own children's college tuition, I'd say.

Don't assume that an argument is weakened because the person making the argument is attacked. This is called an *ad hominem* attack because it goes after the speaker rather than the argument itself.

> Dionne: My mechanic, Mac, tells me my car needs a new transmission.
>
> Brent: You shouldn't listen to Mac; after all, he's been divorced twice.

Mac may not be a sterling example of family values, but as a mechanic, he may know what he's talking about when it comes to transmissions. Brent's argument fails to weaken Dionne's statement.

I Love Happy Endings: Finding the Conclusion

One type of question gives you a few sentences and then asks you to find the conclusion to the last sentence or to identify which of the answer choices would most probably be the next sentence in the paragraph. Here are a few examples:

The reputation for excellence of a European college is supported by the facts, such as the superiority of its faculty and the good academic records of its students. European schools have been in existence much longer than their American counterparts, yet they often lag behind American schools in such matters as research and invention.

Which of the following would most logically follow as the next sentence to the paragraph above?

- (A) European colleges and universities have to take pride in their own records rather than harboring jealousy about the records of the American universities.

- (B) Perhaps the pioneering spirit of the Americans is reflected in their academic successes.

- (C) European colleges need an infusion of American students with their enthusiasm and drive if the European colleges are to survive to serve the needs of future generations.

- (D) American colleges are superior to European colleges in all areas except cost management; American colleges are proportionately much more expensive to attend than are European colleges.

- (E) European and American colleges have different strengths and weaknesses, but each can learn from the others.

The best way to get this question correct is to plug in each answer choice. That is, read the passage and add choice A on the end. Then reread the passage and add choice B on the end. Then reread the passage and add choice C, and so on. You must reread the passage five times. If you read just the answer choices out of context, either all of them will look good or you will fall for the trap answer. The trap answer usually works well with the last sentence in the paragraph but does not fit in with the paragraph as a whole. Either commit the time necessary to answer this style of question conscientiously or make a quick random guess and go on. Remember: The GMAT doesn't have a penalty for guessing, but if you spend a lot of time agonizing over a question only to guess at it in the long run anyway, you've penalized yourself by wasting time.

Do not choose an answer merely because it is true. The answer must flow logically from the preceding paragraph. If the passage is about aviation and one answer choice is "The GMAT is for the birds," the answer choice is true, but it is not really a logical continuation of the passage.

A Sound Foundation: The Assumption

Another type of question may ask you to identify the assumption the author makes. Knowing how to identify an assumption is also useful for answering questions that ask you to weaken the argument, because if you can disprove the assumption, you can disprove the argument. Here's an example:

Despite what critics say, *Citizen Kane* cannot be classified as a great movie. The movie lost money at the box office, and it did not win the Academy Award for best picture.

The author's argument depends upon which of the following assumptions?

(A) The public will flock to and pay a lot of money to see only movies that are great.

(B) Movies that win the Academy Award for best picture are great movies.

(C) A movie must make money at the box office and win the Academy Award for best picture to be considered a great movie.

(D) The public should never take the opinion of a film critic seriously.

(E) Critics consider Citizen Kane to be a great movie.

A special note to international students: This question is particularly difficult if English is not your first language. An assumption is a "given," something that the author accepts as true and doesn't even think about. To identify an assumption, you usually have to understand the entire paragraph, the tone, the reasoning, everything. Guess quickly at this question if the answer isn't immediately obvious to you. Don't waste any time trying to analyze it.

An assumption is sometimes known as a *premise*. It is the foundation of the whole passage. One type of assumption is a *progression,* sometimes called a *factual* assumption, which means that the author assumes that one fact led to another. Suppose that the statement says, "My finger is bleeding; when Brandy handed me the scissors, she must have sliced me." The author assumes the finger is bleeding from being cut by the scissors and not from some other cause. A second type of assumption is a *values* assumption, in which the author implicitly supports certain values. Maybe the sentence says this: "We should divert funds from street cleanup to the SPCA to take care of lost and abandoned pets." The author apparently values the lives of animals over the neatness of a street. Notice that these values are not explicitly stated; they are just general background.

It's All in Your Head: The Inference Question

To *infer* is to deduce something by reading between the lines. Students often get upset over Inference questions, thinking they are being asked to spend a lot of time making deductions and reasoning out obscure matters. Not so. In fact, the word *inferred* has been given a bum rap. Ignore that word. Just ask yourself, "What do I know from reading the preceding material?" This question often pulls together other types of questions, such as assumptions or conclusions. In other words, you can infer what the author concludes, based on what you have identified as his assumptions. (Confused yet? An example will help to clarify matters.)

I heard Dr. Ewing's speech last week, a stirring tirade in which he chastised parents for not teaching children how to set and attain goals. He spent a lot of his speech discussing the importance of having goals. While I would not disagree with him on that point, I feel compelled to ask him: Where is all this parental influence to come from? Today's families often have but one parent, a mother who works two jobs to provide financial support for her children and is not around enough to provide the type of parenting Dr. Ewing demands.

Which of the following can be correctly inferred from the statements above?

(A) The author believes that Dr. Ewing is unqualified to speak on parenting skills.

(B) Dr. Ewing's underlying premise is fatally flawed, destroying the remainder of the argument.

(C) Dr. Ewing assumes a cause-and-effect relationship with which the author disagrees.

(D) Dr. Ewing and the author have defined their terms differently.

(E) An argument is weakened by a lack of statistical evidence.

Questions Only Mr. Spock Could Love: Pure Logic

Pure logic questions have become increasingly rare on the Critical Reasoning portion of the GMAT. I won't be surprised if you don't see any of these at all. However, I'll spend a few minutes discussing them because I don't want *you* to be surprised if you do encounter one or two (and with so few questions in a section, one or two can make a difference).

Everyone who has ever bought a bottle of Flab Away tablets to decrease her appetite has been able to walk away from the table with food still left on her plate. The last time I bought Flab Away tablets, I not only finished all my food but went back for seconds. Therefore, Flab Away tablets don't work at all.

Which of the following most closely parallels the reasoning found in the preceding paragraph?

(A) No one in professional sports has ever won a tournament wearing Brand X sportswear. I won an amateur tournament wearing Brand X sportswear. Therefore, Brand X sportswear should be worn only by amateurs.

(B) All workers get the same number of paid sick days per year. I took six extra sick days last year and didn't get paid for them. Therefore, I must work six more days next year.

(C) All singers squirt their throats with soothing sprays before a concert. I squirted my throat but didn't sing well at all. Therefore, the squirt doesn't work.

(D) No one who has not been on television understands how the TelePrompTers work. I have been on television. Therefore, I understand how the TelePrompTers work.

(E) Everyone who has been to China has been impressed with the vastness of the land. I have not been to China. Therefore, I am not impressed with the vastness of the land.

To answer this question, put the reasoning in the original paragraph in A-B form. It may be something like this: All A do B. I don't do B. Therefore, B doesn't work. In this example, choice C has that same reasoning.

A second type of pure logic — which again is very rare on the GMAT — is a *syllogism,* which contains three statements. The first two are usually premises; the third is the conclusion.

> All football players are athletic.
>
> Brink is athletic.
>
> Therefore, Brink is a football player.

This type of syllogism may be hidden in a more narrative passage. If this is the case, it may also be presented as a *false syllogism,* giving a conclusion that does not necessarily proceed from the premises.

It is a commonly accepted fact at our school that all football players are athletic. My best friend Brink is very athletic and is probably in the best shape of anyone at the school. Therefore, it follows that my friend Brink is a football player.

Do you see the error? True, all football players are athletic. But that does not mean that all athletic people are football players. Brink can be athletic and be a swimmer or a soccer player, not a football player.

Working toward Your Goals: Identifying What the Question Is Asking You

Finally, a word about knowing what you're supposed to do. Here is a very important suggestion that can lessen your reading time and lower your stress levels.

Read the question before the paragraph. It is easy to get confused about what you are supposed to be looking for or thinking about as you go through the passage. Find the question first. It can be difficult to find, buried at the bottom of a paragraph or two. Take your time; don't get frustrated, and skip over this very important step. Mentally underline exactly what the question is asking. Your goal is to know before you jump into the paragraph why you are reading that paragraph. Are you to identify an assumption? Find a strengthening argument? Predict what would weaken the argument?

A Logical Conclusion: Review

- ✔ Critical Reasoning questions look like mini-Reading Comprehension passages but test logic and analytical skills.

- ✔ The most common question asks you to find a strengthening or weakening argument. To weaken an argument

    - destroy its foundation

    - show an incorrect cause-and-effect argument

    - search for overgeneralizations

    - look for circular reasoning, using the argument to make the argument

    - cite inappropriate or irrelevant experts or authority

✔ Some questions ask you to identify a logical conclusion to the passage.

✔ Know how to identify the assumption (which is another word for the basic premise). If a statement would not be true if one concept were changed, that concept is the assumption.

✔ An Inference question is like a typical Reading Comprehension question that tests your understanding of the passage.

✔ Pure Logic questions (syllogisms, parallel reasoning, and so on) are tested infrequently.

✔ Read the questions before the passages to identify what you're looking for.

Chapter 8

Reality Check: Critical Reasoning Practice Questions

If you are going bananas at this stage, at least you know your studying isn't, uh, fruitless. . . . Hey, if you're feeling totally irrational and unreasonable, I sympathize with you. But I have to ask you to please postpone your breakdown for another half hour or so. Get through the following practice questions first.

This chapter features a dozen questions that cover the question styles you are most likely to see on the Critical Reasoning portion of the GMAT, along with a few question styles that are rare but ones you may encounter. The majority of questions in this section are variations on the weakening questions that I discussed at length in the lecture.

Practice Questions

Directions: Choose the best answer to each question.

1. *Ricardo:* My wife and I tried to get marital counseling. The counselors who could see us were too expensive, and the counselors whose fees were reasonable were too busy to fit us into their schedules. My wife and I have decided that counseling cannot help us.

   Which of the following statements, if true, would most weaken Ricardo's conclusion?

   (A) Marital counseling succeeds only with motivated people who are willing to do the exercises and role playing suggested by the counselors.

   (B) People who go to expensive counselors have better results than those who go to more moderately priced counselors.

   (C) Ricardo and his wife will eventually find an affordable counselor who has time for them.

   (D) Husbands are often more critical of marital counseling than are wives, who are willing to continue even when frustrated.

   (E) Counselors are only human and cannot be as unbiased as they would like to be because they have feelings of their own.

   First, identify the conclusion. It is that counseling can't help Ricardo and his wife. Ricardo uses his current inability to find a counselor to leap to this conclusion. He assumes that his wife and he will never see a counselor. The best way to weaken an argument is to contradict the assumption. Choice C does just this. This choice points out that Ricardo can't use the current unavailability of counselors to make a conclusion about future effectiveness.

Eliminate choices D and E right away, because they do nothing to indicate that counseling may succeed, which is necessary to contradict Ricardo's conclusion. If you're in a rush and don't have time to figure out the answer, you can guess among choices A, B, and C.

Next, eliminate choice A. Nothing in Ricardo's tale of woe talked about role-playing. In fact, Ricardo was highly motivated to make the counseling work; it wasn't as if he was unwilling to do exercises or to make an effort. Choice B is the tricky answer because the cost of counseling was in fact mentioned in the passage. However, Ricardo never went to counseling at all. *Correct Answer:* C.

2. *Skating coach:* In my two decades of experience, I have found that taking children out of school to skate full time is actually counterproductive. Children, especially adolescents, need to have a broad range of activities and interests, and friends outside of the skating community. Children who skate full time burn out quickly and drop the sport just at the time they should be approaching their peak. Thus, if children are to reach their full potential, they should be kept in a regular school and not simply have tutors and no classroom experience.

The skating coach makes which of the following assumptions in drawing the preceding conclusion?

(A) Students will suffer emotional distress if they are isolated from their peers.

(B) Children who are physically skilled at skating are often academically gifted as well and would be stars in a classroom setting.

(C) It is easier to coach a well-rounded child than one who has no interests outside of skating.

(D) Children need a full range of activities to realize their ultimate ability as skaters.

(E) Parents who spend all their money on skating lessons cannot afford private tutoring for their children and must be satisfied with a public school education for the children.

The speaker is a skating coach whose primary interest is in the skating abilities of his students. Everything he says, therefore, should be interpreted in that context. When he talks about students "reaching their full potential," he probably means as ice skaters, not as human beings. He assumes that by exposing the child to a wide variety of activities, the child has a higher probability of realizing her potential later on.

Choice A is too extreme. "Emotional distress" is a very intense and evocative expression, too strong for an exam like this. Correct answer choices are usually weak and wishy-washy, rarely this dramatic.

The speaker simply claims that skaters need a regular school environment to become good skaters who will stick with the sport. He assumes that they are good enough academically to stay in school while continuing to skate, but he doesn't assume that they will shine in the classroom, as choice B suggests.

Choice C is somewhat illogical. If anything, a student who is totally committed to spending time at the ice rink may be easier to coach — at least until she burns out.

Choice E is backward. The coach seems to assume the opposite, which is that parents can afford tutoring and have been giving their children too much tutoring. *Correct Answer:* D.

3. *Mr. Janowski:* Adolescents today should be steered away from a career in dentistry. There are so many breakthroughs in cavity prevention that the need for a dentist will soon be minimal.

Mrs. Hogan: That's true. The last time I went to a dentist it wasn't for a cavity at all but to get an implant when I knocked out my tooth playing street hockey with my son.

Which of the following may be said of Mrs. Hogan's comment?

(A) It contradicts the point made by Mr. Janowski.

(B) It gives an example that supports the assumption made by Mr. Janowski.

(C) It assumes facts not in evidence.

(D) It erroneously assumes a cause-and-effect relationship.

(E) It uses an invalid definition to buttress a weak assumption.

Mrs. Hogan appears to agree with what Mr. Janowski says, but her words in fact contradict his premise. He is saying that dentists are not necessary because children no longer get cavities. She shows that a dentist has functions other than to fill a cavity, thus disproving his statement that dentists are no longer necessary.

If you chose B, you fell for the trap. You probably read the "That's true," uttered by Mrs. Hogan, and got no further. Reading the whole statement tells you that while she thought she was agreeing with Mr. J., she was actually proving his premise wrong.

Choice C means nothing. What facts? What evidence? If you chose this answer, you went for the "best-sounding" choice, the one that sounded the most pretentious and analytical. Choice E is wrong because there are no definitions given in the passage, let alone undefined or defined incorrectly. *Correct Answer:* A.

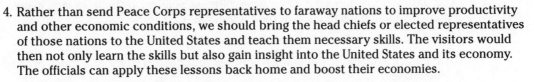

4. Rather than send Peace Corps representatives to faraway nations to improve productivity and other economic conditions, we should bring the head chiefs or elected representatives of those nations to the United States and teach them necessary skills. The visitors would then not only learn the skills but also gain insight into the United States and its economy. The officials can apply these lessons back home and boost their economies.

The conclusion above may be based on which of the following assumptions?

(A) The danger involved in sending American citizens abroad is not worth the benefits that might accrue to the people who receive American help.

(B) The American economic system would be functional in another country.

(C) American tax money should not be used to bring over visitors who may return home with only an incomplete idea of our government and thus may create governments of their own that use the worst rather than the best of our country's principles.

(D) If necessary, American military procedures can be adapted for use in civilian economic endeavors and taught to representatives of foreign countries.

(E) The cost of training someone to help people overseas is prohibitive; it is cheaper to bring over the representatives from other countries.

The conclusion is that people should come to the United States to learn how the system works here and then take those lessons home and apply them in their own countries. The underlying assumption is that the system would work in other countries.

If you're having trouble identifying the assumption, think of it as the "absolute must." Read through each statement and pretend that it is not true. Would the conclusion of the passage still stand? For example, if the American economic system would *not* be functional in another country, would the author still argue that people from other nations should come here to learn our system and take it home to their countries? Of course not. If the opposite of a statement makes the argument false, that statement must be integral to the argument and is an assumption or premise upon which the argument rests.

Choice A is too broad. Nowhere in the paragraph does the author mention the dangers of sending American citizens abroad. Choice C is really reaching. It sounds like the raving of some radio talk show host who is trying to stir up trouble just to increase ratings. Again, nothing in the passage leads you to believe the author is concerned with the best versus the worst of the American system.

Choice D introduces another new element: the military. The passage does not distinguish between civilian and military help. Choice E is tempting. If you chose this, you probably imposed your own beliefs on the arguments of the author. It may or may not be true that it is cheaper to bring someone here than to send Americans abroad; however, nothing in the passage implies that cost is a consideration. The only assumption you can make is that the author believes the American system would work abroad; otherwise, he would not be exhorting us to find better ways of exporting it. *Correct Answer:* B.

5. Americans lead the world in traveling outside of one's homeland. This makes Americans the most open-minded people in the world. Travel enables one to understand the people of different countries. Such understanding allows one to appreciate the differences between the lifestyles of one's native country and those of other nations. Once one sees how the economic, religious, and political systems of another country differ from those with which one is more familiar, one is able to work toward supplanting other nations' systems with those of one's native country. This is ultimately what well-traveled Americans try to do.

The preceding argument has which of the following significant flaws?

(A) It assumes that foreign nations have different political systems; in fact, many of them are nearly identical to that of the United States.

(B) It presents a chain of evidence that contradicts the conclusion.

(C) It fails to explain the differences between American systems and those of other countries.

(D) It assumes what it intends to prove and is therefore a circular argument.

(E) It uses words that are ambiguous without clarifying the definitions of those terms.

The key, once again, is to identify the conclusion. It is that Americans are the most open-minded people in the world. The author supports this by presenting evidence about their frequency of travel.

Some test takers think that the last sentence is the conclusion, but does the stimulus provide support for the observation that Americans try to supplant other nations' systems with their own? No, the author does not provide specific examples of this happening or statistics that show how often other countries become "Americanized." You must remember that the conclusion presents the "what" of the argument while the evidence presents the "why." For a phrase or sentence to be a conclusion, some other part of the argument must attempt to explain why that phrase or sentence is true.

For a few sentences, the evidence about travel does a reasonable job of supporting the author's notion about Americans being open-minded. However, the author finishes up by explaining how Americans use their travel experiences to push their system on other people. This attitude is anything but open-minded.

Choice A does not point to a flaw in the reasoning. The author's argument would still flow even if this assumption were false. It doesn't matter how different foreign nations' systems are from American systems. This does not contradict the need to travel to learn about the other systems.

Choice C is a true statement, but it isn't a flaw in the reasoning. It is not important to explain how the systems differ; what is important is that Americans want to learn about these differences and use them to their advantage.

Choice D does not apply to this argument. Circular reasoning basically involves presenting evidence that is, in fact, the same thing as the conclusion. Here's an example: The government should stay out of my life because my affairs are none of the government's business. The first part of the sentence is the conclusion, and the second part (note the word *because*) is the evidence. Did you notice that the evidence and conclusion are the same? The author of this argument clearly takes it as a given (in other words, he or she assumes) that the government should not intrude. The argument about travel and open-mindedness is not circular because the author does move from point A to point B. The evidence about travel differs from the conclusion about open-mindedness.

Choice E is completely off base: Nothing in the argument in the passage is ambiguous (capable of being interpreted in two or more ways) and in need of a definition. This flaw can appear on the GMAT, but it is not the problem here. *Correct Answer:* B.

At this stage, many of you may be shrugging your shoulders and dismissing critical reasoning, saying that you're never going to see this type of question anywhere in the world other than the GMAT. Boy, are you ever wrong! When you get into the MBA program (notice that I didn't say *if* you get into the MBA program — I have confidence in you), you will often work on case analyses. In them, you are asked to identify what went wrong, what destroyed the company. To do so, you have to identify the underlying assumptions that the company made in determining its policy and what would have strengthened or weakened its policies. Learning these reasoning skills now will help you immensely once you start the actual MBA work.

I know many MBA students get a joint MBA-JD (Juris Doctorate, which is the basic law degree). This style of question is also on the LSAT (Law School Admission Test) although there it is called *logical reasoning*. Developing these critical reasoning skills now will help you not only on the LSAT but also when you are asked to do a case analysis in law school. In short, even though you may be frustrated right about now, hang in there. The time you put into learning these skills now will save you hours and hours of frustration and grief later on in graduate and/or law school.

6. Computers in schools cut the need for homework time in half, because the computers can do most of the basic calculations that students used to spend a lot of time doing by hand. With more computers in the classroom, students will learn more material and process it more quickly, going on to the difficult subjects more rapidly than they would have without the use of computers.

Which of the following, if true, would be a flaw in the reasoning in the preceding paragraph?

(A) Students need to do the work themselves to understand the fundamentals before proceeding to the next level of work.

(B) Students have enough time to do their homework and should agree to do a set number of hours of homework every night.

(C) If they wanted computers, students would have already purchased their own.

(D) Students never do calculations by hand anymore but always use calculators.

(E) Computers are exorbitantly expensive and will force budget restrictions that could hurt the schools in other areas.

First, identify the conclusion. It is that students will learn more material and process it more quickly than they would have without computers and thus will proceed to the difficult subjects more rapidly. Predict a flaw by finding the opposite of the reasoning. Say that students will not go on to the difficult material more quickly. Now think of a reason or two why that would be so. How about the fact that students still have to understand the material, still have to think about it and learn it? While taking away the busywork of doing the calculations by hand, the computers still don't force the knowledge into the students' brains; the students have to take the time to learn the fundamentals before they can proceed.

Choice B is irrelevant. Just because students do have enough time to do their homework at home doesn't mean that they can't learn faster in the classroom. This answer is comparing apples and oranges.

Choice C is also irrelevant. Whether the students want computers or not doesn't address the issue of computers increasing students' progress. Always keep in mind what the argument is that you are trying to refute. (Choice C may also be false in the Real World, but remember that the question asked you to assume that each answer choice is true.)

Choice D is extremely tempting. True, students rarely do any calculations by hand anymore and often use calculators; however, that isn't the major flaw in the reasoning, just one small weakness. The main flaw, again, is that students still must learn the basics, whether they do the work by hand, by calculator, or by computer.

Choice E is an example of a statement that looks good and is probably true but doesn't specifically address the main premise of the argument. The premise is that computers will help students progress to difficult subjects more rapidly. The fact that other areas of the school curriculum will be hurt doesn't weaken the effectiveness of computers. *Correct Answer:* A.

7. People see only what they want to see and live in blindness of the future, even though they pay lip service to it. It is important to continue preparing for the future, something that today's highly paid professionals in their early twenties often do not consider. Just as an ant stores food away for the winter that it knows must inevitably come, adults should save money for the retirement years that they know will follow their moneymaking years.

The author does which of the following to make her point?

(A) Gives specific examples

(B) Clarifies an ambiguous term

(C) Disproves an opposing point of view

(D) Uses an analogy

(E) Cites an authority

I warned you in the introduction to this section that I would ask you questions that are rare on the exam. This question is more pure logic than the others. You are unlikely to see this question, but anything's possible.

To answer the question, you need to know the terminology. In choice D, an *analogy* is a figure of speech involving a comparison. Here, the author compares an ant's food storage to a worker's monetary savings.

You probably could answer this question by process of elimination. No specific examples are given; eliminate choice A. No *ambiguous* (meaning capable of being interpreted in two or more ways) terms are clarified (made clear); eliminate choice B. No opposing views are given, let alone disapproved; eliminate choice C. And no authorities (experts) are cited; eliminate choice E. *Correct Answer:* D.

8. People are intrinsically honest when they see the reason for a law. Most people would never park in a metered space without putting change into the meter, because they realize that the meter is not assessing a penalty but charging a fee to maintain the parking space and the highways and roads in general. People have no compunction however, about speeding on a deserted highway on a safe stretch of road because they believe the 55 mph speed limit at that time and in that place is unnecessary.

Which of the following, if true, would most seriously weaken the conclusion drawn in the preceding paragraph?

(A) Some areas have speed limits as high as 70 mph.

(B) A recent survey showed that as many as 10 percent of the people do regularly forget to put change in the parking meter.

(C) A speeding ticket is much more expensive than a ticket for an expired parking meter.

(D) Most people do not follow the speed limit even on a crowded highway in the pouring rain.

(E) Speeding laws are more rigorously enforced than are parking meters.

First, identify the conclusion. It is that people are intrinsically honest when they see the reason for a law. State the opposite conclusion: People are not intrinsically honest, even when they see the reason for a law. Then look for something that supports the hypothesis that people are not intrinsically honest. Choice D shows that even when there is a valid reason for following a law — a crowded, rainy highway — people still break the law.

Choice A is irrelevant. The fact that some highways have speed limits of 70 mph doesn't alter the fact that some people speed; maybe those people go 90 mph, so they are still speeding even if the limit is 70 mph. Choice B is the major trap. If you chose it, you probably thought that you were weakening the premise by showing that not everyone feeds a meter. However, the answer says that people *forget* to feed the meter. This does not weaken the conclusion that people are intrinsically honest; they just forget. And besides, 10 percent is too small of a sample to make the gross generalization that most people are crooks.

Choice C is probably a true statement but is the opposite of the argument. If it costs more to get caught speeding and less to get caught cheating a meter, then more people are going to cheat a meter and fewer people are going to speed. The same is true for choice E. If speeding laws are more rigorously enforced than parking meters' fees, fewer people will speed, and more people will cheat the meters. *Correct Answer:* D.

9. There is absolutely no doubt in my mind that men with "outties," belly buttons that protrude, are much sexier than men with "innies," belly buttons that go in. A look at any fan magazine shows you that almost all the movie and television actors who are hunky, leading men have "outties" and are proud to show them off. My husband wants to be a movie star and is taking acting classes, but he will never achieve his dream because his belly button is an "innie."

The author of the preceding paragraph makes which of the following assumptions?

(A) Belly buttons are a consideration for male movie stars but are irrelevant for female stars.

(B) Belly buttons are a critical factor in determining which actors will become stars.

(C) Acting classes are wholly irrelevant to ultimate star status.

(D) Articles in fan magazines always tell the truth.

(E) Most actors have had plastic surgery to change their belly buttons from "innies" to "outties," even if they don't broadcast the fact.

The author, who is probably an *omphaloskeptisist* in her spare time (a person who meditates while looking at her navel), believes her husband will never be a movie star because his belly button is an "innie" rather than an "outtie." Because she mentions that her husband is taking acting classes, she must believe that the acting classes are not as important for success as the configuration of one's belly button.

Choice A is too broad; nothing was mentioned about female stars. Don't overgeneralize info you've been given. Choice C is too dramatic. Just because acting doesn't seem to this woman as important as belly buttons does not mean that it is wholly irrelevant.

A dramatic word such as "wholly" or "entirely" is often too strong for a correct answer choice. Eliminate choices with such dramatic words.

Choice D is put in for comic relief. Does anyone really believe fan magazines tell the truth? Besides, the dramatic word *always* makes the choice a bad bet. Choice E is outside the scope of the reading. Nothing was mentioned about plastic surgery. *Correct Answer:* B.

10. *Linguistics scholar:* Throughout the non-English-speaking world, most schools select English as the second language they teach to their students. The schools make this choice because they feel that English will best serve their students as they interact with the international community. According to some simple facts though, these schools are choosing the wrong language to teach their students. Only 325 million people speak English as their native language whereas 840 million people are native speakers of Mandarin Chinese. To facilitate communication throughout the world, schools should require their students to learn Mandarin Chinese instead of English.

Which of the following best serves to undermine the scholar's conclusion?

(A) When native and nonnative speakers are added, Mandarin Chinese speakers outnumber English speakers by just more than 450 million.

(B) In China, the world's most populous nation, many people speak Chinese dialects other than Mandarin.

(C) English is more widely distributed throughout the world than is Mandarin Chinese and is the language most often used in international relations.

(D) Both Hindi and Spanish have more native speakers than does English.

(E) China has a rapidly growing economy and will soon be one of the world's major economic powers.

The scholar uses statistics about the number of native speakers to conclude that schools should teach Mandarin Chinese rather than English as a second language. This connection relies on the assumption that the numbers are the key factor to consider. A great way to undermine what the scholar is saying is to show that there are other points to consider as well. Choice C introduces factors suggesting that English is more useful than Mandarin Chinese in communications throughout the world.

Choice A does not go far enough. The statistics in this choice, along with the stimulus, show that there are more nonnative speakers of English than of Mandarin Chinese. However, Mandarin Chinese speakers still outnumber the English speakers, so the scholar's argument still stands.

All choice B says is that Mandarin Chinese may not help a person to communicate with all Chinese. Mandarin Chinese speakers still outnumber English speakers.

Quickly eliminate choice D because it is completely off the topic. How does information about Hindi and Spanish help you to decide whether schools should teach Mandarin Chinese rather than English?

Choice E strengthens the scholar's argument in that it suggests that Mandarin Chinese will become even more widespread. If choice E is true, China will become a major player in the world's affairs, and knowledge of Mandarin Chinese will become useful or even integral, as knowledge of English is today. *Correct Answer:* C.

11. Lotteries have been won by people who play the game regularly, often buying as many as 100 tickets every week. Therefore, no one who buys at least 100 tickets a week will fail to win the lottery.

The best criticism of the preceding material is which of the following statements?

(A) The argument fails to recognize that not everyone can afford to purchase 100 lottery tickets a week.

(B) The argument doesn't tell the readers which state or national lottery is being discussed; readers may purchase tickets for the wrong lottery.

(C) The argument may not be generalized; the writer fails to realize that there may be many people who buy at least 100 lottery tickets each week and still don't win.

(D) The argument is based on a false premise: that all 100 tickets are purchased at the same time.

(E) The argument fails to differentiate between lotteries in which numbers must be selected and "instant win" lotteries in which scratch-off tickets reveal prizes.

You should have shaken your head in disbelief as you read the author's conclusion. How can someone think that merely buying 100 lottery tickets can guarantee a win? If that were the case, then of course everyone would purchase 100 lottery tickets.

Choice A is irrelevant. The fact that someone can't afford to buy 100 lottery tickets does not address the conclusion that doing so would guarantee a win. In choice B, the fact that the particular lottery is not identified is irrelevant. It is erroneous to assume that winning any lottery can be guaranteed with the purchase of 100 tickets (unless, of course, the whole lottery consists of 100 tickets). (There's a system for you: Buy all the tickets and you are guaranteed to win, rather like betting on every horse in a race.)

Choice D is completely illogical. The fact that people do buy 100 lottery tickets at once does not address the point that they are supposedly guaranteed to win. Choice E is basically the same as choice B. If it makes no difference whether the lottery is a state or national lottery, it certainly makes no difference whether the lottery is played by choosing numbers or by scratching off cards. *Correct Answer:* C.

12. The Supreme Court of the United States can strike down legislation only if it conflicts with the United States Constitution. A constitutional amendment is legislation that becomes part of the United States Constitution. When Congress supports a law that the Supreme Court rules against, the legislators often try to write the law into a constitutional amendment so that the law will become immune to Supreme Court action.

Which of the following can be inferred from the preceding information?

(A) Constitutional amendments are permanently part of the law of the United States.

(B) Legislators can easily work around Supreme Court decisions to pass laws they find necessary.

(C) Constitutional amendments are the main check that Congress has on Supreme Court power.

(D) The Supreme Court cannot strike down any part of the Constitution itself.

(E) The Supreme Court will always strike down a law that conflicts with the United States Constitution.

The first two sentences of this stimulus are adequate to answer this question. The Supreme Court can strike down laws only if they conflict with the Constitution, but a constitutional amendment is part of the Constitution itself. Because the amendment cannot conflict with what it is part of, the Supreme Court cannot strike down the amendment.

Choice A is out because it encompasses too much. The Supreme Court cannot strike down the amendment, but that doesn't mean that there is no other way to do so. For example, the eighteenth amendment (prohibition) was made null and void by the twenty-first amendment (and in case you're wondering, no, I am not old enough to remember that personally, thank you very much!).

Choice B is wrong primarily because of the word *easily*. Just because the legislators propose making a law part of the Constitution doesn't mean that it will easily be done.

Clearly, constitutional amendments are a check that Congress has on the Supreme Court, but how do you know that it is the main check? (Aha! *Main* is another dramatic word, as discussed in the preceding paragraph.) This reasoning eliminates choice C. The Senate (part of Congress) must approve Supreme Court appointments. That is quite a check.

There is no information in the stimulus to support choice E. The Supreme Court can strike down laws that conflict with the Constitution, but it may not *always* (another dramatic word, worth double-checking because it is so often wrong) do so. *Correct Answer:* D.

Part IV

Right Writing and the GMAT: Analytical Writing Assessment

The 5th Wave   By Rich Tennant

"So, on that analytical writing test, how'd you do with that 'existence of God' question?"

In this part . . .

The GMAT features two 30-minute essay sections called the Analytical Writing Assessment. One essay is called Analysis of an Issue; the other is Analysis of an Argument. For the Analysis of an Issue essay, you need to analyze the issue or opinion, state your point of view on the opinion or issue, and then support your point of view. For the Analysis of an Argument essay, you need to state the assumptions the author of the statement makes and analyze whether you consider those assumptions sound or unsound, identify evidence in the argument that strengthens or weakens it, and then provide outside counter examples or supporting information to strengthen or weaken the argument.

The Analytical Writing Assessment is evaluated very differently by schools. Some schools place almost no importance on the writing; others give it great credence. Before you pull your hair out over this section of the GMAT, find out the policy of the schools to which you are applying.

Yes, you do create your essay on computer. The CAT does *not* have a spell checker or a grammar checker (sorry about that!) It does, however, have a very simple "cut 'n' paste" function that allows you to move paragraphs or sentences around. This section is probably the only portion of the GMAT in which good or fast typists have an advantage over the rest of us. If your typing skills are truly atrocious and if the school to which you are applying really scrutinizes the writing sample, you may want to hone your typing skills before you take the test.

Chapter 9

It's Not What You Say, It's How You Say It: Analytical Writing Assessment

In This Chapter

▶ Analysis of an issue

▶ Analysis of an argument

▶ Scoring

▶ Writing the essay

The GMAT features two 30-minute essay sections given the pretentious name Analytical Writing Assessment. One essay is called Analysis of an Issue; the other is Analysis of an Argument.

Your Opinion Counts: Analysis of an Issue

In the Analysis of an Issue section, you are given an issue and asked to explain your views on it.

> "People argue that more money and effort should be spent on developing recycling programs. Their priorities are misplaced. Our goals would be better met by reducing excess packaging on products in the first place."

Which argument are you more in agreement with, the one that more money should be spent on recycling programs, or the one that reducing excess packaging should be emphasized? Using your own experiences, reading, or background in general, explain your reasoning.

How do you get started? If your writer's block looks as big as Cheop's pyramid, you're welcome to use the following organized plan of attack. (**Note:** A much more detailed discussion of writing the essays comes later in this section. The following material is just an overview to get you going.)

✔ Begin by analyzing the issue or opinion: Just what exactly is the point being made? (In the preceding example, the point is that recycling is less important than reducing excess packaging.)

✔ Specifically state your point of view on the opinion or issue: Do you agree or disagree; do you think that the author has gone too far or not far enough?

✔ Support your point of view with examples from personal or professional experiences, reading, or general background: What have you seen, done, or heard about that formed your opinion?

Full of Sound and Fury, Signifying Nothing: Analysis of an Argument

The second writing section is called Analysis of an Argument and consists of a paragraph with a specific conclusion or argument. Your job is to analyze that argument.

Laws should require that sprinkler systems be placed in all buildings. Sprinkler systems, if properly installed and distributed throughout homes and schools and office buildings, will virtually eliminate deaths and injuries from fires because the fires will be stopped before they have had an opportunity to cause any damage. The systems will, at the first hint of excess heat or smoke, let loose cascades of water that will effectively douse the flames or the smoldering hot spot.

Discuss how compelling you find the above argument. Analyze the reasoning presented in the argument, paying special attention to the evidence that supports the argument. Explain your point of view, addressing points that would make the argument more convincing or evidence that, in fact, weakens the conclusion.

Your opinion counts for zilch here; no one cares. Don't confuse the two writing samples. Here, you are not asked to express a personal preference (are sprinkler systems the best way to prevent fire damage?) but to analyze the author's argument. The only opinion you are giving is whether you find the author's arguments valid and sound. Proceed by doing the following:

- Begin by stating the assumptions the author of the statement makes and analyzing whether you consider those assumptions sound or unsound.

- Identify evidence in the argument that strengthens or weakens it.

- Provide outside counterexamples or supporting information to strengthen or weaken the argument.

Half a Dozen Is Better than None: Scoring

You are given a score from zero to six on each passage. The final score on your score report is an average of four separate evaluations of your passages. Zero (0) is the lowest possible score. Almost the only way to receive a score that low is not to write on the assigned topic. (I know someone who wrote, "While pollution is a valid concern, our society has that under control. The real topic our generation is worried about is the economy; therefore, I will address that point." Guess what her score was?) A score of six (6) is considered outstanding. It demonstrates your grasp of writing cogently, developing a position on an issue, and supporting your position with well-argued statements.

Hunting for the next Hemingway: What do evaluators look for?

Apart from offering them huge bribes (Just kidding, evaluators — unless of course — nah, forget it. Really.), the evaluators want you to do the following:

✔ **Take a position on the issue.** Make it clear to the evaluator whether you think the statement has merit or is weak and unsubstantiated.

TIP

There's nothing the evaluators hate more than not knowing where you stand. While good writers address both sides of an argument and anticipate objections and counter-examples, the evaluator must clearly know which side you are supporting and which side you are refuting. It's a common trap for students to be so concerned about being PC (politically correct) or fair-minded that they fail to take and support a position.

✔ **Make sure that your content is logical.** The evaluators want to be certain that your supporting statements are reasonable and feasible. For example, if you state that capital punishment is useless as a deterrent against crime, you should cite instances in which many people have been executed, then explain the crime rate has gone up anyway. Do not give a wholly emotional argument, such as "Too many people are upset when there is an execution, and the other prisoners don't like it."

✔ **Clearly organize your essay.** This is probably the most salient or outstanding feature of any essay. The points must flow logically from one to another. If you don't write an outline before beginning your essay, you may get into the "Oops, I just thought of something else I'd better add" mode. Creating an outline can help you to organize your thoughts, but don't spend too much time on it because the evaluators don't read the outline. Your score is based on your complete essay only, not on the outline, brilliant though it may be.

✔ **Use proper grammar, diction, usage, and spelling.** If you're not sure how to spell or use a word, dump it. Use words you are comfortable with, words you use every day. Evaluators find it especially grating on their nerves to read usage errors that are included in the Sentence Correction portion of the GMAT, such as affect versus effect or lie versus lay (don't ask me how you would work lie or lay into an essay; the thought is mind-boggling). The Grammar Review in Chapter 2 is full of rules that you should review to help you not only with the Sentence Correction portion but also with the Analytical Writing Assessment.

Pointless information: What drives the evaluators crazy

A pointless paper is one that gets zero points. There are several things you can do to end up with nothing or next to nothing.

1. **Avoid taking a stand.**

   Although it is good to argue both sides of an issue or show strengthening and weakening arguments, it is imperative that you make your opinion or conclusion clear. Remember that there is no right or wrong answer. You can be against Mom and apple pie and still receive an outstanding score. It is important only that you take a stand and support your stand.

2. **Peregrinate and meander (sounds like spices found in hot sauce, doesn't it?).**

   Organization, organization, organization! Think of this suggestion as the GMAT version of the real estate axiom: location, location, and location! Put your thoughts in logical order. The writers' philosophy "tell 'em what you're going to tell 'em; tell 'em; and then tell 'em what you told 'em," works well here. Do not put your conclusion in the middle paragraph and then remember a few more points to add at the end. Follow your outline.

3. **Improperly use** *pedantic sesquipedalianism.* (*Sesqui* **means one and a half; for example, a sesquicentennial celebration is a 150-year anniversary.** *Ped* **means foot. Sesquipedalianism is using foot and a half long words . . . in other words, putting your foot in your mouth!**)

You are not paid by the word; you are not credited by the syllable. Don't outsmart yourself by using big words. (If you wind up using a word that the evaluator doesn't know, he or she may feel insecure, humiliated, and possibly vindictive. Not a good idea to alienate the evaluator.)

4. **Use off-color language, slang, or inappropriate humor.**

You say you're the Seinfeld of your crowd? Well, there's no accounting for taste. The joke that absolutely cracked up your friends at the Commons will not necessarily appeal to the evaluators. Scatological humor (anything dealing with bodily functions and bathrooms) is definitely out. Even if a joke is pure and wholesome, it may drop like a lead balloon and annoy the evaluators. Play it safe: Be as dull and boring as the exam itself.

Aerobic Writing: Follow these Steps

Had enough of my generalities? Okay, let's get down to specifics. The following is a boiler-plate or standard format you may use to practice writing good GMAT essays.

Analysis of an Issue

Paragraph one. Use your first sentence to restate the issue. For example, if the point is that capital punishment does not serve as a deterrent to crime, your topic sentence may be, "Many people believe that capital punishment fails in its stated purpose of deterring crime." In your topic sentence, make it obvious that you are, in fact, addressing the topic given. Remember: The most egregious mistake you can make is to fail to address the topic. In your second sentence, show that you recognize that there are two sides to the issue, that you will, in fact, anticipate and address objections to your point of view, crushing them under your brilliant logic and reasoning. Here's a good second sentence: "While capital punishment may have, in specific instances, failed to deter people who would otherwise have committed a crime, I argue that these instances are infrequent and insignificant." Although a two-sentence paragraph technically is sufficient (a one-sentence paragraph is *not*), add one or two more sentences to flesh out this first paragraph.

First impressions count. A super-strong first sentence can cover a multitude of weaknesses later in the paper. If the evaluator is impressed by your opening gambit, he or she is probably going to score your paper higher than if you start off slowly and warm up. Ever hear of the "halo effect" in psychology? Roughly stated, it means that the person who thinks highly of you in one area transfers that high opinion of you over into other areas; your halo surrounds everything you do. Take the time to write a *great* first sentence or two.

Paragraph two. Your second paragraph introduces a specific point that supports your argument. For example, the first sentence of your second paragraph may be, "In states such as Texas that have carried out the death penalty, violent crime has dropped significantly." Give a *specific* state. Good writing is specific, not vague like, "States with no death penalties have higher violent crime rates than states with death penalties." Oh yeah, sez who?

You do not need to be 100 percent correct in your statements. You can fudge a little bit as long as what you are saying sounds feasible. The evaluator is not going to head to the newspaper archives to find out exactly how many executions took place in which state last year.

The next two or three sentences in this paragraph support the topic sentence. Give more information on how the violent crime rate has dropped in Texas: Are murders down? Are rapes down? Are armed robberies down?

International students, here's your chance to shine. The evaluators, who are understandably bored by reading a thousand similar essays from American students, will be intrigued if you discuss a problem from a foreign perspective. Talk, for instance, of how capital punishment has or has not worked in your own country.

Paragraph three. The third paragraph gives yet another supporting example. You may say something such as, "According to articles written by psychologists, interviews with criminals have consistently shown that the criminals did, in fact, stop to consider the consequences of their actions prior to committing the crimes and took precautions not to let the crime develop to extremes, such as murder. In these instances, the criminals were deterred by the threat of capital punishment." List places in which you have read (or feasibly *might* have read, if you are not being entirely truthful) such statements.

The middle of your essay often has more "filler" than the beginning and ending. I'm not suggesting that you add a passel of prattle (a bushel of babble?) just to fill up space, but if you know that your essay is heading towards being only about ten lines long, you have to flesh it out somewhere. The middle paragraphs are the place.

Paragraph four. The fourth paragraph addresses the opposite side: "There have been instances in which capital punishment did *not* serve as a deterrent. In medieval England, criminals were hanged, yet their hangings served as occasions for other criminals to work the crowds, committing even more crimes." Develop this topic a little further with one or two sentences.

Paragraph five. This paragraph pulls everything together. Don't merely rehash your point vaguely, saying something such as, "Therefore, based on these arguments, it is my opinion that capital punishment works well in civilized societies." Instead, "Tell 'em what you told 'em." Continuing with the preceding example, I'd say, "Therefore, while capital punishment occasionally fails to deter criminal behavior, there has been statistical and empirical evidence in dropping crime rates and in interviews with the criminals themselves that capital punishment is an effective deterrent." Another sentence or two finishes up a concise but effective essay.

Question: How long does this essay have to be?

Answer: Obviously, much depends on your typing skills. However, I suggest a minimum of five paragraphs with at least three sentences each. If you are a quick thinker and an even quicker typist, you may come up with an essay of six to eight paragraphs. If your essay is any longer than that, you probably are just inserting a lot of extraneous filler.

Don't chat with the evaluators. If you run out of time, DO NOT write some little note such as, "EVALUATOR: I have more stuff to say, but I'm out of time — sorry." Good grief! All you've done there is call the evaluator's attention to your shortcomings.

Analysis of an Argument

Paragraph one. Paragraph one states your analysis of the argument, whether you found the argument valid and sound or completely ridiculous and unsupported by even a modicum of evidence. Suppose that the passage argues that putting a 25-cent tax on every bottle will provide an incentive for the consumer to recycle bottles and cans and thus cut down on waste. Here's a good opening line: "This author's statement that a tax on bottles and cans will cut down on their waste is unsupported by evidence and is illogical given current recycling parameters set by the government and consumer behavior."

Continue the first paragraph by telling *why,* in your opinion, the argument is incorrect. Perhaps the author gives no facts or statistics to buttress his argument but appears to base it on unsound assumptions. Perhaps the author argues from a personal point of view and doesn't address broader concerns. Perhaps the author is quixotic, assuming an ideal that society has not yet reached.

I suggest that you have a grab bag of several refutations ready before you ever get to the exam. The preceding ones are very good; you can always attack a writer's source of facts or personal biases. Think of several tactics that you yourself use to shoot down an argument when you debate with friends (writing is easier if you use what comes naturally) and have them handy.

Paragraphs two and three. Your second and third paragraphs address each assumption that you believe the author makes. If the author assumes that a financial incentive is more important than any other type of incentive, say so and then either support or refute that assumption. If the author makes the assumption that people will not do what is right unless a law tells them to do so, state that assumption and then argue for or against it.

Paragraph four. In the fourth paragraph, provide possible counterexamples. If the author says that a tax of 25 cents per can would double the recycling rate, cite a situation in which increased taxes on bottles have not led to a significant increase in recycling. If the author states that people want to do the right thing but need a financial incentive, refute the argument by saying that a tax would have to be so large as to be prohibitive.

Don't fall into your own trap. If you argue that the writer's assumption is based on personal logic, unsupported by facts, be sure that *your* refutation is not based on personal logic, unsupported by facts. The last thing you need to do is point out the author's weakness and then make the evaluator chuckle as he marks you down for having the exact same weakness.

Paragraph five. In the final paragraph, give your conclusions. Say once again whether the author makes a valid point or is just wasting everyone's time. Reiterate briefly your reasons for thinking so.

If you can't think of a different way to write the material in the last paragraph, skip the last paragraph. You do *not* want to parrot the first paragraph entirely. You want to summarize the passage, but not by rote, simply repeating what you say earlier. Either put a new slant on the material, packaging it neatly, or eliminate this paragraph entirely.

Question: How long should an Analysis of an Argument essay be?

Answer: The Analysis of an Argument essay is about the same length as the Analysis of an Issue paper, but it may have fewer paragraphs. Don't worry if you have only three or four long paragraphs rather than five or six shorter ones as you had in the Analysis of an Issue essay (for example, you may want to combine paragraphs two and three that I discussed earlier). You are doing more in-depth analysis here and may have more to say on each point.

Keep in mind that everything you have read here about length is simply a suggested format. There is no one right or wrong length (although too short can definitely be a problem). I give you these pointers as guidelines you can use in practicing essay writing. After a few practice essays, you will know your comfort zone — the length of the passage you can write in the allotted time without going crazy.

And speaking of practice essays, turn the page and get ready to try a few on your own. Please, please write these essays using a word processing program on a computer, as that is how you'll be writing them on test day. That is, don't grab some lined paper and bang these essays out when you're in the library one afternoon. Sit down at your computer, type them as you will be doing on the real test, and be sure to time yourself. For most people, it's not the writing itself that's difficult, but coming up with a decent essay in just 30 minutes. After you finish, ask a friend to evaluate each essay on a scale of zero to six and discuss his or her reasoning with you.

Chapter 10

Do You Have the Write Stuff? Analytical Writing Practice Questions

I promised you in the Introduction to this book that each lecture, including the practice exam, would take you about two hours. Going through the material in this part should have taken you less than an hour. Use your remaining hour to write two essays: one about an analysis of an issue and one about an analysis of an argument.

Set your timer for 30 minutes, but if you can't finish what you want to say, just this once go ahead and ignore the time constraint. Finish your writing. After you finish, check out how long you took. If you took only 35 minutes, you should be able to speed up your writing enough to cover that extra inspiration. However, if you took 45 minutes or an hour, you have to decide how you're going to cut your time. Here are a few suggestions:

✔ **Don't spend too long on the outline.** Although the outline helps to clarify your thoughts, it does not count towards your score. Evaluators don't look at your outline at all; too much time spent on it is counterproductive.

✔ **Cut out the middle few paragraphs.** Your most important points should be in the beginning and ending of your essay. ("Tell 'em what you're gonna tell 'em; tell 'em what you told 'em.") Although you do have to provide some support for your thesis, you can present it in one or two paragraphs rather than three or four.

✔ **Limit yourself to three-sentence paragraphs.** Many of us end up saying the same thing over and over, making an important point in a different way. Here's an example from one of my own students: "Community service instead of jail time serves no purpose as the criminals learn no lesson from their service. The people who commit the crimes don't take community service time seriously. There is nothing learned by the criminals who have to serve only community service time." Although the writer obviously has a point, she makes it three times — once would have been enough.

✔ **Have a boilerplate format in your mind before you get to the test and have several refutations or support statements prewritten.** It would be nice if you came up with some astonishingly creative piece of writing that blew away the evaluators, but creativity is not what this section tests you for. It tests your ability to write well. It's not what you think that's important, but how well you express those thoughts. If you can come up with some basic support statements at home, you'll be pleasantly surprised at how well they work into an essay. For example, I almost always put in something about the financial repercussions. Everything has financial repercussions. I also write about individual rights versus the power of the government; I can find something to say about that on nearly every topic. If timing is a problem, have a few stock phrases in mind that you can adapt to your essay as needed.

Ready? Computer fired up and cursor blinking at you? Fingers limber? Set your timer for 30 minutes and go.

Analysis of an Issue

"Smoking causes illness. The evidence that even secondhand smoke can cause many different forms of illness is irrefutable. Accepting this as true, the government has a duty to forbid smoking in all places where children are present. People who argue that citizens have a right to smoke forget that after all, the duty of a government is to protect those citizens who cannot protect themselves, especially children."

Which argument are you more in agreement with: the one about people having a right to smoke or the one about the government having a duty to protect children by disallowing smoking around children? Using your own experiences, reading, or background in general, explain your reasoning.

Analysis of an Argument

"A flat rate income tax is the most fair means of taxing in a democracy. Disallowing all deductions and assessing a 10-percent tax on all income, individual and corporate, regardless of the source, would increase our tax revenues and decrease the current discriminatory effect of taxation."

Discuss how compelling you find the preceding argument. Analyze the reasoning presented in the argument, paying special attention to the evidence that supports the argument. Explain your point of view, addressing points that would make the argument more convincing or giving evidence that in fact weakens the conclusion.

 Here are two additional practice topics for you, just for fun. These are not an official part of this practice exam. If you are doing well in the writing, don't take the time to go through these. They are here just for those of you who want to (okay, *need* to) do more writing, to get your "system" down pat before you get into the exam.

Analysis of an Issue

"Affirmative action programs were beneficial, even critical, 20 years ago, but they have served their function and are now actually counterproductive. Both minorities and nonminorities are hurt by the quota system, which should be abolished. Those people who say that affirmative action programs should continue in place indefinitely fail to recognize that the workplace can regulate itself without governmental interference."

Which argument are you more in agreement with: the one that states that affirmative action programs should be discontinued or the one that states that affirmative action programs should continue indefinitely? Using your own experiences, reading, or background in general, explain your reasoning.

Analysis of an Argument

"The government cannot run a school as well as a private corporation can. Students will be better served by removing all governmental restraints and simply turning over to the schools the same per capita fees they currently get. Schools then could use those fees to pay private corporations, which could run the schools more efficiently and inexpensively."

Discuss how compelling you find the preceding argument. Analyze the reasoning presented in the argument, paying special attention to the evidence that supports the argument. Explain your point of view, addressing points that would make the argument more convincing or giving evidence that in fact weakens the conclusion.

Grading

There are no right or wrong answers to these essay questions. Go to Chapter 9 and review the portion on how the essays are scored.

Make copies of your essays. Give one copy of each of them to four evaluators (Choose people who know something about writing, such as a professor or a journalist friend, not just your buddy down the hall.) and ask each one to rate them on a scale of zero to six. Average the scores.

 Ask each evaluator to focus on a different part of your writing. For example, ask one evaluator to read the passage for content and organization. Ask another to pay attention to grammar, usage, and diction. Ask the next to evaluate the spelling, punctuation, and neatness. The final evaluator can do the "holistic" grading, giving you an overall score. The feedback from each person can help you work on your strengths and weaknesses.

When you have collated the comments, criticism, and carping from your evaluators, rewrite the essay. *Don't* time yourself; take all the time you want and do the job right. You'll need to go slowly to integrate the feedback. Speed can come later.

Part V
Two Years of Math in 58 Pages: The Dreaded Math Review

In this part . . .

No, no, please don't go get your pillow and PJs. I promise that this math review won't put you to sleep. I'm not going to start at $1 + 1 = 2$ and take you through every math concept you've learned since kindergarten; I have more respect for you than that. This math review neither insults you nor wastes your time. Here, I keep the instruction down to what you really need for the GMAT. And before you ask, no, you are not allowed to use a calculator, and no, the computer's calculator function isn't available to you for the test. Sorry about that. You are, however, given scratch paper that you can doodle on to help you solve the problems.

If you've been out of school for a while, don't despair. After you go through the math review, do as many of the math problems as you can. The answer explanations review the formulas and concepts again and again and again; some of them are bound to come back to you.

Chapter 11

More Figures than a Beauty Pageant: Geometry Review

- -

In This Chapter

▶ Angles

▶ Triangles

▶ Similar figures

▶ Area problems

▶ Quadrilaterals and other polygons

▶ Shaded-area problems

▶ Circles

- -

*I*f you've been watching your figure(s), this chapter is a breeze. If not, don't worry. We'll have you back in shape in no time.

You Gotta Have an Angle: Angles

Angles are a big part of the GMAT geometry problems. Fortunately, understanding angles is easy after you memorize a few basic concepts. And keep in mind the best news: You don't have to do proofs. Finding an angle is usually a matter of simple addition or subtraction. These three rules generally apply to the GMAT:

✔ There are no negative angles.

✔ There are no zero angles.

✔ It is extremely unlikely that you'll see any *fractional angles.* (For example, an angle won't measure 45 ½ degrees or 32 ¾ degrees.)

Angles are whole numbers. If you're plugging in a number for an angle, plug in a whole number such as 30, 45, or 90.

1. **Angles greater than zero but less than 90 degrees are called *acute.*** Think of an acute angle as being *a cute* little angle.

45°

Acute angle

2. **Angles equal to 90 degrees are called *right angles*.** They are formed by perpendicular lines and are indicated by a box in the corner of the two intersecting lines.

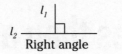
Right angle

A common GMAT trap is to have two lines appear to be perpendicular and look as if they form a right angle. Do not automatically assume that angles that look like right angles are right angles. Without calculating it, you know that an angle is a right angle only if (A) you're expressly told, "This is a right angle"; (B) you see the perpendicular symbol (⊥) indicating that the lines form a 90-degree angle; or (C) you see the box in the angle. Assume otherwise, and you may be headed for a trap!

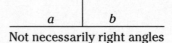
Not necessarily right angles

3. **Angles that total 90 degrees are called *complementary angles*.** Think of *C* for *corner* (the lines form a 90-degree corner angle) and *C* for *complementary*.

Complementary *x* and *y* angles

4. **An angle that is greater than 90 degrees but less than 180 degrees is called *obtuse*.** Think of obtuse as *obese;* an obese (or fat) angle is an obtuse angle.

110°
Obtuse angle

5. **An angle that measures exactly 180 degrees is called a *straight angle*.**

180°
Straight angle

6. **Angles that total 180 degrees are called *supplementary angles*.**

y *x*
Supplementary angles

Think of *S* for *supplementary* (or *straight*) angles. Be careful not to confuse complementary angles (*C* for *complementary* or *corner*) with supplementary angles (*S* for *supplementary* or *straight*). If you're likely to get these confused, just think alphabetically. *C* comes before *S* in the alphabet; 90 comes before 180 when you count.

7. **An angle that is greater than 180 degrees but less than 360 degrees is called a *reflex angle*.**

320°
Reflex angle

Think of a reflex angle as a reflection or mirror image of an acute angle. It makes up the rest of the angle when there's an acute angle.

Reflex angles are rarely tested on the GMAT.

8. Angles around a point total 360 degrees.

360 degrees

9. Angles that are opposite each other have equal measures and are called *vertical angles*.
Note that vertical angles may actually be horizontal. Just remember that vertical angles are *across* from each other, whether they are up and down (vertical) or side-by-side (horizontal).

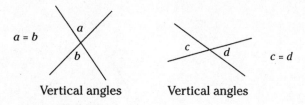

Vertical angles   Vertical angles

10. Angles in the same position (corresponding angles) around two parallel lines and a transversal have the same measures.

When you see two parallel lines and a transversal, number the angles. Start in the upper-right corner with 1 and go clockwise. For the second batch of angles, start in the upper-right corner with 5 and go clockwise. Note that all the odd-numbered angles are equal and all the even-numbered angles are equal.

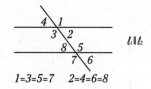

$1=3=5=7$ $2=4=6=8$

Be careful not to zigzag back and forth when numbering, like this:

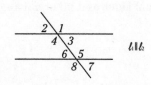

If you zig when you should have zagged, you can no longer use the tip that all even-numbered angles are equal to one another and all odd-numbered angles are equal to one another.

11. **The exterior angles of any figure are supplementary to the interior angles and total 360 degrees.**

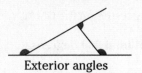

Exterior angles

Exterior angles can be very confusing. They always total 360 degrees, no matter what type of figure you have. Many people think that angles are exterior angles when they aren't. *Remember:* To be called an exterior angle, an angle must be supplementary to an interior angle.

Triangle Trauma: Triangles

1. **A triangle with three equal sides and three equal angles is called *equilateral*.**

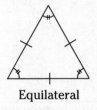

Equilateral

2. **A triangle with two equal sides and two equal angles is called isosceles.**

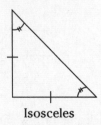

Isosceles

3. **Angles opposite equal sides in an isosceles triangle are also equal.**

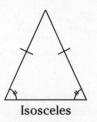

Isosceles

4. **A triangle with no equal sides and no equal angles is called *scalene*.**

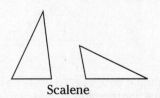

Scalene

5. In any triangle, the largest angle is opposite the longest side.

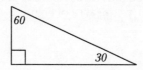

6. In any triangle, the sum of the lengths of two sides must be greater than the length of the third side. This statement is often written as $a + b > c$, where a, b, and c are the sides of the triangle.

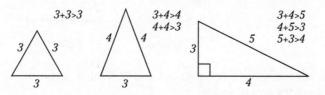

7. In any type of triangle, the sum of the interior angles is 180 degrees.

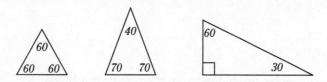

A trap question may want you to assume that different-sized triangles have different angle measures. Wrong! A triangle can be seven stories high and have 180 degrees or be microscopic and have 180 degrees. The size of the triangle is irrelevant; every triangle's internal angles add up to 180 degrees.

8. The measure of an exterior angle of a triangle is equal to the total of the two remote interior angles.

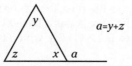

When you think about this rule, it makes sense. The sum of supplementary angles is 180. The sum of the angles in a triangle is 180. Therefore, angle $x = 180 - (y + z)$ or angle $x = 108 - a$. That must mean that $a = y + z$.

Similar figures

1. The sides of similar figures are in proportion. For example, if the heights of two similar triangles are in a ratio of 2:3, then the bases of those triangles are in a ratio of 2:3 as well.

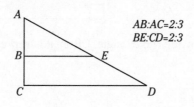

2. **The ratio of the areas of similar figures is equal to the square of the ratio of their sides.** For example, if each side of Figure A is $\frac{1}{3}$ the length of each side of similar Figure B, then the area of Figure A is $\frac{1}{9}\left[\left(\frac{1}{3}\right)^2\right]$ the area of Figure B.

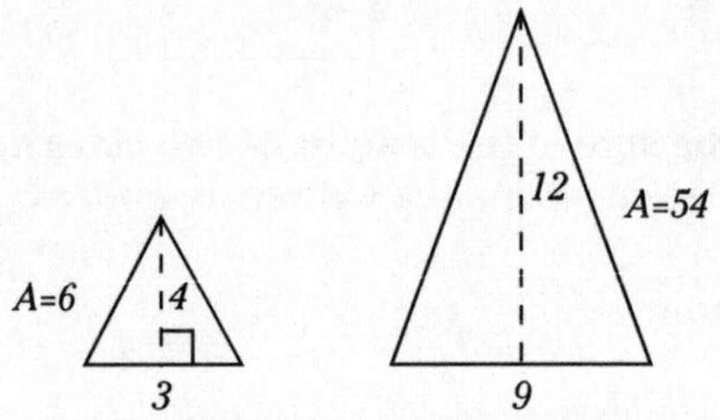

Figure A Figure B

Two similar triangles have bases of 5 and 25. Which of the following expresses the ratio of the areas of the two triangles?

(A) 1:5

(B) 1:15

(C) 1:25

(D) 1:30

(E) It cannot be determined from the information given.

The ratio of the sides is $\frac{1}{5}$. The ratio of the areas is the square of the ratio of the sides: $\frac{1}{5} \times \frac{1}{5} = \frac{1}{25}$. Note that answer E is a trap for the unwary. You can't figure out the exact area of either figure because you don't know the height (the area of a triangle is $\frac{1}{2}$ *base* $\times$ *height*). However, you aren't asked for an area, only for the ratio of the areas, which you can deduce from the formula discussed. *Correct Answer:* C.

Bonus: What do you suppose the ratio of the volumes of two similar figures is? Because volume is found in cubic units, the ratio of the volumes of two similar figures is the cube of the ratio of their sides. If figure A has a base of 5 and similar figure B has a base of 10, then the ratio of their volumes is 1:8 ($[1:2^3]$, which is $\frac{1}{2} \times \frac{1}{2} \times \frac{1}{2} = \frac{1}{8}$).

Don't assume that figures are similar; you must be told that they are.

Area

1. **The area of a triangle is $\frac{1}{2}$ *base* $\times$ *height*.** The height is always a line perpendicular to the base. The height may be a side of the triangle, as in a right triangle.

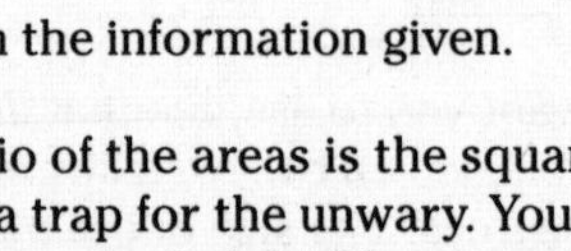

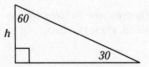

The height may be inside the triangle. Often, it is represented by a dashed line and a small 90-degree box.

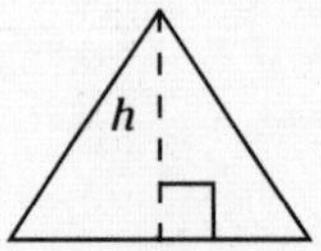

The height may be outside the triangle. This is very confusing and can be found in trick questions. *Remember:* You can always drop an altitude. That is, mentally put your pencil on the tallest point of the triangle and draw a line straight from that point to where the base would be if it were extended. The line can be outside the triangle.

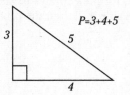

2. **The perimeter of a triangle is the sum of the lengths of the sides.**

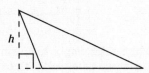

Pythagorean theorem

You have probably studied the Pythagorean theorem (known colloquially as PT). Keep in mind that it works only on *right* triangles. If a triangle doesn't have a right, or 90-degree, angle, you can't use any of the following information.

In any right triangle, you can find the lengths of the sides with the formula

$$a^2 + b^2 = c^2$$

where *a* and *b* are the sides of the triangle and *c* is the hypotenuse. The hypotenuse is always opposite the 90-degree angle and is always the longest side of the triangle. Why? If one angle in a triangle is 90 degrees, no other angle can be more than 90 degrees. All the angles must total 180 degrees, and there are no negative or 0 angles. Because the longest side is opposite the largest angle, the hypotenuse is the longest side.

Pythagorean triples

It's a pain in the posterior to have to do the whole PT formula every time you want to find the length of a side. You'll find five very common PT ratios in right triangles.

1. **Ratio 3:4:5** If one side of the triangle is 3 in this ratio, the other side is 4 and the hypotenuse is 5.

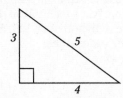

Because this is also a ratio, the sides can be in any multiple of these numbers, such as 6:8:10 (twice 3:4:5), 9:12:15 (three times 3:4:5), or 27:36:45 (nine times 3:4:5).

2. **Ratio 5:12:13** If one side of the right triangle is 5 in this ratio, the other side is 12 and the hypotenuse is 13.

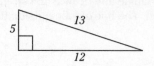

Because this is a ratio, the sides can be in any multiple of these numbers, such as 10:24:26 (twice 5:12:13), 15:36:39 (three times 5:12:13), or 50:120:130 (ten times 5:12:13).

3. **Ratio s:s:$s\sqrt{2}$ where s stands for the side of the figure.** Because two s's are alike or two sides are the same, this formula applies to an isosceles right triangle, also known as a 45:45:90 triangle. If one side is 2, then the other side is also 2 and the hypotenuse is $2\sqrt{2}$.

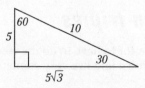

 This formula is great to know for squares. If a question tells you that the side of a square is 5 and wants to know the diagonal of the square, you know immediately that it is $5\sqrt{2}$. Why? A square's diagonal cuts the square into two isosceles right triangles (*isosceles* because all sides of the square are equal; *right* because all angles in a square are right angles). What is the diagonal of a square of side 64? $64\sqrt{2}$. What is the diagonal of a square of side 12,984? $12,984\sqrt{2}$.

 There's another way to write this ratio. Instead of s:s:$s\sqrt{2}$, you can write it as $\left(\frac{s}{\sqrt{2}}\right):\left(\frac{s}{\sqrt{2}}\right):s$, in which s still stands for the side of the triangle, but now you've divided everything by $\sqrt{2}$. Why do you need this complicated formula? Suppose that you're told that the diagonal of a square is 5. What is the area of the square? What is the perimeter of the square?

If you know the formula $\left(\frac{s}{\sqrt{2}}\right):\left(\frac{s}{\sqrt{2}}\right):s$, you know that s stands for the hypotenuse of the triangle, the same as the diagonal of the square. If $s = 5$, then the side of the square is $\frac{5}{\sqrt{2}}$, and you can figure out the area or the perimeter. After you know the side of a square, you can figure out just about anything.

4. **Ratio s:$s\sqrt{3}$:$2s$:** This special formula is for the sides of a 30:60:90 triangle.

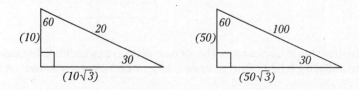

This type of triangle is a favorite of the test makers. The important thing to keep in mind here is that the hypotenuse is twice the length of the side opposite the 30-degree angle. If you get a word problem saying, "Given a 30:60:90 triangle of hypotenuse 20, find the area" or "Given a 30:60:90 triangle of hypotenuse 100, find the perimeter," you can do so because you can find the lengths of the other sides.

Thanks 4 Nothing: Quadrilaterals

1. Any four-sided figure is called a *quadrilateral.*

Quadrilateral

The interior angles of any quadrilateral total 360 degrees. Any quadrilateral can be cut into two 180-degree triangles.

2. A *square* is a quadrilateral with four equal sides and four right angles.

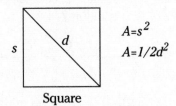
Square

The area of a square is *side*^{2} (also called *base* × *height*), or $\frac{1}{2}d^2$, where *d* stands for diagonal.

3. A *rhombus* is a quadrilateral with four equal sides and four angles that are not necessarily right angles. A rhombus often looks like a drunken square, tipsy on its side and wobbly.

The area of a rhombus is $\frac{1}{2}d_1 d_2$ (or $\frac{1}{2}$ *diagonal*1 × *diagonal*2).

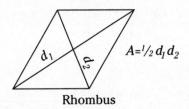
Rhombus

Any square is a rhombus, but not all rhombuses are squares.

4. A *rectangle* is a quadrilateral with two opposite and equal pairs of sides. That is, the top and bottom sides are equal, and the right and left sides are equal. All angles in a rectangle are right angles (*rectangle* means "right angle").

The area of a rectangle is *length* × *width* (which is the same as *base* × *height*).

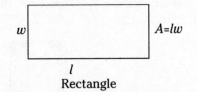
Rectangle

5. A *parallelogram* is a quadrilateral with two opposite and equal pairs of sides. The top and bottom sides are equal, and the right and left sides are equal. Opposite angles are equal but not necessarily right (or 90 degrees).

The area of a parallelogram is *base × height*. Remember that the height always is a perpendicular line from the tallest point of the figure down to the base. Diagonals of a parallelogram bisect each other.

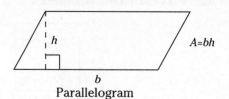

$A=bh$

Parallelogram

All rectangles are parallelograms, but not all parallelograms are rectangles.

6. **A *trapezoid* is a quadrilateral with two parallel sides and two nonparallel sides.**

The area of a trapezoid is $\frac{1}{2}(base1 + base2) \times height$. It makes no difference which base you label base 1 and which you label base 2, because you're adding them together anyway. Just be sure to add them *before* you multiply by ½.

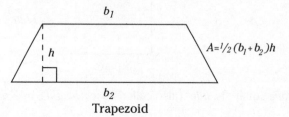

$A = \frac{1}{2}(b_1 + b_2)h$

Trapezoid

Quaint quads: Bizarre quadrilaterals

Some quadrilaterals don't have nice neat shapes or special names.

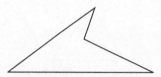

Don't immediately see a strange shape and say that you have no way to find the area of it. You may be able to divide the quadrilateral into two triangles and find the area of each triangle. You may also see a strange quadrilateral in a shaded-area problem.

Leftovers again: Shaded-area problems

Think of a shaded area as a *leftover*. It is "left over" after you subtract the unshaded area from the total area.

Shaded areas are often very unusual shapes. Your first reaction may be that you can't possibly find the area of that shape. Generally, you're right, but you don't have to find the area directly. Instead, be sly, devious, and sneaky; in other words, think the GMAT way! Find the area of the total figure, find the area of the unshaded portion, and subtract.

1. $s = 8$ (because the side of the square is the length of 2 radii).

   Area of square $= 64$

2. $r = 4$

   Area of circle $= 16\pi$

3. Shaded area $= 64 - 16\pi$ (the exam will leave the answer in this form; you don't have to work out π)

Missing Parrots and Other Polly-Gones: More Polygons

Triangles and quadrilaterals are probably the most common polygons tested on this exam. Here are a few other polygons you may see:

Number of Sides	Name
5	pentagon
6	hexagon (think of *x* in *six* and *x* in *hex*)
7	heptagon
8	octagon
9	nonagon
10	decagon

1. **A polygon with all equal sides and all equal angles is called** *regular.* For example, an equilateral triangle is a regular triangle and a square is a regular quadrilateral.

   You are rarely asked to find the areas of any polygons with more than four sides. In those rare instances, break the figure into 3- and 4-sided figures, find the area of each, and then add them together.

2. **The** *perimeter* **of a polygon is the sum of the lengths of all the sides.**

   The exterior angle measure of any GMAT polygon is 360°. Note that some unusual shapes break this "rule," but they are not tested on the GMAT, so you don't need to worry about them.

Total interior angle measure

To find the interior angle measure, use the formula $(n-2)\,180°$, where n stands for the number of sides.

For example, the interior angles of the following polygons are

> ✔ **Triangle:** $(3-2)180 = 1 \times 180 = 180°$
>
> ✔ **Quadrilateral:** $(4-2)180 = 2 \times 180 = 360°$
>
> ✔ **Pentagon:** $(5-2)180 = 3 \times 180 = 540°$
>
> ✔ **Hexagon:** $(6-2)180 = 4 \times 180 = 720°$
>
> ✔ **Heptagon:** $(7-2)180 = 5 \times 180 = 900°$
>
> ✔ **Octagon:** $(8-2)180 = 6 \times 180 = 1,080°$
>
> ✔ **Nonagon:** $(9-2)180 = 7 \times 180 = 1,260°$
>
> ✔ **Decagon:** $(10-2)180 = 8 \times 180 = 1,440°$

Have you learned that proportional multiplication is a great timesaving trick? Numbers are in proportion, and you can fiddle with them to make multiplication easier.

For example, suppose that you're going to multiply 5×180. Most people have to write down the problem and then work through it. However, you can double one and halve the other: Double 5 to make it 10. Halve 180 to make it 90. Now your problem is 10×90, which you can multiply in your head: 900.

Try another one: $3 \times 180 = ?$ Double the first number: $3 \times 2 = 6$. Halve the second number: $\frac{180}{2} = 90$. $6 \times 90 = 540$. You can do this shortcut multiplication in your head very quickly and impress your friends.

One interior angle

1. **To find the average measure of one angle in a figure, use the formula**

$$\frac{(n-2)180}{n}$$

where n stands for the number of sides (which is the same as the number of angles).

Pentagon: $\dfrac{(5-2) \times 180}{5} = \dfrac{3 \times 180}{5} = \dfrac{540}{5} = 108$

Because all angles are equal in a regular polygon, the same formula applies to one angle in a regular polygon.

2. **If you are given a polygon and are not told that it's regular, you can't solve for just one angle.**

What's the measure of angle *x?* It cannot be determined. You cannot assume that it is

$$\frac{(7-2)180}{7} = \frac{900}{7} = 128.57$$

Be sure to divide through by *n*, the number of sides (angles), not by $(n-2)$. If you divide through by $(n-2)$, you always get 180.

$$\frac{900}{5} = 180$$

Knowing this, triple-check your work if you come up with 180 for an answer to this type of problem; you may have made this very typical, but careless error.

Volume

The volume of any polygon is $(area\ of\ the\ base) \times height$. If you remember this formula, you don't have to memorize any of the following more specific formulas.

1. **Volume of a cube:** e^3

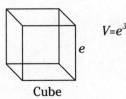

$V = e^3$

Cube

A cube is a three-dimensional square. Think of a die (one of a pair of dice). All of a cube's dimensions are the same; that is, *length = width = height*. In a cube, these dimensions are called *edges*. The volume of a cube is $edge \times edge \times edge = edge^3 = e^3$.

2. **Volume of a rectangular solid:** $l \times w \times h$

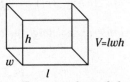

$V = lwh$

Rectangular solid

A rectangular solid is a box. The base of a box is a rectangle, which has an area of *length × width*. Multiply that by height to fit the original formula: $Volume = (area\ of\ base) \times height$, or $V = l \times w \times h$.

3. **Volume of a cylinder:** (πr^2) **height**

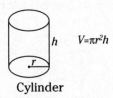

$V = \pi r^2 h$

Cylinder

Think of a cylinder as a can of soup. The base of a cylinder is a circle. The area of a circle is $(area\ of\ base) \times height = (\pi r^2) \times height$.

Multiply that by the height of the cylinder to get $(area\ of\ base) \times height = (\pi r^2) \times height$. Note that the top and bottom of a cylinder are identical circles. If you know the radius of either the top base or the bottom base, you can find the area of the circle.

Total surface area (TSA)

The total surface area, logically enough, is the sum of the areas of all the surfaces of the figure.

1. TSA of a cube: $6e^2$

Cube

A cube has six identical faces, and each face is a square. The area of a square is *side*^{2}. Here, that is called *edge*^{2}. If one face is *edge*^{2}, then the total surface area is $6 \times edge^2$, or $6e^2$.

2. TSA of a rectangular solid: $2(lw) + 2(wh) + 2(hl)$

Rectangular solid

A rectangular solid is a box. You need to find the area of each of the six surfaces. The bottom and top have the area of *length* $\times$ *width*. The left side and the right side have the area of *width* $\times$ *height*. The front side and the back side have the area of *height* $\times$ *length*. Together, they total $2(lw) + 2(wh) + 2(hl)$ or $2(lw + wh + hl)$.

3. TSA of a cylinder: $(circumference \times height) + 2(\pi r^2)$

Cylinder

This is definitely the most difficult TSA to figure out. Think of it as pulling the label off the can, flattening it out, finding its area, and then adding that to the area of the top and bottom lids. The *label* is a rectangle. Its *length* is the length of the circumference of the circle.

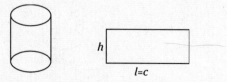

Its *height* is the height of the cylinder. Multiply *length* $\times$ *height* to find the area of the label.

You also need to find the area of the top and bottom of the cylinder. Because each is a circle, the TSA of the top and bottom is $2(\pi r^2)$. Add everything together.

I'm Too Much of a Klutz for Coordinate Geometry

1. The horizontal axis is the *x*-axis. The vertical axis is the *y*-axis.

2. Points are labeled (*x,y*), with the first number in the parentheses being how far to the right or left of the vertical line the point is and the second number being how far above or below the horizontal line the point is.

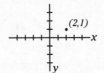

3. The intersection of the *x*- and *y*-axes is called the *point of origin,* and its coordinates are (0,0).

4. A line connecting points whose *x*- and *y*-coordinates are the same forms a 45-degree angle.

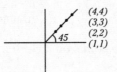

5. To find the distance between two points, you can use the distance formula:

$$\sqrt{\left(x_2 - x_1\right)^2 + \left(y_2 - y_1\right)^2}$$

To find the distance from (9,4) to (8,6), for example, follow these steps:

$$9 = x_1$$
$$8 = x_2$$
$$4 = y_1$$
$$6 = y_2$$
$$\left(8 - 9\right)^2 = -1^2 = 1$$
$$\left(6 - 4\right)^2 = 2^2 = 4$$
$$\sqrt{1 + 4} = \sqrt{5}$$

The distance between the two points is $\sqrt{5}$.

Running Around in Circles

Did you hear about the rube who pulled his son out of college, claiming that the school was filling his head with nonsense? As the rube said, "Joe Bob told me that he learned πr^2. But any fool knows that pie are round; *cornbread* are square!"

Circles are among the least-complicated geometry concepts. The most important things are to remember the vocabulary and to be able to distinguish an arc from a sector and an inscribed angle from a central angle. Here's a quick review of the basics.

1. A *radius* goes from the center of a circle to its circumference (perimeter).

Radius

2. A circle is named by its *center* (midpoint).

Center

3. A *diameter* connects two points on the circumference of the circle, going through the center, and is equal to two radii.

Diameter

4. A *chord* connects any two points on a circle.

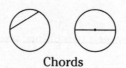

Chords

5. **The longest chord in a circle is the diameter.**

Here's a lovely question you may see in the Data Sufficiency section. The directions are given below.

(A) if statement 1 ALONE is sufficient to answer the question, but statement 2 alone is not sufficient to answer the question asked

(B) if statement 2 ALONE is sufficient to answer the question, but statement 1 alone is not sufficient to answer the question asked

(C) if BOTH statements 1 and 2 TOGETHER are sufficient to answer the question asked, but NEITHER statement ALONE is sufficient

(D) if EACH statement alone is sufficient to answer the question asked

(E) if statements 1 and 2 TOGETHER are NOT sufficient to answer the question asked, and additional data specific to the problem are needed

What is the area of the circle?

(1) The longest chord of the circle is 12.

(2) The radius of the circle is 6.

Either statement 1 alone or statement 2 alone is sufficient to answer the question. The one piece of info you need to find the area of a circle is the radius because the formula for the area of a circle is πr^2. If the longest chord of a circle is 12, the diameter (which is the longest chord) is 12, and the radius (which is half the diameter) is 6. Of course, you don't bother actually finding the area of the circle. You rest content knowing that you could do so if you wanted to. *Correct Answer:* D.

Here's another example.

What is the area of the circle?

   (1) The circle has a chord of 20.

   (2) The circle has a radius of 10.

If you chose D, you fell for a trap. Yes, statement 2 alone is sufficient. To find the area of a circle, you need the radius. But statement 1 alone is not sufficient. Just because *a* chord is 20 does not mean that the *longest chord* is 20, making the diameter 20 and the radius 10.

Oh, you say the answer is C? Congratulations on falling for the second built-in trap. Tut, tut — save your breath; it's no use arguing with me. Yes, based on info in statement 2, you can deduce that a chord of 20 is in fact the diameter and therefore the longest chord. However, you don't need that information to find the answer. The data given in statement 2 alone is sufficient. Just because you get additional information as a bonus doesn't mean that information is necessary. *Correct Answer:* B.

6. **The perimeter of a circle is called the circumference.** The formula for the length of a circumference is $2\pi r$ or πd (logical, huh, because two radii equals one diameter).

Bonus: You may encounter a wheel question in which you're asked how much distance a wheel covers or how many times it revolves. The key to solving this type of question is knowing that one rotation of a wheel equals one circumference of that wheel.

A child's wagon has a wheel of radius 6 inches. If the wagon wheel travels 100 revolutions, approximately how many feet has the wagon rolled?

   (A) 325

   (B) 314

   (C) 255

   (D) 201

   (E) 200

One revolution is equal to one circumference: $C = 2\pi r = 2\pi6 = 12\pi =$ approximately 37.68 inches. Multiply that by 100 = 3,768 inches = 314 feet. *Correct Answer:* B.

7. **The area of a circle is** $\pi\ radius^{2}$.

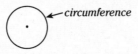

8. **A *central angle* has its endpoints on the circumference of the circle and its center at the center of the circle. The degree measure of a central angle is the same as the degree measure of its intercepted arc.**

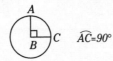

9. An *inscribed angle* has both its endpoints and its center on the circumference of the circle. The degree measure of an inscribed angle is half the degree measure of its intercepted arc.

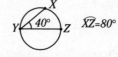

You may see a figure that looks like a string picture you made at summer camp, with all sorts of lines running every which way. Take the time to identify the endpoints of the angles and the center point. You may be surprised at how easy the question suddenly becomes. In this figure, for example, find the sum of $a+b+c+d+e$.

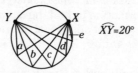

Note: Figure not drawn to scale.

(A) 65°

(B) 60°

(C) 55°

(D) 50°

(E) 45°

Each angle is an inscribed angle; it has half the degree measure of the central angle, or half the degree measure of its intercepted arc. If you look carefully at the endpoints of these angles, they're all the same. They are along arc *XY*, which has a measure of 20 degrees. Therefore, each angle is 10 degrees, for a total of 50. *Correct Answer:* D.

10. When a central angle and an inscribed angle have the same endpoints, the degree measure of the central angle is twice that of the inscribed angle.

11. The degree measure of a circle is 360.

12. An *arc* is a portion of the circumference of a circle. The degree measure of an arc is the same as its central angle and twice its inscribed angle.

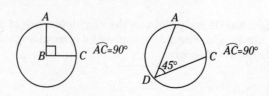

To find the length of an arc, follow these steps:

    a. Find the circumference of the entire circle.

    b. Put the degree measure of the arc over 360 and then reduce the fraction.

    c. Multiply the circumference by the fraction.

Find the length of arc *AC*.

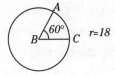

(A) 36π

(B) 27π

(C) 18π

(D) 12π

(E) 6π

Take the steps one at a time. First, find the circumference of the entire circle. $C = 2\pi r = 36\pi$. Don't multiply π out; problems usually leave it in that form. Next, put the degree measure of the arc over 360. The degree measure of the arc is the same as its central angle, 60 degrees.

$$\frac{60}{360} = \frac{1}{6}$$

The arc is ⅙ of the circumference of the circle. Multiply the circumference by the fraction: $36\pi \times \frac{1}{6} = 6\pi$. *Correct Answer:* E.

After you get the hang of these, they're kinda fun. Try another one.

Find the length of arc *RS* in this figure.

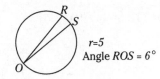

(A) ⅓π

(B) π

(C) 3π

(D) 4π

(E) 12

First, find the circumference of the entire circle. $C = 2\pi = 10\pi$. Second, put the degree measure of the arc over 360. Here, the inscribed angle is 6°. Because an inscribed angle is ½ of the central angle and ½ of its intercepted arc, the arc is 12°. Then $^{12}\!/_{360} = \frac{1}{30}$. The arc is ¹⁄₃₀ of the circle. Finally, multiply the circumference by the fraction: $10\pi \times \frac{1}{30} = {}^{10}\!/_{30\pi} = \frac{1}{3\pi}$. The length of the arc is ⅓π. *Correct Answer:* A.

Be very careful not to confuse the *degree measure* of the arc with the *length* of the arc. The length is always a portion of the circumference, always has a π in it, and always is in linear units. If you chose E in this example, you found the degree measure of the arc rather than its length.

13. A *sector* **is a portion of the area of a circle. The degree measure of a sector is the same as its central angle and twice its inscribed angle.**

To find the area of a sector, do the following:

a. **Find the area of the entire circle.**

b. **Put the degree measure of the sector over 360 and then reduce the fraction.**

c. **Multiply the area by the fraction.**

Finding the area of a sector is very similar to finding the length of an arc. The only difference is in the first step. Whereas an arc is a part of the *circumference* of a circle, a sector is a part of the *area* of a circle. Try a few examples for sectors.

Find the area of sector *ABC*.

(A) 64π

(B) 36π

(C) 16π

(D) 12π

(E) 6π

First, find the area of the entire circle. $A = \pi r^2 = 64\pi$. Second, put the degree measure of the sector over 360. The sector is 90°, the same as its central angle. $^{90}\!/_{360} = \frac{1}{4}$. Third, multiply the area by the fraction: $64\pi \times \frac{1}{4} = 16\pi$. *Correct Answer:* C.

Find the area of sector *XYZ* in this figure.

(A) 9.7π

(B) 8.1π

(C) 7.2π

(D) 6.3π

(E) 6π

First, find the area of the entire circle. $A = \pi r^2 = 81\pi$. Second, put the degree measure of the sector over 360. A sector has the same degree measure as its intercepted arc, here 36 degrees: $^{36}\!/_{360} = \frac{1}{10}$. Third, multiply the area by the fraction: $81\pi \times \frac{1}{10} = 8.1\pi$. *Correct Answer:* B.

Chapter 12

Gotta Catch Some (Xs, Ys, and) Zs: Algebra and Other Sleeping Aids

Trivia Question: Where was algebra supposedly invented?

Answer: Muslim scholars invented Algebra in Zabid, Yemen. See — you can't blame the Greeks for everything!

The Powers That Be: Bases and Exponents

Many GMAT questions require you to know how to work with bases and exponents. The following sections explain some of the more important concepts.

1. **The *base* is the big number (or letter) on the bottom. The exponent is the little number (or letter) in the upper-right.**

   In x^5, x is the base, and 5 is the exponent.

   In 3^y, 3 is the base, and y is the exponent.

2. **A base to the zero power equals one.**

   $x^0 = 1$

   $5^0 = 1$

   $129^0 = 1$

There is a long, boring explanation as to why a number to the zero power equals 1, but you don't really care, do you? For now, just memorize the rule.

3. A base to the second power is $base \times base$.

This is pretty familiar stuff, right?

$$x^2 = x \times x$$

$$5^2 = 5 \times 5$$

$$129^2 = 129 \times 129$$

The same is true for bigger exponents. The exponent tells you how many times the number is repeated. For example, 5^6 means that you write down six 5's and then multiply them all together.

$$5^6 = 5 \times 5 \times 5 \times 5 \times 5 \times 5$$

4. A base to a negative exponent is the reciprocal of itself.

This one is a little more confusing. A *reciprocal* is the upside-down version of something. When you have a negative exponent, just put the base and exponent under a 1 and make the exponent positive again.

$$x^{-4} = \frac{1}{(x^4)}$$

$$5^{-3} = \frac{1}{(5^3)}$$

$$129^{-1} = \frac{1}{(129^1)}$$

The *number* is *not* negative. When you flip it, you get the reciprocal, and the negative just sort of fades away. *Don't* fall for the trap of saying that $5^{-3} = -\left(\frac{1}{5}\right)^3$ or $-\frac{1}{125}$.

When you take a base of 10 to some power, the number of the power equals the number of zeroes in the number.

$$10^1 = 10 \text{ (one zero)}$$

$$10^4 = 10,000 \text{ (four zeroes)}$$

$$10^0 = 1 \text{ (zero zeroes)}$$

5. To multiply like bases, add the exponents.

You can multiply two bases that are the same; just add the exponents.

$$x^3 \times x^2 = x^{(3+2)} = x^5$$

$$5^4 \times 5^9 = 5^{(4+9)} = 5^{13}$$

$$129^3 \times 129^0 = 129^{(3+0)} = 129^3$$

You cannot multiply *unlike* bases. Think of it as trying to make dogs multiply with cats — it doesn't work. All you end up with is a miffed meower and a damaged dog.

$$x^2 \times y^3 = x^2 \times y^3 \text{ (no shortcuts)}$$

$$5^2 \times 129^3 = 5^2 \times 129^3 \text{ (you actually have to work it out)}$$

6. To divide like bases, subtract the exponents.

You can divide two bases that are the same by subtracting the exponents.

$$x^5 \div x^2 = x^{(5-2)} = x^3$$

$$5^9 \div 5^3 = 5^{(9-3)} = 5^6$$

$$129^4 \div 129^0 = 129^{(4-0)} = 129^4$$

(Did I getcha on that last one? It should make sense. Any base to the zero power is 1. Any number divided by 1 is itself.)

Did you look at the second example, $5^9 \div 5^3$, and think that it was 5^3? It's easy to fall into the trap of dividing instead of subtracting, especially when you see numbers that just beg to be divided, like 9 and 3. Keep your guard up.

7. Multiply the exponents of a base inside and outside the parentheses.

That's quite a mouthful. Here's what it means:

$$\left(x^2\right)^3 = x^{(2 \times 3)} = x^6$$

$$\left(5^3\right)^3 = 5^{(3 \times 3)} = 5^9$$

$$\left(129^0\right)^3 = 129^{(0 \times 3)} = 129^0$$

Here's a Data Sufficiency question testing this concept. Remember that you have the following answer choices:

(A) if statement 1 ALONE is sufficient to answer the question, but statement 2 alone is not sufficient to answer the question asked

(B) if statement 2 ALONE is sufficient to answer the question, but statement 1 alone is not sufficient to answer the question asked

(C) if BOTH statements 1 and 2 TOGETHER are sufficient to answer the question asked, but NEITHER statement ALONE is sufficient

(D) if EACH statement alone is sufficient to answer the question asked

(E) if statements 1 and 2 TOGETHER are NOT sufficient to answer the question asked

Is $x^3 = y$?

(1) $\dfrac{x^7}{x^4} = y$

(2) $x = y$

Statement 1 alone is sufficient. When dividing like bases, subtract the exponents: $7 - 4 = 3$. Statement 1 is another way of saying $x^3 = y$. Because statement 1 alone is sufficient, eliminate choices C and E.

Statement 2 alone is not sufficient. If $x = 1$, then $x^3 = y$. If x is not 1, then x^3 is not equal to y. Because you cannot give a definite answer to the question, the data are not sufficient, eliminating choices B and D. Only choice A remains. *Correct Answer:* A.

8. **To add or subtract like bases to like powers, add or subtract the numerical coefficient of the bases.**

The *numerical coefficient* (a great name for a rock band, don't you think?) is simply the number *in front of* the base. Notice that it is *not* the little exponent in the upper-right but the full-sized number to the left of the base.

In $31x^3$, 31 is the numerical coefficient.

In $-8y^2$, -8 is the numerical coefficient.

In x^3, what is the numerical coefficient? One, because any number is itself times 1; the 1 is not always written out. Good trap.

In $37x^3 + 10x^3 = 47x^3$, just add the numerical coefficients: $37 + 10 = 47$.

In $15y^2 - 10y^2 = 5y^2$, just subtract the numerical coefficients: $15 - 10 = 5$.

You cannot add or subtract like bases with *different exponents.*

$13x^3 - 9x^2$ is *not* equal to $4x^3$ or $4x^2$ or $4x$. All it is equal to is $13x^3 - 9x^2$. The bases *and* exponents must be the same for you to add or subtract the terms.

9. **You cannot simply add or subtract the numerical coefficients of unlike bases.**

Even though I'm the Queen of Shortcuts, I want to be sure you know that not every shortcut works. Some can sabotage your efforts.

$$16x^2 - 4y^2 = 16x^2 - 4y^2$$

It is *not* $12x^2$ or $12y^2$ or $12xy^2$.

Keep It in Proportion: Ratios

After you know the tricks, ratios are some of the easiest problems to answer quickly. I call them "heartbeat" problems because you can solve them in a heartbeat. Of course, if someone drop-dead gorgeous sits next to you and makes your heart beat faster, it may take you two heartbeats to solve a ratio problem. So sue me.

1. **A *ratio* is written as $\frac{of}{to}$ or *of:to*.**

The ratio *of* umbrellas *to* heads $= \dfrac{\text{umbrellas}}{\text{heads}}$

The ratio *of* sunflowers *to* roses = sunflowers : roses

2. **A *possible total* is a multiple of the sum of the numbers in the ratio.**

You may be given a problem like this: At a party, the ratio of blondes to redheads is 4:5. Which of the following can be the total number of blondes and redheads at the party?

Mega-easy. Add the numbers in the ratio: $4 + 5 = 9$. The total must be a multiple of 9, such as 9, 18, 27, 36, and so on. If this "multiple of" stuff is confusing, think of it another way: The sum must divide evenly into the total. That is, the total must be divisible by 9. Can the total, for example, be 54? Yes, 9 goes evenly into 54. Can it be 64? No, 9 does not go evenly into 64.

After a rough hockey game, Bernie checks his body and finds that he has three bruises for every five cuts. Which of the following can be the total number of bruises and cuts on poor ol' Bernie's body?

(A) 53

(B) 45

(C) 35

(D) 33

(E) 32

Add the numbers in the ratio: $3 + 5 = 8$. The total must be a multiple of 8 (or, looking at it another way, the total must be evenly divisible by 8). Only choice E is a multiple of 8: $8 \times 4 = 32$. *Correct Answer:* E.

Did you notice the trap answers? The answer 53 is a good trap because it features both 5 and 3, the numbers in the ratio. The answer 45 is a trap. If you multiply $3 \times 5 = 15$, you may think that the total has to be a multiple of 15. No, the total is a multiple of the *sum,* not of the product. *Add* the numbers in the ratio; don't multiply them. 35 (like 53) has both terms of the ratio. 33 is a multiple of 3. Only 32 is a multiple of the *sum* of the terms in the ratio.

Here is one more because you should always get this type of problem correct.

Trying to get Willie to turn down his stereo, his neighbor pounds on the ceiling and shouts up to his apartment. If she pounds seven times for every five times she shouts, which of the following can be the total number of poundings and shouts?

(A) 75

(B) 57

(C) 48

(D) 35

(E) 30

Add the numbers in the ratio: $7 + 5 = 12$. The total must be a multiple of 12 (it must be evenly divisible by 12). Here, only 48 is evenly divisible by 12. Of course, the numbers 75 and 57 may trick you by using the numbers 7 and 5 from the ratio. Choice D is the product of 7×5. *Correct Answer:* C.

Here's an example of how ratios can be tested in Data Sufficiency questions. (If you forgot the answer choices, look above the example on page 123.)

How many tapes does Kit have?

(1) The ratio of her tapes to CDs is 2:9.

(2) Kit has only tapes and CDs.

Just because the ratio of tapes to CDs is 2:9 does not mean that Kit has 2 tapes and 9 CDs. She could have any multiple of those numbers, such as 4 and 18, or 6 and 27, or 200 and 900. Statement 1 alone is not sufficient; eliminate choices A and D.

It should be pretty obvious that statement 2 alone is not sufficient. Knowing that Kit has only tapes and CDs does not tell you how many tapes she has. Eliminate choices B and D.

Could both statements be used together to answer the question? No. You still don't know how many times the ratio 2:9 Kit has: 2? 4? 100? You don't have enough data to answer the question even with everything thrown in. Eliminate choice C. *Correct Answer:* E.

When given a ratio and a total and asked to find a specific term, do the following, in order:

1. **Add the numbers in the ratio.**

2. **Divide that sum into the total.**

3. **Multiply that quotient by each term in the ratio.**

4. **Add the answers to double-check that they equal the total.**

Pretty confusing stuff. Take it one step at a time. Here's an example to help.

Yelling at the members of his team, who had just lost 21–0, the irate coach pointed his finger at each member of the squad, calling everyone either a wimp or a slacker. If there were 3 wimps for every 4 slackers, and every member of the 28-man squad was either a wimp or a slacker, how many wimps were there?

1. **Add the numbers in the ratio:** $3 + 4 = 7$.

2. **Divide that sum into the total:** $^{28}/_7 = 4$.

3. **Multiply that quotient by each term in the ratio:** $4 \times 3 = 12$; $4 \times 4 = 16$.

4. **Add to double-check that the numbers equal the total:** $12 + 16 = 28$.

Now you have all the information you need to answer a variety of questions: How many wimps were there? Twelve. How many slackers were there? Sixteen. How many more slackers than wimps were there? Four. How many slackers would have to be kicked off the team for the number of wimps and slackers to be equal? Four. The GMAT's Math Moguls can ask all sorts of things, but if you have this information, you're ready for anything they throw at you.

Be sure that you actually do Step 4, adding the terms to double-check that they equal the total again. Doing so catches any careless mistakes you may have made. For example, suppose that you divided 7 into 28 and got 3 instead of 4. Then you said that there were 3×3, or 9, wimps, and 3×4, or 12, slackers. That means that the total was $9 + 12 = 21$ — *ooooops!* You know that the total has to be 28, so you can go back and try again. You'll also catch a careless mistake in your multiplication. Suppose that you correctly divide 7 into 28 and get 4. But when you multiply 4×3, you get 43 instead of 12. (Hey, when the adrenaline's flowing during the exam, you'd be surprised at the kinds of mistakes you can make.) When you add the numbers, you get $43 + 16 = 59$ instead of the 28 that you know is the total.

Things Aren't What They Seem: Symbolism

You may encounter two basic types of symbolism problems. If so, do one of the following:

✔ Substitute the number given for the variable in the explanation.

✔ Talk through the explanation to see which constraint fits and then do the indicated operations.

1. Substitute for the variable in the explanation.

You see a problem with a strange symbol. It may be a variable inside a circle, a triangle, a star, or a tic-tac-toe sign. That symbol has no connection to the Real World at all. Don't panic, thinking that your teachers forgot to teach you something. Symbols are made up for each problem.

The symbol is included in a short explanation. It may look like this:

$$a\#b\#c = \frac{(a+b)^c}{b+c}$$

$$x*y*z = z/x + \left(\frac{y}{z}\right)^x$$

$$m@n@o = mn + no - om$$

Again, the symbols don't have any meaning in the outside world; they mean only what the problem tells you they mean, and that meaning holds true only for this problem.

Below the explanation is the question itself:

$$3\#2\#1 =$$

$$4*6*8 =$$

$$2@5@10 =$$

Your job is one of substitution. Plug in a number for the variable in the equation. Which number do you plug in? The one that's in the same position as that variable. For example:

$$a\#b\#c = \frac{(a+b)^c}{b+c}$$

$$3\#2\#1 = \frac{(3+2)^1}{2+1} = \frac{5}{3}$$

Because *a* was in the first position and 3 was in the first position, substitute a 3 for an *a* throughout the equation. Because *b* was in the second position and 2 was in the second position, substitute a 2 for a *b* throughout the equation. Because *c* was in the third position and 1 was in the third position, substitute a 1 for a *c* throughout the equation.

Do the same for the other problems.

$$x*y*z = \left(\frac{z}{x}\right) + \left(\frac{y}{z}\right)^x$$

$$4*6*8 = \left(\frac{8}{4}\right) + \left(\frac{6}{8}\right)^4 = 2 + \left(\frac{6}{8}\right)^4 = 2 + .316 = 2.316$$

and

$$m@n@o = mn + no - om$$

$$2@5@10 = (2 \times 5) + (5 \times 10) - (10 \times 2) = 10 + 50 - 20 = 40$$

This is the simpler of the two types of symbolism problems. Just substitute the number for the variable and work through the equation.

2. Talk through the explanation and do the operations.

This type of symbolism problem may seem more confusing until you've done a few. Then they become so easy that you wonder why you didn't see it before. Following are two possibilities.

$$\boxed{x} = 3x \text{ if } x \text{ is odd}$$

$$\boxed{x} = x/2 \text{ if } x \text{ is even}$$

Solve for $\boxed{5} + \boxed{8}$

First, talk through the explanation. You have something in a circle. If that something in the circle is odd, you multiply it by 3. If that something in the circle is even, you divide it by 2.

In the question, there's a 5 in the circle. Because 5 is odd, you multiply it by 3 to get $5 \times 3 = 15$. In the second half of the question, there's an 8 in a circle. Because 8 is even, you divide it by 2. $\frac{8}{2} = 4$. Now add: $15 + 4 = 19$.

Don't keep going. Do *not* say, "Well, 19 is odd, so I have to multiply it by 3, getting 57." You can bet that 57 is one of the trap multiple-choice answers.

You may still think of this second type of problem as a plug-in or substitution problem because you are plugging the number into the equation for x and working it through. However, you first have to figure out which equation to plug it into. That requires talking things through. You have to understand what you're doing in this type of problem. Try another.

$$\triangle x = 3x + \tfrac{1}{3}x \text{ if } x \text{ is prime}$$

$$\triangle x = x^2 + \sqrt{x} \text{ if } x \text{ is composite}$$

$$\triangle 16 + \triangle 3 =$$

Aha! Now you have to know some math vocabulary. Prime numbers are not the numbers that have stars next to them in your little black book. *Prime numbers* are numbers that cannot be divided evenly other than by 1 and themselves, such as 2, 3, 5, 7, 11, and 13. *Composite numbers* are numbers that *can* be divided evenly other than by just 1 and themselves, such as 4, 6, 8, 9, 10, and 12. The first thing you do is decide whether the term in the triangle is a composite number or a prime number.

$\triangle 16$: Because 16 is a composite number, use the second equation. Square 16: $16 \times 16 = 256$. Take the square root of 16: $\sqrt{16} = 4$. Add them together: $256 + 4 = 260$.

$\triangle 3$: Because 3 is a prime number, use the first equation. $3(3) + \tfrac{1}{3}(3) = 9 + 1 = 10$. Add the two solutions: $260 + 10 = 270$.

Sometimes, the solutions have symbols in them as well. Here's an example:

$$\text{\textcircled{x}} = \tfrac{1}{2}x \text{ if } x \text{ is composite}$$

$$\text{\textcircled{x}} = 2x \text{ if } x \text{ is prime}$$

Solve for $\text{\textcircled{5}} \times \text{\textcircled{10}}$.

(A) $\text{\textcircled{15}}$

(B) $\text{\textcircled{25}}$

(C) $\text{\textcircled{50}}$

(D) $\text{\textcircled{100}}$

Because 5 is prime, you multiply it by 2: $5 \times 2 = 10$. Because 10 is composite, you multiply it by $\tfrac{1}{2}$: $10 \times \tfrac{1}{2} = 5$ Multiply: $10 \times 5 = 50$.

Noooo! Don't choose C; that's the trap answer. Choice C doesn't say 50; it says $\text{\textcircled{50}}$. The 50 is in a circle. That means that you have to solve the answer choice to see what **circle** 50 is. Because 50 is even, you take half of it: $50 \div 2 = 25$. That's not the answer you want. Now go through the rest of the choices:

$\textcircled{15}$: Because 15 is composite, multiply it by $\frac{1}{2}$: $15 \times \frac{1}{2} = 7.5$

$\textcircled{25}$: Because 25 is composite, multiply it by $\frac{1}{2}$: $25 \times \frac{1}{2} = 12.5$

$\textcircled{100}$: Because 100 is composite, multiply it by $\frac{1}{2}$: $100 \times \frac{1}{2} = 50$. You have a winner!

Whenever you see a symbol, get to work. That symbol may be in the question or in the answer choices. You still follow the explanation. But remember the trap I already discussed: *Be super careful not to keep on going.* That is, when you come up with 50 as your answer, don't say, "Well, 50 is composite, so I have to multiply it by $\frac{1}{2}$, getting 25." Stop when there are no more symbols. *Correct Answer:* D.

Have you studied functions? Maybe not in school, but if you've read the preceding material on symbolism, you have just studied functions. A function is very much like the symbolism you've just read about. You may see a problem like this:

$f(x) = (2x)^3$. Solve for $f(2)$

The *f* stands for function. Do the same thing you did before: Talk through the problem. You say, "I have something in parentheses. My job is to multiply that something by 2 and then cube the whole disgusting mess." In other words, just plug in the 2 where you see an *x* in the explanation.

$$f(2) = (2 \times 2)^3 = 4^3 = 64$$

Try another one.

$f(x) = x + x^2 + x^3$. Solve for $f(10)$.

$$2 + 4 + 8 = 14$$

Just plug the 10 in for the *x*: $f(10) = 10 + 10^2 + 10^3 = 10 + 100 + 1,000 = 1,110$

Now that you've acquired this skill, you can call yourself "fully functional."

Abracadabra Algebra

You must be able to do three basic algebra concepts for the GMAT:

✔ Solve for *x* in an equation.

✔ Use the FOIL method.

✔ Take an algebraic expression from its final form back to its original form.

Solve for x in an equation

The first concept to understand is how to solve for *x* in an equation. To solve for *x*, follow these steps:

1. **Isolate the variable, which means get all the *x*'s on one side and all the non-*x*'s on the other side.**

2. **Add all the *x*'s on one side; add all the non-*x*'s on the other side.**

3. **Divide both sides of the equation by the number in front of the *x*.**

Now you try it: $3x + 7 = 9x - 5$.

1. **Isolate the variable. Move the $3x$ to the right, *changing the sign* to make it $-3x$.**

   Forgetting to change the sign is one of the most common careless mistakes students make. The test makers realize that and often include trap answer choices to catch this mistake.

   Move the -5 to the left, *changing the sign* to make it $+5$. You now have $7 + 5 = 9x - 3x$.

2. **Add the x's on one side; add the non-x's on the other side.**

   $12 = 6x$

3. **Divide both sides by what is next to the x.**

   $\frac{12}{6} = \frac{6x}{6}$

   $2 = x$

If you're weak on algebra or know that you often make careless mistakes, plug the 2 back into the equation to make sure that it works.

$3(2) + 7 = 9(2) - 5$

$6 + 7 = 18 - 5$

$13 = 13$

If you absolutely hate algebra, see whether you can simply plug in the answer choices. If this were a Problem-Solving question with multiple-choice answers, you could plug 'n' chug.

Curses! FOILed again

The second thing you need to know to do algebra is how to use the *FOIL* method. *FOIL* stands for *First, Outer, Inner, Last* and refers to the order in which you multiply the variables in parentheses. You can practice by using this equation $(a + b)(a - b) =$.

1. **Multiply the *First* variables: $a \times a = a^2$.**

2. **Multiply the *Outer* variables: $a \times -b = -ab$.**

3. **Multiply the *Inner* variables: $b \times a = ba$ (which is the same as ab).**

4. **Multiply the *Last* variables: $b \times -b = -b^2$.**

Add like terms: $-ab + ab = 0ab$. (Remember that you can multiply numbers forward or backward, such that $ab = ba$.) The positive ab and negative ab cancel each other out. You're left with only $a^2 - b^2$.

Try another one: $(3a + b)(a - 2b) =$

1. **Multiply the *First* terms: $3a \times a = 3a^2$.**

2. **Multiply the *Outer* terms: $3a \times -2b = -6ab$.**

3. **Multiply the *Inner* terms: $b \times a = ba$ (which is the same as ab).**

4. **Multiply the *Last* terms: $b \times -2b = -2b^2$.**

5. **Combine like terms: $-6ab + ab = -5ab$.**

The final answer is $3a^2 - 5ab - 2b^2$.

You should out-and-out *memorize* the following three FOIL problems. Don't bother to work them out every time; know them by heart.

$$(a+b)^2 = a^2 + 2ab + b^2$$

You can prove this equation by using FOIL: $(a+b)(a+b)$

1. **Multiply the *First* terms:** $a \times a = a^2$.
2. **Multiply the *Outer* terms:** $a \times b = ab$.
3. **Multiply the *Inner* terms:** $b \times a = ba$ **(which is the same as ab).**
4. **Multiply the *Last* terms:** $b \times b = b^2$.
5. **Combine like terms:** $ab + ab = 2ab$.

The final solution is $a^2 + 2ab + b^2$.

$$(a-b)^2 = a^2 - 2ab + b^2$$

You can prove this equation by using FOIL: $(a-b)(a-b)$

1. **Multiply the *First* terms:** $a \times a = a^2$.
2. **Multiply the *Outer* terms:** $a \times -b = -ab$.
3. **Multiply the *Inner* terms:** $-b \times a = -ba$ **(which is the same as $-b \times -b = +b^2$).**
4. **Multiply the *Last* terms:** $-b \times -b = +b^2$.
5. **Combine like terms:** $-ab + -ab = -2ab$.

The final solution is $a^2 - 2ab + b^2$.

Be careful to note that the b^2 at the end is *positive,* not negative, because multiplying a negative times a negative gives a positive.

$$(a-b)(a+b) = a^2 - b^2$$

You can prove this equation by using FOIL: $(a-b)(a+b)$

1. **Multiply the *First* terms:** $a \times a = a^2$.
2. **Multiply the *Outer* terms:** $a \times b = ab$.
3. **Multiply the *Inner* terms:** $-b \times a = -ba$ **(which is the same as $-ab$).**
4. **Multiply the *Last* terms:** $-b \times b = -b^2$.
5. **Combine like terms:** $ab + -ab = 0ab$.

The final solution is $a^2 + b^2$. Note that the middle term drops out because $+ab$ cancels out $-ab$. You add ab and subtract ab, thus canceling $-ab$.

Again, *memorize* these three equations:

$$(a+b)^2 = a^2 + 2ab + b^2$$

$$(a-b)^2 = a^2 - 2ab + b^2$$

$$(a-b)(a+b) = a^2 - b^2$$

Doing so saves you time, careless mistakes, and acute misery on the actual exam.

Fact or Fiction Factoring

Now you know how to do algebra forward; are you ready to do it backward? You need to be able to factor down a *quadratic equation* (an equation with a variable to the second power) and take an algebraic expression from its final form back to its original form of two sets of parentheses.

Given $x^2 + 13x + 42 = 0$, solve for x. Take this problem one step at a time.

1. **Draw two sets of parentheses.**

   $(\ )(\ ) = 0$

2. **You know that to get x^2 the *First* terms have to be x and x. Fill those in.**

   $(x)(x) = 0$

3. **Look now at the *Outer* terms.**

   You need two numbers that multiply together to be +42. Well, there are several possibilities: 42×1, 21×1, or 6×7. You can even have two negative numbers: -42×-1, -21×-2, or -6×-7. You aren't sure which one to choose yet. Go on to the next step.

4. **Look at the *Inner* terms.**

   You have to add two values to get +13. What's the first thing that springs to mind? $6 + 7$, probably. Hey, that's one of the possibilities in the preceding step! Plug it in and try it.

   $$(x+6)(x+7) = x^2 + 7x + 6x + 42 = x^2 + 13x + 42.$$

5. **Great, but you're not done. If the whole equation equals zero, then either $(x+6) = 0$ or $(x+7) = 0$. That's because any number times zero equals zero. Therefore, x can equal −6 or −7.**

Again, if you have a multiple-choice problem, you can simply try the answer choices. Never start doing a lot of work until you absolutely have to.

Too Hip to Be Square: Roots and Radicals

To simplify working with square roots (or cube roots or any roots), think of them as variables. You work the same way with $\sqrt{7}$ as you do with x, y, or z.

Addition and subtraction

1. **To add or subtract *like radicals* (for the purpose of this exam, think of "radicals" as "roots"), add or subtract the number in front of the radical (your old friend, the numerical coefficient).**

   $2\sqrt{7} + 5\sqrt{7} = 7\sqrt{7}$ $2x + 5x = 7x$

   $9\sqrt{13} - 4\sqrt{13} = 5\sqrt{13}$ $9x - 4x = 5x$

2. **You *cannot* add or subtract unlike radicals (just as you cannot add or subtract unlike variables).**

   $6\sqrt{5} + 4\sqrt{3} = 6\sqrt{5} + 4\sqrt{3}$. You cannot add the two and get $10\sqrt{8}$.

   $6x + 4y = 6x + 4y$. You cannot add the two and get $10xy$.

Don't glance at a problem, see that the radicals are not the same, and immediately assume that you cannot add the two terms. You may be able to simplify one radical to make it match the radical in the other term.

$$\sqrt{52} + \sqrt{13} = 2\sqrt{13} + \sqrt{13} = 3\sqrt{13}$$

1. **Begin by simplifying. Take out a perfect square from the term.**

$$\sqrt{52} = \sqrt{4} \times \sqrt{13}$$

2. **Because** $\sqrt{4} = 2$, $\sqrt{52} = 2\sqrt{13}$

Try this one: $\sqrt{20} + \sqrt{45} = \left(\sqrt{4} \times \sqrt{5}\right) + \left(\sqrt{9} \times \sqrt{5}\right) = 2\sqrt{5} + 3\sqrt{5} = 5\sqrt{5}$

You must simplify *first*. You can't say that $\sqrt{20} + \sqrt{45} = \sqrt{65} = 8.06$. If you work out the correct answer, $5\sqrt{5}$ (which you don't have to do on the GMAT), you see that it's not 8.06 but 11.18.

Multiplication and division

Just do it. When you multiply or divide radicals, you just multiply or divide the numbers and then pop the radical sign back onto the finished product.

$$\sqrt{5} \times \sqrt{6} = \sqrt{30}$$

$$\sqrt{15} \div \sqrt{5} = \sqrt{3}$$

If you have a number in front of the radical, multiply it as well. Let everyone in on the fun.

$$6\sqrt{3} \times 4\sqrt{2} =$$

$$6 \times 4 = 24$$

$$\sqrt{3} \times \sqrt{2} = \sqrt{6}$$

The answer is $24\sqrt{6}$

Here's a pretty typical problem: $37\sqrt{5} \times 3\sqrt{6}$

(A) $40\sqrt{11}$

(B) $40\sqrt{30}$

(C) $111\sqrt{11}$

(D) $111\sqrt{30}$

(E) 1,221

This problem takes straightforward multiplication: $37 \times 3 = 111$ and $\sqrt{5} \times \sqrt{6} = \sqrt{30}$, so $111\sqrt{30}$. *Correct Answer:* D.

Inside out

When there is an operation under the radical, do the operation first and then take the square root.

$$\sqrt{\frac{x^2}{40} + \frac{x^2}{9}}$$

First, solve for $x^2/_{40} + x^2/_9$. You get the common denominator of $360(40 \times 9)$ and then find the numerators: $9x^2 + 40x^2 = {}^{49x^2}/_{360}$. *Now* take the square roots: $\sqrt{49x^2} = 7x$ (because $7x \times 7x = 49x^2$). $\sqrt{360} = 18.97$. Gotcha, I bet! Did you say that $\sqrt{360} = 6$? Wrong! $\sqrt{36} = 6$, but $\sqrt{360} =$ approximately 18.97. Beware of assuming too much; you can be led down the path to temptation.

By the way, you don't really have to do square roots. The answer choices will be far enough apart for you to estimate. It's a good idea, however, to know the perfect squares of numbers from 1 to 20. If you knew that $19 \times 19 = 361$, for example, you'd know that the square root of 360 was just slightly less than 19.

Your final answer is $^{7x}/_{18.97}$. Of course, you can bet that the answer choices will include $^{7x}/_6$.

Probably Probability

Probability questions are usually word problems. They may look intimidating, with a lot of words that make you lose sight of where to begin. Two simple rules can solve nearly every probability problem tossed at you on the GMAT.

1. **Create a fraction.**

   To find a probability, use this formula:

   $$P = \frac{Number \ of \ possible \ desired \ outcomes}{Number \ of \ total \ possible \ outcomes}$$

   Make a probability into a fraction. The denominator is the easier of the two parts to begin with. The denominator is the total possible number of outcomes. For example, when you're flipping a coin, there are two possible outcomes, giving you a denominator of 2. When you're tossing a die (one of a pair of dice), there are six possible outcomes, giving you a denominator of 6. When you're pulling a card out of a deck of cards, there are 52 possible outcomes (52 cards in a deck), giving you a denominator of 52. When 25 marbles are in a jar and you're going to pull out one of them, there are 25 possibilities, giving you a denominator of 25. Very simply, the denominator is the whole shebang — everything possible.

   The numerator is the total number of the things you want. If you want to get a head when you toss a coin, there is exactly one head, giving you a numerator of 1. The chances of tossing a head, therefore, are ½, one possible head, two possible outcomes altogether. If you want to get a 5 when you toss a die, there is exactly one 5 on the die, giving you a numerator of 1. Notice that your numerator is *not* 5. The number you want happens to be a 5, but there is only *one* 5 on the die. The probability of tossing a 5 is ⅙: There is one 5 out of six possible outcomes altogether.

   If you want to draw a jack in a deck of cards, there are four jacks: hearts, diamonds, clubs, and spades. Therefore, the numerator is 4. The probability of drawing a jack out of a deck of cards is ⁴⁄₅₂ (which reduces to ¹⁄₁₃). If you want to draw a jack of hearts, the probability is ¹⁄₅₂ because there is only one jack of hearts in a 52-card deck.

A jar of marbles has 8 yellow marbles, 6 black marbles, and 12 white marbles. What is the probability of drawing out a black marble?

Use the formula. Begin with the denominator, which is all the possible outcomes: $8 + 6 + 12 = 26$. The numerator is how many there are of what you want: six black marbles. The probability is ⁶⁄₂₆, which can be reduced or (as is more customary) changed to a percentage. The correct answer is ⁶⁄₂₆, or ³⁄₁₃, or 23 percent. What's the probability of drawing out a yellow marble? ⁸⁄₂₆ or ⁴⁄₁₃. A white marble? ¹²⁄₂₆ or ⁶⁄₁₃.

Here's another problem: A drawer has 5 pairs of white socks, 8 pairs of black socks, and 12 pairs of brown socks. In a hurry to get to school, Austin pulls out a pair at a time and tosses them on to the floor if they are not the color he wants. Looking for a brown pair, Austin pulls out and discards a white pair, a black pair, a black pair, and a white pair. What is the probability that on his next reach into the drawer he will pull out a brown pair of socks?

This problem is slightly more complicated than the preceding one, although it uses the same formula. You began with 25 pairs of socks. However, Austin, that slob, has thrown four pairs on to the floor. That means that there are only 21 pairs left. The probability of his pulling out a brown pair is $^{12}/_{21}$, or $^{4}/_{7}$, or about 57 percent.

A cookie jar has chocolate, vanilla, and strawberry wafer cookies. There are 30 of each type. Bess reaches in, pulls out a chocolate and eats it, and then in quick succession pulls out and eats a vanilla, chocolate, strawberry, strawberry, chocolate, and vanilla. Assuming that she doesn't get sick or get caught, what is the probability that the next cookie she pulls out will be a chocolate one?

Originally, there were 90 cookies. Bess has scarfed down 7 of them, leaving 83. Careful! If you're about to put $^{30}/_{83}$, you're headed for a trap. There are no longer 30 chocolate cookies; there are only 27, because Bess has eaten 3. The probability is now $^{27}/_{83}$, or about 33 percent.

Probability must always be between 0 and 1. You cannot have a negative probability, and you cannot have a probability greater than 1, or 100 percent.

2. Multiply consecutive probabilities.

What is the probability that you'll get two heads when you toss a coin twice? You find each probability separately and then *multiply* the two. The chance of tossing a coin the first time and getting a head is $\frac{1}{2}$. The chance of tossing a coin the second time and getting a head is $\frac{1}{2}$. Multiply those consecutive probabilities: $\frac{1}{2} \times \frac{1}{2} = \frac{1}{4}$. The chance of getting two heads is one out of four.

What is the probability of tossing a die twice and getting a 5 on the first toss and a 6 on the second toss? Treat each toss separately. The probability of getting a 5 is $\frac{1}{6}$. The probability of getting a 6 is $\frac{1}{6}$. Multiply consecutive probabilities: $\frac{1}{6} \times \frac{1}{6} = \frac{1}{36}$.

Chapter 13

Miscellaneous Math You Probably Already Know

••

In This Chapter

▶ Time, rate, and distance problems

▶ Averages

▶ Percentages

▶ Number sets and prime and composite numbers

▶ Mixture, interest, and work problems

▶ Absolute value

▶ Order of operations

▶ Units of measurement

▶ Decimals and fractions

▶ Statistics

▶ Graphs

••

*Y*ou've survived two rather technical math review chapters; this more fundamental one should be a piece of cake. In this chapter, you review those concepts you haven't even thought of since about junior high, basics such as averages and percentages. Although this material is simple, it's important that you go through it carefully — especially because it's so often found in the students' bane, the Dreaded Word Problem.

DIRTy Math: Distance, Rate, and Time

D.I.R.T. stands for *Distance* Is *Rate × Time*. So, $D = RT$. When you have a time, rate, and distance problem, use this formula. Make a chart with the formula across the top and fill in the spaces on the chart.

Jennifer drives 40 miles an hour for two and a half hours. Her friend Ashley goes the same distance but drives at one and a half times Jennifer's speed. How many *minutes* longer does Jennifer drive than Ashley?

Do *not* start making big, hairy formulas with *x*'s and *y*'s. Jennifer has no desire to be known as Madame *x;* Ashley refuses to know *y.* Make the DIRT chart.

Distance	=	Rate	×	Time

When you fill in the 40 mph and 2½ hours for Jennifer, you can calculate that she went 100 miles. Think of it this simple way: If she goes 40 mph for one hour, that's 40 miles. For a second hour, she goes another 40 miles. In a half hour, she goes ½ of 40, or 20 miles. (See? You don't have to write down $40 \times 2\frac{1}{2}$ and do all that pencil-pushing; use your brain, not your yellow #2.) Add them together: $40 + 40 + 20 = 100$. Jennifer has gone 100 miles.

Distance	Rate	×	Time
100 (Jennifer)	40 mph		2½ hours

Because Ashley drives the same distance, fill in 100 under distance for her. She goes one and a half times as fast. Uh-uh, put down that pencil. Use your brain! 1×40 is 40; $\frac{1}{2} \times 40$ is 20. Add $40 + 20 = 60$. Ashley drives 60 mph. Now this gets really easy. If she drives at 60 mph, she drives one mile a minute. (60 minutes in an hour, 60 miles in an hour. You figure it out, Einstein.) Therefore, to go 100 miles takes her 100 minutes. Because your final answer is asked for in minutes, don't bother converting this to hours; leave it the way it is.

Distance	Rate	×	Time
100 (Ashley)	60 mph		100 minutes

Last step. Jennifer drives 2½ hours. How many minutes is that? Do it the easy way, in your brain. One hour is 60 minutes. A second hour is another 60 minutes. A half hour is 30 minutes. Add them together: $60 + 60 + 30 = 150$ minutes. If Jennifer drives for 150 minutes and Ashley drives for 100 minutes, Jennifer drives 50 minutes more than does Ashley. However, Ashley gets a speeding ticket, has her driving privileges taken away by an irate father, and doesn't get to go to this weekend's party. Jennifer goes and gets her pick of the hunks, ending up with Tyrone's ring and frat pin. The moral of the story: Slow . . . but steady!

Distance	Rate	×	Time
100 (Jennifer)	40 mph		150 minutes
100 (Ashley)	60 mph		100 minutes

Be careful to note whether the people are traveling in the *same* direction or *opposite* directions. Suppose that a question asks how far apart drivers are at the end of their trip. If you are told that Jordan travels 40 mph east for 2 hours and Connor travels 60 mph west for 3 hours, they are going in opposite directions. If they start from the same point at the same time, Jordan has gone 80 miles one way, and Connor has gone 180 miles the opposite way. They are 260 miles apart. The trap answer is 100, because careless people (not *you!*) simply subtract $180 - 80$.

It All Averages Out: Averages

You can always do averages the way Ms. Jones taught you when you were in third grade: Add all the terms, and then divide by the number of terms.

$$5 + 11 + 17 + 23 + 29 = 85$$

$$\frac{85}{5} = 17$$

Or you can save wear-and-tear on the brain cells and know the following rule:

1. The average of evenly spaced terms is the middle term.

First, check that the terms are evenly spaced. That means that there is an equal number of units between each term. In the previous example, the terms are six apart. Second, circle the middle term, which is 17. Third, go home, make popcorn, and watch the late-night movie with all the time you've saved.

Try another one. Find the average of these numbers:

32, 41, 50, 59, 68, 77, 86, 95, 104

Don't reach for your pencil. You look and see that the terms are all nine units apart. Because they are evenly spaced, the middle term is the average: 68.

This is an easy trick to love, but don't march down the aisle with it yet. The tip works only for *evenly spaced* terms. If you have just any old batch of numbers, such as 4, 21, 97, 98, and 199, you can't look at the middle term for the average. You have to find the average of those numbers the old-fashioned way.

Find the average of these numbers:

3, 10, 17, 24, 31, 38, 45, 52

First, double-check that they are evenly spaced. Here, the numbers are spaced by sevens. Next you look for the middle number . . . and there isn't one. You can, of course, find the two central terms, 24 and 31, and find the middle between them. That works, but what a pain. Not only that, but suppose that you have 38 numbers. It's very easy to make a mistake as to which terms are the central ones. If you're off just a little bit, you miss the question. Instead, use rule number two:

2. The average of evenly spaced terms is $\frac{(first+last)}{2}$.

Just add the first and the last terms, which are obvious at a glance, and divide that sum by 2. Here, $3+52=55$. $\frac{55}{2}=27.5$.

Note: Double-check using your common sense. Suppose that you made a silly mistake and got 45 for your answer. A glance at the numbers tells you that 45 is not in the middle and therefore cannot be the average.

This tip works for *all* evenly spaced terms. It doesn't matter whether there is a middle number, as in the first example, or no middle number, as in the second example. Go back to the first example.

32, 41, 50, 59, 68, 77, 86, 95, 104

Instead of finding the middle term, add the first and last terms and divide by 2, like this: $32+104=136$, and $\frac{136}{2}=68$. Either way works.

Missing term average problem

You are likely to find a problem like this:

A student takes seven exams. Her scores on the first six are 91, 89, 85, 92, 90, and 88. If her average on all *seven* exams is 90, what did she get on the seventh exam?

This is called a *missing term average problem* because you are given an average and asked to find a missing term. Duh.

1. **You can do this the basic algebraic way.**

$$\text{Average} = \frac{\text{Sum}}{\text{Number of Terms}} \cdot$$

$$90 = \frac{\text{Sum}}{7}$$

Because you don't know the seventh term, call it x. Add the first six terms (and get 535) and x.

$$90 = \frac{(535 + x)}{7}$$

Cross-multiply: $90 \times 7 = 535 + x$

$$630 = 535 + x$$

$$95 = x$$

The seventh exam score was 95.

2. **You can do these problems the common-sense way.**

There is another quick way to do this problem. You've probably done it this way all your life without realizing what a genius you are.

Suppose that your dad tells you that if you average a 90 for the semester in advanced physics, he'll let you take that summer trip through Europe with your buddies that the two of you have been arguing about for months (he figures he's safe because there's no way you're going to get such a high grade in that incredibly difficult class). You take him at his word and begin working hard.

On the first exam, you get 91 and you're +1 point. That is, you're one point above the ultimate score you want, a 90. On the second exam, you get 89 and you're −1. On that test, you're one point below the ultimate score you want, a 90. On the third exam, you get an 85, which is −5. You're five points below the ultimate score you want, a 90.

Are you getting the hang of this? Here's how it looks.

$$91 = +1$$
$$89 = -1$$
$$85 = -5$$
$$92 = +2$$
$$90 = 0$$
$$88 = -2$$

The +1 and −1 cancel each other out, and the +2 and −2 cancel each other out. You're left with −5, meaning you're five points in the hole. You have to make up those five points on the last exam; that is, you must get five points *above* what you want for your ultimate score. Because you want a 90, you need a 95 on the last test.

Try another, using the no-brainer method. A student takes seven exams. She gets an 88 average on all of them. Her first six scores are 89, 98, 90, 82, 88, and 87. What does she get on the seventh exam?

Average = 88

89 = +1

98 = +10

90 = +2

82 = −6

88 = 0

87 = −1

The +1 and −1 cancel. Then you have $(10+2) = +12$ and −6, for a total of +6. You are six points *above* what you need for the ultimate outcome. You can afford to lose six points on the final exam or to be six points *below* the average. That gives you an 82.

You may be given only five out of seven scores and asked for *the average of the missing two* terms. Do the same thing and then divide by 2.

Average of seven exams: 85

Scores of the first five exams: 86, 79, 82, 85, 84

Find: The average score of each of the remaining exams

Algebraic way: $85 = \dfrac{(86+79+82+85+84)+x+x}{7}$

Cross-multiply: $595 = 416 + 2x$

$595 - 416 = 2x$

$179 = 2x$

$89.5 = x$

Common-sense way:

Average = 85

86 = +1

79 = −6

82 = −3

85 = 0

84 = −1

The +1 and −1 cancel each other out. You are left with −9 for *two* exams or −4.5 per exam. If you are *down* four and a half points, you must *gain* those four and a half points on each of the two exams:

$85 + 4.5 = 89.5$

The shortcut, common-sense way is quick and easy, but don't forget to make the change at the end. That is, if you decide that you are *minus eight* points going into the final exam, you need to be *plus eight* points on that last exam to come out even. If you subtract eight points from the average rather than add them, you'll probably come up with one of the trap answers.

Weighted averages

In a *weighted average,* some scores count more than others.

Number of Students	Score
12	80
13	75
10	70

If you are asked to find the average score for the students in this class, you know that you can't simply add 80, 75, and 70 and divide by three because the scores weren't evenly distributed among the students. Because 12 students got an 80, multiply $12 \times 80 = 960$. Do the same with the other scores:

$$13 \times 75 = 975$$
$$10 \times 70 = 700$$
$$960 + 975 + 700 = 2,635$$

Divide *not by three* but by the total number of students: $35 \ (12+13+10)$

$$\frac{2635}{35} = 75.29$$

You can often answer a Data Sufficiency question on weighted averages without doing all the work, as demonstrated in the following example. Remember that you have the following answer choices:

(A) if statement 1 ALONE is sufficient to answer the question, but statement 2 alone is not sufficient to answer the question asked

(B) if statement 2 ALONE is sufficient to answer the question, but statement 1 alone is not sufficient to answer the question asked

(C) if BOTH statements 1 and 2 TOGETHER are sufficient to answer the question asked but NEITHER statement ALONE is sufficient

(D) if EACH statement alone is sufficient to answer the question asked

(E) if statements 1 and 2 TOGETHER are NOT sufficient to answer the question asked.

What is the average cost of clothing per piece for 5 black T-shirts and 8 denim shirts?

(1) Black T-shirts cost $20 each.

(2) Denim shirts cost $25 each.

You probably saw the answer almost immediately. You can predict that to find an average you need the total and the number of items. The question stem gives you the number of items: $5+8=13$. Statement 1 lets you find the total amount spent on the T-shirts; statement 2 lets you find the total amount spent on the denim shirts. You need both amounts to figure the total. Don't actually *do* the work. Just know that you can use both statements 1 and 2 together to solve the problem. *Correct Answer:* C.

Percentage Panic

The mere mention of the word *percent* may strike terror in your heart. There's no reason to panic over percentages; there are ways of getting around them.

1. **Ignore their very existence.** You can express a percentage as a decimal, which is a lot less intimidating. You do so by putting a decimal point two places to the left of the percentage and dropping the % sign.

$$35\% = .35 \qquad 83\% = .83 \qquad 50\% = .50 \qquad 33.3\% = .333 \qquad 66.6\% = .666$$

If you have a choice of working with percentages or decimals, it's better to choose decimals.

2. **Convert it to a fraction.** The word *percent* means *per cent,* or *per hundred.* Every percentage is that number over 100.

$$50\% = \frac{50}{100} \qquad 33\% = \frac{33}{100} \qquad 75\% = \frac{75}{100}$$

If you can't ignore the percentage, remember that a percent is

$$\frac{\text{Part}}{\text{Whole}} \times 100, \text{ or } \frac{is}{of} \times 100$$

What percent *is* 45 *of* 90? Put the part, 45, over the whole, 90. Or put the *is,* 45, over the *of,* 90:

$$\frac{45}{90} = \frac{1}{2} \times 100 = \frac{100}{2} = 50\%$$

42 *is* what percent *of* 126? Put the part, 42, over the whole, 126. Or put the *is,* 42, over the *of,* 126.

$$\frac{42}{126} = \frac{1}{3} \times 100 = \frac{100}{3} = 33\frac{1}{3}\%$$

Here's a little harder one: What is 40% of 80? You may be tempted to put the *is,* 40, over the *of,* 80, and get $\frac{40}{80} = \frac{1}{2} \times 100 = \frac{100}{2} = 50\%$. However, when the problem is worded this way, you don't know the *is.* Your equation must be $\frac{x}{80} = \frac{40}{100}$. Cross-multiply: $3200 = 100x$. $x = 32$. There's an easier way to do it: *of* means times, or multiply. Because $40\% = .40$, multiply $.40 \times 80 = 32$.

Life has its ups and downs: Percent increase/decrease

You may see a problem asking you what percent increase or decrease occurred in the number of games a team won or the amount of commission a person earned. To find a percent increase or decrease, use this formula:

$$\text{percent increase or decrease} = \frac{\text{number increase or decrease}}{\text{original whole}}$$

In basic English, to find the percent by which something has increased or decreased, you take two simple steps:

1. **Find the *number* (amount) by which the thing has increased or decreased.** For example, if a team won 25 games last year and 30 games this year, the number increase was 5. If a salesperson earned $10,000 last year and $8,000 this year, the number decrease was 2,000. Make that the numerator of the fraction.

2. Find the *original whole*. This figure is what you started out with before you increased or decreased. If a team won 25 games last year and won 30 games this year, the original number was 25. If the salesperson earned $10,000 last year and $8,000 this year, the original number was 10,000. Make that the denominator.

You now have a fraction. Make it a decimal, and multiply by 100 to make it a percentage.

In 1992, Coach Jarchow won 30 prizes at the county fair by tossing a basketball into a bushel basket. In 1993, he won 35 prizes. What was his percent increase?

(A) 100

(B) 30

(C) 16⅔

(D) 14.28

(E) .1̄6̄6̄

The number by which his prizes increased, from 30 to 35, is 5. That is the numerator. The original whole, or what he began with, is 30. That is the denominator.

$$\tfrac{5}{30} = \tfrac{1}{6} = 16\tfrac{2}{3}\%$$

If you chose E, I fooled you. The question asks what *percent* increase there was. If you say E, you're saying that there was a .1̄6̄6̄ percent increase. Not so. The .1̄6̄6̄ increase *as a percentage* is 16⅔%. If you chose D, you fell for another trap. You put the 5 increase over the 35 instead of over the 30. *Correct Answer:* C.

Two years ago, Haylie scored 22 goals at soccer. This year, she scored 16 goals. What was her approximate percentage decrease?

(A) 72

(B) 37.5

(C) 27

(D) 16

(E) .2̄7̄

Find the number of the decrease: $22 - 16 = 6$. That is the numerator. Find the original whole from which she is decreasing: 22. That is the denominator. $\tfrac{6}{22} \approx .2̄7̄$, or approximately 27 percent. *Correct Answer:* C.

If you chose A, you put 16 over 22 instead of putting the decrease over the original whole. If you chose E, again you forgot the difference between .27 and .27 *percent*. If you chose B, you put the decrease of 6 over the new amount, 16, rather than over the original whole. Note how easy these traps are to fall for. My suggestion: Write down the actual formula and then plug in the numbers. Writing down the formula may be boring, but doing so takes only a few seconds and may save you points.

Here's a tricky question that many people do in their heads (instead of writing down the formula and plugging in numbers) and then blow it big time.

Carissa has three quarters. Her father gives her three more. Carissa's wealth has increased by what percent?

(A) 50

(B) 100

(C) 200

(D) 300

(E) 500

Did you fall for the trap answer, C? Her wealth has doubled, to be sure, but the percent increase is only 100. You can prove that with the formula: The number increase is 75 (she has three more quarters, or 75 cents). Her original whole was 75. $^{75}\!/_{75} = 1 = 100\%$. _Correct Answer:_ B.

When you double something, you increase it by 100 percent because you have to subtract the original "one" you began with. When you triple something, you increase it by 200 percent because you have to subtract the original you began with. For example, if you had three dollars and you now have nine dollars, you have tripled your money but increased it by only 200 percent. Do the formula: _number increase_ = 6 dollars. _Original whole_ = 3 dollars, and $^{6}\!/_{3} = 2 = 200$ percent. Take a wild guess at what percent you increase when you quadruple your money? That's right, 300 percent. Just subtract the original 100 percent.

Ready, Sets, Go: Number Sets

There's no escaping vocabulary. Even on the math portion of the test, you need to know certain terms. How can you solve a problem that asks you to "state your answer in integral values only" if you don't know what integral values are? Here are the number sets with which you'll be working.

- ✔ **Counting numbers:** 1, 2, 3, . . . Note that 0 is _not_ a counting number.

- ✔ **Whole numbers:** 0, 1, 2, 3, . . . Note that 0 _is_ a whole number.

- ✔ **Integers:** . . . –3, –2, –1, 0, 1, 2, 3, . . . When a question asks for _integral values,_ it wants the answer in integers only. For example, you can't give an answer like 4.3 because that's not an integer. You need to round down to 4.

- ✔ **Rational numbers:** Rational numbers can be expressed as $^{a}\!/_{b}$, where _a_ and _b_ are integers.

    Examples: 1 (because $1 = ^{1}\!/_{1}$ and 1 is an integer), ½ (because 1 and 2 are integers), $^{9}\!/_{2}$ (because 9 and 2 are integers), and $-^{4}\!/_{2}$ (because –4 and 2 are integers).

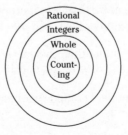

Notice that every number set so far has included the previous number sets. Whole numbers include counting numbers, integers include counting numbers and whole numbers, and rationals include counting numbers, whole numbers, and integers.

- **Irrational numbers:** The highly technical definition here is *anything not rational.* That is, an irrational number cannot be written as ⁰⁄₀, where *a* and *b* are integers. Numbers whose decimals do not terminate and do not repeat can't be written as a fraction and therefore are irrational.

   Examples: π cannot be written *exactly* as 3.14; it is nonterminating and nonrepeating. $\sqrt{2}$ is approximately 1.4142 but is nonterminating and nonrepeating.

   Irrational numbers *do not* include the previous number sets. That is, irrational numbers don't include counting numbers, whole numbers, integers, or rational numbers.

- **Real numbers:** Briefly put, all the above. Real numbers include counting numbers, whole numbers, integers, rationals, and irrationals. For all practical purposes, real numbers are everything you think of as numbers. When a question tells you to "express your answer in real numbers," don't sweat it. That's almost no constraint at all, because nearly everything you see is a real number.

There are such critters as *imaginary* numbers, which are *not* on the GMAT. (Most of you probably stopped reading right there, figuring that you don't even want to hear about them if they're not going to be tested. I don't blame you.) Imaginary numbers are expressed with a lowercase *i* and are studied in upper-division math classes. I won't go into them here because, once again, *they are not tested on the GMAT.* All numbers on the GMAT are real numbers.

Prime and Composite Numbers

Prime numbers are positive integers that have exactly two positive integer factors; they cannot be divided by numbers other than 1 and themselves. Examples include 2, 3, 5, 7, and 11.

Here are a few lovely tricks to prime numbers:

- Zero is *not* a prime number (by definition). Why? Because it is divisible by more than two factors. Zero can be divided by 1, 2, 3, and on to infinity. Although division by zero is undefined (and isn't tested on the GMAT), you can divide zero by other numbers; the answer of course is always zero. $0 \div 1 = 0$; $0 \div 2 = 0$; $0 \div 412 = 0$.

- One is *not* a prime number (by definition). There are not two factors of 1. It cannot be divided only by 1 *and* itself. Confused? Don't worry about it. Just memorize the fact that 1 is not a prime number.

- Two is the *only* even prime. People tend to think that all prime numbers are odd. Well, almost. Two is prime because it has only two factors; it can be divided only by 1 and itself.

- Not all odd numbers are prime. Think of 9 or 15; those numbers are odd but not prime because they have more than two factors and can be divided by more than just 1 and themselves. For example, $9 = (1 \times 9)$ *and* (3×3), and $15 = (1 \times 15)$ *and* (3×5).

Composite numbers have more than two factors and can be divided by more than just 1 and themselves. Examples: 4, 6, 8, 9, 12, 14, and 15.

Note that composite numbers (called that because they are *composed* of more than two factors) can be even or odd.

Don't confuse *prime* and *composite* and *even* and *odd* with *positive* and *negative.* That's an easy mistake to make in the confusion of the exam. If a problem that you know should be easy is flustering you, stop and ask yourself whether you're making this common mistake.

I said that 0 and 1 are not prime. They are also not composite. What are they? Neither. You express this as "0 and 1 are neither prime nor composite." It's rather like wondering whether zero is positive or negative. You say, "Zero is neither positive nor negative." Why should you know this? Here's an example when the information can win you ten points (the approximate value of one correct math question).

Is x a prime number?

(1) $-1 < x < 3$

(2) x is not a composite number

Statement 1 alone is not sufficient to answer the question. Because x could be prime (if it were 2) or could not be prime (if it were 1), you don't have enough information in this statement. Eliminate answer choices A and D. Statement 2 alone is not sufficient. Just because a number is not a composite number does not mean that it is a prime number. The number could be 0 or 1, which are neither prime nor composite. Because statement 2 alone isn't sufficient, eliminate choices B and E. (See answer choices for Data Sufficiency questions earlier in this chapter.)

Using both statements together still isn't sufficient (choice C). x could be 1, which is between -1 and 3 and is neither a composite nor a prime number. Or x could be 2, which is between -1 and 3, is not composite, and is prime. When you can't give a definite answer to the question, choose E. *Correct Answer:* E.

I'm All Mixed Up: Mixture Problems

A mixture problem is a word problem that looks much more confusing than it actually is. There are two types of mixtures: those in which the items remain separate (when you mix peanuts and raisins, you still have peanuts and raisins, not pearains or raispeans) and those in which the two elements blend (these are usually chemicals, like water and alcohol). Check out the separate mixture first.

Marshall wants to mix 40 pounds of beads selling for 30 cents a pound with a quantity of sequins selling for 80 cents a pound. He wants to pay 40 cents per pound for the final mix. How many pounds of sequins should he use?

The hardest part for most students is knowing where to begin. Make a chart.

	Pounds	Price	Total
Beads	40	$.30	$12.00
Sequins	x	$.80	$.80x$
Mixture	$40 + x$	$.40	$.40(40 + x)$

Reason it out. In pennies, the cost of the beads (1200) plus the cost of the sequins ($80x$) must equal the cost of the mixture ($1600 + 40x$). Note that you dump the decimal point (officially, you multiply by 100 to get rid of the decimal point, but really, you dump it). Now you have a workable equation:

$$1200 + 80x = 1600 + 40x$$

$$80x - 40x = 1600 - 1200$$

$$40x = 400$$

$$x = 10$$

Careful! Keep in mind what x stands for. It represents the number of pounds of sequins, what the question asks for.

Go back and double-check by plugging this value into the equation. You already know that Marshall spent $12 on beads. If he buys 10 pounds of sequins for 80 cents, he spends $8, for a total of $20. He spends that $20 on 50 pounds: $2000 \div 50 = 40$. How about that? It works!

Greed Is Great: Interest Problems

This is a pretty problem: PRTI, to be exact. $P = Principle$, the amount of money you begin with, or the amount you invest. $R = Rate$, the interest rate you're earning on the money. $T = Time$, the amount of time you leave the money in the interest-bearing account. $I = Interest$, the amount of interest you earn on the investment. A problem usually asks you how much interest someone earned on his or her investment.

The formula is $PRT = I$. $Principal \times Rate \times Time = Interest$.

Janet invested $1,000 at 5 percent annual interest for one year. How much interest did she earn?

This is the simplest type of problem. Plug the numbers into the formula.

$PRT = I$

$1,000 \times .05 \times 1 = 50$. She earned $50 interest.

The answer choices may try to trap you with variations on a decimal place, making the answers 5, 50, 500, and so on. You know that $5\% = \frac{5}{100} = .05$; be careful how you multiply.

These problems are not intentionally vicious (unlike 99 percent of the rest of the GMAT, right?). You won't see something that gets crazy on interest rates, like "5 percent annual interest compounded quarterly for 3 months and 6 percent quarterly interest compounded daily," blah, blah, blah.

(Useless but fascinating trivia: In Bulgarian, the word for *thank you* is pronounced *blah-go-dah-ree-uh.* But a shortened form, like *thanks,* is simply *blah.* If your mother takes you to task for being a smart aleck and going "blah, blah, blah" when she talks, you can innocently claim that you're practicing your Bulgarian and are just thanking her for her wisdom.)

All Work and No Play: Work Problems

The formula most commonly used in a work problem is

$$Work = \frac{Time\ put\ in}{Capacity\ (time\ to\ do\ the\ whole\ job)}$$

Find each person's contribution. The denominator is the easy part; it represents how many hours (minutes, days, weeks, and so on) it would take the person to do the whole job, working alone. The numerator is how long the person has already worked. For example, if Janie can paint a house in four days and has been working for one day, she has done ¼ of the work. If Evelyn can paint a house in nine days and has been working for five, she has done ⅚ of the project.

So far, so good. The problem comes when more than one person works at the task. What happens when Janie and Evelyn work together?

Janie working alone can paint a house in six days. Evelyn working alone can paint it in eight days. Working together, how long will it take them to paint the house?

Find Janie's work: $x/6$. Find Evelyn's work: $x/8$. Together, the two fractions must add up to 1, the entire job.

$$\tfrac{x}{6} + \tfrac{x}{8} = 1$$

Multiply by the common denominator, 48, to eliminate the fractions.

$$^{48}\tfrac{x}{6} + {}^{48}\tfrac{x}{8} = 48$$

$$8x + 6x = 48$$

$$14x = 48$$

$$x = \text{approximately } 3.43.$$

It would take the two women working together about 3.43 days to paint the house.

Double-check by using your common sense. If you get an answer of 10, for example, you know that you must have made a mistake because the two women working together should be able to do the job *more quickly* than either one working alone.

Reading between the Lines: Absolute Value

The absolute value is the magnitude of a number. So much for the official definition. The *...For Dummies* definition (that is, the easy way to think about it) of *absolute value* is the positive form of a number. Absolute value is indicated by two vertical parallel lines (like this: $|\;|$).

Any number within those lines is read as "The absolute value of that number." For example, $|3| = 3$ is read as "The absolute value of three equals three." That seems straightforward enough, but what if the number inside the straight lines is negative? Its absolute value is still positive: $|-3| = 3$. Here's a tricky problem you're likely to see on the exam.

$$-|-3| = -3$$

The answer may seem contrary to common sense. Isn't a negative times a negative a positive? True, but you have to work from the inside out. The absolute value of negative three is three. Then you multiple three by the negative to get negative three. Here's another example that's even a little harder.

$$-|-|5|| =$$

Here's the official way to work the problem (*Hint:* The word *official* is a clue that in a minute I'm going to give you an unofficial, much easier way to solve this.) Work from the inside out. Say it to yourself as you go along: "The absolute value of negative five is 5. Then the negative of that is negative 5. But the absolute value of negative 5 is 5. And finally, the negative of that is −5." *Correct Answer:* −5.

Do you see the super-shortcut for the preceding example? You actually don't have to work the problem out at all! Anything and everything inside the absolute value signs is going to be positive. Then the one negative sign outside changes the whole problem to negative. You don't, in other words, have to go through the intermediate steps. With an absolute value, look to see whether a negative sign is outside the first absolute value symbol. If it is, the number is negative. If it's not, the number is positive. Simple as that.

Smooth Operator: Order of Operations

When you have several operations (addition, subtraction, multiplication, division, squaring, and so on) in one problem, there is a definite order in which you must perform the operations:

1. **Parentheses.** Do what's inside the parentheses first.

2. **Power.** Do the squaring or the cubing, whatever the exponent is.

3. **Multiply or divide.** Do these left to right. If multiplication is to the left of division, multiply first. If division is to the left of multiplication, divide first.

4. **Add or subtract.** Do these left to right. If addition is to the left of subtraction, add first. If subtraction is to the left of addition, subtract first.

An easy *mnemonic* (memory) device for remembering these is *Please Praise My Daughter And Son* (PPMDAS): Parentheses, Power, Multiply, Divide, Add, Subtract.

$$10(3-5)^2 + \left(\tfrac{30}{5}\right)^0 =$$

First, do what's inside the parentheses: $3-5 = -2$, and $\tfrac{30}{5} = 6$. Next, do the power: $-2^2 = 4$, and $6^0 = 1$. (Did you remember that any number to the zero power equals one?) Next, multiply: $10 \times 4 = 40$. Finally, add: $40 + 1 = 41$. *Correct Answer:* 41. Try another.

$$3 + (9-6)^2 - 5\left(\tfrac{8}{2}\right)^{-2} =$$

First, do what's inside the parentheses: $9-6 = 3$, and $\tfrac{8}{2} = 4$. Second, do the powers: $3^2 = 9$, and $4^{-2} = \tfrac{1}{(4^2)} = \tfrac{1}{16}$. Multiply: $5 \times \tfrac{1}{16} = \tfrac{5}{16}$. Finally, add and subtract left to right. First, $3 + 9 = 12$. Then $12 - \tfrac{5}{16} = 11\tfrac{11}{16}$. *Correct Answer:* $11\tfrac{11}{16}$.

Measuring Up: Units of Measurement

Occasionally, you may be expected to know a unit of measurement that the test makers deem obvious but which you have forgotten. Take a few minutes to review this brief list.

International students, in particular, need to memorize these as you may not have grown up using some of the same units of measurement as those used in the United States (and on the GMAT).

1. **Quantities**

    16 ounces = 1 pound

    2,000 pounds = 1 ton

    2 cups = 1 pint

    2 pints = 1 quart

    4 quarts = 1 gallon

You can calculate that a gallon has 16 cups, or eight pints. To help you remember, think of borrowing a cup of sugar. Sugar is sweet, and you have a Sweet 16 birthday party: 16 sweet cups of sugar in a gallon. It may be silly, but the best memory aids usually are.

2. Length

> 12 inches = 1 foot
>
> 3 feet (36 inches) = 1 yard
>
> 5,280 feet (1,760 yards) = 1 mile

Everyone knows that there are 12 inches in a foot. How many square inches are there in a square foot? If you say 12, you've fallen for the trap. $12 \times 12 = 144$ square inches are in a square foot.

3. Time

> 60 seconds = 1 minute
>
> 60 minutes = 1 hour
>
> 24 hours = 1 day
>
> 7 days = 1 week
>
> 52 weeks = 1 year
>
> 365 days = 1 year
>
> 366 days = 1 leap year

Leap year is an interesting concept in terms of math problems. It comes around every four years. The extra day, February 29, makes 366 days in the year. Why do you need to know this? Suppose that you see this problem:

Mr. Pellaton's neon sign flashes four hours a day, every day all year, for four years. If it costs him three cents a day for electricity, how much will he owe for electricity at the end of the fourth year?

You may be tempted to say that this problem is super easy — multiply 365×4 to find the number of days and then multiply that number by .03. Wrong-o! You forgot that extra day for leap year, and your answer is off by three cents. You *know* that the test makers will have that wrong answer lurking among the answer choices just to trap you. Whenever there is a four-year period, look out for the leap year with an extra day.

Q: What does a watch repairman do on the weekend?
A: Unwind!

What's the Point: Decimals

Here's where a calculator would be very helpful. Until the test makers join the twentieth century and let you use a calculator, however, you'll have to rely on brain power, not battery power. (By the way, did you know that students taking the SAT and ACT are now allowed to use a calculator? Things are changing.)

Adding and subtracting decimals

Line up the decimal points vertically and add or subtract the numbers.

```
  3.09
  4.72
 31.9
121.046
───────
160.756
```

If you're rushed for time and don't want to do the whole problem, go to extremes. The extremes are the far-left and far-right columns. Often, calculating them alone gives you enough information to choose the right answer to a multiple-choice problem. In this case, you can look at the far right, which is the thousandths column, and know that it has to end in a 6. Suppose that the answer choices are

(A) 160.999

(B) 160.852

(C) 160.756

(D) 159.831

(E) 159.444

You know immediately that C has to be the correct choice.

Maybe more than one of the answer choices uses the correct digit for the far-right column. Okay, you're flexible; head for the far-left column, which here is the hundreds place. You know in this problem it has to be a 1. The answer choices are

(A) 160.756

(B) 201.706

(C) 209.045

(D) 210.006

(E) 301.786

Only choice A has the correct far-left number.

Multiplying decimals

The biggest trap is keeping the number of decimal points correct. The number of decimal places in the product (the number you get when you multiply the terms together) must be the same as the sum of the number of decimal places in all the terms.

$5.06 \times 3.9 =$

$$
\begin{array}{r}
5.06 \\
\times\, 3.9 \\
\hline
19.734
\end{array}
$$

There are two decimal places in the first term and one in the second, for a total of three. Therefore, the final answer must have three decimal places.

The shortcut you learned for addition and subtraction works here as well. Go to extremes. Look at the far-right and far-left terms. You know that $6 \times 9 = 54$, such that the last digit in the answer has to be a 4. You can eliminate wrong answers by using that information. You know that $5 \times 3 = 15$, but you may have to carry over some other numbers to make the far-left value greater than 15 (as it turns out here). At least you know that the far-left digits must be 15 *or more*. An answer choice starting with 14, 13, or anything less than 15 can be eliminated.

Dividing decimals

Turn the decimals into integers by moving the decimal point to the right the appropriate number of places for both terms, the one you are dividing and the one you are dividing by (called the *divisor*, should you happen to care).

$$4.44 \div .06 = \frac{444}{6} = 74$$

I won't spend much time on decimals because you almost certainly won't spend much time on them yourself. Just remember two things:

- Keep a wary eye on the decimal point; its placement is often a trap for the careless.
- Go to extremes: Determine the far-left or far-right digit and use that information to eliminate incorrect answer choices.

Broken Hearts, Broken Numbers: Fractions

Fractions strike fear into the hearts of most mere mortals. Fortunately, the GMAT doesn't have many fraction problems and seems to be having fewer all the time.

Adding or subtracting fractions

1. You can add or subtract fractions only when they have the same denominator.

$$\frac{1}{3} + \frac{4}{3} = \frac{5}{3}$$

$$\frac{3}{8} - \frac{2}{8} = \frac{1}{8}$$

2. When fractions have the same denominator, add or subtract the numerators only.

3. When fractions don't have the same denominator, you have to find a common denominator.

   You can, of course, multiply all the denominators, but that often doesn't give you the *lowest* common denominator. You end up with some humongous, overwhelming number that you'd rather not work with. Instead, use this little trick:

4. To find the lowest common denominator, identify the highest denominator and count by it.

   Find the lowest common denominator of 15 and 6. Sure, you can multiply $15 \times 6 = 90$, but that's not the *lowest* common denominator. Instead, count by 15's because it's the larger of the two numbers. 15? No, 6 doesn't go into that. 30? Yes, both 15 and 6 go into 30. That's the *lowest* common denominator.

   Try another one: Find the lowest common denominator for 2, 4, and 5. Count by 5's: 5? No, 2 and 4 don't go into it. 10? No, 4 doesn't go into it. 15? No, 2 and 4 don't go into it. 20? Yes, all the numbers divide evenly into 20. That number is much smaller than the one you get when you multiply $2 \times 4 \times 5 = 40$.

5. **In many problems, you don't even have to find the lowest common denominator. You can find any common denominator by multiplying the denominators.**

$$\frac{4}{15} + \frac{1}{6} =$$

The common denominator is $15 \times 6 = 90$. Cross-multiply: $4 \times 6 = 24$. The first fraction becomes $^{24}\!/_{90}$. Cross-multiply: $1 \times 15 = 15$. The second fraction becomes $^{15}\!/_{90}$. Now add the numerators: $24 + 15 = 39$. Put the sum over the common denominator: $^{39}\!/_{90}$. Can you reduce? Yes, by 3: $^{13}\!/_{30}$.

Do the same thing when working with variables instead of numbers.

$$\frac{a}{b} - \frac{c}{d}$$

Find the common denominator by multiplying the two denominators: $b \times d = bd$. Cross-multiply: $a \times d = ad$. Cross-multiply: $c \times b = cb$. Put the difference of the results of the cross-multiplication over the common denominator:

$$\frac{(ad - cb)}{bd}$$

Multiplying fractions

This is the easy one. Just do it. Multiply horizontally, multiplying the numerators and then multiplying the denominators.

$$\frac{3}{4} \times \frac{2}{5} = \frac{(3 \times 2)}{(4 \times 5)} = \frac{6}{20} = \frac{3}{10}$$

Always check whether you can cancel before you begin working to avoid having to deal with big, awkward numbers and to avoid having to reduce at the end. In the preceding example, you can cancel the 4 and the 2, leaving you with

$$\frac{3}{{}_2 4} \times \frac{2^1}{5} = \frac{(3 \times 1)}{(2 \times 5)} = \frac{3}{10}$$

You get to the right solution either way; canceling in advance just makes the numbers smaller and easier to work with.

Dividing fractions

To divide by a fraction, invert it (turn it upside down) and multiply.

$$\frac{1}{3} \div \frac{2}{5} = \frac{1}{3} \times \frac{5}{2} = \frac{5}{6}$$

Mixed numbers

A *mixed number* is a whole number with a fraction tagging along behind it, like $2\frac{1}{3}$, $4\frac{2}{5}$, or $9\frac{1}{2}$. Multiply the whole number by the denominator and add that to the numerator. Put the sum over the denominator.

$$2\frac{1}{3} = (2 \times 3) + 1 = 7 \rightarrow \frac{7}{3}$$

$$4\frac{2}{5} = (4 \times 5) + 2 = 22 \rightarrow \frac{22}{5}$$

$$9\frac{1}{2} = (9 \times 2) + 1 = 19 \rightarrow \frac{19}{2}$$

The Stats Don't Lie: Statistics

Don't panic; statistics are tested on the GMAT only in the most rudimentary way. If you can master three basic concepts, you can do any statistics on this exam. Those concepts are median, mode, and range.

Median

Simply put, the *median* is the middle number when all the terms are arranged in order. Think of the median strip, which is the middle of the road. Median = middle. Be sure that you arrange the numbers in order (increasing or decreasing, it makes no difference) before you find the median.

Find the median of –3, 18, –4, ½, 11.

  (A) –3

  (B) 18

  (C) –4

  (D) ½

  (E) 11

Put the numbers in order: –4, –3, ½, 11, 18. The one in the middle, ½, is the median. It's as simple as that. *Correct Answer:* D.

Mode

The *mode* is the most frequent number. I suggest that you put the numbers in order again. Then look for the one that shows up the most often. It's the mode.

Find the mode of 11, 18, 29, 17, 18, –4, 0, 19, 0, 11, 18.

  (A) 11

  (B) 17

  (C) 18

  (D) 19

  (E) 29

There are three 18s but no more than two of any other number. *Correct Answer:* C.

Range

The *range* is the distance from the greatest to the smallest. In other words, you take the biggest term and subtract the smallest term and that's the range.

Find the range of the numbers 11, 18, 29, 17, 18, −4, 0, 19, 0, 11, 18.

(A) 33

(B) 29

(C) 19

(D) 0

(E) −4

Ah, did this one getcha? True, 33 is not one of the numbers in the set. But to find the range, subtract the smallest from the largest number: $29 - -4 = 29 + 4 = 33$. *Correct Answer:* A.

The only trap you are likely to see in the statistics questions is in the answer choices. The questions themselves are quite straightforward, but the answer choices may assume that some people don't know one term from another. For example, one answer choice to a median question may be the mean (the average). One answer choice to a range question may be the mode. Circle the word in the question that tells you what you are looking for to keep from falling for this trap.

A Picture Is Worth a Thousand Words: Graphs

A math section of the GMAT may feature simple graphs. Four basic types of graphs show up frequently:

- **Circle or pie graph:** The circle represents 100 percent. The key to this graph is noting what total the percentages are part of. Below the graph you may be told that in 1994, 5,000 students graduated with Ph.D.s. If a 25-percent segment on the circle graph is labeled "Ph.D.s in history," you know to say that the number of history Ph.D.s is 25 percent of 5,000, or 1,250.

- **Two-axes line graph:** A typical line graph has a bottom and a side axis. You plot a point or read a point from the two axes. This is probably the simplest type of graph you will encounter.

- **Three-axes line graph:** This type of graph is rare. It has a left-side axis, a bottom axis, and a right-side axis. The left axis, for example, may represent the number of crates of a product while the right-side axis represents the percentage that those crates are of the whole shipment. You read the points on the graph the same way as you read them on a two-axes graph, simply paying special attention that you answer what the question is asking you. If the question asks you for the number of crates, read the left side. If the question asks you for the percentage of crates, read the right side.

- **Bar graph:** A bar graph has vertical or horizontal bars. The bars may represent actual numbers or percentages. If the bar goes all the way from one side of the graph to the other, it represents 100 percent.

Part VI
Your Number's Up: Math Questions

The 5th Wave   By Rich Tennant

"WHAT EXACTLY ARE YOU TRYING TO SAY?"

In this part . . .

There are two types of people in the world: Those who never met an equation they didn't like . . . and those who wish they had never met an equation at all. The following math lectures and practice questions can be a lot of fun for both types.

In these chapters, you learn all sorts of good tricks. Please note: The GMAT math has no relation to the Real World. Just review it, ace the math sections, and be done with it.

The CAT has one long math section (as opposed to the two or three shorter sections found in standardized paper-and-pencil tests). The CAT has two types of questions, Data Sufficiency and Problem Solving, interspersed. That is, you may see one DS question, then two PS problems, then another DS question, and so on. For learning purposes, however, this book presents separate lectures and practice exams for each of the two types of math.

Calculators are not allowed on the actual GMAT, so they are not allowed in these lectures. If your willpower is nonexistent, fight the temptation to grab your calculator by asking a friend to hide it for the next few hours.

Chapter 14

Sufficient unto the Problem Are the Data Therein

. . . .

In This Chapter

▶ Finding the elusive Data Sufficiency answer choices

▶ Dividing and conquering

▶ Recognizing and running from built-in traps

▶ Working smarter, not harder

. . . .

A riddle: What do quicksand and Data Sufficiency questions have in common?

Answer: They can both suck you in and pull you down before you realize what's happening.

The Data Sufficiency (DS) questions are notorious for featuring traps. This style of question rarely requires power math; it requires paranoia.

Where Did All the Answers Go? The DS Format

A Data Sufficiency question has three parts. The actual question is called the question *stem*. It may look like this:

Is $a > 1$?

That's all you get. Sometimes the question is literally a question, such as the preceding example. Sometimes the "question" is actually a statement, telling you to do something, like this:

Mrs. Drake drives 60 mph for 3 hours. Solve for how far Mr. Drake drives.

Or like this:

Find the rate at which the water flows into a swimming pool.

While the question form is far more common, don't be surprised if you get a statement form. I've included both in the practice exams at the end of the book to make sure that you're comfortable with both formats.

The second part of the DS question is statement number 1. It may look like this

(1) $b < 1$

or

(1) Mr. Drake drives twice as far as his wife but at half her rate.

or

(1) The swimming pool has a capacity of 12,000 gallons.

The third part of the question is statement 2. It may look like this:

(2) $a + b > 1$

or

(2) Mr. Drake starts 200 miles north of the point at which Mrs. Drake started.

or

(2) The pool is half full by noon.

You need to decide whether the data (the information) are sufficient to answer the questions (hence the title, Data Sufficiency. I bet some rocket scientist got big bucks for thinking this one up!). No answer choices are given at the end of the DS questions. You are to read statements 1 and 2 and choose

(A) if statement 1 ALONE is sufficient to answer the question, but statement 2 alone is not sufficient to answer the question asked

(B) if statement 2 ALONE is sufficient to answer the question, but statement 1 alone is not sufficient to answer the question asked

(C) if BOTH statements 1 and 2 TOGETHER are sufficient to answer the question asked, but NEITHER statement ALONE is sufficient

(D) if EACH statement alone is sufficient to answer the question asked

(E) if neither statement 1 ALONE, nor 2 ALONE, nor statements 1 and 2 TOGETHER are sufficient to answer the question asked

Got all that? Here's an easier way to think of it. You choose A if A alone is good enough. Choose B if B alone is good enough. Choose C if you *have* to have both statements. Choose D if either statement is good enough. Choose E if nothing is good enough. A quick way to say this is "AB TEN": A, B, Together, Either, Neither.

Good news! The CAT has directions for the Data Sufficiency questions on the screen with each problem. That is, you see one problem per screen, with the directions right there on the screen. You should, of course, have these directions down cold by the time you get to the exam, but isn't it reassuring to know that they'll be staring you right in the face in case your brain takes a break?

As Easy as π: Approaching DS Questions

The hardest part of a DS question is knowing where to begin. You can save considerable time and frustration if you develop good habits now that carry over to the exam later. Follow this simple approach.

1. **Read the question stem and determine exactly what you need to know.** Sounds simple, right? You'd be amazed at how many careless mistakes are made right here. Students think a question is asking for an area when in fact it is asking for a perimeter. They worry about finding a common denominator to add $^{13}\!/_{41} + {}^{98}\!/_{111}$ when they only need to know whether the sum of the two terms is greater than one. Develop the habit of mentally circling the actual question. This habit is especially important when the question stem gives a lot of information. Here's an example:

   At a fund-raiser, *x* guests each paid either *y* dollars for admission alone or *z* dollars for admission and dinner. What percent of the money paid by the *x* guests was money from the guests who had paid *z* dollars for both admission and dinner?

   What a lot of words! I'd mentally circle the word *percent,* to remind myself I'm looking for a percent that something is of something else.

2. **If possible, predict what information you're going to need to solve the problem or answer the question.**

   For example, if you are given this question:

   What is the area of the triangle *ABC?*

   You can predict that you need to know the height and the base of the triangle because the area of a triangle is one-half the base times the height.

   Notice how I said "if possible," try to predict. You can't always predict what you're going to need. Don't waste a lot of time trying to predict. As you go through the problems in this chapter and in the practice exams, you'll get a sense for which types of questions you can predict (usually geometry) and which type you can't. Spend a few seconds thinking about the problem, but don't obsess over it.

3. **Read statement 1 alone and see whether you can answer the question.** The word *alone* is integral. The worst, absolute worst, thing you can do is skim through the whole problem reading both statements 1 and 2. You want to focus on just statement 1 as if there were nothing else on the computer screen. If you can answer the question based on information given in only statement 1, make a note on your scratch paper. If you can't, cross it out.

   BEFORE you begin working on the CAT, I suggest that you use your scratch paper to write down a bunch of 1's and 2's to represent your Data Sufficiency choices. Then you can circle or cross out the numbers as necessary to help you narrow down your answer choices. If you think statement 1 alone is sufficient, circle it. If statement 1 alone is not sufficient, cross it out. Following are some examples:

   $a > 1$ (because statement 1 is sufficient)

   2

   ~~1~~

   2

4. **Read statement 2 alone and see whether you can answer the question.** The key word once again is *alone*. Forget that you ever saw statement 1. Put it out of your mind completely. Reread the question to refresh your memory of it. Cover up statement 1 with your hand and just read statement 2. If you can answer the question based on statement 2, circle it on your scratch paper. If you can't, cross it out.

5. **If you have not been able to answer the question based on either statement 1 alone or statement 2 alone, decide whether you could answer the question using both statements together.** This is pretty tricky stuff, and I talk more about it later.

Gotchas and Groaners: Tips, Traps, and Tricks

Data Sufficiency questions have so many tricks and traps that I give you a separate section for each one, with a few examples to show how easily you can fall for the traps.

Don't tell me what I already know: Repetitive info

A statement that only repeats information given in the question stem is not sufficient to answer the question. Sometimes you are given information in a statement that you already know from the question stem.

$x = 3y$

Is y positive?

(1) $y = \frac{1}{3}x$

Because $x = 3y$, you already know that $y = \frac{1}{3}x$. Statement 1 puts a different slant on it to try to trick you, but it's the same tired old stuff you have in the question stem. When a statement gives you nothing new, it can be crossed off. It alone is not sufficient to answer the question.

When a jug is half full, it contains 2 gallons. What is the weight of the jug when full?

(1) The capacity of the jug is 4 gallons.

Well, duh! If the half-full jug is 2 gallons, naturally the full jug is 4 gallons. No new information was given.

TRAPS & TRICKS

Did you notice the trap built into this question? The question stem asked for the *weight* of the jug, not the *capacity*. If you thought you had to find the capacity, you probably thought statement 1 did the job. Always, always, always keep in mind what you are being asked.

The Greeks discovered that years ago: Math rules

A statement that merely states a math formula is not sufficient to answer the question. Sometimes a statement gives you a math rule, something that is just a truism.

Angles x and y are alternate interior angles. What is the measure of angle x?

(1) $x + y = 180$

You already know that $x + y = 180$ because of the basic geometry rule that the sum of alternate interior angles is 180. When a statement repeats a math formula, it doesn't give you any new information and thus isn't sufficient to answer the question or to solve the problem.

What is the area of trapezoid *ABCD*?

(1) The area of a trapezoid is $\frac{1}{2}(base\ 1 + base\ 2) \times height$.

Again, statement 1 just gives a math formula. While you *personally* may be delighted with the information because you *personally* don't have a clue what the formula for the area of a trapezoid is, statement 1 alone doesn't give you anything you can use to answer the question.

Separate but equal: Independent statements

Treat each statement separately; do not transfer information from one statement to the other. A problem may give you something useful in statement 1 . . . and then give you a variation of that same information in statement 2. Many people choose A, thinking that statement 1 alone is sufficient. They dump poor statement 2, thinking they don't need it because they already have the info. True, you don't *need* statement 2. However, keep in mind that one of the answer choices, choice D to be exact, states that *either* statement 1 or statement 2 alone is sufficient. Don't rush off just because you've already answered the question. If statement 2 works as well, choose D.

What is the area of square *ABCD*?

(1) The side of the square is 10.

(2) The perimeter of the square is 40.

You know that the area of a square is found by multiplying side times side. Because statement 1 gives you the length of the side, you circle the 1. However, don't immediately choose A, thinking that your job is finished. You must continue reading statement 2. If the perimeter of a square is 40, each side is 10. Again, you have enough information. Circle the 2. Because either statement alone is sufficient, the final answer to the question is D. *Correct Answer:* D.

Thanks, but I can do it myself

Choice C means that both statements must be used. My favorite trap of the many that are built into the DS questions is this one: Don't choose C just because one statement is helpful. To choose C, you must absolutely, positively *need* both statements. Choice C must be something that you can't live without.

What is the perimeter of a rectangle of area 50?

(1) The ratio of the length to the height is 2:1.

(2) The sum of the interior angles of the rectangle is 360.

If you chose C, you fell for the trap. The correct answer is A, because statement 1 alone is sufficient to answer the question. To find a perimeter, you add the lengths of the sides. You already have one solid piece of information from the question stem: that the area is 50. The area of a rectangle is *length* × *width*. If the ratio of the length to the height is 2 to 1, you can experiment with numbers: Could the sides be 2 and 1? No, because then the figure would have an area of 2. Jump up to bigger numbers: How about 6 and 12? No, too big; the area would be 72. Try 10 and 5: The area is now $10 \times 5 = 50$. The perimeter is $10 + 5 + 10 + 5 = 30$, if you care to know. (You don't have to come up with the actual number, just determine whether the data are sufficient to do so. More about that concept in another tip.) Circle statement 1 and go on to statement 2. You should *always* read both statements.

Statement 2 gives you the sum of the interior angles. First, decide whether that alone is sufficient information to answer the question. It is not. How about using both statements together? Statement 2 is nice to know, but it certainly isn't necessary to know. (Besides, you already know that the interior angles of any rectangle total 360°.) Don't fall for the trap of choosing C just because both statements are true. You choose C only when one statement alone is not sufficient and it takes the combined efforts of both statements to get you where you want to go. *Correct Answer:* A.

Lite math: Reduced calories, no workout needed

As soon as you know that the data are sufficient to answer the question, stop. Don't work out these Data Sufficiency problems through to the bitter end. No one cares what the final answer is, least of all you. The name of the game here is not problem solving, in which you — logically enough — actually solve the problem. The section is called Data Sufficiency. You need only a simple yes or no: Are the data sufficient?

What is the volume of a right circular cylinder?

> (1) The area of the base of the figure is 87.

> (2) The height of the figure is 14.

For heaven's sake, don't actually work out the volume. The volume of a cylinder is the *area of the base × the height*. You know the area of the base from statement 1 and the height from statement 2. You don't want to multiply 87 times 14, do you? You know that statement 1 alone is not sufficient, and statement 2 alone is not sufficient. But both statements together give you everything. *Correct Answer:* C.

How old is Larry?

> (1) In sixteen more years, Larry will be twice as old as he is today.

> (2) Four years ago, Larry was ¾ as old as he is today.

Once again, you could go ahead and solve for Larry's age, but you don't have to and shouldn't take the time to do so. Statement 1 alone is sufficient. Okay, for ye of little faith: Set up the equation $x + 16 = 2x$, where x stands for Larry's current age. Move the x to the right, making it $-x$. Then you find that $x = 16$. While it doesn't take long to set up the equation and prove the answer, why do so if you don't have to? Every second counts, and besides, what if you set up the wrong equation, get a weird answer, and get frustrated? You waste even more time "trying to get it right."

The same is true for statement 2. You can set up the equation $x - 4 = \frac{3}{4}x$. Move the $\frac{3}{4}x$ to the left and the -4 to the right, remembering to change the signs. Then you find that $x - \frac{3}{4}x = 4$; $\frac{1}{4}x = 4$; and finally, $x = 16$. As soon as you know you could solve the problem, you're done. The correct answer to this example is D because either statement 1 alone or statement 2 alone is sufficient. *Correct Answer:* D.

Learn to take no for an answer

If you can answer the question stem "no," you have sufficient data to answer the problem. All you need to know about a problem is whether the data are sufficient to answer the question or solve the problem. If the answer to the question is yes *or* if the answer is no, you have enough data.

Is *x* even?

> (1) $x + y$ is odd
>
> (2) *y* is even

Statement 1 alone is not sufficient to answer the question. Knowing that $x + y$ is odd won't tell you whether *x* is even. If *y* is even, then *x* is odd, because an even plus an odd equals an odd. If *x* is even, then *y* is odd, because an even plus an odd equals an even. Put the two statements together. If *y* is even and $x + y$, then *x* must be odd. The answer to the question is no, but there *is* an answer to the problem. Let me repeat that because this is important and often gets overlooked. The answer to the question "Is *x* even?" is "No, *x* is not even." Because you can give an answer, even though that answer is negative, you do have enough data to answer the problem. *Correct Answer:* C.

Is Bruce older than Robin?

> (1) The ratio of Robin's age to Bruce's age is 5:3.
>
> (2) In six years, Robin will be half again as old as he is now.

Statement 1 alone is sufficient to answer the question. If the ratio of the two ages is 5:3, then Robin, the 5 part, is older than Bruce, the 3 part. It makes no difference that the answer to the question is no; you are able to solve the problem. A "no" is as good as a "yes." Statement 2 alone is not sufficient. You can use it to find out how old Robin is now (if you want to plod through the algebra, which I certainly don't intend to do), but you have no information about his age relative to Bruce's age. *Correct Answer:* A.

Did you choose C? If so, you thought you actually had to find the exact ages of the dynamic duo. True, you would need the info in statement 2 to get the age of Robin, and then the info in statement 1 to find the age of Bruce. But you don't have to find the exact ages. You are not asked for the ages, only whether Bruce is older than Robin. Answer the question, and don't put anything more into it.

They're dropping like flies: Eliminating as you go

Based on statement 1, your answer choices can be narrowed down to A or D, or to B, C, or E. Begin by evaluating statement 1. If the data in statement 1 are sufficient to answer the question, the answer is going to be either A (statement 1 alone is sufficient, but statement 2 alone is not) or D (either statement 1 alone or statement 2 alone is sufficient). A 50–50 guess is a great guess, especially if you're confused by the rest of the question or in too much of a rush to finish the rest of the work.

If the data in statement 1 are not sufficient to answer the question, the answers are narrowed down to B, C, or E. Your next step is to cover up statement 1 and look only at statement 2. If that alone is sufficient to answer the question, choose B. If not, your answers are narrowed down still further to C (you can answer the question using both pieces of information) or E (nothing helps; you can't solve the problem even when you throw everything you've got at it).

C you later

Don't forget to try both statements 1 and 2 together. Students in a big rush (most of us, in other words) often eliminate choice A because statement 1 doesn't work. Then they eliminate choice B because statement 2 doesn't work. They immediately head to choice E, thinking that there is no way to answer the question. They forget that there's one more possibility: Maybe combining the two pieces of information will do the job.

Is $a > b$?

    (1) $a^2 = b^2$

    (2) $a, b > 0$

Look at statement 1 alone. You may be tempted to say that if the squares of two numbers are identical, why of course those two numbers are identical. Wrong. One of those numbers could be positive while the other could be negative. Say that $a = 2$ and $b = -2$. Then $a^2 = b^2$, but a is *not* equal to b (and you don't know whether $a > b$ because a could be negative and b positive, or b could be negative and a positive). Statement 1 alone is not sufficient to answer the question. Eliminate choices A and D.

Look at statement 2 alone. Certainly knowing that a and b are greater than zero doesn't tell you which is greater, a or b. Eliminate choice B.

Here's where many students make the mistake of choosing E, saying there's not enough information to answer the question. Wrong! Combine the two statements. If both a and b are greater than zero, then they must be the same number for their squares to be equal. In other words, they would no longer be 2 and -2; they would be 2 and 2 (or any other number; I just plugged in 2 arbitrarily). Both statements together are necessary to answer the question. *Correct Answer:* C.

Are you arguing with me right about now that the answer must be E because the answer to the question "Is $a > b$?" is "No, a is not greater than b"? Keep in mind that the answer to the question can be yes or no, as long as an answer is possible.

Is x a prime number?

    (1) $x > 10$

    (2) x divided by 2 has a remainder of 0

Statement 1 alone is not sufficient. Some numbers greater than 10 are prime, such as 11. Some numbers greater than 10 are composite, such as 12. Eliminate choices A and D.

Statement 2 alone is not sufficient. When a number divided by 2 has no remainder, that number is even. You may be thinking that there are no even prime numbers and that statement 2 alone is sufficient. Sorry; I trapped you. There is one even prime number: 2. Therefore, statement 2 alone is not sufficient because the answer could be yes or no. Eliminate choice B.

Here is where most students get lazy and choose E. Put the two statements together. You know from statement 2 that the number must be even. You know from statement 1 that the number must be greater than 10. Because the only even prime is 2, any even number greater than 2 must be composite, not prime. The answer to the question is no, x is not prime. Because you can answer the question based on both statements, the answer is C. *Correct Answer:* C.

Familiarity Breeds Content (ment): A Review

Before going on to the sample questions in the following chapter, review the approach and the tricks described here.

Approach

1. **Read the question stem and determine exactly what the question wants to know.**

2. **If possible, predict what information you're going to need to solve the problem or answer the question.**

3. **Read statement 1 alone and see whether you can answer the question.**

4. **Read statement 2 alone and see whether you can answer the question.**

5. **If you have not been able to answer the question based on either statement 1 alone or statement 2 alone, decide whether you could answer the question using both statements together.**

Tricks

✔ A statement that only repeats information given in the question stem is not sufficient to answer the question.

✔ A statement that merely states a math formula is not sufficient to answer the question.

✔ Treat each statement separately; do not transfer information from one statement to the other.

✔ A choice C means that both statements *must* be used.

✔ As soon as you know that the data are sufficient to answer the question, stop.

✔ A "no" answer provides sufficient data.

✔ Based on statement 1, your answer choices can be narrowed down to A or D, or to B, C, or E.

Chapter 15

The Dirty Dozen: Data Sufficiency Practice Questions

Data "Sufficiency" *must* be a misnomer, because who could *ever* get enough of these wonderful, wonderful questions, right? (Yeah, right!) Here's a practice exam (12 questions) to let you fall for all the traps now and get them out of your system before the real test. Enjoy!

Directions: Following each question are two numbered statements. Determine whether the information given in the statements is sufficient to answer the question. Choose

- (A) if statement (1) ALONE is sufficient to answer the question, but statement (2) alone is not sufficient to answer the question asked
- (B) if statement (2) ALONE is sufficient to answer the question, but statement (1) alone is not sufficient to answer the question asked
- (C) if BOTH statements (1) and (2) TOGETHER are sufficient to answer the question asked, but NEITHER statement ALONE is sufficient
- (D) if EACH statement alone is sufficient to answer the question asked
- (E) if either statement alone is sufficient to answer the question asked

Information:

1. Unless the problem specifically states otherwise, all figures lie in a plane.
2. Angles measure more than zero.
3. Lines that appear to be straight are straight.
4. A figure will follow information given in the question stem but will not necessarily follow additional information given in statement 1 or statement 2.
5. Angles and points are in the order shown.
6. All numbers used in this section are real numbers.
7. If more than one value for a quantity is possible, the data given in the statements may not be sufficient to determine the value of a quantity.

Example:

$3x + y = 25$. What is the value of x? (x, $y > 0$)

- (1) $25 - y = 15$
- (2) $2y^2 = 200$

Statement 1 alone is sufficient to answer the question. If $25 - y + 15$, $y = 10$. Plug 10 back into the original equation and solve for x. First, $3x + 10 = 25$. Then $3x = 15$. Finally, $x = 5$.

Statement 2 alone is sufficient to answer the question. If $2y^2 = 200$, $y^2 = 100$. $y = 10$. Plug 10 back into the original equation and solve for x. First, $3x + 10 = 25$. Then $3x = 15$. Finally, $x = 5$.

Because either statement 1 alone or statement 2 alone is sufficient to answer the question, the answer is D. *Correct Answer:* D.

1. What is the value of x? $(x \neq 0)$

    (1) $x^2 + 0 = x^2$

    (2) $x^3 - x^2 = x^2$

Statement 1 simply restates the truism that zero added to any number is the same as that number $(1^2 + 0 = 1^2; 2^2 + 0 = 2^2)$. In this case, you are no closer to finding x than you were before. Because statement 1 alone is not sufficient to answer the question, eliminate choices A and D. For statement 2, plug in numbers to try to make the statement true. Start with 1: $1^3 - 1^2 = 1$? No, that's not a true statement; therefore, x cannot be 1. Try 2: $2^3(8) - 2^2(4) = 4$? Yes, that's true; x could be 2. Could it be anything else? Try plugging in a few more times. Let $x = 3$: $3^3(27) - 3^2(9)$ does *not* equal 9. Make a jump to a big number: $100^3(1,000,000) - 100^2(10,000)$ does *not* equal 10,000. Because statement 2 alone is sufficient to give you the answer, choose B. *Correct Answer:* B.

How can you be absolutely, positively, bet-your-retirement-fund sure that statement 2 alone is sufficient? After all, you've plugged in only three or four numbers out of an infinite quantity. You can't be totally sure, but you have to make a choice: Do you sit here and plug in numbers, having a jolly old time like a child stringing beads all afternoon, or do you go on and hope things work out for the best? Don't waste too much time. As a rule of thumb, plugging in three times is good enough. I plugged in 100 here just in case a big number made a difference, but doing so wasn't really necessary.

2. What is the volume of a right cylinder?

    (1) The radius of the cylinder is 5 units.

    (2) The height of the cylinder is equal to two radii of the cylinder.

PREDICT! You know (or should know, if you were awake during the math review — and how could anyone sleep through those thrilling formulas?) that the formula for the volume of a cylinder is $\pi r^2 h$ (the volume of such a solid is the area of the base times the height). Predict, therefore, that you need to know the radius of the base (because the base of a cylinder is a circle, and the area of a circle is πr^2) and the height of the figure. Statement 1 gives you the radius. That lets you find the area of the base, but that alone isn't enough to find the volume of the figure. Knowing that statement 1 alone isn't enough allows you to give the heave-ho to choices A and D. Statement 2 alone is useless; it gives no numbers whatsoever. Throw choice B on the same trash heap as choices A and D. Finally, play matchmaker and join statement 2 to statement 1. Because the height of the cylinder is equal to 2 radii of the cylinder and because the radius is 5, the height of the cylinder is 10. You now know the height and the radius, which are all you need to find the volume of the cylinder. Both statements together were necessary. *Correct Answer:* C.

Don't actually work out the problem; why waste time doing so? The name of the game is not Problem Solving; you don't care how much the actual volume comes out to be. The name of the game is Data Sufficiency: Are the data sufficient to solve the problem, should you decide to do so (even if it's summer and the TV has nothing but reruns that were boring even the first time around)?

3. Is Chico going to the movies?

    (1) If Jeannie isn't going to the movies, Chico isn't going to the movies.

    (2) Jeannie is going to the movies.

For statement 1, make a little note: If no J, no C. Well, because you don't know whether J is or is not going, you don't know whether C is or is not going. Statement 1 alone is not sufficient to answer the question; eliminate choices A and D. Now jot down a note for statement 2. You know J is going to the movies. Maybe your note would read "J = movies." All by itself, that's not enough to know whether C will also be dishing out $7 or not. The hard part here is knowing that even the two statements together won't give you enough info. Just because J is going doesn't necessarily mean C is going. We know only the negative side: If J doesn't go, C doesn't go. But if J goes, maybe C decides not to go to the movie anyway (J picks a three-hanky film, while C's silver screen tastes run more towards the Stooges flicks). The two statements together don't give enough information. *Correct Answer:* E.

This is a great type of question to guess at quickly and go on. It doesn't test nice, neat, straightforward math; it tests nasty and *nefarious* (wicked, evil) logic. It's bad enough that you're expected to be able to spew out esoteric math formulas on demand; how dare the test makers expect you to *think* during a test as well! Seriously, keep track as you go through practice questions of the ones that test logic, as opposed to making you work through an equation or plug in a formula. If you know that you stink at logic, don't waste time on a problem you'd probably miss anyway. Make a quick guess and go on to greener pastures. Remember that the computer doesn't let you continue until you've chosen an answer.

The wording of this question is exceedingly confusing. If the English in this question bothers you, don't waste time trying to figure it out. Students from Albania to Zimbabwe (and all points in between) should just make a quick, random guess at this question and go *on*.

4. What is $a + b$? (a, $b > 0$)

   (1) $a^2 + 2ab + b^2 = 64$

   (2) $a^2 - b^2 = 32$

Statement 1 is another way of saying $(a + b)(a + b)$ or $(a + b)^2$. Because $8 \times 8 = 64$, you know that $a + b = 8$. Statement 1 alone is sufficient to answer the question, narrowing your answers down to A and D. If you are running short on time or brain capacity, taking a 50–50 guess is a good idea.

If you were not told that a, $b > 0$, you couldn't assume that $a + b = 8$. It could have equaled NEGATIVE 8 because $-8 \times -8 = 64$.

Factor statement 2 down into $(a + b)(a - b) = 32$. All by itself, that doesn't tell you how much $(a + b)$ equals. Eliminate answers B and D. Because you had previously narrowed the answers down to A and D, the only answer left is A. Note that you don't have to waste time deciding whether statement 2 adds anything to statement 1; as long as statement 1 alone is sufficient, you're on your way.

Did you forget that $a^2 + 2ab + b^2$ factors into $(a + b)^2$? Did you forget that $a^2 - b^2$ factors into $(a + b)(a - b)$? Pack your bags; you're going on a guilt trip. These expressions were discussed in detail in the math review. *Correct answer:* A.

5. By what percentage did the team's wins increase this year over last year's wins?

   (1) Last year the team won 36 games; this year it won 72 games.

   (2) The team doubled the number of wins this year from last year.

PREDICT! The formula for a percent increase or decrease is number increase/decrease divided by the original whole (what you are increasing or decreasing from). Therefore, you need to know the number increase or decrease and the original whole. Keep in mind what you need as you're going through the statements.

Statement 1 gives you the original whole (36 games) and enough information for you to find the number increase $(72-36)$. Statement 1 alone is sufficient, narrowing your choices down to A or D.

Statement 2 looks less forthcoming, but beneath that chaste appearance beats a very accommodating sentence. If something doubles, it increases by 100 percent. (This concept also was covered in the percentage section of the math review in Chapter 13. If you've forgotten it, go back to it right now and review. Don't procrastinate; going back immediately will fix the information in your mind.) Statement 2 alone is sufficient, making the choices B or D. Because each statement alone is sufficient, the answer is D. *Correct Answer:* D.

If all of this math is flooding your mind, don't worry. There's a remedy for water on the brain: a tap on the head!

6. Is quadrilateral *MNOP* a square?

    (1) The area of *MNOP* is 16 square units.

    (2) The perimeter of *MNOP* is 16 units.

Statement 1 alone is not sufficient. The quad could be a rectangle of sides 1 and 16, for example, or a parallelogram of heights 2 and 8, or many other possibilities. Statement 1 alone is not sufficient to answer the questions, eliminating choices A and D.

Statement 2 alone is also pretty useless. The figure could be, for example, a rhombus of side 4 or a parallelogram of sides 1 and 7. Because statement 2 alone is not sufficient to answer the question, eliminate choices B and D. The only choices left are C (you need both statements to answer the question) or E (the quest is futile). Here, putting the information together tells you that the area and the perimeter have the same number of units. That can be written algebraically as $base \times height = 4\ sides$. $bh = 4s$. If you plug in, you should be able to see that the side of the figure must be 4 and that only 4 could work in this situation. Therefore, all sides are equal, and both statements together give you enough information to answer the question. *Correct Answer:* C.

Note: What about a rhombus? All sides are equal in a rhombus, right? Right, but the height of a rhombus is not the same as its side.

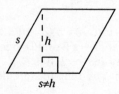

$s \neq h$

7. When one sock is taken at random from a sock drawer, what is the probability it will be white?

    (1) The drawer contains three times as many non-white socks as white socks.

    (2) The drawer has white, brown, and black socks.

The formula for probability (covered in the math review) is

$$\frac{number\ of\ possible\ desired\ outcomes}{number\ of\ total\ possible\ outcomes}$$

In this case, the desired outcomes are white socks; the total possible outcomes are all the socks. (Who says the GMAT has no sox appeal?)

Statement 1 tells you that the white socks are ¼ of the total socks in the drawer (for you algebra mavens: $3x$ = nonwhite socks; x = white socks). White/total = $x/4x$. The probability of drawing out a white sock is ¼. Statement 1 alone is sufficient, narrowing the choices down to A and D.

You do *not* have to have an actual, concrete number of how many socks are in the drawer. There could be 4 socks or 400 socks; the chance of getting a white sock is still ¼ or 25 percent. Don't immediately think that there is not enough information given just because you don't have a number; a proportion is as good as a number in a probability problem any day.

Statement 2 alone is not sufficient. The drawer has only three colors of socks; well, isn't that nice? There's a dandy topic of conversation to bring up on a date the next time you have a gap in the conversation. Unfortunately, the information is about as useless here as it would be on a date. How many socks are there altogether? How many socks are white? You don't know either fact needed for probability, a total or a subtotal. You can't answer the question based on statement 2 alone, so eliminate choices B and D. Because the choices were already narrowed down to A and D, and D is now shot down, the answer must be A.

If you chose C, you lost track of just what C is all about. Choose C only when you absolutely, positively, desperately have to have both statements, when you can't live without both of them. If you can get along with only statement 1, and statement 2 just adds a nice interesting tidbit, thank statement 2, but don't pay it any royalties. Here you can manage fine with just statement 1; choose A. *Correct Answer:* A.

8. Is x an even number?

   (1) x^2 is odd.

   (2) $x^2 - x$ is even.

An even number times itself is even ($4 \times 4 = 16$; $10 \times 10 = 100$). An odd number times itself is odd ($3 \times 3 = 9$; $11 \times 11 = 121$). If x^2 is odd, x must be odd. Statement 1 alone is sufficient to solve the problem *even though the answer to the question is "no."*

Remember: As long as you can answer the question, the data is sufficient. It makes no difference whether the answer is yes or no, just that you can come up with an answer. If you eliminated choices A and D, saying that statement 1 alone wasn't sufficient because it answered the question in the negative, you fell for a very common trap.

Statement 2 alone is not sufficient, as you can tell by plugging in a few numbers. Let's try 1: $1^2 - 1 = 0$; 0 is even. Therefore, x could be 1, which is odd. Plug in 2: $2^2 - 2 = 2$, which is even. Therefore, x could be 2, which is even. Because x could be odd or even, statement 2 alone is not sufficient to answer the question. *Correct Answer:* A.

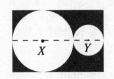

9. What is the area of the shaded portion of the preceding figure?

   (1) The ratio of the area of circle X to the area of circle Y is 4:1

   (2) The radius of circle $X = 6$

PREDICT! A shaded area problem is a "gimme," a freebie. You know (because you read the shaded area portion of the math review in Chapter 11) that the shaded area is a leftover, what's left over after you have subtracted the unshaded portion from the whole figure. You can predict here that you have to find the area of each circle, which means you need to know the radius. If you have the radii of the circles, you can find the lengths of the sides of the rectangle as well. Everything depends on the radii.

Statement 1 alone gives no info on the radius. Eliminate choices A and D. Statement 2 alone is not sufficient. Knowing the radius of Circle X is 6 tells us that the area of Circle $X = 36\pi$. But what about the area of Circle Y? Eliminate choices B and D.

Put the two statements together. Knowing that Circle X has four times the area of Circle Y allows you to find that the area of Circle $Y = 9\pi$. You could add the areas of the two circles. *But* could you find the area of the rectangle? If you chose trap answer E, you didn't think so. And you were wrong. If the area of circle Y is 9π, the radius of circle Y is 3 (because the area of a circle is $\pi\ radius^2$). If the radius of Circle Y) is 3, the diameter is 6 and the length of the rectangle is 18, which is 12 (diameter of circle X) + 6 (diameter of Circle Y). The height of the rectangle is 12 (diameter of Circle X). You could find the area of the whole rectangle, the area of the two circles, and then subtract to find the shaded area. Don't bother doing so; just sleep better tonight knowing you *could* do so. *Correct Answer:* C.

10. If x is a positive whole number, is $\frac{x}{18}$ a whole number?

   (1) x is divisible by 9.

   (2) x is divisible by 2.

Plug in numbers for x. Statement 1 says that x is divisible by 9: Make $x = 9$ (don't fight it; give in and take the path of least resistance). If $x = 9$, the answer to the question is no because $\frac{9}{18} = \frac{1}{2}$, which is not a whole number. But when plugging numbers, always plug in more than once. What if $x = 18$? Then the answer to the question is yes because $\frac{18}{18} = 1$, which is a whole number. Because the statement allows us to answer yes and no, it doesn't provide enough information. Eliminate choices A and D.

Plug in numbers based on statement 2. Let $x = 2$. Then $\frac{2}{18} = \frac{1}{9}$, which is not a whole number. Let $x = 18$, then $\frac{18}{18} = 1$, which is a whole number. The information in statement 2 alone is not sufficient; eliminate choices B and D.

Your choices are now narrowed down to C or E. If x is divisible by 2, x is even. If x is divisible by 9, x is a multiple of 9. Plug in even multiples of 9: 18, 36, 54, 72. They all can be divided evenly by 18. Both statements together are sufficient. *Correct Answer:* C.

11. Jensen and Mike working together can file 600 papers in an hour. How many can Mike file in an hour working alone?

   (1) Jensen works half as fast as Mike.

   (2) Jensen, working alone, takes three hours to file 600 papers.

Statement 1 alone is sufficient to answer the question. If Jensen works half as fast as Mike and together they file 600 papers in an hour, then Jensen does 200 and Mike does 400, for a total of 600. (For those of you who can't live without algebra, think of Jensen as x and Mike as $2x$. First, $x + 2x = 600$, and $3x = 600$. Finally, $x = 200$; $2x = 400$. Same concept, just taking matters to x-ess.) Because statement 1 alone is sufficient, your choices are narrowed down to A and D.

Statement 2 alone is also sufficient. If Jensen takes 3 hours to file 600 papers, he can file 200 papers in one hour $\left(\frac{600}{3} = 200\right)$. If he files 200 papers in an hour, Mike must file the other 400 in an hour.

Don't get confused between which information is given in the question stem and which information is given in the statements. The question stem tells you that Jensen and Mike working together can file 600 papers in an hour. That information is solid, not dependent on what you learn in either statement. If the information that Jensen and Mike working together can file 600 papers in an hour were given as additional information in statement 1 (but not in the question stem), for example, then statement 1 alone would be sufficient, but statement 2 would not. *Correct Answer:* D.

12. How far is a round trip to the basketball court from Coach Fetzner's home?

(1) Ms. Fetzner leaves home at 9:00 a.m. and arrives at the court 20 minutes later, driving nonstop.

(2) Ms. Fetzner drives at 30 mph.

PREDICT! This question lets you get down and DIRTy: Use the DIRT formula: Distance Is Rate × Time. To find out the distance, you need to know the rate and the time. Look for them.

Statement 1 alone is not sufficient because you don't know Ms. Fetzner's rate. If she drives 65 miles per hour (She'd never dream of exceeding the speed limit any more than you would, right?) and arrives in 20 minutes, the distance is obviously greater than if she were to drive at a sedate 30 mph (ignoring the honking serenades and digital salutes of the drivers behind her) and arrive in 20 minutes. Because statement 1 alone is not sufficient to answer the question, eliminate choices A and D.

Statement 2 alone is not sufficient. You know the rate but not the time. Ms. Fetzner drives at 30 mph . . . but for how long? An hour? Two hours? Ten minutes? Eliminate choices B and D; statement 2 doesn't give you enough information on its own to answer the question.

Combine the statements: Statement 1 gives you the time, and statement 2 gives you the rate. Using them, you could find distance (don't actually do so, just know that you have sufficient info to do so). *Correct Answer:* C.

Q: Why did the coach flood the court?

A: She wanted to send in the subs.

Chapter 16

Real Math at Last: Problem Solving

In This Chapter

▶ Developing a plan of attack for Problem Solving questions

▶ Side stepping snares and avoiding built-in traps

▶ Separating the boring from the bewildering

Problem Solving is a rather ritzy name for "regular" math problems. A Problem Solving question, amazingly enough, actually expects you to solve a problem. This is different from the Data Sufficiency questions (see Chapter 14), in which you often don't need to solve the problem through to the bitter end — you just decide whether the data are sufficient to answer the question. (Who thinks of these catchy names anyway? How much do they get paid, and where can I apply for the job?)

Strategic Planning: The Attack Strategy

Are you an Algebra Ace? Mathematics Master? Geometry Guru? Me neither. Isn't it lucky that you don't have to be any of those things to do well on the Problem Solving questions? To improve your chances of acing the material, try to understand and apply the strategies that I discuss here.

Senior Discount: I realize that some of you reading this book haven't taken a math class in a long, long time. Maybe you are a senior in college, and because you tested out of math in high school, never took any math in college at all. Maybe you're returning to school after spending several years working or having a family or traveling or pursuing the idle and decadent lifestyle of the independently wealthy. Whatever the case, you may be so rusty in math that your pencil creaks when you pick it up. I realize that you are not going to get every single math question correct; you should realize that you don't have to. The following suggestions help you to maximize your points with a minimum of time and bother.

1. **Read the problem through carefully and mentally circle what the question is asking for.**

   This crucial point is missed very often, especially by people who are math-phobic. It's easy to predict or anticipate what the question is asking for and not take note of what it really wants. Your goal is to give 'em what they want. If the question asks for a circumference, mentally circle the word *circumference* and don't solve for an area. If the question wants you to find the number of hours already worked rather than the total number of hours a job would take, be sure that you supply that figure.

   Of course, *of course,* the answer choices feature trap answers; this goes without saying on the GMAT. The area of a figure will be a trap answer choice to a question that asks for the volume. Just because you calculated an answer that is staring you in the face does not mean that answer is correct. It may be correct . . . or it may be a trap.

2. **Preview the answer choices; look to see how precise your answer has to be and how careful you have to be about the decimal points.**

   If the answer choices are 4, 5, 6, 7, and 8, you probably will have to solve the problem to the bitter end, calculating rather than estimating. This type of problem may take a long time. If the answer choices are .05, .5, 5, 50, and 500, you know that the digit is definitely going to be a 5 and that you have to keep your decimal point straight. You may be able to use common sense on that problem and estimate the answer without working it out.

3. **Solve the problem forwards and backwards.**

   Work out the problem and get an answer; then plug that answer back into the problem to make sure that it makes sense. If you found the average of 4, 6, 7, 9, and 10 to be 36, you can look at the answer and reason that you made a mistake somewhere because the average can't be bigger than the biggest number.

Three Commonsense Suggestions

The Problem Solving questions are much more straightforward than the Data Sufficiency problems (covered in Chapter 14). There aren't as many tricks or traps, but you can learn a few good, fairly commonsense techniques that can speed up your work or prevent you from making careless mistakes.

Eliminate illogical (dumb) answer choices

You know how some professors always reassure students by saying, "Oh, there's no such thing as a dumb question or answer; just try!" Wrong. There *are* such things as dumb answers. If you're asked for the temperature of a liquid and one of the answer choices is −200° Fahrenheit, it's unlikely that a liquid would be that cold; it would freeze and no longer be a liquid! If you're asked for the age of a person and one answer is 217, I'd like to know what kind of vitamins he's been taking! When you preview the answers, dump the ones that seem to make no sense.

Don't choose a "close enough" answer

Suppose that you do a ton of calculations and get the answer 36. One of the answer choices is 38. Don't shrug and say, "Ahh, close enough; I must have made a mistake somewhere." You sure did, and you're about to make a second mistake by being lazy and choosing an answer that's close. *Remember:* Close counts only in horseshoes (which you may want to bring to the exam for luck, come to think of it) and hand grenades (which may be what you feel has hit you when you see some of these math questions!).

Don't let me scare you too much about the math. The GMAT does not, I repeat, *does not* test trigonometry or calculus. It tests basic arithmetic, algebra, and geometry. Even if you haven't had those subjects in years, you can learn enough to do well. I had one student in her 60s who wanted to go back to graduate school after her husband passed away. She had never taken geometry in her life because the subject wasn't a requirement when she applied to college 40 years ago. She memorized formulas, plowed her way through some sample problems, kept an eye open for tricks, and did just as well as anyone else.

Give your pencil a workout

Although you get no paper and pencil exam, you do get scratch paper. Use it! Draw and doodle as necessary. As you'll see when you go through the sample questions and practice exams, writing down formulas and plugging numbers into them or drawing pictures and putting numbers on the pictures is an excellent means of avoiding careless errors and clarifying and organizing thoughts. Don't think you're wasting time by using your pencil; you may actually be saving time by avoiding confusion.

Summary

Before going on to the sample questions, let's review the approach and the tricks.

Approach

1. **Read the problem through carefully and mentally circle what the question is asking for.**

2. **Preview the answer choices.**

3. **Solve the problem forwards and backwards (plugging in the multiple-choice answers).**

Tricks

- Eliminate illogical (dumb) answer choices.

- Don't choose a "close enough" answer.

- Plug in numbers, write down formulas, and draw pictures: Give your pencil a workout.

Chapter 17

A Chance to Show Off: Problem-Solving Practice Questions

So you think you understand everything from the lecture? Prove it! I'm calling your bluff. Let's see you ace these practice questions.

Note: Please go through the answer explanations for *every* question, not just for the ones you miss. (How dare I assume that you'll miss any!)

1. $5/7 < x$. The x may be which of the following?

   (A) $1/6$

   (B) $1/3$

   (C) $1/2$

   (D) $3/5$

   (E) $5/6$

   You could, of course, divide this whole problem out and figure out that $5/7$ is .714, and then figure out the decimal equivalents of the answer choices. But that's too much pencil pushing. The purpose of the exam is to find those students who use their brains, not their yellow #2s. You know that because 3.5 is half of 7, 5 out of 7 is more than half. You can immediately eliminate choices A, B, and C. As quickly as that, you narrow your choices down to two. If you're really in a rush, you may decide that a 50–50 guess is good enough and not even bother solving the problem through to its ultimate solution. But make that decision intelligently, not just out of haste. ***Remember:*** You *cannot* go back to a problem later. After you hit the Confirm button, that problem is history.

   Okay, you've decided to solve the problem. You still don't have to work out all the arithmetic. You know that the bigger the denominator (the number on the bottom) of a fraction, the smaller the fraction. For example, $1/7$ is smaller than $1/6$. Therefore, $5/7$ is smaller than $5/6$, and you have your answer without ever having to do any calculations. Life is worth living again. *Correct Answer:* E.

2. One-half of all the tourists in Africa are from the United States. Of those, two-thirds are women. Of the women, three-fifths are from California. What fraction of all the tourists in Africa are women from California?

   (A) $1/6$

   (B) $1/5$

   (C) $1/3$

   (D) $3/4$

   (E) $4/5$

   Multiply the fractions together. The word *of* means to multiply: $\frac{1}{2} \times \frac{2}{3} \times \frac{3}{5}$. When you see that the 2s and the 3s cancel, you know you're on the right track. *Correct Answer:* B.

TIP

If you absolutely hate, loathe, and despise fractions, there's a way to get around them. Plug in numbers. You want a nice round number that's divisible by 2, 3, and 5. How about 30? Then ½ or 15 tourists are from America. Two-thirds or 10 tourists are women. Three-fifths or 6 women are from California. Your total of California girls is ⁶⁄₃₀, which reduces to ⅕. Note that the key to this problem is choosing the right number to plug in; a number that is divisible by all the denominators. Plugging in numbers can take more time, but if you are a complete fraction-phobe, it may be worth the investment.

3. Last year the newspaper printed 63 retractions. This year it printed 42. What percent decrease was there in the number of retractions printed by the newspaper?

(A) 21

(B) 33⅓

(C) 50

(D) 66⅔

(E) 90

The percent increase or decrease is the number increase or decrease over the original whole. That is, you find the number difference between the two terms. In this case, it's $63 - 42 = 21$. (Trap answer A. You didn't really think the problem was that easy, did you?) Put that number over the original whole, or what you are increasing or decreasing from: ²¹⁄₆₃. That reduces to ⅓ or 33⅓ percent. *Correct Answer:* B.

This percentage increase/decrease jazz is covered in detail in the percentage section of the math review in Chapter 13.

4. Gigi, Maryalyse, and Tommy make contributions to the fund-raiser in the ratio of 2:3:5. If altogether they contribute $50,000, how much more money does Tommy contribute than Gigi?

(A) $5,000

(B) $10,000

(C) $15,000

(D) $25,000

(E) $35,000

No need for gray-cell gridlock; this problem is actually pretty simple. Add the numbers in the ratio: $2 + 3 + 5 = 10$. Divide the total amount contributed by 10 to find that each "part" is equivalent to $5,000. Gigi pays two parts, or $10,000. Tommy pays 5 parts, or $25,000. The difference between them is $15,000. *Correct Answer:* C.

5. How many circles of circumference 10π feet can fit completely into a rectangle measuring 25 feet by 45 feet?

(A) 15

(B) 12

(C) 11

(D) 8

(E) 4

The circumference of a circle is 2π radius, or π diameter (two radii equal one diameter). The diameter of this circle, therefore, is 10. If the width (height) of the rectangle is 25, only two circles can fit into it vertically. (Yes, space will be left over. The problem did not say that the circles were "perfectly inscribed," meaning that the circles had to fill the rectangle.) If the length (base) of the rectangle is 45, then only four circles will fit into it. Two rows of four circles each total eight circles.

The answer choices are full of traps. If you thought that three circles could fit in vertically and five horizontally, you chose A. If you thought you could put in three circles vertically and four horizontally, you chose B. If you got really desperate and worked with fractions or decimals, saying that 3.5 circles fit in vertically and 4.5 fit in horizontally, you got 15.75 (and a headache from doing too much work) and rounded it down to choice A. *Correct Answer:* D.

Because so many geometry problems expect you to know how to work "forwards and backwards," be sure that you can get from a circumference to a diameter or radius or area, and from an area to a circumference. If you know even one measure of a figure, you should be able to manipulate it to get other measures.

6. Bob's constant monthly income was 250 percent greater than Anthony's constant monthly income in 1994. If Anthony's income of $1,000 in January of 1995 was unchanged from his monthly income in 1994, but Bob's income showed a 20 percent increase over his previous monthly income, what percentage of Anthony's monthly income is Bob's income in 1995?

    (A) 420

    (B) 350

    (C) 200

    (D) 4.2

    (E) 3.5

If Anthony earned $1,000 a month and Bob earned 250 percent more, Bob earned $3,500 a month.

If you thought Bob earned $2,500, you got confused on the difference between percent OF and percent MORE. For example, 10 is 200 percent of 5, but only 100 percent more than 5. (If this is totally confusing to you, go back to the math review section on percentages. All will become clear.) If Bob's income rose 20 percent, it went up ⅕, or $700, for a total of $4,200. The question now is what percent of Anthony's income is Bob's income. To find this, use the IS/OF formula: What percent OF Anthony's income (so that goes on the bottom, 1,000) IS Bob's income? That goes on the top, giving you the fraction 4,200/1,000. Cancel the zeros to get 42/10 or 4.20. If you chose D, you fell for a major trap of confusing numbers and percentages. For example, 1 doesn't mean 1 percent; it means 100 percent. Therefore, 4.2 is not 4.2 percent, but 420 percent. *Correct Answer:* A.

This is a difficult problem for non-native speakers of English. Even people who have spoken English all their lives shake their heads and have to read this sort of problem over a half a dozen times. If the wording is confusing to you, make a quick guess and go on. It's a time-waster and has so many traps that it's easy to miss even when you think you've figured it out.

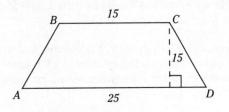

7. What is the area of trapezoid *ABCD* in square units?

    (A) 600

    (B) 450

    (C) 310

    (D) 300

    (E) 150

The area of a trapezoid is $\frac{1}{2}(base\ one + base\ two) \times height$. You know that *base one* and *base two* are $15 + 25 = 40$. (Because you're adding the terms, it makes no difference which side you call *base one* and which you call *base two*. Don't spend any time fretting over the labeling. The top and bottom are the bases.) Half of 40 is 20.

A height or altitude is defined as a line from the tallest point down to the base. The line from point C down is the height. Multiply it by the 20 you calculated earlier: $20 \times 15 = 300$. *Correct Answer:* D.

TRAPS & TRICKS

If you chose A, you forgot to take half of the sum of the bases. If you chose E, you did way too much work and found half of the height as well ($7.5 \times 20 = 150$).

TIP

Learn the geometry formulas by heart. They are the foundation of all the geometry questions. While it's unfair to say that you can answer all the geometry questions merely by memorizing the formulas, it's completely fair to say that if you don't memorize the formulas, you can't answer the questions. My suggestion is that you write down the appropriate formula: Just jot it down on the scratch paper in front of you and then fill in the numbers. The problem practically solves itself. (I know, I know: easy for me to say!)

8. A hiring office is filled with job seekers. Forty of the job seekers are looking for clerical work. Thirty-three and a third percent are looking for manual labor. The remaining 20 people aren't seriously looking for work but are in the office just to get out of the rain. How many people are in the office altogether?

   (A) 120

   (B) 100

   (C) 90

   (D) 85

   (E) 60

Begin by eliminating the stupid choice, E. You know that there are 40 job seekers and 20 deadbeats just looking to escape the rain. That means there are 60 people in that group alone and there are other people in the office, those looking for manual labor. Try to eliminate the obviously incorrect choices as quickly as possible.

Because manual laborers are 33⅓ percent or ⅓ of the people in the office, the clerical workers and the deadbeats must be the other ⅔. Your equation is $60 = \frac{2}{3}x$, or two-thirds of the total. Now, you can just talk this through. If 60 is TWO-thirds, then ONE-third would be 30, and the total, THREE-thirds, is 90. (If you insist on doing the math, divide both sides through by what is next to the variable: ⅔. The right side cancels out to be 1. The left side is 60/(⅔). When you divide by a fraction, invert or turn it upside down and multiply. $60 \times \frac{3}{2} = \frac{180}{2} = 90$.) *Correct Answer:* C.

9. A parking lot contains 85 Chryslers, 131 Volvos, and 615 Fords. The lot contains no other cars. A lucky contestant wins the chance to pick any car of his choice. What is the probability that he will pick either a Chrysler, Volvo, or Ford?

   (A) 85

   (B) 100

   (C) 131

   (D) 615

   (E) 831

Probability is expressed as a percentage, and it can never be more than 100. Let me repeat that because it is the crux to this whole problem: Probability can never be more than 100 percent. The probability of doing something is between 0 (you absolutely will not do it) and 100 (you absolutely will do it) percent. Immediately eliminate answers C, D, and E. (If you chose E, you did too much work, adding up all the items.)

Because the cars mentioned are the only ones in the lot, the lucky contestant is going to take out one of those cars. Therefore, he positively will select one, making the probability 100 percent. *Correct Answer:* B.

Question: Did you hear about the new model Ford called Amnesia?
Answer: It'll never be recalled!

10. Two cans in the shape of right circular cylinders are in a factory waiting to be filled with prunes. The volume of the second can is twice that of the first can, although their radii are both equal. Which of the following expresses the ratio of the height of the first can to that of the second can?

 (A) 4:1

 (B) 3:1

 (C) 2:1

 (D) 4:9

 (E) 1:2

The formula for the volume of a solid is (*area of the base*) × *height*. The base of a cylinder is a circle. The area of a circle is $\pi\ radius^2$. Therefore, the volume of a cylinder is $\pi\ radius^2 \times height$. Plug in numbers to make your life easier. Say that the radii of both cans are 4, and the height of the first can is 10. (You can plug in any number your heart desires, but why not use numbers that are easy to work with?) The volume of the first cylinder is $16\pi \times 10 = 160\pi$. The second cylinder has twice that volume or 320π. If the radii are the same, the area of the base of the second cylinder is also 16π. Divide 320π by 16π to get 20 for the height of the second cylinder. $10:20 = 1:2$. (If you chose C, you got sloppy.) *Correct Answer:* E.

Still skeptical about plugging in numbers? Plug in different terms and try the problem again. It'll be good practice for you, and it'll prove to you that the ratio comes out to be the same.

11. $x > 0$. Solve for $\dfrac{x^{12}x^{12}x^{-3}}{x^7}$

 (A) x^{425}

 (B) x^{16}

 (C) x^{14}

 (D) x^{5}

 (E) x^{3}

To multiply like bases, add the exponents: $12 + 12 + (-3) = (24 - 3) = 21$. To divide like bases, subtract the exponents: $21 - 7 = 14$. *Correct Answer:* C.

If you chose E, you divided the exponents in the last step: $21/7 = 3$. If you chose A, you multiplied the exponents in the numerator (completely ignoring the negative sign) and then subtracted the exponent in the denominator.

Exponents are one of the simpler types of math problems . . . if you know the technique. If you don't, they can be vile. Take a few minutes now to return to the math bases and exponents section of the math review.

12. Two-thirds of the area of isosceles right triangle *ABC* is equal to 48. What is the perimeter of the triangle?

(A) 144

(B) 48

(C) $36\sqrt{2}$

(D) $2\sqrt{3}$

(E) $24+12\sqrt{2}$

Instead of heading for equations, talk the problem through. If two-thirds of a number is 48, then one-third of the number is 24. Three-thirds would be 3×24, or 72. The area of a triangle is one-half base times height. Therefore, 72 is one-half base times height; 144 is base times height.

An isosceles right triangle has two equal sides, the base and the height, and $base\times height=144$; the square root of 144 is 12. If one side is 12, the other side is 12, then the hypotenuse is $12\sqrt{2}$. Add them. (You can either find that using the Pythagorean theorem or answer by memorizing the Pythagorean triples, one of which is side:side:side $\sqrt{2}$ for an isosceles right triangle.) *Correct Answer:* E.

If you're uncomfortable with finding the area of a triangle or with using the Pythagorean Triples, return to the breathtaking excitement of the geometry math review in Chapter 11.

If you have a limited amount of time to spend studying, I suggest you invest it in the geometry review. The exam is roughly one-third algebra, one-third arithmetic, and one-third geometry. Most of the geometry problems can be answered merely by knowing a few basic formulas and then plugging the numbers from the problem into the formulas. Have those formulas down pat, able to access them in a nanosecond.

Part VII

It All Comes Down to This: Full-Length Practice GMATs

The 5th Wave   By Rich Tennant

"I guessed my way to a perfect score on the GMAT, then I guessed my way through grad school and several middle management jobs. So—would you like me to guess your weight?"

In this part . . .

*J*ust when you think your brain can't be stuffed with one more factoid, relief is at hand. You finally get to download some of the information you've been inputting for the past 17 chapters. Trust me; you'll feel better when you let it all out.

This unit has two full-length practice exams that are as close to the actual GMAT as I can get without having briefcase-bearing barristers battering down my door. I take these tests seriously, and you should, too — do them under actual test conditions, sitting in a quiet room and timing yourself. Open books are definitely out (sorry!). I have spies everywhere; I'll know if you cheat on these tests — there will be a knocking at your door one foggy night. . . . After you've done your duty on these practice exams, you'll have a good time going through the answer explanations, which are nowhere near as dry and stuffy as the exams themselves.

After the practice exams, it's back to Party Central with Part VIII, "The Part of Tens." Do yourself a favor and don't miss it; it's a lot of fun (who says you have nothing to live for?).

Chapter 18

How to Ruin a Perfectly Good Day, Part I: Practice Exam 1

Are you bloody but unbowed, ready to have a go at it? You are now ready to take a sample *hard* GMAT. The following exam consists of two 75-minute sections with multiple-choice questions and two 30-minute essay questions for a total of four sections. *Note:* This exam consists of one verbal section (Reading Comprehension, Critical Reasoning, and Sentence Correction questions), one quantitative section (Problem-Solving and Data Sufficiency questions), and two essays. (On the CAT, the essays will be first.)

You have no choice but to guess at everything — the key to success is guessing quickly. Don't waste time on problems you know you can't do.

Please take this test under normal exam conditions. This is serious stuff here!

1. **Sit where you won't be interrupted (even though you'd probably welcome any distractions).**

2. **Use the answer grid provided for the multiple-choice questions; write your essays on lined paper.**

3. **Pretend each question is on a computer screen and must be answered before you see the next question. Do not skip ahead or go back.**

4. **Set your alarm clock for the 30- to 75-minute intervals.**

5. **Do not go on to the next test until the time allotted for the section you are taking is up.**

6. **If you finish early, check your work for that section only.**

7. **Do not take a break in the middle of any section.**

8. **Give yourself one five-minute break between sections 1 and 2 and a second five-minute break between sections 3 and 4.**

When you complete the entire test, check your answers with the answer key at the end of the chapter. Record your scores on the scoring worksheet provided. To grade your essays, ask a friend or teacher to read them and give you a score ranging from 0 to 6.

Chapter 19 gives detailed explanations of the answers. Go through the answer explanations to ALL the questions, not just the ones you miss. There is a wealth of worthwhile information there, material that provides a good review of everything you've learned in the lectures. I've even tossed in a few good (you'll be the judge of that!) jokes to keep your brain from exploding. Good luck!

Practice Exam 1 Answer Sheet

Section 1	Section 2

Section 1

1. Ⓐ Ⓑ Ⓒ Ⓓ Ⓔ
2. Ⓐ Ⓑ Ⓒ Ⓓ Ⓔ
3. Ⓐ Ⓑ Ⓒ Ⓓ Ⓔ
4. Ⓐ Ⓑ Ⓒ Ⓓ Ⓔ
5. Ⓐ Ⓑ Ⓒ Ⓓ Ⓔ
6. Ⓐ Ⓑ Ⓒ Ⓓ Ⓔ
7. Ⓐ Ⓑ Ⓒ Ⓓ Ⓔ
8. Ⓐ Ⓑ Ⓒ Ⓓ Ⓔ
9. Ⓐ Ⓑ Ⓒ Ⓓ Ⓔ
10. Ⓐ Ⓑ Ⓒ Ⓓ Ⓔ
11. Ⓐ Ⓑ Ⓒ Ⓓ Ⓔ
12. Ⓐ Ⓑ Ⓒ Ⓓ Ⓔ
13. Ⓐ Ⓑ Ⓒ Ⓓ Ⓔ
14. Ⓐ Ⓑ Ⓒ Ⓓ Ⓔ
15. Ⓐ Ⓑ Ⓒ Ⓓ Ⓔ
16. Ⓐ Ⓑ Ⓒ Ⓓ Ⓔ
17. Ⓐ Ⓑ Ⓒ Ⓓ Ⓔ
18. Ⓐ Ⓑ Ⓒ Ⓓ Ⓔ
19. Ⓐ Ⓑ Ⓒ Ⓓ Ⓔ
20. Ⓐ Ⓑ Ⓒ Ⓓ Ⓔ
21. Ⓐ Ⓑ Ⓒ Ⓓ Ⓔ
22. Ⓐ Ⓑ Ⓒ Ⓓ Ⓔ
23. Ⓐ Ⓑ Ⓒ Ⓓ Ⓔ
24. Ⓐ Ⓑ Ⓒ Ⓓ Ⓔ
25. Ⓐ Ⓑ Ⓒ Ⓓ Ⓔ
26. Ⓐ Ⓑ Ⓒ Ⓓ Ⓔ
27. Ⓐ Ⓑ Ⓒ Ⓓ Ⓔ
28. Ⓐ Ⓑ Ⓒ Ⓓ Ⓔ
29. Ⓐ Ⓑ Ⓒ Ⓓ Ⓔ
30. Ⓐ Ⓑ Ⓒ Ⓓ Ⓔ
31. Ⓐ Ⓑ Ⓒ Ⓓ Ⓔ
32. Ⓐ Ⓑ Ⓒ Ⓓ Ⓔ
33. Ⓐ Ⓑ Ⓒ Ⓓ Ⓔ
34. Ⓐ Ⓑ Ⓒ Ⓓ Ⓔ
35. Ⓐ Ⓑ Ⓒ Ⓓ Ⓔ
36. Ⓐ Ⓑ Ⓒ Ⓓ Ⓔ
37. Ⓐ Ⓑ Ⓒ Ⓓ Ⓔ
38. Ⓐ Ⓑ Ⓒ Ⓓ Ⓔ
39. Ⓐ Ⓑ Ⓒ Ⓓ Ⓔ
40. Ⓐ Ⓑ Ⓒ Ⓓ Ⓔ
41. Ⓐ Ⓑ Ⓒ Ⓓ Ⓔ
42. Ⓐ Ⓑ Ⓒ Ⓓ Ⓔ
43. Ⓐ Ⓑ Ⓒ Ⓓ Ⓔ
44. Ⓐ Ⓑ Ⓒ Ⓓ Ⓔ
45. Ⓐ Ⓑ Ⓒ Ⓓ Ⓔ
46. Ⓐ Ⓑ Ⓒ Ⓓ Ⓔ
47. Ⓐ Ⓑ Ⓒ Ⓓ Ⓔ
48. Ⓐ Ⓑ Ⓒ Ⓓ Ⓔ
49. Ⓐ Ⓑ Ⓒ Ⓓ Ⓔ
50. Ⓐ Ⓑ Ⓒ Ⓓ Ⓔ

Section 2

1. Ⓐ Ⓑ Ⓒ Ⓓ Ⓔ
2. Ⓐ Ⓑ Ⓒ Ⓓ Ⓔ
3. Ⓐ Ⓑ Ⓒ Ⓓ Ⓔ
4. Ⓐ Ⓑ Ⓒ Ⓓ Ⓔ
5. Ⓐ Ⓑ Ⓒ Ⓓ Ⓔ
6. Ⓐ Ⓑ Ⓒ Ⓓ Ⓔ
7. Ⓐ Ⓑ Ⓒ Ⓓ Ⓔ
8. Ⓐ Ⓑ Ⓒ Ⓓ Ⓔ
9. Ⓐ Ⓑ Ⓒ Ⓓ Ⓔ
10. Ⓐ Ⓑ Ⓒ Ⓓ Ⓔ
11. Ⓐ Ⓑ Ⓒ Ⓓ Ⓔ
12. Ⓐ Ⓑ Ⓒ Ⓓ Ⓔ
13. Ⓐ Ⓑ Ⓒ Ⓓ Ⓔ
14. Ⓐ Ⓑ Ⓒ Ⓓ Ⓔ
15. Ⓐ Ⓑ Ⓒ Ⓓ Ⓔ
16. Ⓐ Ⓑ Ⓒ Ⓓ Ⓔ
17. Ⓐ Ⓑ Ⓒ Ⓓ Ⓔ
18. Ⓐ Ⓑ Ⓒ Ⓓ Ⓔ
19. Ⓐ Ⓑ Ⓒ Ⓓ Ⓔ
20. Ⓐ Ⓑ Ⓒ Ⓓ Ⓔ
21. Ⓐ Ⓑ Ⓒ Ⓓ Ⓔ
22. Ⓐ Ⓑ Ⓒ Ⓓ Ⓔ
23. Ⓐ Ⓑ Ⓒ Ⓓ Ⓔ
24. Ⓐ Ⓑ Ⓒ Ⓓ Ⓔ
25. Ⓐ Ⓑ Ⓒ Ⓓ Ⓔ
26. Ⓐ Ⓑ Ⓒ Ⓓ Ⓔ
27. Ⓐ Ⓑ Ⓒ Ⓓ Ⓔ
28. Ⓐ Ⓑ Ⓒ Ⓓ Ⓔ
29. Ⓐ Ⓑ Ⓒ Ⓓ Ⓔ
30. Ⓐ Ⓑ Ⓒ Ⓓ Ⓔ
31. Ⓐ Ⓑ Ⓒ Ⓓ Ⓔ
32. Ⓐ Ⓑ Ⓒ Ⓓ Ⓔ
33. Ⓐ Ⓑ Ⓒ Ⓓ Ⓔ
34. Ⓐ Ⓑ Ⓒ Ⓓ Ⓔ
35. Ⓐ Ⓑ Ⓒ Ⓓ Ⓔ
36. Ⓐ Ⓑ Ⓒ Ⓓ Ⓔ
37. Ⓐ Ⓑ Ⓒ Ⓓ Ⓔ
38. Ⓐ Ⓑ Ⓒ Ⓓ Ⓔ
39. Ⓐ Ⓑ Ⓒ Ⓓ Ⓔ
40. Ⓐ Ⓑ Ⓒ Ⓓ Ⓔ
41. Ⓐ Ⓑ Ⓒ Ⓓ Ⓔ
42. Ⓐ Ⓑ Ⓒ Ⓓ Ⓔ
43. Ⓐ Ⓑ Ⓒ Ⓓ Ⓔ
44. Ⓐ Ⓑ Ⓒ Ⓓ Ⓔ
45. Ⓐ Ⓑ Ⓒ Ⓓ Ⓔ
46. Ⓐ Ⓑ Ⓒ Ⓓ Ⓔ
47. Ⓐ Ⓑ Ⓒ Ⓓ Ⓔ
48. Ⓐ Ⓑ Ⓒ Ⓓ Ⓔ
49. Ⓐ Ⓑ Ⓒ Ⓓ Ⓔ
50. Ⓐ Ⓑ Ⓒ Ⓓ Ⓔ

Section 1

Time: 75 minutes

41 questions

Directions: Each of the Sentence Correction sentences is either entirely or partially underlined. Following the sentence are five ways of restating that sentence. Select the one that best expresses the meaning of the original sentence in a succinct and grammatically correct manner. Choice A is the same as the original sentence; select it if you think the original is preferable to the alternative choices.

Each Reading passage is followed by questions pertaining to that passage. Read the passage and answer the questions based on information stated or implied in that passage.

With each Critical Reasoning question, choose the best answer.

1. A company that once held a virtual monopoly found itself losing market share to a new, aggressive competitor. Outside consultants hired by the older company credited the competitor's success to the wide use of effective marketing strategies. Nevertheless, the older company decided not to change its current marketing plan and chose instead to invest heavily in improving product delivery.

   Which of the following, if true, provides the strongest reason to predict that the investment decision made by the older company will allow it to regain market share?

   (A) A company's market share is obtained by dividing the amount of revenue earned by the company by the total of amount of money consumers spend on products made by the company and its competitors.

   (B) The decision to invest in product delivery rather than marketing will save the company several million dollars.

   (C) Other companies that have hired the outside consultants used by the older company have quickly regained market share.

   (D) If the older company does not regain its market share, it can still increase its revenue by simply increasing the size of the market.

   (E) Ultimately, the surest way to attract new customers and convince them to choose your company over others is to satisfy current customers, who then provide effective word-of-mouth marketing.

2. No true artist would compromise his integrity by painting anything so plebeian as a landscape. Pierre has just had a showing of ten of his finest landscapes.

   Assuming the above statement to be true, which of the following must also be true?

   (A) Pierre's landscapes are so good they are not considered plebeian.

   (B) Pierre is not a true artist.

   (C) Pierre has much integrity.

   (D) Landscapes are not considered plebeian by most artists, including Pierre.

   (E) Landscapes are plebeian only when painted by those artists who have not had a show of their own.

Go on to next page

3. <u>A school administrator may have difficulty predicting the amount of students before they have registered for the semester.</u>

(A) A school administrator may have difficulty predicting the amount of students before they have registered for the semester.

(B) A school administrator may be difficult to predict the amount of students before they have registered for the semester.

(C) Before registering for the semester, a school administrator may have difficulty predicting the number of students.

(D) A school administrator may have difficulty predicting the number of students prior to their registering for the semester.

(E) A school administrator, having difficulty predicting the number of students prior to their registering for the semester.

4. <u>Alive with vibrant colors, the New England countryside is visited every fall by thousands of tourists from all around the world.</u>

(A) Alive with vibrant colors, the New England countryside is visited every fall by thousands of tourists from all around the world.

(B) Alive with vibrant colors, thousands of tourists visit the New England countryside every fall.

(C) Alive with vibrant colors and thousands of tourists, the New England countryside is every fall visited.

(D) Thousands of tourists every fall visit the New England countryside, alive with vibrant colors.

(E) Thousands of tourists visit every fall the vibrantly alive and colorful New England countryside.

5. <u>The mastery of computers is as important a skill to elementary schoolchildren today that mastering</u> slide rules and typewriters was to children of an earlier generation.

(A) The mastery of computers is as important a skill to elementary schoolchildren today that mastering

(B) Mastering computers is as important a skill to elementary schoolchildren today as mastering

(C) The mastery of computers, as important a skill to elementary schoolchildren today, and the mastery of

(D) Mastering computers, an important skill to elementary schoolchildren today, is like the mastery of

(E) Computers mastering elementary schoolchildren today is as important as mastering

The results of this study show that the organic matter content of a soil can be altered to a depth of 10 cm or more by intense campfire heat. As much as 90 percent of the original organic matter may be oxidized in the top 1.3 cm (05) of a soil. In the surface 10 cm, the loss of organic matter may reach 50 percent if the soil is dry and the temperature exceeds 250 degrees C. The loss of organic matter reduces soil fertility and water-holding capacity and renders the soil more sus- (10) ceptible to compaction and erosion.

Sandy soils attain higher temperatures and retain heat longer than clayey soils under similar fuel, moisture, and weather conditions. From this standpoint, it is desirable to locate campgrounds (15) in an area with loam or clay-loam soil. Sandy soils are less susceptible to compaction damage, however, and are more desirable for camp-grounds from this standpoint.

A water-repellent layer can be created in a (20) soil by the heat from the campfire. This condi-tion was noted only in sandy soils where the temperature remained below 350 degrees C during the campfire burn. Campfires often pro-duce temperatures above this level. By compari- (25) son, forest fires are a shorter-duration event, and soil temperatures produced are more likely to create water repellency-inducing conditions. The greater areal extent of forest fires makes them a more serious threat than campfires in terms of (30) causing soil water repellency.

If the soil remained moist for the duration of the campfire, the increased heat capacity of the soil and heat of water vaporization kept the soil

Line (to right of "altered to")

Go on to next page

(35) temperature below 100 degrees C. At this temperature, little loss of organic matter occurred, and no water repellency was created. For areas where the soil remains very moist, campfires probably have little effect on the soil properties.

(40) Study has shown that softwood fuels burn faster and produce less heat flow into the soil than do hardwood fuels under the same conditions. Elm and mesquite were the hottest burning and longest lasting fuels tested. In areas

(45) where some choice of fuels is available, the use of softwood fuels should be encouraged in an effort to minimize the effect of campfires on soil properties.

The effects of campfires on the soil in a

(50) campground can be lessened by restricting the fire site to the same area, even if permanent concrete fireplaces are not installed. In this manner, any harmful effects are restricted to a minimum area. If users are allowed to start campfires any-

(55) where, the harmful effects tend to be spread over a larger part of the campground. The placement of a stone fire ring in the chosen location is one way to accomplish the objective.

These data support the decision to install

(60) permanent fireplaces in many areas and to restrict the use of campfires elsewhere in the park. This eliminates the harmful effects of campfires on the soil and allows the campground to be located on sandy soil with low compactibil-

(65) ity and good drainage.

6. The primary purpose for this passage is to discuss

(A) the dangers of campfires.

(B) soils of america.

(C) dousing campfires with soil.

(D) the best woods to use in campfires to protect soil.

(E) how campfire heat affects soil.

7. It can be inferred from the passage that campfire users generally

(A) evaluate the amount of soil damage that can result before they build a campfire.

(B) are concerned with the possibility that their campfire can cause a forest fire.

(C) have no regard for the biological consequences that result from their campfire.

(D) consider many areas of a campground to be suitable for a campfire.

(E) favor sandy soil over clay-loam soil as a campfire site.

8. Long-lasting campfires are more likely than short-lived ones to

(A) create water repellency-inducing conditions.

(B) maintain soil fertility.

(C) occur with softwood fuels.

(D) restrict damage to the top 1.3 cm of soil.

(E) produce higher soil temperatures.

9. The author suggests that elm and mesquite

I. conduct relatively high heat flow into the soil.

II. should never be used in campfires.

III. can substantially damage the soil if used in campfires.

(A) I only

(B) III only

(C) I and III only

(D) II and III only

(E) I, II, and III

10. The purpose of lines 52–65 is to

(A) demand stringent enforcement of fire safety laws.

(B) support the banning of campfires outside fire rings in public parks.

(C) summarize the effects of campfires on soil properties.

(D) describe means of reducing the harmful effects of campfires.

(E) encourage exploitation of alternative energy sources.

Go on to next page

11. Last year, there was only one fatality among circus performers who did acts on the trapeze or the high wire without the net. There were more than five hundred deaths from skateboarding accidents. Therefore, it is more dangerous to skateboard than to perform without a net on the trapeze or high-wire in a circus.

The absurdity of the conclusion in the preceding material would be best illustrated by which of the following?

(A) comparing the death rates as percentages of all skateboarders versus all circus performers on the trapeze or high wire

(B) graphing the history of the number of deaths from circus acts versus the number of deaths from skateboarding over a longer period, such as 10 years

(C) identifying more specifically the causes of the deaths: lack of qualification for the task, equipment failure, outside forces, and so on

(D) counting severe injuries as well as deaths from the two activities

(E) comparing the age groups of the average trapeze or high wire artist to the age group of the average skateboarder and finding the number of deaths as a percentage of that age group

12. Obstetricians report that only 10% of the deliveries that they attend are by way of Caesarian section whereas more than 40% of obstetrician-assisted deliveries were via Caesarian section fifty years ago. These statistics, however, may not be used as evidence that the rate of delivery by Caesarian section has decreased over the past fifty years because - - - - - - -.

(A) many non-Caesarian births fifty years ago, unlike today, took place without the aid of an obstetrician

(B) fifty years ago, many Caesarian deliveries were performed by physicians not specialized to practice obstetrics

(C) a greater percentage of the Caesarian deliveries today are deemed medically necessary

(D) the definition of what constitutes a Caesarian delivery has not changed over the past fifty years

(E) a greater percentage of births take place in hospitals today than fifty years ago

13. A school district with particularly low test scores found that those students who scored the lowest were those who were habitually truant. To raise test scores, the district implemented a strict attendance policy, which greatly decreased the number of truancies. Nevertheless, one year after the attendance policy had been in effect, district scores were the lowest ever.

Which of the following, if true, best reconciles the seeming discrepancy described above?

(A) Over half the students in the district had been truant at least once during the school year, and only a small percentage of these students were not considered habitually truant.

(B) The strict attendance policy also reduced the number of district-approved absences.

(C) The majority of the district's students are from poor neighborhoods, and children from such neighborhoods are generally absent more often than are children from wealthier areas.

(D) The students who had been truant were unmotivated to learn while in school and when these students attended school, they interfered with other students' attempts to learn.

(E) At the same time the district implemented its attendance policy, it also took several steps to improve campus and classroom discipline.

Go on to next page

14. The simplicity of the exam enabling the students to complete it early and double-check their work for careless mistakes.

   (A) The simplicity of the exam enabling the students to complete it early and double-check their work for careless mistakes.

   (B) The simplicity of the exam, enabling the students' completing it early and double-checking their work for careless mistakes.

   (C) The simplicity of the exam enabled the students to complete it early, and double-checking their work for careless mistakes.

   (D) The simplicity of the exam enabled the students to complete it early and double-check their exam for careless mistakes.

   (E) The simplicity of double-checking their exams for careless mistakes enabled the students to finish early.

15. By the time that my friend will have come to the Saturday afternoon beach cleanup, all the hard work will have been done already.

   (A) By the time that my friend will have come to the Saturday afternoon beach cleanup, all the hard work will have been done already.

   (B) By the time my friend comes to the Saturday afternoon beach cleanup, all the hard work will have been done.

   (C) By the time my friend came to the Saturday afternoon beach cleanup, all the hard work will have been done.

   (D) By the time my friend is coming to the Saturday afternoon beach cleanup, all the hard work will have been done.

   (E) By the time my friend, coming to the Saturday afternoon beach cleanup, all the hard work will be done.

16. Even though the average citizen rarely uses more than just a fraction of their brain cells is no reason for us not to continue studying and learning throughout our lives.

   (A) Even though the average citizen rarely uses more than just a fraction of their brain cells is no reason for us not to continue studying and learning throughout our lives.

   (B) Even though the average citizen rarely uses more than just a fraction of his brain cells, he has no reason not to continue studying and learning throughout his life.

   (C) Because the average citizen rarely uses more than just a fraction of their brain cells, that is no reason for him not to continue studying and learning throughout his life.

   (D) Although using rarely more than a fraction of their brain cells, the average citizen cannot reasonably continue studying and learning throughout their lives.

   (E) While not using more than a fraction of his brain cells, the average citizen, reasonably, should continue studying and learning throughout his life.

17. It's fascinating to see how the data the scientists collected is opening new possibilities of alternative medicines that heretofore had been scoffed at by practitioners of traditional medicine.

   (A) It's fascinating to see how the data the scientists collected is opening

   (B) Its fascinating to see how the data the scientists collected is opening

   (C) Its fascinating to see how the data, collected by the scientists, is opening

   (D) It's fascinating to see how the data collected by the scientists are opening

   (E) Its fascinating to see how the data collected by the scientists are opening

Go on to next page

A topographic map tells you where things are and how to get to them. These maps describe the shape of the land. They define and locate natural and manmade features like wood-
(05) lands, waterways, important buildings, and bridges. They show the distance between any two places, and they also show the direction from one point to another.

Distances and directions take a bit of figur-
(10) ing, but the topography and features of the land are easy to determine. The topography is shown by contours. These are imaginary lines that follow the ground surface at a constant eleva-tion; they are usually printed in brown, in two
(15) thicknesses. The heavier lines are called index contours and are usually marked with numbers, which give the height in feet or meters. The con-tour interval, a set difference in elevation between the brown lines, varies from map to
(20) map; its value is given in the margin of each map. Natural and manmade figures are represented by colored areas and by a set of standard symbols on all U.S. Geological Survey topographic maps.

A convenient way of representing map dis-
(25) tance is by a graphic scale. Most Survey topo-graphic maps have a scale, or scales, in the margin, such as 1:24,000 or 1:62,500. To use these scales, select the one that matches the scale of the map you are using. Distance is measured
(30) between points on the map by aligning the scale with 0 on one point and the scale bar extending toward the other point. If these points are close enough to each other, you can read the number of feet or miles between them on the scale. If
(35) they are too far apart for that, put a strip of plain paper down on your map, and mark the strip where it touches the two points. Then match this marked strip with the appropriate scale printed in the margin of the map and figure the distance
(40) from a series of comparisons with the scale. Read the distance on a curving road or fence line the same way. Mark a strip of plain paper at the ends of relatively straight stretches of road or fence, and then compare the marked strip with
(45) the scale.

To determine the direction, or bearing, from one point to another, you need a compass as well as a map. Most compasses are marked with the four cardinal points — north, east, south, and
(50) west — but some are marked additionally with the number of degrees in a circle (360 degrees: north is 0 degrees or 360 degrees; east is 90 degrees; south is 180 degrees; and west is 270 degrees). Both kinds are easy to use with a little
(55) practice.

One thing to remember is that a compass does not really point north — not true north, except by coincidence in some areas. The com-pass needle is attracted by magnetic force, which varies in different parts of the world and (60) is constantly changing. When you read north on a compass, you're really reading the direction of the magnetic north pole.

18. With which of the following would the author most likely agree?

(A) Map reading is a technique that requires years of study.

(B) Topography is easier to master than distance calculation on a map.

(C) The U.S. Geological Service maps are outdated too quickly and should be upgraded more frequently.

(D) It is easier to read a map if you use a compass at the same time.

(E) It is imperative to determine magnetic north before beginning to read a map.

19. The author of the passage probably expects her audience to be which of the following?

(A) professional cartographers

(B) students

(C) professors

(D) surveyors

(E) hunters

20. The primary concern of the passage is to

(A) compare and contrast topographical and other types of maps.

(B) lament the fact that few people know how to interpret topographical maps.

(C) discuss topographical maps and how to use them.

(D) deride topographical maps and those who use them.

(E) urge that classes in topographical map reading be made mandatory in schools.

Go on to next page

21. Many fans would agree that Alice Walker is one of the most insightful writers <u>who ever put</u> pen to paper, or fingers to keyboard.

    (A) who ever put

    (B) that ever put

    (C) which ever put

    (D) ever putting

    (E) whoever put

22. Voters each year give interviews in which they say they are <u>repulsed by what they see as the lack of integrity of the candidates, unhappy with mud-slinging politics, and complain about the paucity of choices.</u>

    (A) repulsed by what they see as the lack of integrity of the candidates, unhappy with mud-slinging politics, and complain about the paucity of choices.

    (B) repulsed by what they see as the lack of integrity of the candidates, unhappy with mud-slinging politics, and dissatisfied with the paucity of choices.

    (C) repulsing what they see as the lack of integrity of the candidates, unhappy with mud-slinging politics, and complaining about the paucity of choices.

    (D) repulsing what they see as the lack of integrity of the candidates, unhappy with mud-slinging politics and the paucity of choices.

    (E) repulsed, unhappy, and complaining about what they see as the lack of integrity of the candidates, mud-slinging politics, and the paucity of choices.

23. <u>If the contestant would have known the answer</u> to the last question on the quiz show, she would have won over twenty thousand dollars and been able to go back to school and finish her degree without having to work part-time to earn the tuition money.

    (A) If the contestant would have known the answer

    (B) If the contestant answered

    (C) If the contestant, knowing the answer,

    (D) The contestant, had she known the answer

    (E) Had the contestant known the answer

24. Photo lab customer: I have two, developed rolls of film here, and you are charging me double for one of them because you used a more expensive process to develop it. I did not request the more expensive process when I dropped off the film; therefore, I should not have to pay double for it.

    Photo lab clerk: We are entirely justified in charging you double for the roll because you ordered double prints.

    The clerk's response depends logically on which of the following assumptions?

    (A) The more expensive process costs twice as much as the other process.

    (B) The photo lab is responsible for any costs associated with mistakes on its part.

    (C) The customer actually requested the more expensive process.

    (D) Double prints cost less than twice as much as single prints.

    (E) The customer did not order double prints on the less-expensive roll.

25. Cancer is more deadly now than it was 100 years ago. In 1895, only 5 percent of all deaths were caused by cancer, whereas cancer is responsible for 25 percent of all deaths today.

    Which of the following most weakens the argument?

    (A) More money is spent on cancer research now than was spent 100 years ago.

    (B) Immunizations and other health care measures protect humans from non-cancer diseases that were fatal 100 years ago.

    (C) Heart disease causes a higher percentage of deaths now than it did 10 years ago.

    (D) New technologies produce many cancer-causing agents.

    (E) Modern medicine alleviates the pain that cancer patients endure.

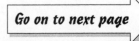*Go on to next page*

26. <u>Because her second exam had fewer mistakes on it than the first,</u> the student was allowed to progress to the next level of class, even though it was clear she had not yet fully mastered all the aspects of the subject.

    (A) Because her second exam had fewer mistakes on it than the first,

    (B) Because her second exam had less mistakes on it than did her first,

    (C) Because her second exam, with fewer mistakes on it than her first,

    (D) Her second exam had less mistakes on it than her first, because

    (E) With making less mistakes on her second exam than on her first,

27. A few years ago, clouded leopards <u>were disappearing just about so fast, or even faster than, they had</u> in their recorded history, making their survival problematic.

    (A) were disappearing just about so fast, or even faster than, they had

    (B) were disappearing just about as fast as, or even faster than, they had

    (C) disappeared as fast than they had

    (D) disappeared, fast and faster than, they had

    (E) disappeared (fast), and they had

Sulfur dioxide, a colorless and odorless gas in typical outdoor concentrations, is formed naturally through biological decay and volcanic eruptions. Sulfur dioxide becomes most dangerous to people when, clinging to small particulates, it is carried into the lungs. (05)

Particulates have both natural and man-made sources. Natural sources include the sea, volcanoes, forest fires, and wind blown silt. Important man-made sources include incinerators, manufacturing and industrial processes, fossil-fueled power plants, mining and materials processing, the internal combustion engine, and agricultural activities. (10)

The health effects of particulates depend on their size and composition. The larger particulates are usually filtered out in the nose and throat and rapidly cleared from the body. Smaller particles may be carried deeper into the lungs. Particles reaching sensitive deep lung areas are considered relatively more important for health purposes. (15) (20)

Acid rain, or more accurately, acidic deposition (which refers to both wet and dry deposition of acidifying compounds), is one of the most controversial and important environmental issues of the day. (25)

The principal causes of high rainfall acidity are sulfuric, nitric, and hydrochloric acids. The major manmade sources of pollutants that cause these acids are fossil-fueled utility and industrial boilers and the internal combustion engine. Proposed efforts to control man's contributions to acid rain concentrate on controlling these acidifying pollutants, especially sulfur dioxide. (30) (35)

Acidity is measured using a logarithmic scale of 0 to 14 called the pH scale. On this scale, a neutral substance has a pH of 7. An acidic substance, like vinegar, has a pH value less than 7. An alkaline or basic substance, like baking soda, has a pH value greater than 7. Theoretically, pure rainfall has a pH of 5.6 and is acidic because the water has combined with carbon dioxide in the air to form weak carbonic acid. Rain with a lower pH than 5.6 is called acid rain. Recent evidence suggests that natural rain (in the absence of manmade pollution) is several times more acidic than previously thought. In several remote areas of the globe, rainfall pHs of 4.5 to 5.0 are routinely encountered. Some scientists suggest that these low pH values indicate the global extent of the acid rain problem. (40) (45) (50)

Clearly something must be done. It would be unwise to investigate every aspect of acid rain before action is taken. (55)

Go on to next page

28. According to the passage, the dangers of sulfur dioxide are increased when

    (A) people participate in arduous exercise, like marathons.

    (B) pollution laws are rescinded.

    (C) particulates carry it into the lungs.

    (D) acid rain increases.

    (E) drought conditions exist for extended periods of time.

29. In his discussion of sulfur dioxide, particulates, and acid rain, the author describes

    (A) the solution to the problem.

    (B) the leading scientists working on the problem.

    (C) the economic repercussions of the problem.

    (D) the sources of the problem.

    (E) the number of deaths attributable to the problem.

30. Which of the following would be the best title for the passage?

    (A) Sulfur Dioxide: The Silent Killer

    (B) The Effects of Sulfur Dioxide and Acid Rain

    (C) How Chemistry Is Destroying Our Universe

    (D) The Benefits of Clean Air

    (E) Why New Stronger Anti-Pollution Laws Are Needed

31. By stating in lines 50–52 that "some scientists suggest that these low pH values indicate the global extent of the acid rain problem," the author

    (A) indicates there may be disagreement on the point.

    (B) denigrates as scaremongers those scientists who are attempting to frighten us.

    (C) lampoons the scientists who claim acid rain is a theory, not a fact.

    (D) predicts that global warming is finally coming under control.

    (E) proves that global warming is the most serious consequence of acid rain.

32. The next paragraph of this passage would most likely discuss which of the following?

    (A) the steps to take to decrease acid rain

    (B) the importance of swift action to work on the problems

    (C) the economic difficulties in implementing acid rain controls

    (D) the programs that have already been attempted and have failed to decrease acid rain

    (E) the folly of being too hasty in enacting stringent antipollution laws

33. <u>Being that</u> under 30 percent of the population, on average, votes in any given election, politicians have learned to target their political policies to that vocal minority.

    (A) Being that

    (B) Due to

    (C) Despite the fact that

    (D) Because

    (E) In spite of the fact that

34. <u>The first-time father claimed that, of all the babies in the nursery, his was the most perfect, beaming with pride.</u>

    (A) The first-time father, claimed that, of all the babies in the nursery, his was the most perfect, beaming with pride.

    (B) The first-time father, beaming with pride, claimed that of all the babies in the nursery, his was the most perfect.

    (C) The first-time father, claiming that his baby was the most perfect of all the babies in the nursery, beaming with pride.

    (D) The first-time father, beaming with pride, claimed that his baby in the nursery was perfect.

    (E) The first-time father and his perfect baby in the nursery, beaming with pride.

Go on to next page

35. When the television commentator finished giving what he had hoped would be a provocative report, he was extremely disappointed that neither the station's editors <u>nor the public were</u> calling to complain.

    (A) nor the public were

    (B) or the public were

    (C) or the public was

    (D) nor the public was

    (E) nor the public would be

36. Parents and other citizens across the country frequently criticize schools for not doing their job. Most notably, they blame schools for low student achievement scores. Surprisingly, the most frequent and vociferous complaints come from those who live in districts where the achievement scores are high.

    All of the following, considered individually, help to explain the apparent paradox EXCEPT

    (A) Parents from districts of high achievers are very involved with the schools and are therefore more likely to make critical comments.

    (B) Parents and other citizens have no knowledge of their district's own scores.

    (C) High scores cause parents' expectations to rise, leading parents to demand that students achieve even more.

    (D) High-scoring districts contain low-achieving students whose parents are very likely to complain when they observe that their children's scores do not match those of children who live nearby.

    (E) Most complaints about schools come from political activists, most of whom live in high-achieving districts.

37. You will not take Economics 101C unless you took Economics 101B. You will take Economics 101B only if you took Economics 101A.

    If the statements above are true, which of the following must also be true?

    (A) You are taking Economics 101C, so you took Economics 101A.

    (B) You took Economics 101A, so you will take Economics 101B.

    (C) Other than Economics 101A, there are no requirements to take Economics 101B.

    (D) If you take Economics 101A and 101B, you will take Economics 101C.

    (E) Economics 101B is a prerequisite only for Economics 101C.

38. When the philogynist was forced <u>to choose between Kerry and I,</u> he disappointed me by choosing Kerry, saying it was time to promote a woman into the executive ranks.

    (A) to choose between Kerry and I,

    (B) to choose among Kerry and I,

    (C) to choose between Kerry and me,

    (D) to choose among Kerry and me,

    (E) to choose I or Kerry,

39. The hospital nurse told the patient that <u>laying</u> in bed without moving, he might get bed sores, and volunteered to help him turn if doing so were difficult for him.

    (A) laying

    (B) if he laid

    (C) if he layed

    (D) if he lyed

    (E) if he lies

Go on to next page

40. The sailor telephoned his wife from aboard ship <u>and said that hopefully his deployment would end soon</u> and he could return home.

    (A) and said that hopefully his deployment would end soon

    (B) saying that hopefully his deployment would end soon

    (C) to say that hopefully his deployment would end soon

    (D) and said that he hoped his deployment would end soon

    (E) and was saying that he hoped his deployment would end soon

41. Census undercounts are most pronounced in areas in which people are unlikely to receive, read or respond to their mail, the method by which most American citizens are counted. In an attempt to obtain more accurate counts in such areas, census bureau officials will count residents at monthly meetings at local elementary schools and will publicize these meetings in community newspapers.

    Which of the following, if true, casts the most doubt on the effectiveness of the plan described above?

    (A) The citizens who attend monthly meetings at local elementary schools are usually incapable of solving community problems.

    (B) People who are counted in the census will not necessarily fully participate in American democracy.

    (C) The newspapers are delivered to everybody in the communities, including those who mail in their census responses.

    (D) The census undercount is greater among senior citizens than among families with schoolchildren.

    (E) People who are unlikely to use the mail for the census are also unlikely to read the newspaper and attend a meeting.

Section 2

Time: 75 minutes

37 questions

Directions: Following each Data Sufficiency question are two numbered statements. Determine whether the information given in the statements is sufficient to answer the question. Choose

(A) if statement 1 alone is sufficient to answer the question, but statement 2 alone is not sufficient to answer the question.

(B) if statement 2 alone is sufficient to answer the question, but statement 1 alone is not sufficient to answer the question.

(C) if both statements are needed to answer the question, but neither statement alone is sufficient to answer the question.

(D) if either statement 1 alone or statement 2 alone is sufficient to answer the question.

(E) if neither statement 1 alone nor statement 2 alone nor both statements together give enough information to answer the question.

Information:

1. Unless the problem specifically states otherwise, all figures lie in a plane.

2. Angles measure more than zero.

3. Lines that appear to be straight are straight.

4. A figure will follow information given in the question stem but will not necessarily follow additional information given in statement 1 or statement 2.

5. Angles and points are in the order shown.

6. All numbers used in this section are real numbers.

7. If more than one value for a quantity is possible, the data given in the statements may not be sufficient to determine the value of a quantity.

Example:

$3x + y = 25$. What is the value of x?

   (1) $25 - y = 15$

   (2) $2y^2 = 200$

Statement 1 alone is sufficient to answer the question. If $25 - y = 15$, then $y = 10$. Plug 10 back into the original equation and solve for x. First $3x + 10 = 25$. Then $3x = 15$. Finally, $x = 5$.

Statement 2 alone is not sufficient to answer the question. If $2y^2 = 200$ and $y^2 = 100$, $y = \pm 10$. Plug 10 back into the original equation and solve for x. First, $3x + 10 = 25$. Then $3x = 15$. Finally, $x = 5$. But if $y = -10$, then $x = {}^{35}\!/_3$.

Because statement 1 alone is sufficient and statement 2 alone is not sufficient to answer the question, the answer is A. *Correct Answer:* A

For each problem-solving question, solve the problem and then choose the correct answer from the choices given. You may use the exam booklet for scratchwork.

Notes:

- All numbers used in this exam are real numbers.

- All figures lie in a plane.

Go on to next page

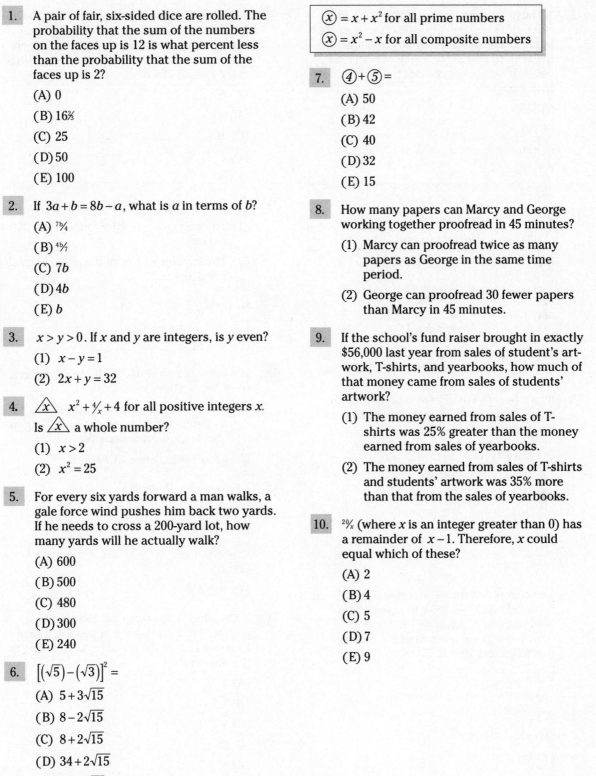

1. A pair of fair, six-sided dice are rolled. The probability that the sum of the numbers on the faces up is 12 is what percent less than the probability that the sum of the faces up is 2?

   (A) 0

   (B) 16⅔

   (C) 25

   (D) 50

   (E) 100

2. If $3a + b = 8b - a$, what is a in terms of b?

   (A) $7\tfrac{b}{4}$

   (B) $4\tfrac{b}{7}$

   (C) $7b$

   (D) $4b$

   (E) b

3. $x > y > 0$. If x and y are integers, is y even?

   (1) $x - y = 1$

   (2) $2x + y = 32$

4. $\triangle\!\!x\!\!\triangle$ $x^2 + \tfrac{4}{x} + 4$ for all positive integers x. Is $\triangle\!\!x\!\!\triangle$ a whole number?

   (1) $x > 2$

   (2) $x^2 = 25$

5. For every six yards forward a man walks, a gale force wind pushes him back two yards. If he needs to cross a 200-yard lot, how many yards will he actually walk?

   (A) 600

   (B) 500

   (C) 480

   (D) 300

   (E) 240

6. $\left[\left(\sqrt{5}\right) - \left(\sqrt{3}\right)\right]^2 =$

   (A) $5 + 3\sqrt{15}$

   (B) $8 - 2\sqrt{15}$

   (C) $8 + 2\sqrt{15}$

   (D) $34 + 2\sqrt{15}$

   (E) $34 - \sqrt{15}$

$$\textcircled{x} = x + x^2 \text{ for all prime numbers}$$
$$\textcircled{x} = x^2 - x \text{ for all composite numbers}$$

7. $\textcircled{4} + \textcircled{5} =$

   (A) 50

   (B) 42

   (C) 40

   (D) 32

   (E) 15

8. How many papers can Marcy and George working together proofread in 45 minutes?

   (1) Marcy can proofread twice as many papers as George in the same time period.

   (2) George can proofread 30 fewer papers than Marcy in 45 minutes.

9. If the school's fund raiser brought in exactly $56,000 last year from sales of student's artwork, T-shirts, and yearbooks, how much of that money came from sales of students' artwork?

   (1) The money earned from sales of T-shirts was 25% greater than the money earned from sales of yearbooks.

   (2) The money earned from sales of T-shirts and students' artwork was 35% more than that from the sales of yearbooks.

10. $\tfrac{20}{x}$ (where x is an integer greater than 0) has a remainder of $x - 1$. Therefore, x could equal which of these?

    (A) 2

    (B) 4

    (C) 5

    (D) 7

    (E) 9

Go on to next page ⟹

11. Jill buys 16 cookies, Kent buys 12 cookies, and Catharine buys x cookies. The average number of cookies the three bought is between 19 and 23, inclusive. What is the smallest number of cookies Catharine could have bought?

    (A) 35

    (B) 31

    (C) 30

    (D) 29

    (E) 28

12. What is the perimeter of triangle ABC?

    (1) Triangle ABC is isosceles.

    (2) The radius of the circle is 5.

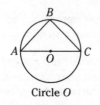

Circle O

13. If four pencils cost x cents and nine pens cost y cents, what is the cost of one pencil and three pens?

    (A) $\dfrac{3x+4y}{12}$

    (B) $\dfrac{4x+3y}{12}$

    (C) $12xy$

    (D) $\frac{1}{12}xy$

    (E) $\frac{1}{4}x+y$

14. The cost of a textbook increased by 25% from 1998–1999. In 2000, the cost of the textbook was ¼ below its 1998 cost. By what percent did the cost of the textbook decrease from 1999 to 2000?

    (A) 0

    (B) 20

    (C) 25

    (D) 40

    (E) 75

15. Set A has six terms, beginning with 1. Each term subtracts half of the preceding term. Set B has six terms, beginning with 1. Each term adds double the preceding term. What is the sum of $A+B$?

    (A) 63½₂

    (B) 60⅔₂

    (C) 10½₂

    (D) 2

    (E) ½₂

16. How many sides are there in the polygon?

    (1) The polygon's exterior angles total 360 degrees.

    (2) The interior angles of the polygon total 900 degrees.

17. Is $x>0$?

    (1) $x^2+yx+24=0$

    (2) $y=10$

18. How far is a round trip to the grocery store from Ms. DeFilio's home?

    (1) Ms. DeFilio leaves home at 9:00 a.m. and arrives to the grocery store 20 minutes later, driving nonstop.

    (2) Ms. DeFilio drives at 30 mph.

19. $\boxed{x} = x^2+2$, then $\boxed{4}$

    (A) 16

    (B) 18

    (C) 324

    (D) 326

    (E) 106,278

20. If a machine can stamp out 15 metal parts per second, how many minutes will it take to stamp out 36,000 metal parts (working at this same rate)?

    (A) 9

    (B) 3.5

    (C) 4

    (D) 35

    (E) 40

Go on to next page

21. From the beginning to the end of 1990, the price of a rare book rose 20 percent. In 1991, it dropped 25 percent. In 1992, it rose 20 percent. What percent of 1990's starting price is 1992's price?

    (A) 80

    (B) 90

    (C) 95

    (D) 100

    (E) 108

22. Is $\dfrac{x^4 \times x^7}{x^4} > 1$?

    (1) $x > 0$

    (2) x is a whole number.

23. Georgia buys q quarts of milk at d dollars per quart and b boxes of cereal at $d+1$ dollars per box. Which of the following expressions represents the total amount spent?

    (A) $qd + bd + 1$

    (B) $(q+b)\ (d+1)$

    (C) $(q+b)\ (2d+1)$

    (D) $d(q+b) + b$

    (E) $bd\ (q+b)$

24. Hakeem takes seven exams for the semester. His semester grade is 80. If his first five exam scores were 75, 69, 81, 90, and 73, what was his average score for the last two exams?

    (A) 78

    (B) 81

    (C) 82

    (D) 86

    (E) 65

25. It takes three painters ten hours to paint four rooms. How many hours would it take nine painters to paint twelve rooms?

    (A) 1⅓

    (B) 3⅓

    (C) 6

    (D) 10

    (E) 30

26. Rachel and Shayna are looking at a shelf of 84 books at the library. The difference between the number of books that they look at and put back and the number of books that they look at and check out is 20. How many books did they put back? (They put back more books than they checked out.)

    (A) 24

    (B) 32

    (C) 35

    (D) 52

    (E) 64

27. What is $x + y$?

    (1) x and y are the degree measures of two angles in an isosceles triangle.

    (2) $x = 2y$

28. What is $a + b$?

    (1) $a^2 + b^2 = 125$

    (2) $a^2 - b^2 = -75$

29. In the figure below, if the diameter of the circle is 10, then the area of the shaded portion of the square is

    (A) $100 - 25\pi$

    (B) $100 - 10\pi$

    (C) $40 - 25\pi$

    (D) $40 - 10\pi$

    (E) It cannot be determined from the information given.

    d=10

30. Michael traveled 40 percent of the distance of his trip alone, went another 20 miles with Cameron, and then finished the last half of the trip alone. How many miles long was the trip?

    (A) 240

    (B) 200

    (C) 160

    (D) 100

    (E) 50

Go on to next page

31. A salesman makes a commission of $1.50 per shirt sold and $2.50 per pair of pants sold. In one pay period, he sold ten more shirts than pairs of pants. If his total commission for the pay period were $215, what was the total number of shirts and pairs of pants he sold?

(A) 40

(B) 50

(C) 60

(D) 110

(E) 150

32. In the figure below, what is the area of the shaded portion of square *ABCD?*

(1) The area of circle *O* is 36π.

(2) The circumference of circle *O* is 12π.

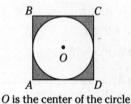

O is the center of the circle

33. The average of *x, y,* and *z* is one-third greater than *x.* The sum $y + z$ is what percent greater than *x*?

(A) 50

(B) 100

(C) 200

(D) 300

(E) 400

34. A plane flies from Los Angeles to New York at 600 miles per hour and returns along the same route at 400 miles per hour. What is the average (arithmetic mean) flying speed for the entire route?

(A) 460 mph

(B) 480 mph

(C) 500 mph

(D) 540 mph

(E) It cannot be determined from the information given.

35. Is $\frac{1}{x} > 1$?

(1) $0 < x < 1$

(2) $\frac{x}{1} = \frac{x}{4}\left(\frac{1}{x}\right)$

36. Is $a > b$? (*a, b* are integers)

(1) $a^2 > b^2$

(2) $a^3 > b^3$

37. Two cans of equal height are wrapped with labels. The ends of the labels on each can just touch with no overlap. The label for the large can is 10 cm high and 8 cm wide. The label for the small can is 10 cm high and 4 cm wide. What is the ratio of the volume of the large can to the volume of the small can? (Volume of a cylinder $= \pi r^2 h$)

(A) 1:2

(B) 2:1

(C) 4:1

(D) 6:1

(E) 8:1

STOP You may check your work on this section only. Do not go on to the next section until you are told to do so.

Section 3

Time: 30 minutes

One essay

Directions: Present and explain your view on the following issue. While there is no one right or wrong answer to the question, be sure to consider various points of view as you explain the reasons behind your own perspective.

"Many people believe affirmative action programs should be a permanent part of our hiring system. They don't realize that the goals of affirmative action programs have been met and that the needs of minorities (for whom the affirmative action programs were first developed) would be better served by eliminating quotas and allowing the hiring market to regulate itself."

Which point of view do you agree with — that affirmative action programs should be permanent or that they should be abolished? Justify your position using examples from your personal or professional experience, reading, or general observation.

Section 4

30 minutes

One essay

Directions: Critique the following argument. Identify evidence that will strengthen or weaken the argument, point out assumptions underlying the argument, and offer counterexamples to the argument.

The following statements were part of a speech made to a group of school administrators.

"The government cannot run a school as well as a private corporation, motivated by profit to work efficiently, can. Students of all ages will be better served by schools that are held accountable to stockholders to show results. Private schools in the Midwest, run as part of an experiment, have resulted in reading score increases of as much as 10%."

Discuss your point of view on the above argument. Analyze the evidence used as well as the general reasoning. Present points that would strengthen the argument or make it more compelling.

Answer Key for Practice Exam 1

Section 1
Verbal Section

1. E	26. A
2. B	27. B
3. D	28. C
4. A	29. D
5. B	30. B
6. E	31. A
7. D	32. B
8. E	33. D
9. C	34. D
10. D	35. D
11. A	36. B
12. A	37. A
13. D	38. C
14. D	39. E
15. B	40. D
16. B	41. E
17. D	
18. B	
19. B	
20. C	
21. A	
22. B	
23. E	
24. E	
25. B	

Section 2
Math Section

1. A	20. E
2. A	21. E
3. B	22. E
4. B	23. D
5. D	24. D
6. B	25. D
7. B	26. D
8. C	27. E
9. C	28. E
10. D	29. A
11. D	30. B
12. C	31. D
13. A	32. D
14. D	33. C
15. A	34. B
16. B	35. D
17. C	36. B
18. C	37. C
19. D	

Scoring

Here's the way GMAT questions are scored:

✔ You get one point for each question you answer correctly.
✔ You get zero points for each incorrect answer.

To determine your Verbal and Math converted scores, complete Worksheet 18-1 by following these steps:

1. **If you have not already done so, compare your answers with the preceding answer key and mark each correct answer with a plus or star and circle each incorrect answer.**
2. **Add the number of verbal questions correct. This is your raw verbal score.**
3. **Add the number of math questions correct. This is your raw math score.**
4. **Add your raw verbal score and your raw math score. This is your raw total score.**

Note: Return to Chapter 9 to review how schools use the Writing Assessment scores.

Worksheet 18-1	GMAT Scaled (Converted) Scoring Worksheet	
	Verbal	*Math*
Correct answers	_____	_____

Table 18-1	GMAT Scaled (Converted) Scoring Chart		
Raw Verbal Score	**GMAT Verbal**	**Raw Math Score**	**GMAT Math**
41	60		
40	59		
39	58		
38	56		
37	55	37	60
36	53	36	58
35	51	35	57
34	50	34	55
33	48	33	54
32	47	32	51
31	45	31	50
30	44	30	48
29	42	29	47
28	41	28	45
27	39	27	43
26	38	26	42
25	36	25	40
24	35	24	38
23	33	23	37
22	32	22	35
21	31	21	33
20	29	20	31
19	28	19	30
18	26	18	28
17	25	17	27
16	23	16	25
15	22	15	23
14	20	14	21
13	19	13	20
12	17	12	18
11	16	11	17
10	14	10	15
9	13	9	14
8	12	8	12
7	10	7	10
6	9	6	8
5	7	5	6
4	6	4	5
3	5	3	4
2	3	2	2
1	1	1	1
0	0	0	0

Find your converted scores for both Verbal and Math in Table 18-1. Add them together and use that sum to find your converted total score in Table 18-2.

These charts are a *very* rough estimate. Your actual score is determined by the difficulty level of the questions you personally encounter. The test is adaptive for each test taker. (Return to Chapter 1 for a more complete explanation of scoring the CAT.)

Table 18-2	GMAT Total Scaled (Converted) Scoring Chart		
Raw Score	*GMAT Total Score*	*Raw Score*	*GMAT Total Score*
78	800	39	490
77	790	38	480
76	780	37-36	470
75	770	35	460
74	760	34	450
73	750	33-32	440
72	740	31	430
71-70	730	30	420
69	720	29-28	410
68	710	27	400
67-66	700	26	390
65	690	25-24	380
64	680	23	370
63-62	670	22	360
61	660	21-20	350
60	650	19	340
59	640	18	330
58-57	630	17-16	320
56	620	15	310
55	610	14	300
54	600	13-12	290
53-52	590	11	280
51	580	10	270
50	570	9-8	260
49-48	560	7	250
47	550	6	240
46	540	5-4	230
45-44	530	3	220
43	520	2	210
42	510	1-0	200
41-40	500		

Chapter 19

Practice Exam 1: Answers and Explanations

• •

Section 1

1. **E.** Look for a choice that connects investment in product delivery with company success. Choice E is the only answer that makes this connection. In fact, choice E is the only answer that even includes both terms.

   Choice A defines market share but makes no attempt to demonstrate that the company will increase its fraction of the market revenue with its new strategy. Choice B provides some evidence that the company has made a sound financial decision (because it will save on costs), but the scope of the argument has to do with bringing in more money, not spending less of it. Choice C is not compelling because the company has not followed the consultants' advice. In addition, choice C is too vague. Just because other companies have succeeded after hiring the consultants does not provide much assurance that this company will succeed. Choice C needs to include some details before one can evaluate whether those other cases are relevant to this one. Choice D shows another way that the company can succeed, but the issue here is whether the money put into product delivery will lead to increased market share.

2. **B.** The question uncompromisingly states that no true artist would do what Pierre has just done; therefore, Pierre must not be a true artist. To put this into A – B form: No A does B. Pierre does B; therefore, Pierre is not A.

   Choice A argues against the basic premise of the statement, which you cannot do. The question says that you are to assume the above statement to be true. In other words, you can't rewrite the author's opinion; if he thinks landscapes are plebeian, you have to accept that as true.

   Choice C at first glance looks good because it mentions integrity, which is mentioned in the question. However, the answer is exactly the opposite of what you'd want. If Pierre has a lot of integrity, he would not compromise it by painting a landscape. Had the question said that Pierre had little integrity, it would have made more sense. Choice D again argues against the author's definition, which the question stem asks you to believe is true. You can't change the definition given in the question. Choice E adds additional facts and tries to change the definition of plebeian again.

3. **D.** This question tests the difference between *number* and *amount*. *Number* is plural, referring to countable units — like the number of students. *Amount* is singular, referring to a measurable bulk — like the amount of intelligence of the students. Immediately eliminate any answer choices with the word *amount*, choices A and B. Choice C is wrong because it sounds as if the school administrator has registered for the semester. Choice E is a fragment — an incomplete sentence. It does not complete the thought but just leaves you there wondering, "Well? What *about* the school administrator?"

4. **A.** Ask yourself: *What* is alive with vibrant colors? It's the New England countryside, not the tourists. Choices B and D sound as if the tourists are colorful, not the countryside. Choice C is awkward. Choice E changes the meaning, and is awkward.

5. **B.** The correct construction of a comparison is *as . . . as.* It is wrong to say *as . . . that.* You would not, for example, say you were "as happy that a lark" but "as happy as a lark." The rest of the sentence is excellent as is; change only the offending part (if thy pronoun offend thee, cut it off). Choice C is completely awkward when reinserted into the sentence. Choice D may be true, but it changes the meaning of the sentence. Choice E makes it sound as if the computers are mastering the children instead of the children mastering the computers. Things may come to that soon, but let's not rush matters!

6. **E.** The primary purpose of a passage is its main idea, found in the topic sentence (usually the first or last sentence of the passage). Here, the passage is about campfires; choose an answer with that specific word. Doing so eliminates choice B. The passage also discusses soil; look for an answer with that word, eliminating choice A. Choice C was never discussed in the passage. Choice D is a trap. Using softwoods rather than hardwoods was discussed as a means of protecting the soil. However, discussing hardwoods was not the author's purpose, just one fact among many presented. The primary purpose was to discuss something much more general: how campfires affect soil.

Remember the Big Three for a Primary Purpose or Main Idea or Best Title question (same concept, different aliases):

   1. **Use key words from the topic sentence (usually the first sentence).**

   2. **Be general, not specific.**

   3. **Be positive or neutral, not negative.**

7. **D.** The last two paragraphs of the passage urge measures to restrict campfire location. Without such measures, the author claims that campfires will be built just about everywhere and that soil damage will be widespread. It can be inferred from this that campfire users, when left to their own devices, will build a campfire just about anywhere. This leads to choice D as the answer. Because the opposite of choice A appears to be true, eliminate this choice. Choice B is plausible, but there is no mention of a connection between campfire users and forest fires. Forest fires were discussed briefly in paragraph three in relation to water repellency. Choice C goes overboard. There is no information to indicate whether campfire users favor a certain type of soil, eliminating choice E. The scientific findings discussed in paragraph two point to an advantage of one type or the other, but you can't tell whether the campfire users actually consider this evidence.

8. **E.** Common sense suggests that E is the right answer. Paragraph three helps to confirm this. This paragraph mentions that short-lived forest fires are more likely than campfires to create water repellency-inducing conditions (knocking out choice A). This information implies that campfires last longer. Combine this reasoning with the explicit mention that campfires typically exceed 350 degrees and you have your answer. Choice C is directly contradicted by paragraph five. Choices B and D don't make sense. The passage often mentions that heat flow into the soil damages it. A long-lasting campfire will produce more heat flow than will a short-lived one.

While you certainly do not need to have any background knowledge to answer Reading Comprehension questions (all information necessary is given or implied in the passage), don't hesitate to use your common sense, especially with science passages. Common sense is a good place to start, but do be sure to check your "logical" answer with the facts given in the passage.

9. **C.** All the information needed to answer this question comes from the fifth paragraph. The author does not directly state option I but comes close by saying that elm and mesquite are the hottest burning fuels. In addition, the author says that elm and mesquite are long-lasting, suggesting that they are not softwoods, which burn quickly. Because they are not softwoods, elm and mesquite will not be associated with little heat flow into the soil. Statement II goes too far. The author recommends that softwood use be encouraged when there is a choice of wood available. The author would probably permit elm and mesquite use if that was all that was available. Statement III follows from statement I and is consistent with the entire paragraph. Elm and mesquite conduct heat into the soil, which damages it, and as hardwoods, are not the woods of choice. With I and III in and II eliminated, the answer has to be C.

10. **D.** Did you notice that this question is almost the same question as number 6, and very similar to number 8? The questions following reading passages are often very similar, like variations on a theme. Think of them as all spokes emanating from the hub, or the central idea. After you've identified the central idea, the other answers may cover the same territory. Here, the central idea is that campfires have negative effects on soil. The last few paragraphs get very specific on how to reduce that negative impact, via proper fuel selection and using campfire rings.

Choice B looks good at first glance, but it's too dramatic, too strong, and too intense. Lines 56–61 talk about using fire rings but don't say anything about banning fires outside of them. Be sure not to "take the next step," reading too much into a statement. Most passages don't get that demanding.

Answer C is also tricky. If you didn't actually go back and skim over specific lines again, you probably chose this answer. Summarizing the effects of campfires on soil properties was the theme of the *first* half of the passage, not of the second. The second half shifts ideas, from what campfires do to soil, to how to prevent their doing it.

Choice E has a few problems. The author does suggest using softwoods, but is that really "an alternative energy source"? Even if it is, the suggestion isn't the theme of all of lines 48–65, just one paragraph's worth. This answer is too specific for the question. Just because your answer was mentioned in the passage does not mean it's the best answer to this specific question.

11. **A.** The absurd conclusion is that skateboarding is more dangerous than performing on a trapeze or high wire (without a net) in the circus. This conclusion is based on the fact that in one year, more skateboarders died than did trapeze and high wire performers. You can show the writer's conclusion to be flawed (with apologies to circus performers in my reading audience) by showing the number of deaths among those performers as a percentage of all performers versus the number of deaths of skateboarders as a percentage of all skateboarders. If there are, for example, 100 trapeze artists and 3 died, that's a much larger percentage than if there are 10 million skateboarders and 3,000 died.

Choice B addresses the problem of a longer time span but still does not deal with the deaths as a percentage of all involved in the activity. That would be like saying because more people have died in traffic accidents in the past decade than from jumping out of planes without a parachute, riding in a car is more dangerous than jumping out of a plane without wearing a parachute. Choice C does not change the conclusion. The causes for the death rate do not show that it is illogical to conclude that skateboarding is more dangerous than working the trapeze. Choice D is tempting; however, unless it compares the injuries as a percent of those people involved in the activity, you're right back to the original problem. Choice E talks about a percentage but then goes overboard and brings in the age group question. The original conclusion dealt with everyone in the activity as a whole, not people in various age groups.

12. **A.** The statistics at first glance indicate a decrease in Caesarian deliveries, but you should notice a change in scope between the first and second sentences. The first sentence deals with obstetricians involved with deliveries while the second discusses <u>all</u> deliveries. The second statement says that the first sentence does not allow for a definitive conclusion about deliveries in general, and your job is to fill in the reason after the word *because*.

Often, one of the answer choices is the exact opposite of what you want. In this instance, that's Choice B. Choice B actually provides evidence that the Caesarian rate was even higher than reported in the first sentence, suggesting that there is even more of a drop in the Caesarian delivery rate. You want to come up with something that brings up the possibility that the drop wasn't all that great.

Some test takers may be tempted to go with choice C because they may think that the number of medically necessary Caesarians fifty years ago may have been comparable to the number today, but the passage deals with <u>all</u> Caesarians, not subtypes. Choice D supports the notion that the statistics from the two time periods can be readily compared and, if anything, supports the notion that the Caesarian rate has decreased. Remember, your job is to cast doubt on the conclusion that the Caesarian rate has gone down. Choice E is irrelevant because the passage is not concerned with where births in general (or even Caesarians) have taken place.

13. **D.** First, identify the discrepancy. The district saw a relationship between truancies and low scores. It figured that with fewer truancies, there would be fewer low scores and overall scores would go up. The score results were contrary to the district's expectations. You need to find the choice that explains how the scores could go down with fewer truancies even though it was reasonably expected that scores should have improved with fewer truancies.

Think about the truant students. Are they doing poorly in school simply because they are truant? Perhaps, but their poor performance may be because they don't care, and this lack of concern explains why they are often truant. Such students are not likely to do well even when they do show up. Furthermore, when they do attend, they may cause trouble and make it harder for teachers to teach and students to learn. The choice that matches this line of reasoning (and remember, reasoning is key; that's why they call this type of question "Critical Reasoning"), is choice D.

Choice A accentuates how bad the truancy problem was, giving more reason to think that the attendance policy would help, not hurt, test scores. Choice B simply says that attendance improved in more ways than one. You don't know how students with excused absences perform. If anything, better attendance from non-truants should improve test scores. Choice C provides a possible reason for the truancies; it does not resolve the discrepancy between improved attendance and decreased performance. You can eliminate choice E because you have no information about how discipline affects test scores. Common sense tells you that better discipline should improve test scores, so Choice E, if anything heightens the discrepancy.

14. **D.** Choices A, B, and C are all sentence fragments, portions that don't express a complete thought. Choice E changes the meaning of the sentence. Note that the correct answer, choice D, properly uses parallel structure: *complete... double-check*, rather than the careless mixed forms of *complete... double-checking*.

15. **B.** This question tests verb tense. The hard work occurred before the friend's arrival; therefore, the latter clause must have a "more in the past" verb than the former clause: "Will have been done . . . comes." You don't need to clutter your brain with all the rules about *pluperfect,* future *pluperfect,* and so on. Simply read the sentences aloud, and your ear will catch which is the correct verb.

This is one of the hardest types of questions to get correct. If all the answers look good to you, skip this question (especially if English is not your native tongue). It is a time-waster that can make you mutter each sentence over and over and over. It is better to blow off this question and go on to the ones that ask you to find one easily identifiable error, such as *affect* versus *effect* or *amount* versus *number*.

16. **B.** *Average* is a red flag word. *Average* indicates that the verb and pronoun to follow must both be singular because "the average" is one person. The "average" man is doing *his* best. Eliminate answers with the plural words *they* or *their*. That scratches off choices A, C, and D. The choices are narrowed down to B and E. Choice E is wrong because it changes the meaning of the sentence and is awkward as well.

Have you noticed how often I have used the expression "is awkward"? A sentence must flow trippingly off the tongue. You should be able to read the sentence without stumbling and stuttering. If the sentence is awkward to say, it is probably incorrect.

17. **D.** This question tests two concepts: *its/it's* and the plurality of *data*. The sentence uses *its* to mean it is, which requires the form *it's*. (*Its/it's* is one of the twosomes discussed in the grammar review.) Eliminate answers with *its,* choices A, C, and E. The word *data* is plural (the singular form is *datum*). Use the plural verb, *are*. (Unusual singular/plurals, like *data/datum, media/medium,* and so on, are also covered in the grammar review. Hmmm . . . kinda makes you want to go back to the grammar review and see what else you missed, doesn't it?)

18. **B.** Lines 9–11 tell you that "distances and directions take a bit of figuring, but the topography and features of the land are easy to determine."

19. **B.** The passage explains how to use a map. Students would learn such a thing. Professional cartographers — map makers — would certainly know how to read a map. Professors wouldn't be spoken to in this rather elementary tone. Surveyors had better know how to read a map already. Hunters are tempting, but there is no clue to indicate that the author is addressing them.

20. **C.** The passage introduces topographical maps and explains what they are and how to use them.

The word *discuss* is a nice vague word that is often the correct answer to a main purpose or primary concern question.

Choices B and D should be eliminated quickly; they are both negative. To *lament* is to regret, to grieve over, or to deplore. To *deride* is to ridicule, to laugh contemptuously at.

The word *urge* (choice E) is rarely the correct answer to a primary concern question. That is, few passages "urge" the readers to do anything, especially a straightforward facts passage like this one. An editorial may urge a course of action, but a passage on how to read a map doesn't stimulate any urges that I know of.

21. **A.** The sentence is correct as written. Because Alice Walker is a person, the pronoun required is *who,* not *that* or *which,* eliminating choices B and C. Choice E misuses the word *whoever. Whoever* as one word means an unknown person. Choice D is tempting but changes the tense unnecessarily. Change as little as possible. If a change does not improve the sentence, don't make it.

22. **B.** Adjectives in a series must be in parallel forms. The people are repulsed, unhappy, and dissatisfied. The original changes the form two-thirds of the way through. "Repulsed . . . unhappy . . . and complain about." The "and complain about the paucity of choices" is like a caboose tacked on at the end, just tagging along as an afterthought. Choice C has two *-ing* verbs (you should be allergic to *-ing* verbs by now, getting a headache whenever you see them) and an adjective, "unhappy." Eliminate this answer because of the non-parallel structure. Choice E is very tempting, but it, too, is not parallel. "Repulsed . . . unhappy . . . and complaining: would work if it were changed to "repulsed . . . unhappy . . . and dissatisfied with."

23. **E.** *If* and *would* are archenemies and will not serve together in the same clause. Usually *if . . . would* can be corrected to *had.* Choice B is devious enough to catch careless readers who don't take the time to reinsert the answer choice into the original question. It would read, "If the contestant answered to the last question." Take the time to reinsert your answer into the original.

You do not have to insert every answer into the original sentence; many answer choices can be eliminated very quickly. However, when you have finally made up your mind and selected an answer choice, take the time to insert it into the original sentence. Think of it as the dating game. The vast majority of people you date never get introduced to your family. You can eliminate these dates from the *Future Mate* contest after just a few boring evenings together. But after you have selected your mate, it is imperative you introduce that person into your family to see whether he/she fits in or leaves you incomplete somehow. Choice C has an -*ing* verb and would not fit into the sentence. Choice D again is tempting but repeats the pronoun *she*. "The contestant, had she known the answer to the quiz show, she would have won. . . ."

24. **E.** The clerk uses the evidence of double prints to lead to the conclusion that the roll should cost double the other roll. The potential problem with this argument is that the conclusion brings in the other roll, which is a term that does not appear in her evidence. In order to connect the evidence with the conclusion, the clerk must assume that the two rolls are alike in all respects except the double prints. Choice E points out one of these essential similarities. If choice E is not assumed, there must be some reason other than double prints that one roll is more expensive than the other, meaning that the clerk may not use the double prints to justify the extra charge.

Choices A, B, and C may all be dismissed because they have nothing to do with the clerk's argument. The clerk is using double prints and is ignoring all the other issues that may be involved with the extra charge. Choice B is especially bad because it weakens the lab's position that it is justified in charging more. TIP! Often, one of the answer choices is the "inside-out" choice, one that states almost exactly the opposite or does almost exactly the opposite of what you want. Keep an eye out for it and eliminate it quickly. Choices A and C may be reasons that the lab charged more, but the clerk does not bring them up. Choice D addresses double prints but actually weakens the clerk's argument. If the clerk assumed choice D, all she could say is that the lab charged more because of the double prints. She would not be justified in saying double prints mean double charge.

25. **B.** The argument uses the increase in percentage to conclude that cancer is more deadly. To weaken the argument, find a choice that says that the increased percentage reflects something other than an increase in the virulence of cancer.

Choice B is not obvious at first, but what it is saying is that fewer people are dying from diseases other than cancer. Because everyone has to die, if fewer die from something other than cancer, more will have to die from cancer, even if it is not more deadly. (Maybe there are just more people now.)

You do not need outside knowledge to answer a question, but what you do know can be helpful. The test makers will not put in a question that is contrary to common sense, history, or general knowledge. One hundred years ago, many children died of such diseases as diphtheria, long before cancer could develop in their bodies. The longer one lives, the better one's chances are of developing cancer. More people die of cancer now, not because it's more deadly, but because they live long enough to get the disease.

Choice A does not do the job. The money may not have led to any cure. Perhaps the increased spending is motivated by the increased threat of cancer. Choice C does not weaken the argument that cancer is more deadly now than it was 100 years ago. Heart disease may *also* be more deadly, but that doesn't stop cancer. Choice D strengthens the argument by giving a reason why you must be more concerned about cancer today. Choice E would be a candidate if the medicine *cured* cancer, but all that's discussed is pain relief.

26. **A.** The original, although not a very well-written sentence, is the best of this gene pool. The question tests the distinction between *less* and *fewer*. *Less* is singular and should be followed by a singular noun, for example, less criticism. *Fewer* is plural and should be followed by a plural noun, for example, fewer critics. Because we are talking about mistakes, we need the word *fewer*. (Just think of the Peggy Lee classic tune, "You give me fewer. . . ") Eliminate choices B, D, and E. Choice C, when reinserted into the original sentence, turns the sentence into a fragment. The sentence does not express a complete thought.

27. **B.** None of the choices is very good (if my student turned in an essay with this sentence, I'd ask him or her to rewrite the sentence from scratch), but you don't have an answer of "none of the above; these all stink." You have to choose the best from what you have. Choice B correctly uses the form *". . . as . . . as."* The forms *"so . . . than"* (choice A) and *"as . . . than"* (choice C) are incorrect. Choices D and E are awkward.

28. **C.** "According to the passage" questions usually have their answers stated verbatim (word for word) in the passage. Find the key words in the question and skim for those in the passage. Lines 15–22 tell you that sulfur dioxide is most dangerous when it clings to small particles and is carried into the lungs. Choice A, exercise and running in a marathon, was not mentioned at all in the passage. (Personally, I couldn't run a bath, let alone a marathon!)

29. **D.** This is an excellent question to guess quickly at if the answer isn't obvious to you immediately. If you don't remember that the author talked about the sources of each type of problem, you'd have to go back and reread the entire passage. You just don't have the time to do so, and even if you do have the time, do you really *want* to plod through the passage again? (This is like the old joke: Why is there a clock in the leaning tower of Pisa? *Answer:* What good's the inclination if you don't have the time?!)

30. **B.** A title is broad, general. Choice A is tempting, but B is better because it incorporates *both* sulfur dioxide and acid rain.

    If you chose A, you probably looked *only* at the first sentence of the passage. While the main idea or best title is usually found in the first sentence, a passage of this length presents quite a bit of material. Check all the answer choices to see which one encompasses the most ideas.

    Choice C would not be a good guess because it is negative, and negative answers are rarely correct. Even if something bad is discussed, it will be discussed in an upbeat way — not "How I Lost My Brain Stem Activity the Night Before the GMAT" but "How I Took the GMAT Despite Having Lost My Brain Stem Activity the Night Before."

31. **A.** This is a more common sense question. When "some" people suggest a point, it is fair to assume that *not all* people agree on the point.

    You could eliminate the negative answer choices of B (to denigrate is to criticize) and C (to lampoon is to ridicule) because negative answer choices are rarely correct. Choice E is also a good one to cross off; "prove" is a very strong word and is usually wrong. Choose wishy-washy answers, to hedge your bets.

32. **B.** If it would be unwise to investigate every aspect of acid rain before action is taken, action is important and should be taken sooner rather than later. You need to go back to the last sentence of the passage to answer this question. The next paragraph would continue the theme of its topic or main idea sentence.

33. **D.** The word *being* is so often misused and abused in grammar that the mere sight of it should make you do a double-take. Don't automatically assume that *being* is <u>always</u> used incorrectly, but do check its use very carefully. In this case, *being that* is substandard, slang English. The correct word is *because*. Note that choices C and E change the meaning of the sentence.

34. **D.** The adjective "perfect" is known as an absolute adjective. It cannot be modified; that is, something is not "more perfect" or "most perfect." Something is either perfect or it's not. Eliminate choices A, B, and C. Choice E is a fragment (an incomplete sentence) and sounds as if the baby and the father were both in the nursery, beaming away.

35. **D.** The proper form is *neither . . . nor.* Because *neither* is not underlined, you cannot change the form to *either . . . or.* Eliminate choices B and C. *Public* is a collective noun. It's tricky. It looks plural, but it is actually singular. The public *is,* the public *was,* the public *will be.* Knowing that you want the singular form allows you to eliminate choice A. Choice E changes the meaning of the sentence.

36. **B.** Because of the word *except,* you need to find the one choice that does *not* provide a reason for why those who live in high-achieving districts are likely to complain.

    Choice A is very explicit in presenting a factor that accounts for complaints from high-achieving districts.

    Choice B is the answer because those complaining don't even know what the scores are.

    Choices C and D are especially good at explaining why parents in high-achieving districts are more likely to complain than those in low-achieving districts.

    Choice E doesn't focus on how high scores lead to complaints, in the way that choices C and D do, but it still provides an explanation. For all we know, the activists are complaining about low scores in other districts, but the fact remains that they live in a high-achieving district. The complaints are coming from such a district, even though they're not about that district.

37. **A.** The key to this question is to realize that Economics 101A is *necessary* for Economics 101B and that 101B is *necessary* for 101C, but this does not mean that 101A is *sufficient* for 101B or that 101B is *sufficient* for 101C. When something is necessary, it's required for something else to happen. It does not *guarantee* that the other event will happen. For example, you may have to take the GMAT to get into graduate school, but simply taking the GMAT will not put you in graduate school. You must also apply, have acceptable grades, and so on. This understanding readily eliminates choices B and D. It also wipes out choice C. There is nothing in the question stimulus that states that Economics 101A is the *only* prerequisite. All we know is that it is *a* prerequisite. Choice E is also out. For all we know, Economics 101B is required for many courses besides Economics 101C.

    This leaves choice A. If you are in 101C, you had to meet the requirements, one of which was to take 101B. To be in 101B, you must have taken 101A.

38. **C.** When comparing two items, use *between;* when comparing more than two items, use *among.* Here only two items, Kerry and I, are compared, allowing you to narrow the answer choices down to A and C and maybe E. *Between* is a preposition and requires an object of the preposition. *I* is subjective; change it to the objective form *me.* Eliminate choices A and E.

    Notice that you did not need to know the word *philogynist* to get the sentence correct. It's a fun word, actually: A philogynist is a person who loves women. My boyfriend always uses this word to fill in any form that asks for his occupation!

39. **E.** This sentence tests the distinction between *lie* and *lay.* To *lie* is to recline and does not require an object. To *lay* is to put or place and does require an object. Here the patient is reclining in bed, such that *"if he lies"* is correct. (Chapter 2 discusses *lie* and *lay* in detail.)

40. **D.** Abandon *hopefully,* all ye who enter here (abandon all attempts at humor, all ye stuck with the GMAT). The word *hopefully* is an adverb meaning "full of hope." Hearing the telephone ring, the lonely man looked up hopefully (he looked up "full of hope"). The correct expression here would be "he hoped." Because *hopefully* is wrong, eliminate answer choices A, B, and C. Choice E incorrectly uses an *-ing* verb (*-ing* verbs are worthy of extreme scrutiny, given the number of times they are abused and misused).

41. **E.** The people who are not counted because they don't use the mail will still not be counted if they don't know about and/or care to attend the meetings. Choice E makes this point.

    Eliminate choice A because the issue is not solving community problems in general. Choice B is out because the census officials are trying to get a more accurate count. While they would probably like to see more participation in American democracy, they are not holding meetings for that purpose. How could the delivery of a newspaper to somebody who is already counted hurt the effort to count more people? Scratch off choice C. Don't read too much into choice D. You may think that senior citizens may be less likely than people with school age children to attend a meeting at an elementary school, but you may not justify such an assumption. The senior citizens may be more than eager to attend a meeting. Even if only families with schoolchildren attend a meeting, you can't tell from choice D that the plan for reducing the undercount will fail.

    Keep going back to the question as you read each answer choice. If you read more than one answer choice, you can easily confuse what you learned in the answer choice with what you read in the original question. The questions aren't that long; keep reviewing them over and over and over. You have 25 minutes to do only 16 questions; that means you have, on average, more than a minute and a half per question.

Section 2

1. **A.** This problem looks confusing but is actually ridiculously easy. It's just the wording that's hard. The face of a die has six numbers. The only way to get a total of 12 is to roll two sixes. There is only one chance of doing that. The only way to get a sum of 2 is to roll two ones. There is only one chance of doing that. Therefore, the *difference* between the two chances is 0.

   If you said 100 (100 percent), you didn't answer what the question was asking. It asked for what percent LESS one probability was than the other. Since they are the exact same probability, there is 0 percent less.

2. **A.** Get all the a's on one side and all the non-a's on the other, remembering to change the signs. (Forgetting to change the signs is a common careless mistake.) $3a + a = 8b - b$. Combine like terms: $4a = 7b$. Divide both sides through by 4 to get $a = \frac{7b}{4}$.

3. **B.** Statement 1 alone is not sufficient. It tells you in effect that x is one more than y. Well, if $x = 2$, then $y = 1$, and the answer to the question is no. But if $x = 3$, then $y = 2$, and the answer to the question is yes. It depends on the values you plug in. Eliminate choices A and D.

   Statement 2 alone is sufficient. Two times any number makes it even. No matter what the value of x, $2x$ is even. An even number plus an even number equals an even number, and an even plus an odd is odd. For example, say that $x = 2$. Then $4 + y = 32$; $y = 28$. Say that $x = 3$. Then $6 + y = 32$; $y = 26$. No matter what the value of x, y must be even. Narrow the choices down to B and D.

   Because choice D has already been eliminated, the correct answer is B.

4. **B.** When you encountered this bizarre triangle, was your first response a self-pitying cry of, "What fresh hell is this?" Not to fear; the problem can be quite straightforward if you just plug numbers into the equation.

   Statement 1 alone is not sufficient. What if $x = 8$? Then $\frac{4}{x} = \frac{4}{8} = \frac{1}{2}$ and $\triangle x$ is not a whole number $\left(8^2 + \frac{4}{8} + 4 = 68\frac{1}{2}\right)$. But if $x = 4$, then $\triangle x$ is a whole number $\left(4^2 + \frac{4}{4} + 4 = 21\right)$. The answer to the question could be yes or no, depending on the value of x. If you can't get one definite answer, you don't have sufficient data. Eliminate choices A and D.

   Statement 2 alone is sufficient. If $x^2 = 25$, then $x = 5$. $\triangle x = 25 + \frac{4}{5} + 4$. $\triangle x = 29\frac{4}{5}$, not a whole number.

   If you chose E, you confused "insufficient data" with "the answer is no." It makes no difference whether the answer to the question (in this case, "Is $\triangle x$ a whole number?") is yes or no; if you can definitely answer one way or the other, the data are sufficient.

5. **D.** The man is covering two extra yards for every four yards he gains. The ratio of walk to gain, therefore, is $\frac{6}{4}$ or $\frac{3}{2}$. Multiply $200 \times \frac{3}{2}$ to get 300.

   If this way is difficult for you to see, try doing some small calculations. Talk your way through the problem. If he walks 6 yards, he covers 4. If he walks 12 yards, he covers 8. If he walks 24 yards, he covers 16. Now multiply by 10: If he walks 240 yards, he covers 160. This is pretty close, enough to tell you that huge numbers like 600 and 500 are probably wrong, and enough to tell you that the number of yards he walks must be more than 240. By estimation, you can narrow the answer choices down to C and D. A guess with 50–50 odds is pretty good.

Because the test makers are nice enough to give you multiple-choice answers, you can often use those answers to make an estimate. You don't have to solve the problem out to the bitter end in many instances. If you can get close enough to make a guess from between two choices, save yourself time and do so.

6. **B.** This problem is much easier if you remember one of the algebra formulas I warned you (in Chapter 12) you would encounter again: $(a-b)^2$. Think of the $\sqrt{5}$ as the a, and the $\sqrt{3}$ as the b. You know (or will in a minute) that $(a-b)^2 = a^2 - 2ab + b^2$. Just substitute the $\sqrt{5}$ for the a and the $\sqrt{3}$ for the b.

$\sqrt{5}^2 = \sqrt{5} \times \sqrt{5} = 5$. (*Not* 25; that's a trap.)

$2(\sqrt{5})(\sqrt{3}) = 2\sqrt{15}$ (To multiply square roots, just multiply the numbers under the signs and then put the sign back over the product. In other words, just multiply normally.) Remember to put the $-$ sign in front, as the formula is a squared *minus* $2ab + b$ squared.

$\sqrt{3}^2 = \sqrt{3} \times \sqrt{3} = 3$ (*Not* 9; that's a trap.)

Put them all together: $5 + 3 = 8$, and $8 - 2\sqrt{15}$. Do you see the trap answers? If you thought that $\sqrt{5}^2$ was 25 and $\sqrt{3}^2$ was 9, you added and got 34. And if you didn't keep your $+$ and $-$ straight, you could miss any one of the trap answers.

7. **B.** Understand what the explanation means. (The explanation is made up for this particular problem. There is no such thing as a "circle" operation in the real world, only in the little universe of the GMAT. Lucky you.) The explanation says that you have a number in the circle. If that number in the circle is a prime number (meaning that it can be divided evenly only by itself and 1), you add the number in the circle to the square of the number in the circle.

If the number in the circle is a composite number (one that *can* be divided evenly by something other than just 1 and itself), you square that number and subtract the number in the circle from the square.

Ugh. You may have to repeat those instructions to yourself a few times. You're really just substituting the number in the circle for the x in the appropriate equation.

Because 4 is composite, you use the second line of the explanation. Square 4: $4^2 = 16$. Subtract from that the number in the circle: $16 - 4 = 12$.

Because 5 is prime, you add it to its square: $5 + 25 = 30$.

Add the two results: $12 + 30 = 42$.

The problem has all sorts of trap answers. If you used the first line $(x + x^2)$ for both terms, you got 50. If you used the second line $(x^2 - x)$ for both terms, you got 32. If you confused prime and composite numbers, using the composite rule for 5 and the prime rule for 4, you got 40.

8. **C.** Statement 1 alone is not sufficient; it gives you a ratio (Marcy works twice as fast as George) but never gives you a solid number. Eliminate choices A and D.

Statement 2 alone is not sufficient. Knowing George can proof 30 fewer papers doesn't tell you how many papers he and Marcy proofed together. Eliminate choices B and D.

Could you find the number of papers graded by using both statements 1 and 2? Yes. Deduce that 30 papers is ½ the total Marcy proofs, because she proofs twice as many as George. In other words, George proofs 30 and Marcy proofs 60. Both statements together let you calculate how many papers Marcy and George can proof together.

9. **C.** Statement one alone is not sufficient, because it does not address the question of income from sales of artworks. For example, maybe sales of T-shirts were 4 and sales of yearbooks were 5 (25% greater). On the other hand, maybe sales of T-shirts were 40 and sales of yearbooks were 50, which is also 25% greater. Eliminate choices A and D.

Statement two alone is not sufficient. All it tells you is that T-shirts and artwork sales were 35% more than yearbooks. From that, you could make the equation: $TS + A = 1.35Y$. Then, because everything together equaled 56,000, you could say $1.35Y$ (the sales of T-shirts and artwork) $+Y = 56,000$. Solving for Y (which you definitely would not take the time to do on the real test), you get approximately 23,830. That means that money from yearbook sales was approximately $23,830.00. That still isn't enough information to tell you how much was earned from artwork sales. Eliminate choice B.

What about the two statements together? From statement two, you know how much came from yearbook sales. Using that with statement one, you could find out how much income came from sales of T-shirts. Then whatever is left over must be the income from the sale of artwork. Yes, you finally have enough information!

Note that you are NOT going to do this work, not actually find real numbers. Don't solve the problem, just determine whether in fact the data are sufficient to solve the problem.

10. **D.** If you saw the shortcuts and reasoned this out rather than doing the algebra, this should have been a very easy problem. Because 20 can be divided evenly by 2, 4, and 5, there will be no remainder. Dump those choices quickly. Now just try plugging in the remaining two choices. $\frac{20}{7} = 2$ remainder 6, and $x - 1 = (7 - 1) = 6$. That answer works. Check the last choice just to be sure that you didn't make a careless mistake somewhere. $\frac{20}{9} = 2$ remainder 2, and $x - 1 = (9 - 1) = 8$. Nope, that answer wouldn't work.

11. **D.** Often, you can estimate answers without doing any work. However, you should always look at the answer choices first. In this case, you see that the answers are all too close together, alerting you to the fact that you had better just sit down and do the actual calculations. No shortcuts this time.

An average may be written as *Avg = Sum ÷ Number of items*. If the smallest average is 19, you work with that number. (The 23 is there as a red herring, just to confuse and mislead you. Ignore it and it'll go away.) $19 = Sum \div 3$ (because there are three people purchasing cookies). Cross multiply: $19 \times 3 = Sum$. $Sum = 57$. If the other two people bought 16 and 12, they bought 28 all together. That means that Catharine must have bought the difference: $57 - 28 = 29$.

There is one minor shortcut you can use in the last step. Just look at the units digits: 7 and 8. $7 - 8$ would be $17 - 8 = 9$. Only one answer choice ends in a 9.

12. **C.** Statement 1 alone is not sufficient to answer the question. If the triangle is isosceles, two sides are equal. Great. That gives you no information about the lengths of those sides, which is what you need to find the perimeter of the triangle. Eliminate choices A and D.

Statement 2 alone is not sufficient to answer the question. If the radius is 5, then the diameter *AC* is 10. But you don't have enough information to find the lengths of the other sides of the triangle. Eliminate choices B and D.

Putting the two statements together gives you everything you need. If a triangle is inscribed in a semicircle, it is a right triangle. (That's just a math truism you need to beat into your brain, if you don't already know it. Any triangle inscribed in a semicircle is a right triangle.) If it is an isosceles right triangle, the sides are in the ratio *side: side: side* $\times \sqrt{2}$. Another way to write that ratio is $\frac{side}{\sqrt{2}} : \frac{side}{\sqrt{2}} : side$. (Go back to Chapter 11 if you are hopelessly lost about now.) Because the hypotenuse is "side" in the second formula, your ratio is $\frac{5}{\sqrt{2}} : \frac{5}{\sqrt{2}} : 5$. The perimeter is $2\left(\frac{5}{\sqrt{2}}\right) + 5$. Don't bother to work it out; just know that you *could* do so.

13. **A.** If four pencils cost *x* cents, then one pencil costs $\frac{1}{4}x$. If nine pens cost *y* cents, then one pen costs $\frac{1}{9}y$ cents and three pens cost $\frac{3}{9}y$ or $\frac{1}{3}y$ cents. Put everything in terms of the common denominator 12: $\frac{1}{4}x = \frac{3}{12}x$, and $\frac{1}{3}y = \frac{4}{12}y$. Add: $\frac{(3x + 4y)}{12}$.

If all these x's and y's are giving you a headache, plug in numbers. Say that four pencils cost 4 cents so that each pencil costs 1 cent. That means $x = 4$. Say that nine pens cost nine cents so that each pen costs one cent and three pens cost three cents. $y = 9$. How much are one pencil and three pens? $1 + 3 = 4$. The answer to the whole problem is 4. Now go back and plug the numbers in for the answers. Choice A is

$$[3(4)+4(9)]\big/_{12} = {}^{(12+36)}\big/_{12} = {}^{48}\!/_{12} = 4.$$ Of course, you want to check the rest of the answer choices as well, but doing so takes only a few seconds.

14. **D.** If you chose answer A or answer E, you fell for a trap. Answer A caught careless students who thought, "The price rises 25% then falls ¼ or 25%, for a 0% change." Wrong. An easy way to solve a problem like this is to plug in 100 for the price of the book originally. In 1998, the book cost $100. If it rose by 25%, it went up $25 to a total of $125. In 2000, the price was ¼ or 25% below its 1998 cost. That means it was $25 below the original $100, or $75.

Here's where the trap comes in. Reading the question carefully tells you that you want to know the percent decrease from 1999 to 2000, which here is from 125 to 75. The formula (given in the math review) for percent increase or decrease is:

Number increase or decrease / starting (original) number

In other words, the denominator is the number you began with, which in this case is the 125 (because the question asks for the change from 1999, not from 1998). The number decrease is 50 $(125 - 75 = 50)$. Finally, ${}^{50}\!/_{125} = {}^{4}\!/_{10} = 40\%$.

Choice E trapped readers who forgot you were trying to find a percentage decrease, and found just the year 2000 price.

15. **A.** Draw six dashes to represent the six terms. Then talk through the problem. Set A starts with 1, and then each term subtracts half of the term before it. This gives you set A as $1 - \frac{1}{2} - \frac{1}{4} - \frac{1}{8} - \frac{1}{16} - \frac{1}{32}$. Set B starts at 1, and then each term adds double the term before it. This gives you set B as $1 + 2 + 4 + 8 + 16 + 32$. Set A works out to be ¹⁄₃₂; set B works out to be 63.

For heaven's sake, don't actually work through all that fraction chaos. Just work with the nice whole numbers. When you add those, you get 63. You are *adding* something more to the 63, which means that the answer must be *more* than 63. Only choice A is bigger than 63. If you worked this through, you destroyed living brain tissue for nothing.

16. **B.** Statement 1 alone is not sufficient to answer the question. The *exterior* angles of *any* polygon total 360 degrees. The polygon could have 3 or 5 or 12 sides and could have interior angles from 180 to some ridiculously huge number. Eliminate choices A and D.

Statement 2 alone does have sufficient data. The formula for the interior angles of a polygon is: $(n - 2) \times 180°$, where $n =$ *the number of sides of the polygon*. Don't bother figuring out how many sides there actually are; just know that you could do so if you wanted to.

Okay, okay, for those of you who can't leave things in mid-problem: $(n - 2) \times 180 = 900$; $180n - 360 = 900$; $180n = 1260$; $n = 7$. The figure is a heptagon. If you forgot how to do this type of problem, go back to the geometry portion of the math review (Chapter 11).

17. **C.** This one was a gift to you, after making you fall for so many questions that looked to be C but really weren't.

Statement 1 alone is not sufficient. You cannot factor the equation down without knowing the value of y. For example, the terms could be $(x + 24)(x + 1) = 0$, making x either -24 or -1. Or the terms could be $(x - 24)(x - 1) = 0$, making x either 24 or 1. The answer to the question could be yes or no. Eliminate choices A and D.

Statement 2 alone is not sufficient. Knowing the value of y by itself doesn't give you any information about x. (If you chose B, you transferred information from statement 1 to statement 2, a common mistake.)

Both statements together allow you to answer the question. If $y = 10$, factor the equation down to $(x+4)(x+6) = 0$, making x either –6 or –4.

If you chose E, you forgot that a "no" answer doesn't mean choice E. You choose E only when you can't answer the question at all. Whether the answer is yes or no, if you can answer the question, don't choose E.

18. **C.** Use the DIRT formula for *Distance Is Rate* times *Time*. To find out the distance, you need to know the rate and the time. Look for them.

Statement 1 alone is not sufficient because you don't know Ms. DeFilio's rate. If she drives at 55 miles per hour and arrives in 20 minutes, the distance is obviously greater than if she drives at a sedate 30 mph and arrives in 20 minutes. Because statement 1 alone is not sufficient to answer the question, eliminate choices A and D.

Statement 2 alone is not sufficient. You know the rate, but not the speed. Ms. DeFilio drives at 30 mph . . . but for how long? An hour? Two hours? Ten minutes? Eliminate choices B and D, as statement 2 doesn't give you enough information on its own to answer the question.

Combine the statements: Statement 1 gives you the time, and statement 2 gives you the rate. Using them, you could find distance (don't actually do so, just know that you have sufficient info to do so).

19. **D.** Was your first reaction to say that the only way to solve this problem is with catoptromancy (divination by means of mirrors)? Don't worry; it's not as hard as it looks. It is a symbolism problem (covered in the math review in Chapter 12). First, you say to yourself in words what the triangle means, as explained in the question stem: "I have a number inside of a triangle. That means I square the number first and then add 2 to it." For $\triangle{x}$ you square 4 and add 2 to it: $4^2 + 2 = (16 + 2) = 18$. If you chose A or B, you didn't finish the problem through. Always remind yourself that the mere fact that the answer you got is one of the answer choices does not mean you can stop working. The test makers are notorious for supplying incremental answers among the choices (in other words, if solving the problem takes five steps, the answer to the first step may be choice A, the answer to the second step may be choice B, and so on).

Because the first triangle is inside a second triangle, you have to do the whole operation over again. It's as if you're starting anew with a $\triangle{x}$. Square 18 and add 2 to it: $18^2 = 324 + 2 = 326$. If you chose C, you forgot to add the 2 at the end and did all that work for nothing. If you chose E, you acted as if there were a third triangle, squaring 326 and adding 2 to it. Naturally, the answer you get after doing all that wasted work is among the answer choices. *Tip:* You didn't have to do all the multiplication, you know. Look at the unit's digits: 18×18. Because $8 \times 8 = 64$, the last digit is a 4, and $4 + 2$ means the last digit is a 6. Because 16 is way too small, the answer must be 326.

20. **E.** I call this type of problem a "Nike" problem: Just Do It. There are no tricks, no traps. Given that there are 60 seconds in a minute, if the machine does 15 parts per second, multiply $15 \times 60 = 900$. The machine stamps out 900 parts a minute. It wants 36,000 parts, so divide 36,000 by 900 to get 40.

If you chose C, you made a careless, clerical mistake. TIP! Before you begin doing arithmetic, scan the answer choices. Doing so will tell you how careful you have to be with your decimal point and your 0's. In this problem, you saw you had a 4 and a 40, telling you to double-check your arithmetic.

21. **E.** *Plug in* 100 for percentages, remember? Let the starting price for 1990 be 100. By the end of 1990, the price had risen 20 percent, up to 120. In 1991, the price dropped 25 percent, *but* it dropped from 120, not from the original 100. That means it went from 120 to 90 (25 percent of $120 = 30$; $120 - 30 = 90$). In 1992, it went up 20 percent, *but* it

went up from 90, not from 100 or from 120. That means it went from 90 to 108 (20 percent of $90 = 18$; $18 + 90 = 108$). If 1992 is 108 and 1990's beginning price is 100, then 108 is 108 percent of 100.

The question did not ask how much the price went up (or down), which would lead you to put as an answer 8%. It asked you what percent of 1990's price is 1992's price. A percent = XXX.

You may have been tempted not to work the problem out but to say that the "obvious" answer is 95, because it went up 20, down 25, and up 20 again, for a net loss of 5%. AAAARGH! Any time you think something is obvious, think again.

22. **E.** You know that when you multiply like bases, you add the exponents, giving you $x^4 \times x^7 = x^{11}$. You know that when you divide like bases, you subtract the exponents, giving you $x^{11} - x^4 = x^7$ (a lotta work to get right back where you began). The question, therefore, really is: Is $x^7 > 1$? The answer, obviously, depends on the value of x.

Statement 1 alone is not sufficient to answer the question. If x is ½, then the answer is no. If x is 2, then the answer is yes. If you can answer a question two different ways depending on the value of the variable, there is not enough information. Eliminate choices A and D.

Statement 2 alone is not sufficient. If x is 1, the answer is no. But if x is 2, then the answer is yes. Eliminate choices B and D.

Time to check for C. Does putting the statements together result in anything worthwhile? Nope. The same problem exists: The answer depends on whether x is, for example, 1 or 2. Eliminate choice C. Separately or together, the data are not sufficient to answer the question.

23. **D.** Okay, we can make this easy or we can make it hard. You want to do it the easy way, you say? Great: *Plug in numbers!* I'll discuss the hard algebraic approach in just a minute, but to get through this problem quickly and with a minimum of brain cell destruction, just choose some numbers and plug them into the question. You can choose any numbers your heart desires, but I suggest you keep them small. Why waste time on a lot of multiplication? Let $q = 1$. Georgia buys 1 quart of milk. Let $d = 2$; the milk costs two dollars a quart. (It doesn't have to make fiscal sense; maybe this is rare yak's milk. You have better things to worry about.) Let $b = 3$. She buys three boxes of cereal at 3 dollars a box ($d + 1 = 2 + 1 = 3$). Now you can easily figure out a total: 1 quart of milk at two dollars a quart = 2 dollars. Three boxes of cereal at 3 dollars a box = 9 dollars. Add them up to get 11 dollars. Plug the values for q, d, and b into the answer choices and see which one comes out to be 11. Only choice D works: $2(1 + 3) + 3 = 8 + 3 = 11$.

Keep two important concepts in mind when plugging in numbers: First, keep the numbers small and easy to work with. Second, jot down the numbers as you create them. That is, write to the side: $q = 1$; $d = 2$; $b = 3$. It's very easy to get the numbers confused in the pressure of the exam and say that $d = 3$ or $b = 1$, for example. Take just a nanosecond to put down the assigned values and refer to them. Constantly.

I promised you algebra. Here it is:

Amount spent on milk: (q quarts) (d dollars / quart) = Cancel the "quarts" and get qd.

Amount spent on cereal: (b boxes) ($d + 1$ dollars / box) = cancel the "boxes" = $b(d + 1) = bd + b$. Add these together: $qd + bd + b$. Take out the d: $d(q + b) + b$. If you think the algebra is pretty straightforward, you're right . . . as long as you set up the original equation correctly. Unfortunately, too many people have no idea how to set up the equation and do it upside down, inside out, or whatever. If you plug in numbers, you can talk your way through this relatively difficult problem in just a few seconds.

24. **D.** Because the average is the sum of all the terms divided by the number of terms, your equation should look like this:

$$80 = (75 + 69 + 81 + 90 + 73 + x) \div 7. \text{ Cross multiply: } 80 \times 7 = 560.$$

$$560 = 388 + x; \ x = 172.$$

You're probably lucky that there was no trap answer of 172; you might have chosen it and gone on your merry way. However, the question asks for the average score on the last *two* exams. Divide $172 \div 2 = 86$.

If you just divided 388 (the sum of the six numbers) by 6, you got 64.66 and may have been tempted to choose E, rounding up to 65. But that answer is just the average of those six numbers — not at all what the question is asking for. Besides, that answer would be too easy for a question this close to the end. If you think a question in the second half of the section is super easy, think again. You may be falling for a trap.

25. **D.** Choice E is a sucker bet. Just because both the number of painters and the number of hours are three times as great does not mean that the number of hours by which you can multiply the original is three. A problem towards the end of the section is not going to be that simple and straightforward.

If three times as many painters are working, they can do the job in one-third the time it takes just one painter. If this is confusing, reword the problem in your own terms. Suppose that it takes you three hours to mow a lawn. If your two fraternity buddies chip in and help you, the three of you can work three times as fast and get the job done in just one hour. The same is true here. Three times the number of painters (from 3 to 9) means the job can be done in ⅓ the time: $^{10}\!/_3 = 3\frac{1}{3}$.

If you chose 3⅓, you didn't finish the problem. Nine painters would do the SAME job, that is, paint 4 rooms, in 3⅓ hours. But the number of rooms is three times what it was, so this factor triples the amount of time needed. Triple 3⅓ to get 10 hours. Yup, you're back to the original amount of time, which unfortunately was probably the first answer your "common sense" told you to eliminate.

Think about this logically. It takes ⅓ the time, but the painters do three times the work. The ⅓ cancels out with the 3 to get you right back where you started from.

26. **D.** Make x be the number of books the girls check out; make $(x + 20)$ represent the number of books that they put back. The equation now is $x + (x + 20) = 84$. First, $2x + 20 = 84$. Then $2x = 64$. Finally, $x = 32$.

If you chose B, you forgot to answer the question, which wants to know how many books were put back, not how many were checked out. $84 - 32 = 82$.

You can use a great shortcut to narrow the answers down. You know that more books were put back than were checked out. That means that more than half of the books were put back, and fewer than half the books were checked out. Half 84 is 42; more than that must have been put back. Only choices D and E could fit. Instead of working through all the garbage algebra, use those two choices. If 52 books were put back, 20 fewer than 52, or 32, were checked out. Does $52 + 32 = 84$? Yup, it does, and the problem is finished. If you want to check, try choice E. If 64 books were put back, 20 fewer than 64, or 44, were checked out. Does $64 + 44 = 84$? Nope. Choice D was right all along.

27. **E.** Statement 1 alone is not sufficient. The two angles could be a wide variety of values, such as 45 and 90 (a 45:45:90 triangle), or 70 and 40 (a 70:70:40 triangle), and so on. Eliminate choices A and D.

Statement 2 alone is not sufficient. You don't even know that x and y are angles in a triangle, based on statement 2 alone! If you chose B, you probably subconsciously transferred information from statement 1 to statement 2. Try to cover up one statement with your hand and read the second one as if it were entirely separate. Eliminate choices B and D.

Both statements together appear to give you everything you need. If you chose C, you're normal. Wrong, but normal. You probably thought that if $x = 2y$, then $y = 45$ and $x = 90$. But what if $y = 36$ and $x = 72$? Then $72 + 72 + 36 = 180$, just as $45 + 45 + 90$ would. Therefore, even with both statements, you don't have enough information to answer the question.

28. **E.** By adding, you can see that $2a^2 = 50$, so $a^2 = 25$. Therefore, from 1, $b^2 = 100$. These values both satisfy 1 and 2. However, a can be +5 or –5, and b can be +10 or –10. Four possible values exist for $a + b$: –15, –5, 5, and 15.

29. **A.** To find a shaded area, subtract the area of the unshaded portion from the area of the total figure. If the diameter of the circle is 10, the side of the square is 10.

Because the area of a square is $side^2$, the area of this square is $10 \times 10 = 100$. If the diameter of a circle is 10, the radius is 5. The area of a circle is πr^2, or $5 \times 5 \times \pi = 25\pi$. Subtract: $100 - 25\pi$.

The easy way to do a shaded area problem is to think of it as a "leftover," what remains when the area of the unshaded part has been subtracted from the area of the entire figure. Shaded areas were covered in the math review.

If you got choice B, you found the circumference $2\pi r = 10\pi$ of the circle instead of the area. If you chose C, you used the perimeter of the square $10 + 10 + 10 + 10 = 40$ rather than the area. If you chose D, you messed up absolutely everything (!); you found the perimeter of the square instead of its area and found the circumference of the circle instead of its area. Isn't it vicious how the test makers anticipate just about every mistake you can make? They must be psychic . . . or is that psycho?

30. **B.** If the last half of the trip were alone, the 40% and the 20 miles are the first half, or 50%. Because $50\% - 40\% = 10\%$, 20 miles = 10%. It may be easier to think in terms of fractions: $10\% = \frac{1}{10}$. One-tenth of *something* is 20; that *something* is 200. (Arithmetically: $\frac{1}{10}x = 20$. Divide both sides through by $\frac{1}{10}$, which means inverting and multiplying by $\frac{10}{1}$; $\frac{10}{1}$; $20 \times 10 = 200$.) This was a good problem to talk through; you needed reasoning, not arithmetic.

31. **D.** Let x be the number of pairs of pants the salesman sold. Then the number of shirts is $x + 10$ (because the problem tells you that the salesman sold ten more shirts than pairs of pants). Make the equation:

$\$1.50(x + 10) + \$2.50(x) = \$215$.

Multiply: $\$1.50x + 15 + \$2.50x = 215$

Combine like terms: $4.0x + 15 = 215$

Isolate the x on one side: $4.0x + 15 = 215 - 15$

Subtract: $4.0x = 200$

Divide: $x = \frac{200}{4}$ or $x = 50$

If you chose answer B, you fell for the trap answer (after all that hard work!). Remember to go back and reread what the question is asking for. In this case, it wants to know the total number of pants and shirts sold. You're not done working yet. If x (50) is the number of pairs of pants, then $x + 10(60)$ is the number of shirts sold. (Note that 60 is a trap answer as well.) Combine $50 + 60$ to get the right answer, 110.

32. **D.** Statement 1 alone is sufficient. The area of a circle is πr^2. If the area is 36π, then $r^2 = 36$, and $r = 6$. If the radius of the circle is 6, the diameter (2 radii) is 12, meaning that the side of the square is 12 as well. The area of a square is $side^2$, or 144. The shaded area is found by subtracting the unshaded area (here a circle) from the total (here a square). Narrow the choices down to A or D.

Statement 2 alone is sufficient. The circumference of a circle is πd. If the circumference here is 12π, the diameter is 12. The side of the square is the same as the diameter. The area of a square is $side^2: 12 \times 12 = 144$. If the circumference is 12π, $r = 6$, and area $= 36\pi$, subtract $144 - 36\pi$ to find the shaded area. Narrow the choices down to B or D. Because either statement 1 or statement 2 alone is sufficient, choose D.

33. **C.** Good problem. Set it up as follows:

$(x + y + z) \div 3 = \frac{4}{3}x$. You know that an average is the sum of all the terms divided by the number of terms. You know that one-third more than something is the same as $1\frac{1}{3}$ or $\frac{4}{3}$ of that something.

To get rid of the fraction, multiply both sides through by 3. You now have $x + y + z = 4x$. Subtract an x from both sides. $y + z = 3x$.

If you chose D, you got suckered. If a number is *three times* as much as another number, it is *two times greater,* or 200 percent greater. If this is confusing, talk it through in simple terms, such as dollars and cents. If you have three dollars, you have three times as much as one dollar, but it is only two dollars, or 200 cents, more than one dollar. You have to "subtract" the original 100 cents, or in this case, 100 percent.

The concept of percent greater/lesser (also known as percent increase/decrease) is covered in the percentages portion of the math review.

34. **B.** If you chose C, my work here has been in vain. True, to find an average you add up the terms and then divide by the number of terms. But this is a Distance-Rate-Time DIRT problem, and the terms here aren't simply 600 and 400. You have to find the length of time spent flying at 600 mph and the length of time spent flying at 400 mph, and then add *those* and divide.

If you think logically about this problem and know the answer can't be C, but don't want to spend time working it out, you can eliminate a few more answers. You know that the plane must go more time at the slower rate and less time at the faster rate. That means the average is going to be less than half of the "average" 500 mph. Immediately narrow your answer choices down to A and B. If you're in a hurry, guess and go.

You probably wanted to make a simple Distance-Rate-Time chart for this problem, right? Good thinking . . . but it won't work here. To make a chart of that sort, you have to have at least two of the three variables. For example, if you know rate and distance, you can find time. But here, you have only one variable, rate. You cannot solve for time and distance. What do you do now? Find a ratio.

Use a common multiple of 12 (actually, 1200) miles. In 2 hours, the plane traveling at 600 mph will go 1200 miles. In 3 hours, the plane traveling at 400 miles will go 1200 miles. To find the average, add 600 twice and 400 three times . . . and then divide by *five,* not by two. $600 + 600 + 400 + 400 + 400 = 2400$. Finally, $\frac{2400}{5} = 480$.

Did the words *arithmetic mean* confuse you? They're put there to prevent any lawsuits over confusion of terms. The "average" can mean different things to different people; the "arithmetic mean" is the precise term. Don't worry about it. The info in parentheses is usually there to cover fundamental anatomical regions in case of litigation. You can ignore it.

35. **D.** Statement 1 alone is sufficient to answer the question. Because x is between 0 and 1, it is a fraction. One divided by a fraction is more than 1 (for example: $1 \div \frac{1}{2} = 2$. Narrow the choices down to A and D.

Statement 2 alone is also sufficient to answer the question. To multiply fractions, multiply the numerators (the numbers on top), then the denominators (the numbers on the bottom). That gives you $\frac{1 \times 4}{4 \times x}$, or $\frac{1}{4}$. Because either statement 1 alone or statement 2 alone is sufficient, the answer is D.

36. **B.** Statement 1 alone is not sufficient to answer the question. What if a and b are negative? Maybe $a = -2$ and $b = -1$. Then $a^2 = 4$, which is greater than b^2, which is 1. BUT a as -2 is smaller than b as -1. Yet if $a = 2$ and $b = 1$, then $a^2 > b^2$ and this time $a > b$. Because there are two possibilities, you can't give a definitive answer to the question; eliminate choices A and D.

Statement 2 alone is sufficient to answer the question. Here, for a^3 to be greater than b^3, a must be greater than b. If the terms are negative, maybe $a = -2$ and $b = -4$. Then $a^3 = -8$ which is greater than b^3, which is -64.

When playing the "what if" game, remember to plug in positive, negative, zero, and fractions. The Sacred Six (numbers you always plug in, as you learned in the lecture) are 1, 2, 0, −1, −2, 2, and ½. This particular problem tells you that a and b are integers, eliminating ½, but all the other choices are fair game.

Be absolutely sure that you're comfortable with your math vocabulary. If you didn't know that an integer is a whole number and not a fraction, and that it can be negative as well as positive (and zero, too), you could have missed the previous question. The terminology is all given to you in the Number Sets portion of the math review in Chapter 13; take a moment now to go back and look at it. (I once received a call from an irate mother of one of my students. She was furious because she thought I had taught her son about "number sex." I told her that as far as I knew, there is no sex you can count on. . . .)

37. **C.** Immediately toss choice A into the circular file. The large can has a greater volume than the small can (duh!), so the ratio *large/small* must be greater than 1.

Choice B is too good to be true. Sure, $\frac{10 \times 8}{10 \times 4} = \frac{80}{40} = \frac{2}{1}$, but if the problem were that easy, it probably wouldn't be on the test. Always keep in mind that questions go from easier to harder; the last three questions are superhard, supertricky, or superlong (or all three!).

Here, for those of you who haven't tuned me out yet, is the TMA: Traditional Mathematical Approach (AKA the Tedious Masochistic Approach). If you were to unwrap the label, you would find that its width is the same as the circumference of the circle that is the base of the can. Circumference $= 2\pi r$. That means that in the large can, $2\pi r = 8$. Divide both sides through by 2π to find the radius: $\frac{8}{2\pi}$; reduce by a factor of 2: $\frac{4}{\pi}$. Great, you're halfway home (or halfway to The Home, depending on your mental state right about now).

Next, you need to realize that the height of the label is the same as the height of the can, 10. Because volume $= \pi r^2$ height, the volume of the large can is $\pi \left(\frac{4}{\pi}\right)^2 10$. Work it out: $\frac{\pi \times 16}{\pi^2 \times 10}$. Here comes a tricky part: One of the π's in the denominator cancels, making the volume $= \frac{16}{\pi} \times 10 = \frac{160}{\pi}$. One can down, one to go.

For the small can, the width of the label is also the same as the circumference, making the formula $C = 2\pi r = 4$. Next, $\frac{2}{\pi} = r$. Volume $= \pi r^2 h = \pi \left(\frac{2}{\pi}\right)^2 \times 10$. Cancel one π from the denominator again: $\frac{\pi \times 4}{\pi^2 \times 10} = \frac{4}{\pi} \times 10 = \frac{40}{\pi}$.

Finally, you're ready to set up a ratio: $\text{large/small} = \left(\frac{160}{\pi}\right) / \left(\frac{40}{\pi}\right) = 4{:}1$.

For those of you with a way with words, remember that the circumference of the large can is twice the circumference of the small. That means the radius of the large can is twice the radius of the small can. When figures are similar (like two cylinders, as here), the ratio of their areas is the square of the ratio of their sides (or in this case, of their radii). If the radii are in the ratio $\frac{2}{1}$, the areas of the bases (like the lids of the cylinders) are in the ratio $\frac{4}{1}$. Multiplying *both* cylinders by 10 to get the volume does not change the ratio.

Sections 3 and 4

Note: There are no "right" or "wrong" answers to these essay questions. Go back to Chapter 9 and review the portion on how the essays are scored.

Photocopy your essays. Give a copy of them to four graders (choose people who know something about writing: a professor or a journalist friend, not just your buddy down the hall) and ask each one to rate them on a 0 to 6 scale. Average the scores.

Ask each grader to focus on one different part of your writing. For example, ask one grader to read the passage for content and organization. Ask the next grader to pay attention to grammar and usage and diction. Ask another grader to concern himself with spelling, punctuation, and neatness. The final grader can do the "holistic" grading, giving you an overall score. The feedback from each person will help you work on your strengths and weaknesses.

When you have collated the comments, criticism, and carping from your graders, rewrite the essay. Don't time yourself; take all the time you want and do the job right. You'll need to go slowly to integrate the feedback. Speed can come later.

Chapter 20

How to Ruin a Perfectly Good Day, Part II: Practice Exam 2

● ●

You are now ready to take a GMAT that's slightly easier than Exam 1 (not easy, just easier). The following exam consists of two 75-minute sections with multiple-choice questions and two 30-minute essay questions for a total of four sections. *Note:* This exam consists of one verbal section (Reading Comprehension, Critical Reasoning, and Sentence Correction questions), one quantitative section (Problem-Solving and Data Sufficiency questions), and two essays.

You have no choice but to guess at everything — the key to success is guessing quickly. Don't waste time on problems you know you can't do.

Please take this test under normal exam conditions. This is serious stuff here!

1. **Sit where you won't be interrupted (even though you'd probably welcome any distractions).**

2. **Use the answer grid provided for the multiple-choice questions; write your essays on lined paper.**

3. **Pretend each question is on a computer screen and must be answered before you see the next question. Do not skip ahead or go back.**

4. **Set your alarm clock for the 30- to 75-minute intervals.**

5. **Do not go on to the next test until the time allotted for the section you are taking is up.**

6. **If you finish early, check your work for that section only.**

7. **Do not take a break in the middle of any section.**

8. **Give yourself one five-minute break between sections 1 and 2 and a second five-minute break between sections 3 and 4.**

When you complete the entire test, check your answers with the answer key at the end of the chapter. Record your scores on the scoring worksheet provided. To grade your essays, ask a friend or teacher to read them and give you a score ranging from 0 to 6.

Chapter 21 gives you detailed explanations of the answers. Go through the answer explanations to ALL of the questions, not just the ones you missed. There is a wealth of worthwhile information there, material that provides a good review of everything you've learned in the lectures. I've even tossed in a few good (you'll be the judge of that!) jokes to keep your brain from exploding. Good luck!

Practice Exam 2 Answer Sheet

Section 1

1. Ⓐ Ⓑ Ⓒ Ⓓ Ⓔ
2. Ⓐ Ⓑ Ⓒ Ⓓ Ⓔ
3. Ⓐ Ⓑ Ⓒ Ⓓ Ⓔ
4. Ⓐ Ⓑ Ⓒ Ⓓ Ⓔ
5. Ⓐ Ⓑ Ⓒ Ⓓ Ⓔ
6. Ⓐ Ⓑ Ⓒ Ⓓ Ⓔ
7. Ⓐ Ⓑ Ⓒ Ⓓ Ⓔ
8. Ⓐ Ⓑ Ⓒ Ⓓ Ⓔ
9. Ⓐ Ⓑ Ⓒ Ⓓ Ⓔ
10. Ⓐ Ⓑ Ⓒ Ⓓ Ⓔ
11. Ⓐ Ⓑ Ⓒ Ⓓ Ⓔ
12. Ⓐ Ⓑ Ⓒ Ⓓ Ⓔ
13. Ⓐ Ⓑ Ⓒ Ⓓ Ⓔ
14. Ⓐ Ⓑ Ⓒ Ⓓ Ⓔ
15. Ⓐ Ⓑ Ⓒ Ⓓ Ⓔ
16. Ⓐ Ⓑ Ⓒ Ⓓ Ⓔ
17. Ⓐ Ⓑ Ⓒ Ⓓ Ⓔ
18. Ⓐ Ⓑ Ⓒ Ⓓ Ⓔ
19. Ⓐ Ⓑ Ⓒ Ⓓ Ⓔ
20. Ⓐ Ⓑ Ⓒ Ⓓ Ⓔ
21. Ⓐ Ⓑ Ⓒ Ⓓ Ⓔ
22. Ⓐ Ⓑ Ⓒ Ⓓ Ⓔ
23. Ⓐ Ⓑ Ⓒ Ⓓ Ⓔ
24. Ⓐ Ⓑ Ⓒ Ⓓ Ⓔ
25. Ⓐ Ⓑ Ⓒ Ⓓ Ⓔ
26. Ⓐ Ⓑ Ⓒ Ⓓ Ⓔ
27. Ⓐ Ⓑ Ⓒ Ⓓ Ⓔ
28. Ⓐ Ⓑ Ⓒ Ⓓ Ⓔ
29. Ⓐ Ⓑ Ⓒ Ⓓ Ⓔ
30. Ⓐ Ⓑ Ⓒ Ⓓ Ⓔ
31. Ⓐ Ⓑ Ⓒ Ⓓ Ⓔ
32. Ⓐ Ⓑ Ⓒ Ⓓ Ⓔ
33. Ⓐ Ⓑ Ⓒ Ⓓ Ⓔ
34. Ⓐ Ⓑ Ⓒ Ⓓ Ⓔ
35. Ⓐ Ⓑ Ⓒ Ⓓ Ⓔ
36. Ⓐ Ⓑ Ⓒ Ⓓ Ⓔ
37. Ⓐ Ⓑ Ⓒ Ⓓ Ⓔ
38. Ⓐ Ⓑ Ⓒ Ⓓ Ⓔ
39. Ⓐ Ⓑ Ⓒ Ⓓ Ⓔ
40. Ⓐ Ⓑ Ⓒ Ⓓ Ⓔ
41. Ⓐ Ⓑ Ⓒ Ⓓ Ⓔ
42. Ⓐ Ⓑ Ⓒ Ⓓ Ⓔ
43. Ⓐ Ⓑ Ⓒ Ⓓ Ⓔ
44. Ⓐ Ⓑ Ⓒ Ⓓ Ⓔ
45. Ⓐ Ⓑ Ⓒ Ⓓ Ⓔ
46. Ⓐ Ⓑ Ⓒ Ⓓ Ⓔ
47. Ⓐ Ⓑ Ⓒ Ⓓ Ⓔ
48. Ⓐ Ⓑ Ⓒ Ⓓ Ⓔ
49. Ⓐ Ⓑ Ⓒ Ⓓ Ⓔ
50. Ⓐ Ⓑ Ⓒ Ⓓ Ⓔ

Section 2

1. Ⓐ Ⓑ Ⓒ Ⓓ Ⓔ
2. Ⓐ Ⓑ Ⓒ Ⓓ Ⓔ
3. Ⓐ Ⓑ Ⓒ Ⓓ Ⓔ
4. Ⓐ Ⓑ Ⓒ Ⓓ Ⓔ
5. Ⓐ Ⓑ Ⓒ Ⓓ Ⓔ
6. Ⓐ Ⓑ Ⓒ Ⓓ Ⓔ
7. Ⓐ Ⓑ Ⓒ Ⓓ Ⓔ
8. Ⓐ Ⓑ Ⓒ Ⓓ Ⓔ
9. Ⓐ Ⓑ Ⓒ Ⓓ Ⓔ
10. Ⓐ Ⓑ Ⓒ Ⓓ Ⓔ
11. Ⓐ Ⓑ Ⓒ Ⓓ Ⓔ
12. Ⓐ Ⓑ Ⓒ Ⓓ Ⓔ
13. Ⓐ Ⓑ Ⓒ Ⓓ Ⓔ
14. Ⓐ Ⓑ Ⓒ Ⓓ Ⓔ
15. Ⓐ Ⓑ Ⓒ Ⓓ Ⓔ
16. Ⓐ Ⓑ Ⓒ Ⓓ Ⓔ
17. Ⓐ Ⓑ Ⓒ Ⓓ Ⓔ
18. Ⓐ Ⓑ Ⓒ Ⓓ Ⓔ
19. Ⓐ Ⓑ Ⓒ Ⓓ Ⓔ
20. Ⓐ Ⓑ Ⓒ Ⓓ Ⓔ
21. Ⓐ Ⓑ Ⓒ Ⓓ Ⓔ
22. Ⓐ Ⓑ Ⓒ Ⓓ Ⓔ
23. Ⓐ Ⓑ Ⓒ Ⓓ Ⓔ
24. Ⓐ Ⓑ Ⓒ Ⓓ Ⓔ
25. Ⓐ Ⓑ Ⓒ Ⓓ Ⓔ
26. Ⓐ Ⓑ Ⓒ Ⓓ Ⓔ
27. Ⓐ Ⓑ Ⓒ Ⓓ Ⓔ
28. Ⓐ Ⓑ Ⓒ Ⓓ Ⓔ
29. Ⓐ Ⓑ Ⓒ Ⓓ Ⓔ
30. Ⓐ Ⓑ Ⓒ Ⓓ Ⓔ
31. Ⓐ Ⓑ Ⓒ Ⓓ Ⓔ
32. Ⓐ Ⓑ Ⓒ Ⓓ Ⓔ
33. Ⓐ Ⓑ Ⓒ Ⓓ Ⓔ
34. Ⓐ Ⓑ Ⓒ Ⓓ Ⓔ
35. Ⓐ Ⓑ Ⓒ Ⓓ Ⓔ
36. Ⓐ Ⓑ Ⓒ Ⓓ Ⓔ
37. Ⓐ Ⓑ Ⓒ Ⓓ Ⓔ
38. Ⓐ Ⓑ Ⓒ Ⓓ Ⓔ
39. Ⓐ Ⓑ Ⓒ Ⓓ Ⓔ
40. Ⓐ Ⓑ Ⓒ Ⓓ Ⓔ
41. Ⓐ Ⓑ Ⓒ Ⓓ Ⓔ
42. Ⓐ Ⓑ Ⓒ Ⓓ Ⓔ
43. Ⓐ Ⓑ Ⓒ Ⓓ Ⓔ
44. Ⓐ Ⓑ Ⓒ Ⓓ Ⓔ
45. Ⓐ Ⓑ Ⓒ Ⓓ Ⓔ
46. Ⓐ Ⓑ Ⓒ Ⓓ Ⓔ
47. Ⓐ Ⓑ Ⓒ Ⓓ Ⓔ
48. Ⓐ Ⓑ Ⓒ Ⓓ Ⓔ
49. Ⓐ Ⓑ Ⓒ Ⓓ Ⓔ
50. Ⓐ Ⓑ Ⓒ Ⓓ Ⓔ

Section 1

Time: 75 minutes

40 questions

Directions: Each of the Sentence Correction sentences is either entirely or partially underlined. Following the sentence are five ways of restating that sentence. Select the one that best expresses the meaning of the original sentence in a succinct and grammatically correct manner. Choice A is the same as the original sentence; select it if you think the original is preferable to the alternative choices.

Each Reading passage is followed by questions pertaining to that passage. Read the passage and answer the questions based on information stated or implied in that passage.

With each Critical Reasoning question, choose the best answer.

1. Scratching the rash caused by a skin disease just exacerbates the problem, but one cannot help doing so. The lotions and salves that the doctors prescribe seem to cost too much money and do almost no good. We have found that keeping ice packs on the rash helps, as the skin becomes so numb the itching ceases.

    Assuming the above passage to be correct, with which of the following statements would its author most likely agree?

    (A) Doctors are incapable of estimating the severity of a skin rash on another person.

    (B) Doctors' services are overpriced and do little good.

    (C) Some homemade remedies seem to work better than doctor-prescribed medications.

    (D) Patients have a greater awareness of what feels good to them than their doctors do.

    (E) Money spent on prescription medicines is wasted.

2. Fraud is the intentional misrepresentation upon which a person is intended to rely and upon which he does rely to his detriment. If a person is accidentally misled and suffers an injury (for example, if he is given erroneous financial advice), he may not sue for fraud. If a person relies on something that he was never supposed to find out, the person making the false statement that was not meant to be overheard is not liable for fraud, because there was no intentional misrepresentation. Similarly, if the person were intended to rely on the information, and did, but actually benefited from the information, there is no fraud because there was no detrimental effect of the reliance.

    Which of the following is best supported by the information above (assuming it to be true)?

    (A) If even one element of those required for fraud is absent, there is no fraud.

    (B) Fraud is a tort (a civil wrong) and never a crime.

    (C) A person must act on the information immediately upon receiving it; there is no such concept as "delayed fraud."

    (D) If there is harm from relying on the information but the harm eventually turns to gain, there is no fraud.

    (E) Fraud is an extremely difficult concept to understand and prove in a court of law.

Go on to next page

3. The number of foreign tourists visiting the United States in the past few years has risen from the number in the previous decades. The devalued dollar against foreign currency is primarily responsible for this increase.

   If true, which of the following most seriously weakens the conclusion given above?

   (A) America is granting more work visas to foreign nationals than it ever has before.

   (B) Foreign tourists have been able to get lower airfares due to price wars among the major airlines.

   (C) American colleges and universities are admitting a proportionately larger number of foreign students than they have in the past.

   (D) The number of American tourists visiting foreign countries has doubled in the past ten years.

   (E) Just over eighty percent of tourists visiting America are on their first trip here but say they will come visit again.

4. One may do the work quickly and efficiently, but if you don't do it alright, you've wasted your time entirely.

   (A) One may do the work quickly and efficiently, but if you don't do it alright, you've wasted your time entirely.

   (B) If one doesn't do the work quickly and efficiently and alright, you've wasted your time entirely.

   (C) If you don't want to waste your time entirely, do the work quickly and efficient and alright.

   (D) Wasting your time entirely is what one does when one doesn't do it alright, as well as quickly and efficiently.

   (E) You may do the work quickly and efficiently, but if you don't do it all right, you've wasted your time entirely.

5. The union has stated in their newsletter that a strike is imminent and that members should begin stockpiling food and cutting down expenses in order to save enough money to cover living costs during what will probably be a long period without income.

   (A) has stated in their newsletter that a strike is imminent

   (B) have stated in their newsletter that a strike is imminent

   (C) has stated in its newsletter that a strike is imminent

   (D) has stated in its newsletter that a strike is eminent

   (E) have stated in their newsletter that a strike is eminent

6. The rising rate in teen obesity, as indicated by statistics published in various medical journals, prove that the programs currently in place in schools to teach nutrition, proper eating habits, and exercise, have not achieved the goals that had been set for them.

   (A) prove that the programs currently in place

   (B) prove that the current programs in place

   (C) proves that the programs currently in place

   (D) prove that the current programs, in place

   (E) proves currently that programs in place

Go on to next page ⟶

The UTM grid location, or reference, of a point may easily be found if the point can be located on a map with UTM grid marks along its edges or with a UTM grid superimposed. USGS (05) (United States Geographical Survey) quadrangles published since 1959, and many published before then, have these ticks, which are printed in blue. If no USGS map with UTM ticks exists for a location, then latitude, and longitude coordi-(10) nates, or certain local grid coordinates, may be converted to UTM references by a mathematical formula. However, computer programs are necessary to perform such a task. It is always preferable to record locations initially in UTM terms (15) rather than to use translated values.

The simplicity of the UTM grid method follows from certain assumptions, which do not seriously compromise the accuracy or precision of measurements made on the common types of (20) USGS topographical maps. The primary assumption is that narrow sections of the earth's nearly spherical surface may be drawn on flat maps with little distortion. Larger sections, however, such as the contiguous United States, cannot be (25) drawn on a single flat map without noticeable distortion.

In the UTM system, the earth is divided into 60 zones, running north and south, each six degrees wide. Mapping on flat sheets within one (30) of these narrow zones is satisfactory for all but the most critical needs. Each zone is numbered, beginning with zone 1 at the 180th meridian near the International Date Line with zone numbers increasing to the east. Most of the United States (35) is included in zones 10 through 19. On a map, each zone is flattened, and a square grid is superimposed upon it. Any point in the zone may be referred to by citing its zone number, its distance in meters from the equator ("northing"), (40) and its distance in meters from a north-south reference ("easting"). These three figures — the zone number, easting, and northing — make up the complete UTM Grid Reference for any point and distinguish it from any point on earth.

(45) Northings for points north of the equator are measured directly in meters, beginning with a value of zero at the equator and increasing to the north. To avoid negative northing values for points south of the equator, the equator is arbi-(50) trarily assigned a value of 10 million meters, and points are measured with decreasing, but positive, northing values heading southward. For clarity, a minus sign usually precedes northing figures for points south of the equator. The (55) explanation may seem complicated, but experience has shown that dealing with negative

values for measurements and having to specify the direction of measurements from a reference line are more complex and less reliable. When actually working with maps, especially at the (60) scales commonly used for locating historic sites, the UTM grid system becomes extremely clear and straightforward to use.

7. By "ticks," the author most likely means

(A) beats.

(B) sounds.

(C) insects.

(D) marks.

(E) watches.

8. You may infer from the passage that which of the following is the most likely reason the author prefers not to use translated values?

(A) They are inaccurate.

(B) They are difficult or inconvenient to obtain.

(C) They are appropriate only for large-scale maps.

(D) They measure longitude but not latitude.

(E) They quickly become obsolete.

9. The purpose of the last sentence of this passage is to

(A) list possible uses for UTM grids.

(B) criticize the use of negative numbers in the UTM grid system.

(C) justify the choice of arbitrary values of points.

(D) distinguish northing from easting.

(E) reassure readers as to the feasibility of using the UTM grid system.

Go on to next page

10. The tone and style of this passage are most similar to what would be found in

    (A) an encyclopedia entry on the U.S. Geographical Survey.

    (B) a backpacking and hiking booklet.

    (C) a geography textbook.

    (D) a magazine article about using computers to create more accurate maps.

    (E) an advertisement for a map-reading course.

11. The author's opinion would be most supported by information on which of the following topics?

    (A) how to use the computer system that converts local grid coordinates to UTM references

    (B) specific situations in which mapping on flat sheets does not provide sufficiently accurate data

    (C) the distinctions between the UTM grid system and other map reading systems

    (D) the qualifications of the author to write this passage

    (E) an example of how to find the specific UTM grid location for one city

12. You may infer which of the following from the passage?

    I.   The zone number of Florida is higher than the zone number of California.

    II. The zone numbers of the United States and Mexico are identical.

    III. Zone 15 is farther north of the equator than is zone 10.

    (A) I only

    (B) II only

    (C) III only

    (D) I and II only

    (E) II and III only

13. <u>The famous race car driver with the fluorescent orange car that skis in the Alps to get himself in shape for racing</u> is signing autographs at the downtown mall this afternoon.

    (A) The famous race car driver with the fluorescent orange car that skis in the Alps to get himself in shape for racing

    (B) The famous race car driver who skis in the Alps to get himself in shape for racing his fluorescent orange car

    (C) The famous orange-car race driver that skis in the Alps to get himself in shape for racing

    (D) To get himself in shape for skiing, the famous race car driver with the fluorescent orange car

    (E) To get himself and his fluorescent orange car in shape for racing, the famous race driver is skiing in the Alps

14. The financial planner recommended that her client <u>cut down on electrical costs, landscapers' fees, and maintaining the parking lot.</u>

    (A) cut down on electrical costs, landscapers' fees, and maintaining the parking lot.

    (B) cut down electricity, landscapers, and parking lot maintenance.

    (C) cut down on electricity costs, landscapers' fees, and parking lot maintenance charges.

    (D) reduce the costs of electricity, landscapers, and parking lots.

    (E) be reducing electrical, landscaping, and maintenance fees.

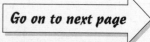

15. In the 1970s, a congregation averaged $467 per year in contributions while 77% of the congregation's members contributed some money during a typical year. In the 1990s, the average annual amount collected in contributions per member was $732, but an average of only 51% of the congregation's members contributed in a given year.

    If the statements above are correct, which of the following additional statements can logically be derived from them?

    (A) The average amount contributed from members who donated increased from the 1970s to the 1990s.

    (B) Congregants' earnings increased between the 1970s and the 1990s.

    (C) The proportion of members who were classified as wealthy was greater in the 1990s than in the 1970s.

    (D) The congregation had more members in the 1990s than in the 1970s.

    (E) The larger the congregation, the greater the likelihood of receiving large contributions from its members.

16. My dentist said that she would use the drill when I visit her today. I know that I will feel pain today.

    The argument above depends on which of the following assumptions?

    (A) The drill emits a high-frequency sound that can hurt ears.

    (B) The drill will be used for a routine teeth cleaning.

    (C) The dentist will extract some teeth.

    (D) The patient has experienced pain at the dentist's office in the past.

    (E) Use of the drill always leads to pain for the patient.

17. The entire global population of the California condor is currently at risk <u>so introducing</u> new bloodlines would help the situation.

    (A) so introducing

    (B) with introducing

    (C) to introduce

    (D) whereas introducing

    (E) because the introduction of

18. Many Californians, <u>concerned about the structural integrity of their homes, are hiring contractors to strengthen the foundations of houses and garages, hoping to be prepared</u> in case another earthquake strikes.

    (A) concerned about the structural integrity of their homes, are hiring contractors to strengthen the foundations of houses and garages, hoping to be prepared

    (B) concerning the structural integrity of their homes, hire contractors to strengthen the foundations of houses and garages, hoping and preparing themselves

    (C) due to concern about the structural integrity of their homes, are hiring contractors to strengthen their foundations, hoping to be prepared

    (D) concerned with the integrity (structural) of their homes, hire contractors to strengthen them, hoping they will be prepared

    (E) concerned about the structural integrity of their homes, are hiring contractors for strength

19. The scientist studying Stacy and Tracy, identical twins, <u>identified which one was oldest and asked her</u> to participate in the experiments first.

    (A) identified which one was oldest and asked her

    (B) identified which one was oldest and asked them

    (C) identifying which one was oldest, asking her

    (D) identifying which one was older, asking her

    (E) identified which one was older and asked her

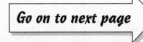
Go on to next page

20. Scientists are still studying the long-term effects of the nuclear disaster at Cherynobl, hoping to garner information they can use in treating all forms of cancer, not only those caused by exposure to radiation.

(A) are still studying the long-term effects of the nuclear disaster at Cherynobl, hoping to garner

(B) are still studying the long-term affects of the nuclear disaster at Cherynobl, hoping to garner

(C) still study the long-term affects of the nuclear disaster at Cherynobl, hopefully garnering

(D) still studying the long-term effects of the nuclear disaster at Cherynobl, garnering

(E) study still the long-term affects of the nuclear disaster at Cherynobl, having garnered

Due to the involuntary simultaneous contraction of 15 facial muscles, the upper lip is raised, partially uncovering the teeth and effecting a downward curving of the furrows that extend from the wings of both nostrils to the corners of the mouth. The eyes undergo reflex lacrimation and vascular engorgement. At the same time, an abrupt strong expiration of air is followed by spasmodic contractions of the chest and diaphragm, resulting in a series of expiration-inspiration microcycles with interval pauses. The whole body may be thrown backward, shaken or convulsed due to other spasmodic skeletal muscle contractions. We call this condition laughter.

Of all human expressive behaviors, laughter has proven a most fascinating enigma to philosophers and scientists alike. Its physiology, neurology, and anthropological origins and purpose are only partially defined. But its effects and uses are becoming increasingly apparent to health care professionals.

Laughter is considered to be an innate human response that develops during the first few weeks of life. Evidence of the innate quality of laughter is seen in its occurrence in deaf and blind infants and children who are completely without visual or auditory clues from their environment. Darwin propounded in his "Principle of Antithesis" that laughter develops as the infant's powerful reward signal of comfort and well-being to the nurturing adult. This signal is totally antithetical perceptually to the screams or cries of distress associated with discomfort. Laughter seems to play an important role in the promotion of social unity, production of a sense of well-being, communication of well-being, and as a mechanism for coping with stressful situations. Physiologically, both reflexive (tickle-response) and heart-felt (mental response) laughter effect changes to the human system, which may be significant in the treatment and prevention of illness. These include laughter's association with an increase in pulse rate, probably due to increased levels of circulatory catecholamines (blood catecholamine levels vary directly with the intensity of laughter). There is an increase in respiration. There is a decrease in blood CO_2 levels. There is a possible increase in secretion of brain and pituitary endorphins — the body's natural anesthetics that relieve pain, inhibit emotional response to pain, and thus reduce suffering. There is a decrease in red blood cell sedimentation rate ("sed rate" is associated with the body's level of infection or inflammation).

Go on to next page

While it is possible that the effect laughter and other salutary emotions have is primarily one of a placebo, this in no way minimizes the therapeutic potential for these emotions. It may (60) be possible that there is a physical chemistry associated with the will to live.

Immanuel Kant, in his "Critique of Pure Reason," wrote that laughter is the physician of the body. Echoing Kant's thesis nearly two cen- (65) turies later, Norman Cousins, author, senior lec- turer at the UCLA School of Medicine, and editor of *Saturday Review,* became the modern- day patron saint of self-healing through the power of laughter.

21. According to the passage, all of the follow- ing are potential benefits of laughter EXCEPT:

    (A) It plays a key part in the advancement of social accord.

    (B) It assures caregivers that they are pleasing the infant under their care.

    (C) It is critical to human development during the first few weeks of life.

    (D) It stimulates the secretion of natural pain relievers found in the brain.

    (E) It helps humans deal with stressful situations.

22. According to the passage, laughter is a con- dition that largely results from

    (A) a desire to treat and prevent illness

    (B) a learning process that takes place over the first few months of life

    (C) decreased red blood cell sedimentation rate

    (D) the contraction of several muscles throughout the body

    (E) complex physiological changes in blood chemistry

23. It can be inferred from the passage that the author considers the possibility that laugh- ter has a positive effect on the body prima- rily by way of a placebo to be

    (A) incidental to the discussion of physio- logical responses presented in the third paragraph

    (B) completely unimportant to achieving a better understanding of the benefits of laughter

    (C) damaging to the hypothesis that laugh- ter helps treat and prevent illness

    (D) a factor that must be dealt with before scientist can achieve a good under- standing of laughter

    (E) evidence that laughter promotes social interaction and individual self-esteem

24. The passage supports which of the follow- ing about human physiology?

    (A) Pulse rate increases only in the pres- ence of increased circulatory cate- cholamine levels.

    (B) Laughter is more effective than other methods of increasing endorphin secretion.

    (C) Intense laughter is associated with a relatively high level of blood cate- cholamines.

    (D) A decrease in red blood cell sedimenta- tion rate reduces inflammation in the body.

    (E) Respiration rate and blood CO_2 levels are typically inversely related.

Go on to next page

25. Which of the following statements is most consistent with Immanuel Kant's belief, presented in lines 62-64?

    (A) A physician who tries to amuse her patients in no way shirks her responsibility to use the latest medical findings.

    (B) People who laugh have certain advantages over those who don't when it comes to protecting their own health.

    (C) Laughter will become more beneficial once more is known about its physiological, neurological, and anthropological origins.

    (D) Ill individuals will get well sooner if they force themselves to laugh.

    (E) Any one episode of laughter will provide only minimal benefit, but several episodes can help significantly.

26. After a four-year survey, we have found that only 12 percent of those studying speed reading actually used what they learned in their day-to-day assignments. Therefore, we have concluded that speed reading is useless and should no longer be taught.

    Which of the following, if true, would most weaken the conclusion of the above passage?

    (A) The students in this survey were less educated than the average students nationwide.

    (B) Most speed-reading surveys cover at least a five-year period.

    (C) Speed reading is most advantageous when used in timed examinations, not for doing homework assignments.

    (D) Speed reading is extremely difficult to learn.

    (E) Only ten percent of anything learned is used daily.

27. Cars are safer than planes. Fifty percent of plane accidents result in death, while only one percent of car accidents result in death.

    Which of the following, if true, would most seriously weaken the argument above?

    (A) Planes are inspected more often than cars.

    (B) The number of car accidents is several hundred thousand times higher than the number of plane accidents.

    (C) Pilots never fly under the influence of alcohol, while car drivers often do.

    (D) Plane accidents are usually the fault of air traffic controllers, not pilots.

    (E) Planes carry more passengers than cars do.

28. As world oil reserves dwindled, politicians, economists, and environmental experts urged consumers to buy fuel-efficient cars. For years, however, most people who purchased an automobile based their decision on the style, performance, and prestige of the car, and only those who could not afford any other car would buy one that was economical with regard to fuel. The trend has finally changed in the last two years as the top-selling high-priced cars are now those that are most fuel-efficient. At last, consumers consider the conservation of fuel to be the most important factor when buying a new car.

    Which of the following, if true, most seriously weakens the conclusion about the factors car buyers consider?

    (A) Five years ago, the top-selling high-priced car was only average with regard to fuel efficiency.

    (B) People who can afford expensive cars deny that they are interested in saving fuel when buying a new car.

    (C) More people have become aware of a worldwide oil shortage in the last two years.

    (D) Automobile designers have now created many fuel-efficient cars that are stylish and prestigious.

    (E) Because of inflation, cars are much more expensive now than they were ten years ago.

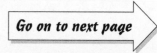
Go on to next page

29. Detective Olson, <u>being worried over some noticeable increase in hot burglaries in his precinct and citizen paranoia rising as a result,</u> has formed a task force of citizens and police officers to study the issue and formulate recommendations.

    (A) being worried over some noticeable increase in hot burglaries in his precinct and citizen paranoia rising as a result,

    (B) worried over the noticeable increase in hot burglaries in his precinct, and with citizen paranoia rising as a result,

    (C) worried over the noticeable increase in hot burglaries and citizen paranoia in his precinct,

    (D) worried over the noticeable increase in hot burglaries in his precinct and being worried over the resulting rising citizen paranoia,

    (E) with some noticeable increase in hot burglaries and rising citizen paranoia in his district worrying him,

30. <u>The last person we expected to see in prison, the warden introduced us to a famous movie star</u> who was secretly spending weekends in jail as part of a work-release program instigated for drunk drivers.

    (A) The last person we expected to see in prison, the warden introduced us to a famous movie star

    (B) The warden introduced us to the last person we expected to see in prison, a famous movie star

    (C) A famous movie star, the warden introduced us to the last person we expected to see in prison,

    (D) Introduced to the famous movie star by the warden, the last person we ever expected to see in prison

    (E) The famous movie star, the last person we ever expected to see in prison, was introduced to us by the warden

31. The hockey player, along with his younger brother and cousin, <u>are going to give</u> a demonstration of stick skills at the new rink on the south side of town.

    (A) are going to give

    (B) should give

    (C) giving

    (D) is going to give

    (E) will have been giving

32. Motivated by the success of his friends, <u>it was decided by the businessman to take his company public.</u>

    (A) it was decided by the businessman to take his company public

    (B) it was decided to take his company public by the businessman

    (C) the businessman decided to take his company public

    (D) the businessman decided to be taking his company public

    (E) the businessman decisively took his company public

Chile's human history apparently began about 10,000 years ago, when migrating Indians followed the line of the Andes and settled in fertile valleys and along the coast. The Incas briefly extended their empire into the north, but the (05) area's remoteness prevented any significant impact. In 1541, the Spanish, under Pedro de Valdivia, encountered about one million Indians from various cultures who supported themselves primarily through slash-and-burn agriculture and (10) hunting. Although the Spaniards did not find the gold and silver they had sought there, they recognized the agricultural potential of Chile's central valley, and Chile became part of the Viceroyalty of Peru. (15)

Chilean colonial society was heavily influenced by the *latifundio* system of large landholdings, kinship politics, the Roman Catholic Church, and an aggressive frontier attitude stemming from Indian wars. The drive for independ- (20) ence from Spain was precipitated by usurpation of the Spanish throne by Napoleon's brother Joseph. A national junta in the name of Ferdinand — heir to the deposed king — was formed on September 18, 1810. Spanish attempts (25) to reimpose arbitrary rule during the Reconquista led to a prolonged struggle under Bernardo O'Higgins, Chile's most renowned patriot. Chilean independence was formally proclaimed on February 12, 1818. (30)

The political revolution brought little social change, however, and 19th century Chilean society preserved the essence of the stratified colonial social structure. The system of presidential absolutism eventually predominated, but the (35) wealthy land owners continued to control Chile.

Although Chile established a representative democracy in the early 20th century, it soon became unstable and degenerated into a system protecting the interests of the ruling oligarchy. (40)

Line

Go on to next page

By the 1920s, the newly emergent middle and working classes were powerful enough to elect a reformist president, but his program was frus-
(45) trated by a conservative congress.

After constitutional rule was restored in 1932, a strong middle-class party, the Radicals, formed. The Radical Party became the key force in coalition governments for the next 20 years.
(50) The 1930s saw the emergence of Marxist groups with strong popular support. During the period of Radical Party dominance (1932–1952), the state increased its role in the economy. However, presidents generally were more conservative
(55) than the parties supporting them, and conservative political elements continued to exert considerable power through their influence over the economy and control of rural voters.

33. The author is primarily concerned with

(A) the Indian-Spaniard South American wars.

(B) why Chile became an independent country.

(C) an overview of Chilean history and culture.

(D) farming in Chile.

(E) American influence in Chile.

34. Which of the following best describes the relationship between congress and the workers in the 1920s?

(A) They were in opposition.

(B) They worked together toward the same goals.

(C) They took turns governing the country.

(D) They united only once to overthrow the government.

(E) Congress was composed of workers; they were one and the same.

35. The tone of the passage is

(A) opinionated.

(B) argumentative.

(C) objective.

(D) urgent.

(E) dolorous.

36. <u>Because everyone is on their best behavior</u> during job interviews, employee relations specialists often recommend meeting applicants in a more informal setting at least once before hiring them.

(A) Because everyone is on their best behavior

(B) Because everyone is being on his best behavior

(C) Everyone, being on his best behavior,

(D) Because they are on their best behavior

(E) Because job applicants are on their best behavior

37. When the manned space program began, astronauts were treated with scorn by engineers, who considered themselves the glamour boys of the program. Astronauts were merely passengers who had to fight the engineers in order to get a window in the capsule and to have piloting control. A few decades later, everyone has heard of John Glenn and Alan Shepard, but how many of us can name even one engineer?

Which of the following conclusions proceeds most logically from the preceding paragraph?

(A) Astronauts are more extroverted than are engineers.

(B) The abilities of engineers have lessened over the years, while those of astronauts have increased.

(C) The public understands the role of the engineer better than it comprehends the role of the astronaut.

(D) Modern astronauts are more qualified than were their earlier counterparts.

(E) People are more interested in the role of the astronaut than in the role of the engineer.

Go on to next page

38. UCLA basketball fan: I am so glad that college basketball changed its rules and put in a shot clock. When there was no clock, a team with inferior ability could keep the ball away from the other team by passing it around the entire game. The winning team should be the one that is better at shooting baskets, not at playing keep away.

North Carolina basketball fan: I disagree. The object of basketball is to win. If playing keep-away is the way for a team to win, it should do so.

The North Carolina fan's response indicates that he has misunderstood the UCLA fan's remark to mean

(A) games without a shot clock are boring.

(B) true basketball does not involve a game of keep-away.

(C) it is unwise to utilize a keep-away strategy, even when permitted to do so.

(D) a game with a shot clock is better than a game without one.

(E) the best team doesn't always win.

39. Scientists believe that the heat from global warming <u>can effect virtually every aspect of the planet, from the birthrates of animals and the growth rates of plants.</u>

(A) can effect virtually every aspect of the planet, from the birthrates of animals and the growth rates of plants.

(B) can effect virtually every aspect of the planet, from the birthrates of animals to the growth rates of plants.

(C) can affect virtually every aspect of the planet, from the birthrates of animals and the growth rates of plants.

(D) can affect every virtual aspect of the planet, the birthrates of animals, and the growth rates of plants.

(E) can affect virtually every aspect of the planet, from the birthrates of animals to the growth rates of plants.

40. By asking for income information, a credit card company will be successful because it will not extend credit to those who are incapable of paying their bills.

The argument above logically depends upon each of the following assumptions EXCEPT

(A) The success of a credit card company is primarily dependent upon the ability of its cardholders to pay their credit card bills.

(B) Credit card applicants will be truthful in reporting their incomes.

(C) A credit card company will not be successful if it extends credit to some people not capable of paying their bills.

(D) People who are capable of paying credit card bills do, in fact, pay them.

(E) The credit card company will know how to use the income information to determine who is capable of paying a credit card bill.

41. An editorial in a newspaper argued that sexual characteristics were limiting and determined irrefutably the different roles of men and women. The author's primary premise was that women are, for example, intrinsically more patient than men. Ms. Faulk threw the paper down in disgust halfway through the editorial.

Ms. Faulk argued against the editorial by

(A) her judicious use of counterpoint.

(B) her actions and boycotting of the rest of the editorial.

(C) her refutation of the editorial.

(D) her example as a very patient woman.

(E) her intention to write a critical letter to the newspaper.

 STOP You may check your work on this section only. Do not go on to the next section until you are told to do so.

Section 2

Time: 75 minutes

37 questions

Directions: Following each Data Sufficiency question are two numbered statements. Determine whether the information given in the statements is sufficient to answer the question. Choose

(A) if statement 1 alone is sufficient to answer the question, but statement 2 alone is not sufficient to answer the question.

(B) if statement 2 alone is sufficient to answer the question, but statement 1 alone is not sufficient to answer the question.

(C) if both statements are needed to answer the question, but neither statement alone is sufficient to answer the question.

(D) if either statement 1 alone or statement 2 alone is sufficient to answer the question.

(E) if neither statement 1 alone nor statement 2 alone nor both statements together give enough information to answer the question.

Information:

1. Unless the problem specifically states otherwise, all figures lie in a plane.

2. Angles measure more than zero.

3. Lines that appear to be straight are straight.

4. A figure will follow information given in the question stem but will not necessarily follow additional information given in statement 1 or statement 2.

5. Angles and points are in the order shown.

6. All numbers used in this section are real numbers.

7. If more than one value for a quantity is possible, the data given in the statements may not be sufficient to determine the value of a quantity.

Example:

$3x - y = 25$. What is the value of x?

(1) $25 - y = 15$

(2) $2y^2 = 200$

Statement 1 alone is sufficient to answer the question. If $25 - y = 15$ then $y = 10$. Plug 10 back into the original equation and solve for x. First $3x + 10 = 25$. Then $3x = 15$. Finally, $x = 5$.

Statement 2 alone is not sufficient to answer the question. If $2y^2 = 200$ and $y^2 = 100$, $y^2 = +10$. Plug 10 back into the original equation and solve for x. First, $3x + 10 = 25$. Then $3x = 15$. Finally, $x = 5$. But if $y = -10$, then $x = {}^{35}\!/_3$.

Because statement 1 alone is sufficient and statement 2 alone is not sufficient to answer the question, the answer is A. *Correct Answer:* A

For each problem-solving question, solve the problem and then choose the correct answer from the choices given. You may use the exam booklet for scratchwork.

1. The remainder when *n* is divided by 5 is 4. What is the remainder when 3*n* is divided by 5?

   (A) 0

   (B) 1

   (C) 2

   (D) 3

   (E) 5

2. The average weight of five friends is 150 pounds. When one friend leaves, the average weight of the remaining people is 160. What is the weight of the friend who left?

   (A) 170

   (B) 150

   (C) 140

   (D) 135

   (E) 110

Go on to next page

3. In four years, Mary Alyce will be twice as old as she was last year. Mary Alyce is how many years old now?

(A) 12

(B) 9

(C) 8

(D) 6

(E) 4

4. Is $m^2 - n^2 > 0$?

(1) $m < 0$

(2) $n > 0$

5. What is the area of trapezoid *ABCD?*

(1) $AD = 5$

(2) $DC = 12$

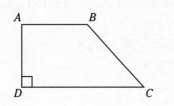

6. This year a $42 coat will be marked up 200 percent. What will be its new price?

(A) $242

(B) $142

(C) $126

(D) $84

(E) $42

7. Lael took seven exams. Her average score was 82. Her first six scores were 75, 91, 85, 89, 74, and 79. What was her seventh score?

(A) 90

(B) 87

(C) 82

(D) 81

(E) 80

8. An 18" loaf of bread is cut into three pieces. How long is each piece?

(1) The shortest piece is 7" less than the second longest piece.

(2) The sum of the first and last pieces is equal to the length of the middle piece.

9. An elementary school teacher walks down the aisle, checking homework. He checks the math for the first student, the English for the second, the science for the third, and the history for the fourth. If he continues this pattern, what homework will he check for the 38th student?

(A) math

(B) English

(C) science

(D) history

(E) It cannot be determined from the information given.

10. Given that $2r = 5s = 3t$, which of the following is a true statement? ($r, s, t > 0$).

I. $3t = 2r + s$

II. $6s = 3t + r$

III. $10s = 3t + 2r$

(A) I only

(B) II only

(C) III only

(D) I and III only

(E) I, II, and III

11. What is the sum of the degree measures of the shaded angles?

(A) 90

(B) 180

(C) 360

(D) 720

(E) 900

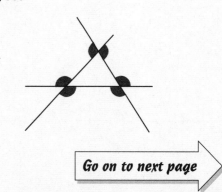

Go on to next page

12. $x > y > z$. Is $y + z = x$?

    (1) $\frac{y}{x} = \frac{1}{2}$

    (2) $y + z = 100$

> Questions 13–14 refer to the following definition: The "price" of any number is the number of positive distinct prime factors that comprise the number. For example, the "price" of 75 is 2, because $75 = 5 \times 5 \times 3$.

13. 5 is the "price" of which of the following?

    (A) 2310

    (B) 2000

    (C) 1550

    (D) 1220

    (E) 1000

14. The "price" of 100 – the "price" of $32 =$

    (A) 68

    (B) 32

    (C) 3

    (D) 1

    (E) –1

15. How much does a crate of pinion nuts cost when it is not on sale?

    (1) The crate of nuts on sale at 60 percent off costs $40.

    (2) The profit on the sale of the crate of nuts is 20 percent of its cost.

16. What is x in the following figure?

    (1) $180 - 2y = 3x$

    (2) $y = 2x$

17. Emily works three times as fast as Russ. Together, they can address x envelopes in y hours. In terms of x, how many envelopes can Emily, working alone, address in y hours?

    (A) $3x$

    (B) $2x$

    (C) x

    (D) $\frac{3}{4}x$

    (E) $\frac{2}{3}x$

18. A box of candy contains three types of candy: 20 cremes, 15 chews, and 12 nuts. Each time LaVonne reaches into the box, she pulls out a piece of candy, takes a bite out of it, and throws it away. She pulls out a creme, a nut, a chew, a nut, a creme, and a chew. What is the probability that on the next reach she will pull out a nut?

    (A) $\frac{15}{47}$

    (B) $\frac{13}{41}$

    (C) $\frac{10}{41}$

    (D) $\frac{13}{15}$

    (E) $\frac{11}{15}$

19. $\dfrac{6a^{10}b^5c^7}{3a^5b^9c^7} =$

    (A) $2a^2b^4c$

    (B) $\dfrac{2a^2b^4}{c}$

    (C) $\dfrac{2a^5b^4}{c}$

    (D) $2a^5b^4$

    (E) $\dfrac{2a^5}{b^4}$

20. From last year to this year, what percent increase was there in the number of games the bowling team won?

    (1) Last year the team won 42 games.

    (2) The team won double the number of games this year that it won last year.

Go on to next page

21. What is m?

    (1) $3m + 2n = 14$

    (2) $2n + 6m = 21$

22. A rectangle of area 32 has perimeter 24. What is the ratio of the sides of the rectangle? (Assume that the sides are integers.)

    (A) 4:1

    (B) 3:1

    (C) 3:2

    (D) 2:1

    (E) 1:1

23. Jessica receives a chain letter, which she copies and sends on to five friends. Each of them sends the letter to five more friends. The cycle continues, with each recipient sending the letter to five more friends. Which of the following represents the number of people receiving letters on the fifth round? (Count Jessica, sending the letters, as round one.)

    (A) 15,625

    (B) 3,125

    (C) 625

    (D) 225

    (E) 125

24. What is the length of line segment RS in the following figure?

    (A) 3

    (B) 4

    (C) 4.5

    (D) 5

    (E) 5.5

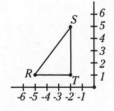

25.
    $9AB5$
    $+ABAB$
    $\overline{1C,667}$

    Which of the following is true of A, B, C?

    (A) $A = 3, B = 3, C = 3$

    (B) $A = 4, B = 3, C = 3$

    (C) $A = 4, B = 2, C = 3$

    (D) $A = 3, B = 2, C = 4$

    (E) $A = 4, B = 2, C = 4$

26. Skip spends $385 on 25 CDs. If all the CDs cost the same, what would he pay for only 11 CDs?

    (A) $295.80

    (B) $260.50

    (C) $169.40

    (D) $125.20

    (E) $101.10

27. If Barney's average (arithmetic mean) score for five tests was 92, what was his highest score?

    (1) His highest score was exactly the same as his two lowest scores combined.

    (2) His highest score was 10 points higher than his second highest score.

28. Jermaine sold $1,000 worth of gold-plated necklaces last year. What percent of costs was his profit?

    (1) Last year his profits were $200 more than his costs.

    (2) His costs last year were 60 percent less than his sales.

29. Is $x + y > 10$?

    (1) $x > 0$; $y < 0$

    (2) $xy = -100$

Go on to next page

30. Pellaton lives 15 miles from Cottam and 35 miles from Roberts. If x is the number of miles between Cottam and Roberts, which of the following represents the possible values of x?

    (A) $10 \le x \le 35$

    (B) $20 \le x \le 35$

    (C) $25 \le x \le 35$

    (D) $20 \le x \le 50$

    (E) $35 \le x \le 50$

31. What is the number of degrees in angle x?

    (A) 360

    (B) 260

    (C) 180

    (D) 110

    (E) 70

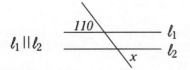

$\ell_1 \parallel \ell_2$

32. If $x = 3a - 4$ and $y = 2$, then for what value of a does $x = y$?

    (A) ½

    (B) ¾

    (C) ⅘

    (D) ⅛

    (E) 1

33. What is the 100th term in the series?

    (1) The fifth term in the series is even.

    (2) The first two terms in the series are 4 and 16.

34. In a high school, 25% of the students are blondes, and 40% of the students are female. If 50% of the females are blondes, how many of the students are blond females?

    (1) The school has 84 males.

    (2) There are 140 students in the school.

Citizen of the Month		
Student	*Points in September*	*Points in October*
Amanda	75	90
Bret	90	100
Carlyse	60	90
Denzil	100	120
Edmund	70	90

35. The chart represents the number of points students get in their quest to be the good citizen of the month for their class. Which of these five students has had the greatest percentage increase in points from September to October?

    (A) Amanda

    (B) Bret

    (C) Carlyse

    (D) Denzil

    (E) Edmund

36. What is the probability of choosing a yellow marble at random out of a jar?

    (1) The jar contains 15 marbles.

    (2) Eight of the marbles are black.

37. The perimeter of a rectangular floor is 36 square feet. What is the length of the floor?

    (1) The length of the floor is twice the width of the floor.

    (2) The sum of the measures of the four sides of the floor is six times the width of the floor.

STOP You may check your work on this section only.
Do not go on to the next section until you are told to do so.

Section 3

Time: 30 minutes

One essay

Directions: Present and explain your view on the following issue. While there is no single right or wrong answer to the question, be sure to consider various points of view as you explain the reasons behind your own perspective.

"People facing higher taxes to support public schools complain that the schools often 'waste' money on 'luxury' courses like art and music and propose that these courses be eliminated from the curriculum. They don't realize that the primary purpose of school is to produce a well-rounded individual, not simply one who understands the basics of math and literature."

Which point of view do you agree with — that courses like art and music should be offered or that they should be abolished? Justify your position by using examples from your personal and professional experiences, reading, or general observations.

_____

_____

_____

_____

_____

_____

_____

_____

_____

_____

_____

_____

_____

_____

_____

_____

Section 4

Time: 30 minutes

One essay

Directions: Critique the following argument. Identify evidence that will strengthen or weaken the argument, point out assumptions underlying the argument, and offer counterexamples to the argument.

The following statements were part of a speech made to a group of voters.

"The proposed law, nicknamed 'Three strikes and you're out,' sends criminals to jail for life upon conviction of a third crime. This law unfairly burdens prisons and removes from the judge the discretion in sentencing that is his or her major role in the court-room. Such laws should not be passed."

Discuss your point of view on the preceding argument. Analyze the evidence used as well as the general reasoning. Present points that strengthen the argument or make it more compelling.

STOP You may check your work on this section only.
Do not go on to the next section until you are told to do so.

Answer Key for Practice Exam 2

Section 1

Verbal Section

1. C	24. C	
2. A	25. B	
3. B	26. C	
4. E	27. B	
5. C	28. D	
6. C	29. C	
7. D	30. B	
8. B	31. D	
9. E	32. D	
10. C	33. C	
11. E	34. A	
12. A	35. C	
13. B	36. E	
14. C	37. E	
15. A	38. C	
16. E	39. E	
17. A	40. C	
18. A		
19. E		
20. A		
21. C		
22. D		
23. A		

Section 2

Math Section

1. C	24. D
2. E	25. C
3. D	26. C
4. E	27. E
5. E	28. D
6. C	29. E
7. D	30. D
8. C	31. D
9. B	32. B
10. C	33. E
11. D	34. D
12. E	35. C
13. A	36. E
14. D	37. D
15. A	
16. B	
17. D	
18. C	
19. E	
20. B	
21. C	
22. D	
23. B	

Scoring

Here's the way GMAT questions are scored:

✔ You get one point for each question you answer correctly.

✔ You get zero points for each incorrect answer.

To determine your Verbal and Math converted scores, complete Worksheet 20-1 by following these steps:

1. **If you have not already done so, compare your answers with the preceding answer key and mark each correct answer with a plus or star and circle each incorrect answer.**

2. **Add the number of verbal questions correct. This is your raw verbal score.**

3. **Add the number of math questions correct. This is your raw math score.**

4. **Add your raw verbal score and your raw math score. This is your raw total score.**

Note: Return to Chapter 9 to review how schools use the Writing Assessment scores.

Worksheet 20-1	GMAT Scaled (Converted) Scoring Worksheet	
	Verbal	*Math*
Correct answers	_____	_____

Table 20-1	GMAT Scaled (Converted) Scoring Chart		
Raw Verbal Score	*GMAT Verbal*	*Raw Math Score*	*GMAT Math*
41	60		
40	59		
39	58		
38	56		
37	55	37	60
36	53	36	58
35	51	35	57
34	50	34	55
33	48	33	54
32	47	32	51
31	45	31	50
30	44	30	48
29	42	29	47
28	41	28	45
27	39	27	43
26	38	26	42
25	36	25	40
24	35	24	38
23	33	23	37
22	32	22	35
21	31	21	33
20	29	20	31
19	28	19	30
18	26	18	28
17	25	17	27
16	23	16	25
15	22	15	23
14	20	14	21
13	19	13	20
12	17	12	18
11	16	11	17
10	14	10	15
9	13	9	14
8	12	8	12
7	10	7	10
6	9	6	8
5	7	5	6
4	6	4	5
3	5	3	4
2	3	2	2
1	1	1	1
0	0	0	0

Find your converted scores for both Verbal and Math in Table 20-1. Add them together and use that sum to find your converted total score in Table 20-2.

These charts are a *very* rough estimate. Your actual score is determined by the difficulty level of the questions you personally encounter. The test is adaptive for each test taker. (Return to Chapter 1 for a more complete explanation of scoring the CAT.)

Table 20-2 GMAT Total Scaled (Converted) Scoring Chart

Raw Score	GMAT Total Score	Raw Score	GMAT Total Score
78	800	39	490
77	790	38	480
76	780	37–36	470
75	770	35	460
74	760	34	450
73	750	33–32	440
72	740	31	430
71–70	730	30	420
69	720	29–28	410
68	710	27	400
67–66	700	26	390
65	690	25–24	380
64	680	23	370
63–62	670	22	360
61	660	21–20	350
60	650	19	340
59	640	18	330
58–57	630	17–16	320
56	620	15	310
55	610	14	300
54	600	13–12	290
53–52	590	11	280
51	580	10	270
50	570	9–8	260
49–48	560	7	250
47	550	6	240
46	540	5–4	230
45–44	530		
43	520	3	220
42	510	2	210
41–40	500	1–0	200

Chapter 21

Practice Exam 2: Answers and Explanations

● ●

Section 1

1. **C.** This is a good, wishy-washy answer. The word *some* is often part of a correct answer choice because it gives more options than *all* or *none*. The passage is telling of one homemade remedy that works better than a doctor's prescription. Don't go overboard and generalize from this that all doctor's prescriptions are useless (choice E) or that doctor's services themselves are useless (choices A and B). Choice D may be a true statement, but it does not address the question as well as choice C.

2. **A.** The passage gives the elements that make up fraud and then provides examples of how not having those elements negates the fraud. Most of the other answer choices take the information too far, discussing points not brought up in the paragraph. Nothing was mentioned about the distinction between a tort and a crime, eliminating choice B. Choice C may be slightly tricky. The passage does say that a person must act upon the fraud, but does not discuss the time frame for doing so. You do not know from the passage whether, in fact, there is such a concept as "delayed fraud." Choice D is the trickiest of the answer choices. The passage does say that there is no fraud if there is no harm. However, it does not say that there is no fraud if the harm eventually turns to gain. Don't take the information and make more of it than is there. Choice E may or may not be true; who knows? The passage gives no information about the difficulty of understanding and proving fraud.

3. **B.** First, identify the conclusion. It is that the devalued foreign currency is primarily responsible for the increase in the number of foreign tourists visiting America. Predict what the opposite of this would be: The devaluation is not primarily responsible for the increase. Predict that therefore something else must be primarily responsible. Lower airfares due to price wars would contribute to increased tourism.

   Choice A is a trap; it seems plausible until careful reading tells you it is talking about foreigners who come here to *work,* not to take tours. Choice C also talks about the wrong group of people, about students, not about tourists. Choice D is completely irrelevant; who cares how many Americans go abroad? The discussion is about how many foreigners come to America. Choice E addresses tourists, but does not say *why* the tourists will come again.

4. **E.** The first mistake is the hodgepodge of *one* and *you.* You can't mix and match these so indiscriminately. The grammar police are as bad as the fashion police are when it comes to clashing ensembles. Use either *one* or *you,* not both. Eliminate choices A and B. The second mistake is one you may not know: There is no such word as *alright.* The correct words are *all right.* You probably have been guilty of writing *alright* many times in your life ("You want to know how I did on the paper? I did alright, I guess."). Ain't no such critter. The word *altogether* is okay; the word *alright* is an abomination. Eliminate choices C and D, all right?

5. **C.** This is my favorite question in this exam. There are three major grammatical concepts. First, *union* is singular and requires a singular verb: the union *has,* not the union *have.* Eliminate choices B and E. Because the union is singular, it requires a singular pronoun as well: the union has stated in *its* newsletter, not in *their* newsletter. Eliminate choice A. And the third grammatical concept tests *imminent* versus *eminent. Imminent* means about to happen. Think of this word as "in a minute." If a woman is nine months pregnant, birth is *imminent,* or will happen "in a minute." *Eminent* means outstanding or distinguished. My *eminent* colleague's maternity leave is imminent.

6. **C.** This is a classic subject-verb question. The subject, "the rising rate," is singular and requires a singular verb, "proves." Eliminate choices A, B, and D. Choice E changes the meaning of the sentence. "Currently" means that the programs are in place now in the school, not that something is now being proven.

7. **D.** The marks along the edge of the maps are the ticks. You can deduce this from the second sentence, which says that ticks are printed in blue. Of the answer choices, only marks can be printed. You can't print a beat or print an insect, for example.

If you chose A, B, or C, you probably didn't go back to the passage to see how the word was used but merely went on instinct. Always go back, back, back to check how the *author* uses the word; often he uses it differently than you'd expect.

8. **B.** In lines 12–13, you learned that computers are necessary for this translation. Use this statement to infer (the passage doesn't come right out and say this) that such translation is not always convenient (where's a computer when you need one?).

Choice A is the trap, but it is illogical. A computer most likely would give better or more precise readings than a human would.

9. **E.** The last sentence reassures readers that the grid system becomes "extremely clear and straightforward to use" with a map. Even if you don't know the meaning of *feasibility* (probability or possibility), you could get the correct answer from the word *reassure.*

If you chose B, you forgot one tip you learned in the reading lecture: The GMAT rarely says anything mean and nasty about anyone. Your answers should be sweet and kind, no matter how grumpy *you* are over having to read all this dull material.

10. **C.** Going back to the passage to look for the answer to this question is a waste of time. This is an inference question, one you can answer only by "reading between the lines" and getting a general idea of the tone and purpose of the passage. Often, the best way to answer this sort of question is by the process of elimination. The passage is not specifically about the U.S. Geographical Survey; the USGS is mentioned only as an example of one type of organization that uses the UTM system. The focus is on the UTM grid location system, not on the USGS, eliminating choice A.

Although hikers need to know how to read maps, the focus of the maps discussed in this passage is on a global scale. If a backpacker or hiker is so lost she doesn't know what zone of the earth she is in, she has bigger problems than understanding the UTM grid system! Dump choice B. Choice D is tempting because computers are mentioned in the passage. However, the focus of the passage is not on using computers, which are mentioned only as being desirable for their accuracy, but on *understanding* how to use the UTM grid system. Eliminate choice D. Choice E can also be superficially tempting. The passage is about reading maps. However, if this were an advertisement for a map-reading course, it went into way too much detail. The student may not need to take the course at all but could make do with just the info gleaned from the passage! Only choice C remains. This is an informational, narrative passage, just giving information on how to read a particular type of map. Such information is likely to be presented in a geography textbook.

11. **E.** This question may seem somewhat subjective. You are asked to use your common sense, your reasoning skills, rather than to go back to the passage and locate a specific sentence or topic. A good way to approach this question is to eliminate wrong answers. Choice A is too comprehensive for this passage. Instructions on using a computer system would be outside the scope of the passage; besides, several different systems may be available. Choice B sounds plausible. However, while it may be somewhat useful to know when the UTM grid system in general doesn't work, the readers probably don't need to know such specific information as why the basic assumption upon which the whole premise rests — that the earth can be mapped on a flat surface — may be flawed. Keep in mind why the passage was written: to acquaint readers with the UTM grid system and how to use it. Choice C would be adding too much information, going outside the scope of the passage. The focus is on the UTM grid system; getting into a discussion of other systems would not enhance the passage but would change it. Choice D is completely extraneous. The passage is not giving a controversial theory, something arguable in which the qualifications of the writer may influence your perception of what is said. Here, the passage gives just the facts. Choice E is the best answer. The passage is about how to use the UTM grid location system. Giving a specific example of that use would clarify the topic in the readers' minds. In general, giving a specific example to supplement the main idea of the passage makes the passage more understandable and relevant to its readers.

12. **A.** Lines 32–35 tell you that the zone numbers increase as they go east. Because Florida is east of California, it's a safe bet that Florida's zone number is higher than California's. Because statement I is correct, eliminate choices B and C. Because the United States goes farther east than Mexico, the two countries probably don't have the same zone numbers. Because statement II is wrong, eliminate choices D and E. Only A is left.

    For those of you who like to finish what you start: Statement III is wrong because the zones measure only from west to east, not north to south. This is a little tricky because you read about northing (measuring the distance in meters from the equator) near the spot where you read about zone numbers. You can avoid this trap by eliminating answers as you go, as I did earlier.

13. **B.** The original sounds as if the orange car goes skiing in the Alps! Choice C sounds as if the race driver himself is an orange car. Choice D changes the meaning of the sentence. The driver is not trying to get in shape for skiing but for racecar driving. Choice E has the orange car skiing to shape up for racing, but it is the driver who skis to get in shape for racing.

14. **C.** The problem with the original is that it does not have parallel structure: "electrical costs, landscapers' fees, and maintaining the parking lot." Predict before you even look at the answers that you will probably have three parallel structures: electrical costs, landscapers' fees, and parking lot maintenance costs. Choice B is wrong because it sounds as if the client is supposed to go out and cut down the landscapers. (Now watch — some political candidate will suggest a three-day waiting period before purchasing an ax!) Choice D is wrong because the client cannot reduce the costs of parking lots. She may be able to reduce the cost of parking lot maintenance, but she probably is not going to bring down the price of the asphalt itself. And choice E is wrong because of the verb formation "be reducing."

    Sentences with -*ing* words are often awkward and incorrect. View them with a jaundiced eye.

15. **A.** If the average amount per member is higher while a smaller percentage of members contribute, the amount collected per contributor has to be higher. Think of it this way: If the amount collected per contributor stayed the same or decreased, the amount collected per member would have to decrease when the contributions come from a smaller part of the congregation. Because the average amount collected was higher, choice A must be true.

Choice B provides a possible reason why the average amount contributed increased, but it does not have to be true. The congregants, for example, could simply have become more generous. In addition, the earnings could have decreased, explaining why a smaller percentage chose to contribute. Choice C is similar to choice B. There may have been a higher proportion of wealthy members, but the key point here is what was contributed, not what people were worth. Choice D is irrelevant because all the information in the passage has to do with average per member. The passage is not about the total amount collected. The major problem with choice E is that there is no information about the congregation's size or the size of any congregations that can be compared to it.

16. **E.** The author's conclusion about feeling pain follows from evidence about the use of a drill. This logically follows only if there is a connection between the drill and pain, which is what choice E provides. If choice E isn't true, you cannot be certain that pain will result.

Choice A is tempting, but it is too specific. The drill can produce pain in a variety of ways. Choice B is wrong because it provides a reason to think that pain *won't* result from the drill. Choice C is out because it doesn't connect the drill to pain. Choice D certainly explains why the patient expects pain, but it does not connect the drill to the pain.

17. **A.** The original is the best of the versions offered. Choices D and E change the meaning of the sentence. Choice C makes the sentence into a fragment (an incomplete thought). Choice B makes no sense at all in the sentence.

If you missed this question, you probably forgot to go back and plug the answer choices into the question. Don't be so concerned about saving a few seconds on a question that you forget this vital step.

18. **A.** You can get this question right by the process of elimination. All the other answers stink. Choice B works until the last part: "hoping and preparing themselves . . . ." Hoping what? You're missing an object. Choice C sounds as if the contractors are strengthening their own foundations ("foundations" can be used as a euphemism for butts; did you know that?) rather than the foundations of the homes. Choice D has an indefinite pronoun, *they:* hoping that *they* will be prepared — who are "they"? The sentence sounds as if the contractors want to be prepared rather than the homeowners. Choice E has the contractors hired for strength. Unless Arnold Schwarzenegger is hired as a contractor, this sentence makes no sense at all.

Whenever you see a pronoun, especially *they, them,* or *their,* double-check the antecedent. Ask yourself to whom or to what the *they, them,* and *their* is referring.

19. **E.** Beware of twins! A comparison between twins is comparing only two items (here, Stacy and Tracy). You need the comparative, or *-er* form (older), not the superlative, or *-est* form (oldest). Looking for *older* immediately narrows the choices down to D and E. Choice D turns the sentence into a fragment.

If you chose D, you may have thought you were choosing parallel verbs: *identifying* and *asking.* However, when you reinsert the answer into the sentence, you see that the sentence just dangles; it does not complete a thought.

20. **A.** The original sentence is perfect; don't change a thing. The question expects you to know the difference between *effects* and *affects.* As you learned in the grammar review, to *affect* is to concern or influence. How will the radiation *affect* (concern or influence) the citizens of Chernobyl? *Effect* means cause or result. What will be the *effect* (result) of the nuclear disaster at Chernobyl? Looking for *effects* allows you to eliminate choices B, C, and E. Choice D turns the sentence into a fragment (and has another of our archenemies: the *-ing* verbs. When you see an *-ing* verb, you should say to yourself, "Sure, I'm paranoid, but am I paranoid *enough?*").

21. **C.** The potential benefits of laughter are discussed in the third paragraph. Choices A and E are mentioned in lines 33–37. Choice B is a paraphrase of lines 28–31, and choice D comes from lines 46–48. Choice C is a <u>distortion</u> of lines 22–24. That sentence says that laughter develops during the first few weeks of life. It does not suggest that laughter is critical to the development of any other factor. Be careful not to read too much into the material.

22. **D.** The answer to this question comes from the first paragraph, which describes the condition of laughter. The rest of the passage is concerned with the effects of laughter. The first and last sentences of the first paragraph describe how muscle contractions trigger key components of the laughter response. Lines 9–10 also mention contractions. *Note:* While the diaphragm is a muscle, you don't have to know this to answer the question. All questions on the GMAT may be answered on the basis of what is stated or implied in the passage; no background knowledge is necessary.

    Choice A is tempting because much of the passage discusses the therapeutic benefits of laughter and also brings up the placebo effect (line 55), suggesting a relationship between mental states and physical responses. However, the passage never says that laughter comes about directly because of a desire to treat and prevent illness. What is more likely the case is that some environmental event (for example, a pathetic Dummies joke, or tickling) stimulates the laughter, which in turn sets up body defenses and treatments.

    Choice B is contradicted at the beginning of the first paragraph, which says that laughter is considered to be an innate response. Choices C and E, which come up in the third paragraph, are results, rather than causes, of laughter.

23. **A.** In the next-to-last paragraph, the author admits that the effect laughter has on someone could very well be one of a placebo. The same paragraph goes on to emphasize that laughter still has therapeutic potential (the point discussed at length in the previous paragraph) and then suggests a possible connection between the will to live and physical chemistry. The author feels that even a placebo effect can result in physiological changes. The author does not back down from what was said earlier, making choice A a good answer.

    Choice B is too extreme (notice the word <u>completely</u>). Think "strong is wrong" as you are answering reading questions. Often, the best choice is the most vague, wishy-washy one, simply because it gives you more room for interpretation. Here, the author doesn't dismiss the idea that laughter works as a placebo. The author could easily work the placebo effect into an explanation of how laughter helps humans. Choices C and D are too negative. The author does not present the placebo effect as a barrier. Choice E brings up a factor that is discussed in lines 33–35. Nothing in the "placebo paragraph" is tied to these lines. The author feels that psychological phenomena can lead to physiological effects, so don't think that the placebo effects must be solely of the psychological variety presented in choice E.

24. **C.** The information is in the third paragraph. The incorrect choices distort what is said there. Choice C is a nice, safe choice (on the GMAT, "safe" choices are often correct) because it simply says that there is an association between intense laughter and high blood catecholamines. Choice C follows from lines 43–44.

    Watch out for choice D. All the passage says in lines 50–52 is that the sed rate decreases during laughter and that there is an association between sed rate and the body's level of infection and inflammation. The passage makes no claim about changes in sed rate actually causing changes in infection or inflammation levels. For all you know, a decrease in inflammation causes a decrease in sed rate.

    The passage provides no information that would allow you to pick choice A as the correct answer. The passage presents increased levels of catecholamine as a probable cause of an increase in pulse rate, but it does not claim that this cause is the only one. Similarly, the passage makes no comparison among the various ways to increase endorphin secretion, so knock out choice B. In lines 44–46, the passage states that, during laughter, respiration increases while blood CO_2 levels decrease, but you do not know whether this relationship typically holds.

25. **B.** This question requires you to extrapolate a bit, meaning you must go beyond the passage. You have to come up with the choice that best follows from the statement "laughter is the physician of the body." Find the choice that simply shows how laughter has medicinal qualities. (By doing so, you will also be consistent with Norman Cousins, who is presented as someone who echoes Kant.)

    Choice A says too much. Certainly, it seems reasonable to support a physician who tries to make her patients laugh, but that would be a problem if she doesn't use the latest medical findings. Choice A does not tell you whether this physicians uses the latest medical findings or not. Choice C is very possibly true and picks up on something mentioned in the second paragraph, but the choice has little to do with what Kant said.

    Just because a statement is true, or was made in the passage, does not mean it is the correct answer. Remember to note what the question is asking for, and provide that information specifically. Kant certainly didn't know everything there is to know about laughter, and he still claimed that laughter is the physician of the body. Why should you hold out for more information when you're trying to be consistent with Kant?

    Choice D could very well work if it weren't for the word *force*. The passage implies that the happy emotions associated with laughter (see lines 38–39 and 53–54) have a lot to do with the healing properties of laughter. To say that forced laughter would also help is going too far. Choice E comes out of nowhere, even though it makes a little sense. The passage does not even provide a hint about how many times one must laugh to feel good in terms of health.

26. **C.** The conclusion is that speed-reading is not useful, based on the information that a low percentage of persons use it in one particular situation (the day-to-day reading assignments). To weaken the conclusion, rebut or give an exception to the information. Showing that speed-reading is most useful in a situation other than that covered in the survey would provide such a rebuttal.

    While choices D and E may be true statements, they do not weaken the conclusion, which is that speed-reading is useless and should no longer be taught. Other things, like Latin and calculus, are difficult to learn, (and some people argue that a lot less than 10 percent of calculus is used daily); but that doesn't necessarily mean those subjects should no longer be taught. Choice A may or may not weaken the argument. Maybe less-educated students are more in need of speed-reading than are educated students. Choice B is the trap answer. This survey took place over four years; if most surveys are for five years, maybe this survey is flawed. However, the question asks for what would *most* weaken the conclusion. Choice C is stronger because it more specifically addresses the crux of the argument, the *use* of speed-reading.

27. **B.** The argument concludes that cars are safer than planes. The evidence used to support this conclusion deals with the percentages of accidents that result in fatalities. To justify the conclusion, one must assume that these percentages are the key statistic, that there isn't some other factor that would overcome the supposed 50 to 1 advantage in favor of cars.

    Choice B wipes out the 50 to 1 advantage. One out of every two plane accidents results in fatalities, but for every two plane accidents, there are approximately one million car accidents. One percent of one million is ten thousand. This means that for every one fatal plane accident, there are about ten thousand fatal car accidents. Suddenly, cars don't seem so safe.

    Choices A and C simply indicate that humans make efforts to ensure that planes and flying are as safe as possible. They do not weaken the argument, though, because it still could be the case that many people die in plane accidents.

    Assigning blame does nothing to show that planes are safer than what is suggested by the statistics. This eliminates choice D.

    If it does anything, choice E strengthens the argument. It could be used to say that there are not only more fatal plane accidents but also more fatalities per fatal accident. The choice goes right along with an argument that claims planes are dangerous because many people die.

28. **D.** The author of this argument observes that high-priced, fuel-efficient cars are more popular now than they were years ago. She assumes that the increase in popularity has come about because people are more interested in saving fuel.

A good way to weaken an argument is to attack the assumption. Find another reason why fuel-efficient cars in the high-priced range have become more popular. It could be that purchasers of such cars don't care about fuel economy and simply consider fuel-efficient, high-priced cars to possess the all-important attributes of style, performance, and prestige. Choice D points out this possibility.

The fastest way to eliminate choice A is to realize that it refers to five years ago. The author makes a claim about the last two years. Choice B is irrelevant because the important factor is what the consumers actually consider, not what they claim to consider. Choice C goes along with the author's reasoning by providing a reason why consumers are more concerned about fuel efficiency (and remember, you are looking for something that <u>weakens</u>, not strengthens, the author's reasoning). Choice E is wrong primarily because it says nothing about fuel efficiency. The argument concerns which models are most popular at any one time. Just because the price of all cars goes up does not weaken the idea that people are now more conscious of how much fuel a car uses.

29. **C.** Did you notice and immediately get suspicious of the dreaded word "being?" That word is often used incorrectly on grammar exams. Don't automatically assume "being" is wrong, but check it out carefully. In choices A and D, "being" is misused. Choice B sounds as if the reason citizen paranoia is rising is that Detective Olson is concerned (whereas the real reason for the rising paranoia is the increase in burglaries). Choice E is borderline acceptable, but not as crisp and close to the original as choice C.

30. **B.** Eliminate answer choices A and D, as they make the warden seem the last person we expected to see. A warden's bailiwick (or his domain) *is* a prison. It is the movie star whose presence surprised us. Eliminate answer choice C because it sounds as if the warden is a famous movie star. Choice E is grammatically correct but is in the passive voice (. . . *was introduced to us*) rather than the active voice (*introduced us to* . . .). While passive and active voice are both grammatically correct, active is preferable.

31. **D.** The subject of the sentence, *the hockey player,* is singular and requires a singular verb, *is*. (*Along with his younger brother and cousin* is a prepositional phrase. Prepositional phrases do not affect subject-verb agreement. Draw a line through prepositional phrases to keep them from confusing you.) Choices B and E change the meaning of the sentence. Choice C changes the sentence into a fragment, an incomplete sentence.

Subject-verb agreement is usually the most frequently tested concept in grammar questions. It's the first thing you know you should check.

32. **D.** When a sentence begins with a subordinate clause (one that can't stand alone, like "motivated by the success of his company"), the first noun or pronoun after the subordinate clause must be doing the action of the clause. For example, in this sentence, "it" is not motivated; the businessman is motivated. Eliminate choices A and B. Choice D is unnecessarily wordy (*-ing* verbs are often wordy and sloppy) and choice E changes the meaning of the sentence.

33. **C.** The author's primary purpose is the same as the main idea or purpose of the passage, which in this case was to provide an overview of Chile. While most of the answers cover topics that were mentioned in the passage, those topics were secondary, not the main idea.

34. **A.** In lines 41–44, you are told that the conservative congress rebuffed or frustrated the program of a reformist president. From this, you may infer that the congress and the president were in opposition.

35. **C.** No way did you miss this one. What's our favorite word? OBJECTIVE! This answer is often (but NOT always!) correct for a *tone or attitude* question. Here, the passage is narrative, neutral. It simply states the facts. Eliminate negative answers like opinionated, argumentative, and dolorous (sad). Also eliminate dramatic, overly intense answers like urgent. It's not too hard to find the right answer now.

36. **E.** This question tests the singular/plural agreement of nouns and pronouns. Although the word *everyone* is singular, requiring a singular pronoun, his or her, if you chose B or C you fell into a trap. The non-underlined portion of the sentence cannot be changed. Because the non-underlined portion uses the plural form *them,* you must use the plural form in the underlined portion as well.

    Choice B is wrong, not only because of *everyone,* but because of the dreaded verb *being.* The word *being* is rarely used correctly on this exam. Choice C is wrong for several reasons: It has *everyone;* it has *being;* and it does not make sense when inserted into the sentence. Choice D is very tempting. The pronoun *they* is correct; it is plural and agrees with the pronoun *them* later in the sentence. However, choice D makes the sentence sound as if the *employee relations specialists* are on their best behavior during job interviews, when in fact we mean the job applicants are on their best behavior. The word *they* often introduces a plethora of problems. Anything that comes into contact with *they* should be checked for contamination.

37. **E.** This is a relatively difficult question because so many of the answers look good. Begin by identifying the main point or premise of the passage: People forget engineers but remember astronauts. Why would that be so? People are probably more interested in astronauts than engineers, and naturally remember better what they are interested in. Choice A may or may not be true, but remember, the GMAT won't offer two correct choices.

    Choice B makes no sense. There's no cause to believe that engineers — who have sent people to the moon and spaceships past Mars — have lost their abilities. Choice C is exactly backwards. If the public understood the role of the engineer, it probably would remember the engineers better. Choice D may or may not be true but has nothing to do with the public's forgetting about engineers.

    If every single answer looks good to you, make a quick guess and go on. Keep reminding yourself that half right is average on this test, and that Critical Reasoning is the hardest of the three verbal sections. You can get most of the Sentence Correction questions correct by memorizing grammar rules. You can get about ⅔ of the Reading Comprehension questions correct by slowing down and focusing on two out of the three passages. In Critical Reasoning, you may be totally bewildered by the confusing wording of a question or may think that all the answers look good. Fight the temptation to obsess over one question. Either narrow down the answers and choose one, or forget about the problem entirely.

38. **C.** The UCLA fan criticizes basketball without a shot clock because he feels that such a rule allows for a game that does not capture the essence of basketball. There is nothing in his statement that criticizes a team's decision to employ a certain strategy. In fact, he implies that a team with inferior talent should play a keep-away game if it is permitted to do so by the rules. He simply says that a team should not be allowed such an option. Nevertheless, the North Carolina fan, by defending the use of a keep-away game, acts as if the UCLA fan said teams shouldn't play such a game. This is what choice C says. For the North Carolina fan to dispute what the UCLA fan said, he should defend the lack of a shot clock, saying something on the order of how such a lack adds intrigue, keeps the game exciting, and so on. Choice A does not really capture the scope of the argument. Neither fan discussed excitement or boredom. The UCLA fan seems to imply that the lack of a shot clock produces a not-so-satisfying game, so if the North Carolina fan thinks choice A, he hasn't misunderstood too much.

    Choices B, D, and E are all stated or implied by the UCLA fan. The North Carolina fan should have picked up on this. If he had, there would have been less misunderstanding.

39. **E.** Did you catch both errors in the original? First, you need the word "affect," meaning to concern or influence, not "effect," meaning to cause. Eliminate choices A and B. Second, the correct expression is "from . . . to" not "from . . . and." Eliminate choices C and D. Only Choice E is left.

40. **C.** Remember that you are looking for the one choice that is <u>not</u> essential to link the conclusion (the credit card company will be successful) with the evidence presented. Choice A has to be assumed because if it weren't (company success is primarily dependent on some other factor), the author would be unable to conclude that once the poor credit risks are eliminated, the company will be successful. Choice B is important in the flow of the argument because the request for income information won't allow the company to weed out the bad credit risks very well (and hence, not be successful) if people give false information about their incomes.

Choice C is the correct answer because the argument simply states that weeding out bad credit risks leads to success. The argument does not claim that not weeding out such risks will lead to failure. (Can you see the distinction? If not, read those last two sentences over and over, until they make sense. This is a very important point.) The argument discusses one way that companies can be successful; it does not discount other paths to success. According to the argument, not granting credit to those incapable of paying their bills is sufficient for the company's success; such an action is not necessary. Understanding the difference between <u>sufficient</u> and <u>necessary</u> is important for success on critical reasoning.

Choice D is assumed because the whole idea of asking for income is to get rid of people who aren't capable of paying their bills and, therefore, won't pay them. If the people who are capable of paying their bills still don't pay them, the credit card company is in the same boat (one that will probably founder) as it was when it had people incapable of paying their bills. Choice E is an essential assumption because the argument links the query for income with the company's move not to extend credit to those who aren't capable of paying their bills. If the company can't use the income information to determine who is capable of paying their bills, it could very well extend credit to people who won't pay their bills.

41. **B.** What is the point of the editorial? Women are more patient than men. What did Ms. Faulk do? She didn't even finish reading the editorial but threw the paper down. Her actions disproved, in her case at least, the main point of the editorial.

Choice A is a trap answer put there to get students who automatically choose the answer with the big words. What on earth does "judicious use of counterpoint" mean, anyway? (For those of you who care, *judicious* means wise, sensible. *Counterpoint* is a pleasing or effective combination of contrasting things. Throwing away a paper in disgust is not particularly judicious.) In this section, as you learned in the lecture, you are not required to know logic terms. Don't choose an answer just because it has pretentious or official-sounding vocabulary in it.

Choice C should have made you laugh. It says absolutely nothing. The question wants to know how Ms. Faulk argued against the editorial; choice C says she argued against the editorial by refuting the editorial. (To *refute* means to argue against, to disprove.) That's just running around in circles, like saying "I didn't like that question because I liked that question not." Choice D is obviously wrong. If she were a patient woman, she would not have thrown the paper down in the first place, and then she would have been supporting, rather than arguing against, the premise. Choice E is irrelevant. Ms. Faulk's deciding to write a letter to the paper has nothing to do with whether her sexual characteristics determine her role in life.

Section 2

1. **C.** You know that the remainder cannot be 5; you cannot have 5 left over when you divide by 5. (Think of $\frac{19}{5}$: It's not "1 remainder 5," but 2.) Eliminate choice E.

   A great way to simplify a remainder problem is to **plug in numbers.** Choose a number that fits the criterion of the problem: A number divided by 5 has a remainder of 4. How about 9 (because $\frac{9}{5} = 1$ with 4 left over)? Make $n = 9$. Then $3n = 27$. When 27 is divided by 5, the remainder is 2 ($\frac{27}{5} = 5$ with 2 left over). Still skeptical? Try another number. Say that $n = 14$ (because $\frac{14}{5} = 2$ remainder 4). Then $3n = 14 \times 3 = 42$. Finally, $\frac{42}{5} = 8$, remainder 2.

2. **E.** An average is a sum divided by the number of items. You can write the formula like this: *Average = Sum ÷ Number*. Now plug the numbers into that formula: With all the friends, you have $150 = Sum \div 5$. Cross multiply: $150 \times 5 = Sum = 750$. All the friends together weigh 750 pounds. Write the same formula and work it through for four people:

$$Aver \quad = Sum \div Number$$
$$160 \quad = Sum \div 4$$
$$160 \times 4 \quad = Sum = 640$$

Subtract the weight of four friends from the weight of five friends to find the weight of the missing friend:

$$750 - 640 = 110$$

3. **D.** The equation is $x + 4 = 2(x - 1)$ where x is the current age. Distribute the terms: $x + 4 = 2x - 2$. Move the x's to the right, the non-x's to the left, remembering to change the signs. $6 = x$. Double-check by putting it back into the problem and talking it through: In four years (when she is 10), Mary Alyce will be twice as old as she was last year (when she was 5).

4. **E.** Statement 1 alone is not sufficient. You don't know how much less than zero m is: Is it -1 or $-1,000,000$? Is m^2 1 or 1 gazillion? Eliminate choices A and D.

   Statement 2 alone is not sufficient. How much greater than 0 is n? Is $n = 1$ or 1,000,000? Is n^2 1 or 1 gazillion? Eliminate choices B and D.

   Choice C is tempting; it is logical to think that a smaller number ($m < 0$) minus a larger number ($n > 0$) is less than 0. But even if you are brilliant and have more degrees than a thermometer, double-check your first reaction by plugging in numbers. What if $m = -10$ and $n = 5$? Then $(m^2 - n^2) = (100 - 25) = 75$. Uh, oh. Everything depends on the magnitude of the numbers. Because the answer could be yes or no, the data are not sufficient to answer the question.

5. **E.** The formula for the area of a trapezoid is $\frac{1}{2}(base\ 1 + base\ 2) \times height$. Predict that you need to know three things: *base 1, base 2*, and *height*.

   Statement 1 alone is not sufficient to answer the question. It gives you just the height. Eliminate choices A and D.

   Statement 2 alone is not sufficient to answer the question. It gives you just the length of one base, the bottom. Eliminate choices B and D.

   Putting the two statements together is not sufficient. You have the height and one base, but no way to find the other base. It looks as if you have a lot of information here, but appearances are deceiving; you're actually left with squat (a TRAP-ezoid, indeed!).

6. **C.** One hundred percent markup is doubling the price; two hundred percent markup is tripling the price. $42 \times 3 = 126$. Choice A just adds 200 to 42, not at all what the problem calls for. A two hundred percent increase does not mean something increases by 200 unless that something were 100. Choice D is also a trap, as it just doubles the original number. Doubling something is a one hundred percent increase, not a two hundred percent increase. If the percent increase/decrease (also tested as percent greater/lesser) concept is confusing to you, return to the percent section of the math review.

7. **D.** Find the total number of points by multiplying the average times the number of items: $82 \times 7 = 574$. Find the subtotal by adding all the numbers: $75 + 91 + 85 + 89 + 74 + 79 = 493$. Subtract total minus subtotal: $574 - 493 = 81$. (The math review has a second, even easier way to do this problem. Check out the section "Missing term average problem" in Chapter 13.)

8. **C.** What a *crumby* question (or as my Spanish friends would say, it doesn't *pan* out). Statement 1 alone is not sufficient to answer the question. If you were to set this up as an equation, you could let the shortest piece equal x and the longest piece equal $x+7$. But you still would have the missing middle piece, which we can call y, and $x+y+(x+7)=18$. Nice equation, but it doesn't answer the question because you are asked for the length of each piece, and there's no way to find y from this one equation. Eliminate choices A and D.

Statement 2 alone is not sufficient to answer the question. Letting the pieces equal x, y, and z, you know that $x+z=y$. You could make the equation $2y=18$ (because $x+y+z=18$, and $x+z=y$. That would allow you to solve for y; the middle piece must be 9 inches long. But you still don't know how long *each* piece is. Eliminate choices B and D.

If you chose B, you accidentally carried over information from statement 1. Remember to cover up statement 1 and forget its shadow ever passed your path before you begin reading statement 2.

Putting the two pieces of information together does the trick. If the middle piece is 9 inches, the sum of the two remaining pieces is 9 inches. The first piece is 7 inches shorter than the longest piece: $x+(x+7)=9$. Then $2x+7=9$, and $2x=2$. Finally, $x=1$. The shortest piece is 1 inch, the second longest piece is 7 inches, and the longest piece is 9 inches.

9. **B.** The pattern is a set of 4. Divide 4 into 38, and you get 9 with a remainder of 2. That means the 36th student ($4 \times 9 = 36$) finishes a set of 4. The 37th student starts a new set, with math. The 38th student has his English homework checked.

Did you forget your times tables? How embarrassing! As a tutor, I see hundreds of students who grew up using calculators to the detriment of their times tables. If you said that $9 \times 4 = 38$, you're not alone. Infantile as it may be, take a few minutes to be sure that you can rattle off your times tables from 1×1 all the way to 12×12. Wouldn't you absolutely hate to miss points just because you forgot what 7×8 or 6×9 was?

10. **C.** You can solve this problem two ways. One easy way is to find a common multiple and then *plug in numbers*. Because 2, 5, and 3 all divide evenly into 30, use that multiple. Next, calculate $2r=30$; $r=15$. Then calculate $5s=30$; $s=6$. Then $3t=30$; $t=10$. Now you can work through each answer choice.

Be sure to write down what each variable equals; don't try to remember these values, even if you do have a lot of unused space in your head.

   a. $3(10)$ is not equal to $2(15)+6$. Eliminate choices A, D, and E. (Eliminating as you go is always a good idea.)

   b. $6(6)$ is not equal to $3(10)+15$, so eliminate choice B. Choice C must be right; you don't have to spend time working the problem through.

   c. If you want proof, however, here it is: $10(6)=3(10)+2(15)$.

These answers will work out, regardless of what numbers you plug in, as long as you plug in something that is true in the equation $2r=5s=3t$. For example, you could have plugged in $r=30$, $s=12$, $t=20$ (although why you'd want to make life that hard, I have no idea).

If you don't want to plug in numbers, you can talk the problem through.

   a. $3t$, you know, is equal to $2r$ on its own; adding s would make the sides unequal. Eliminate answers A, D, and E.

   b. Let's skip to III.

   c. Because $10s$ is twice $5s$, it *would* equal $3t$ ($5s$) plus $2r$ (another $5s$). Because you had already narrowed the answers down to II only or III only, and III works, choice C is correct. Either method — plugging in numbers or talking the problem through — will work.

11. **D.** The exterior angles of any polygon total 360 degrees. This was discussed and shown in the math review. CAUTION! If you said 360 was the answer, you fell for the trap.

The trick here is that the figure represents TWO SETS of exterior angles. Think of them this way:

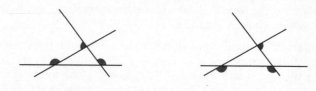

Because each set totals 360, $360 \times 2 = 720$

12. **E.** Statement 1 alone is not sufficient to answer the question. If $y/x = 1/2$, then (in simple English, instead of GMAT-ese), x is twice as great as y. You don't know anything about z so far. Eliminate choices A and D.

Statement 2 alone is not sufficient to answer the question. You have to know whether x equals 100, is more than 100, or is less than 100. Eliminate choices B and D.

The two statements alone are not sufficient to answer the question. Ah, did you choose C? Then you fell into a pretty good trap. You probably thought something like this: Suppose that $y = 99$ and $z = 1$. Then $x = 2y$, $x = 198$, and $z + y$ is NOT equal to x. I wish I could say that I sympathize with you, but if truth be told, I'm sitting here smirking that you fell for my carefully designed trap. *What about negatives?* The data are not sufficient to give one definite answer to the question, and the answer is E.

13. **A.** Wasn't it nice of me to make the first answer correct, to save you the trouble of going through the rest of the numbers? You are often rewarded in this way on the real exam as well.

First, understand what the so-called "explanation" means. The word *price* doesn't have any special mathematical meaning in the real world; it's only made up for this question. The price is how many prime numbers there are in a number, less the repeats. (You *don't* count a prime that repeats.) So, to find the price of something, factor it down to its different primes and add together how many there are.

Factor 2310 down by 10 (which is 2×5) to get 231. Because 3 is a common prime, try it: $231/3 = 77$. Ah, now it's easy to see 7×11. How many primes are there? 2, 5, 3, 7, 11: There are 5. Be very careful to remember to break the 10 down into its primes, 2 and 5.

14. **D.** If you chose A, you completely forgot to go back to the "explanation" and see what "price" means. When more than one problem refers to an explanation or to some central information, I suggest you mentally circle the numbers of those problems to call your attention to the fact that they "go together."

The price of 100 is 2. Factor it down to its primes. You probably thought first of 10×10, which factors down to $2 \times 5 \times 2 \times 5$. Because there are only two *distinct* primes, the price is 2. Factor 32 down to $2 \times 2 \times 2 \times 2 \times 2$. Because there is only one distinct prime, the price is 1, and $2 - 1 = 1$. (And you thought this math was hard!)

15. **A.** Statement 1 alone is sufficient to answer the question. If the crate of pinion nuts is marked down 60 percent, it is now 40 percent of its original price (because 60 percent + 40 percent = 100 percen). Say to yourself, "Forty percent of something is $40.00." Don't bother actually finding out what that "something" is; who cares? Narrow the choices down to A or D.

Statement 2 alone is not sufficient to answer the question. The profit on the crate of pinion nuts is 20 percent. Great. Maybe the crate sells for $10, and $2 is profit. Maybe the crate sells for $100 and $20 is profit. Because statement 2 alone is not sufficient, eliminate choices B and D. Because you've already narrowed the choices to A or D, only A is left.

Question: What do you have when you have two pinion nuts in one hand and three in the other?

Answer: A difference of a pinion!

16. **B.** Statement 1 alone is not sufficient to answer the question. This statement, in fact, tells you something you already know just by looking at the picture. Because all angles along a straight line total 180, $2y + 3x = 180$ and therefore, $180 - 2y$ in fact does equal $3x$. That alone doesn't tell you enough to solve for x. Eliminate choices A and D.

Statement 2 alone is sufficient to answer the question. If $y = 2x$, then you have angles along a straight line that can be written as $x + x + x + 2x + 2x = 180$; $7x = 180$. You could solve for x, but don't bother to do so. It's enough to know you can find x; you don't want to bother doing the actual division. Because statement 2 alone is sufficient, choose B.

If you chose C, you fell into the "free gift with purchase" trap. That is, you get something extra with statement 1, something nice to know, but it's not essential. Remember that you choose C only when you *need* to have both statements in order to answer the question. If one statement alone does the job and the second statement just gives you a little fillip, something extra, C is a trap answer.

17. **D.** Make r stand for the number of envelopes Russ, working alone, can address in y hours. Make $3r$ stand for the number of envelopes Emily, working alone, addresses in y hours (because Emily works three times as fast as Russ). Then $r + 3r = x$, and $4r = x$. Because Emily is $3r$, Emily is $\frac{3}{4}x$.

The key to this problem is the ratio 3:1. The total must be a multiple of the ratio, 4. For example, if Emily and Russ addressed 100 envelopes, she did 75 and he did 25. Because 75 is $\frac{3}{4}$ of 100, you can prove your answer by plugging in numbers.

Choice E is a great trap. Don't focus on the 3:1 ratio and think Emily did $\frac{2}{3}$ and Russ $\frac{1}{3}$. If that's the case, she addressed only twice as many envelopes as Russ, not three times as many.

18. **C.** You can find the probability by using this formula:

# of possible desired outcomes/ # of total possible outcomes.

The first thing to do is to find the denominator: How many candies will be left after LaVonne has chomped into the others? She starts with 47 candies ($20 + 15 + 12$). You know that she throws some of them away, allowing you to eliminate choice A immediately, because the denominator must be less than 47.

She throws away a creme (down to 46), a nut (down to 45), a chew (down to 44), a nut (down to 43), a creme (down to 42), and a chew (down to 41). The denominator for the probability of the next candy that she pulls out will be 41 because she'll have some chance in 41 of pulling out a nut. That narrows the choices down to B and C.

As a shortcut, subtract 6 (the number of candies that she already pulled out) from 47 (the number of candies that were originally in the box). I solved the problem the long way to show you where the 41 really comes from.

Now find the numerator. She starts with 12 nuts, pulls out one (down to 11), and then pulls out another (down to 10). The probability that the next candy will be a nut is $\frac{10}{41}$.

(This type of probability problem was discussed in the math review. If you've forgotten it, go back and review the explanation there.)

19. **E.** If you chose A, you fell for the trap. (Are you getting totally sick and tired of hearing that expression? Don't fall for so many traps, and you won't have to hear it.) Dividing like bases means subtracting the exponents. For $a^{10} \div a^5$, subtract: $10 - 5 = 5$. Divide 6 by 3 to get 2. You know the first term is $2a^5$, narrowing the choices down to C, D, and E.

b^5 divided by b^9 is b^{-4} or $\frac{1}{b^4}$. That result eliminates choices C and D; you can stop now.

Just for fun, though, I'll finish the calculation. $c^7 \div c^7 = 1$. Any number divided by itself is 1. (Or you could think of it as $7 - 7 = 0$; any number to the zero power is 1.) The answer 1 doesn't change anything in the multiplication; ignore it.

Choices A and B were traps for people who tried ¹⁰⁄₅ instead of subtracting the exponents.

Choices C and D were traps for people who forgot that a negative exponent is in the denominator, not the numerator. ***Remember:*** 2^{-3} is really $\frac{1}{2^3}$. If you forgot this, return to the thrilling math review.

20. **B.** Statement 1 alone is not sufficient to answer the question. Knowing how many games the team won in one year is not enough to tell you what percent increase there was from the year before. Eliminate choices A and D.

    Statement 2 alone is sufficient. If the team doubled its wins, it increased them by 100 percent. (If this is confusing to you, go back to the percent portion of the math review. But always keep in mind the glad tidings that, in this section, you don't have to do the questions out to the bitter end. The fact that you *personally* don't have a clue how to do a problem does not mean it's undoable.)

    Did you choose choice C? If so, you probably fell for the "anticipation" trap. You anticipated or predicted that you would have to have both statements, last year's wins and this year's wins, to find the percent increase. Sounds logical, but then statement 2 spoils everything by giving you everything you need in one tidy statement. Choose C only when you HAVE to have both statements.

21. **C.** Statement 1 alone is not sufficient to answer the question. All you can do with the equation is manipulate it a little bit; for example, $3m = 14 - 2n$. $m = 1\frac{4}{3} - \frac{2}{3}n$. But that doesn't tell you the value of *m*. Eliminate choices A and D.

    Statement 2 alone is not sufficient to answer the question. Again, all you can do is manipulate it: $6m = 21 - 2n$, and $m = 2\frac{1}{6} - \frac{2}{6}n$. Eliminate choices B and D.

    Put both statements together into simultaneous equations and subtract to make one of the variables drop out.

$$6m + 2n = 21$$
$$-(3m + 2n = 14)$$

    When you subtract (don't forget to change every sign in the second equation, giving you $-3m$, -2, and -14, you get $3m = 7$. Finally, $m = \frac{7}{3}$.

    When you have two variables with only one equation, chances of solving for either individual variable with just that equation alone are slim. You normally need at least two equations to solve for one of two variables.

22. **D.** The area of a rectangle is *length × width*. The perimeter of any figure is the sum of the lengths of the sides. Solve this problem the easy way by trial and error rather than by equations. Start by thinking of some numbers that can multiply together to make 32: 1×32. If so, then the sides are 1 and 32, and the perimeter is $1 + 32 + 1 + 3$, which does not equal 24. How about 8×4? Then the perimeter is $8 + 4 + 8 + 4$, which does equal 24. You know that one side is 8 and one is 4 — $8:4 = 4:2 = 2:1$.

    I can hear the griping all the way down here in San Diego. Some of you mathletes are wondering why there is no answer like, "It cannot be determined" because you don't know which side is the length and which is the width. If the answer choices had both 2:1 and 1:2, your complaint would be valid. But because the answers have only 2:1, choose that.

    Why am I so anti-equation, you ask? I fear the careless mistakes that people make when they design the equations. Here's how many people would create the equation for this problem:

$$W \times L = 32$$
$$2W + 2L = 24$$
$$W = 32 - L$$
$$2(32 - L) + 2L = 24$$
$$64 - 2L + 2L = 24$$

Uh, oh. Now you have the 2Ls canceling each other out, and you see $64 = 24$, which is nonsense. Do you see the mistake? The third line here should not be $W = 32 - L$ but instead $W = 32 \div L$. This is such an easy mistake to make; I see my students make it all the time. My suggestion is: If you can talk the problem through rather than doing Power Math, do so.

23. **B.** The point of this problem was not to make you do the multiplication but to see whether you were shrewd enough to use the answer choices and so avoid having to do any arithmetic at all. You know that the numbers will be: 5×5; $5 \times 5 \times 5$; $5 \times 5 \times 5 \times 5$; and $5 \times 5 \times 5 \times 5 \times 5$. You know that the first three rounds are 5, and 25, and 125. You can probably figure out 625 quickly and know you still have one more round. Eliminate C, D, and E immediately. Choice A is way, way too big, leaving you with only choice B without doing any actual multiplication.

24. **D.** This is your long-lost bud, the 3:4:5 triangle. I think test makers must get a discount on this triangle; they use it so much. Just count the spaces on the grid. The base of the triangle, *TR*, goes from -2 to -5, a distance of 3. (As soon as you see a 3, you should start getting suspicious, thinking there is a 3:4:5 triangle lurking around somewhere.) The height of the triangle, *TS*, goes from 1 to 5, making its length 4. The triangle is a right triangle (because all lines are perpendicular). If one side is 3 and the other is 4, the hypotenuse must be 5. (Go back to the Pythagorean Triples portion of the math review.)

Of course, you could do this out the old-fashioned, legitimate way using the Pythagorean Theorem. First, $a^2 + b^2 = c^2$. Then $3^2(9) + 4^2(16) = c^2(25)$. Finally, $C = \sqrt{25} = 5$.

25. **C.** Don't be intimidated; this is not nearly as hard as it looks. Just talk it through. Start with the units digits (the ones column). Five plus something equals 7; that something must be 2. Because $B = 2$, you can immediately eliminate choices A and B.

Eliminate as you go; you'll avoid making a careless mistake.

Plug in 2 for *B* in the tens column. Because $2 + \text{something} = 6$, that something must be 4. You now know that $A = 4$; eliminate choice D.

Plug in 4 for *A* and 2 for *B* in the hundreds column. $A + B = 6$. This is a good way to make sure you haven't made any careless mistakes.

Finally, plug in 4 for *A* in the thousands column. Because $9 + 4 = 13$; *C* must equal 3.

This problem is better solved by mouth than by pencil. Make like your friend Brooke and babble your way through it.

26. **C.** You know there must be a shortcut to this problem, as I have been preaching at you that this test does not expect a lot of busywork out of you. The key here is to estimate. Let's say Skip spent $400 instead of $385. Then each of the 25 CDs cost him $16 (you can do this in your mind: There are 4 twenty-fives in a hundred, there would be 4×4 or 16 twenty-fives in four hundreds. Talk it through.) If he bought 10 CDs, he spent $160, so 11 CDs is a tad more than that. Only one answer choice is remotely close.

Before you begin estimating, check out the answer choices. Usually they will be quite far apart, making it easy for you to estimate. In the rare case that the answer choices are close together, you know that you have to pick up your pencil and actually do the work.

27. **E.** To find an average (don't let the words "arithmetic mean" scare you; they just mean a regular old average), you add up all the terms and then divide the sum by the number of terms. Here, you know there are 5 tests. Let them be A, B, C, D and E. That means the average is

$$\frac{A + B + C + D + E}{5}$$

Statement one tells you that Barney's highest score (A) was the same as his two lowest scores combined. That means that $A = D + E$. Your new equation is

$$\frac{D + E + B + C + D + E}{5} = 92$$

That alone is not sufficient information to answer the question. Eliminate choices A and D.

Statement two allows you to note that $A = B + 10$. Your new equation would be:

$$\frac{(B+10)+B+C+D+E}{5} = 92$$

Statement two alone is not sufficient to answer the question. Eliminate choice B.

Combine information from both statements. Because $A = D + E$ and $A = B + 10$, you know that $D + E = B + 10$. Make the new equation:

$$\frac{(B+10)+B+C+(B+10)}{5} = 92$$

Combine like terms: $\dfrac{3B+2+C}{5} = 92$

Soooo close, but still, you don't have enough information. That pesky C is still there, still unknown.

Don't fall into the bad habit of assuming that just because a problem gives a lot of information, it gives sufficient information to answer the specific question. In this case, as you saw, you can do a lot of number crunching and pushing around equations . . . to no avail.

28. **D.** Statement 1 alone is sufficient. The formula required here is $S = C + P$ (Sales equals Cost plus Profits). If Jermaine's sales were $1,000 and his profit was $200 more than his costs, his profit was $600, and his costs were $400. (Some profit margin there! But then again, you have to worry about dealers who sell gold-plated necklaces. They have association by gilt. . . .) Narrow the choices down to A and D.

Statement 2 alone is sufficient. If costs were 60 percent less than Jermaine's sales, the costs were 40 percent of sales. The profit must represent the other 60 percent. Again, don't bother actually figuring this out (if you must, costs = $40) just know that the data are sufficient to do so. Narrow the choices down to B or D. And get me Jermaine's business secrets, will you?

Because either statement alone is sufficient, the answer is D.

29. **E.** Statement 1 alone is not sufficient. The values of x and y could be just about anything. If x and y are 30 and -10, respectively, then the answer is yes. If x and y are 100 and -100, respectively, then the answer is no. If you can't get a definite answer, you don't have enough data. Eliminate choices A and D.

Statement 2 alone is not sufficient. You may have been tempted to choose B, thinking that $x = 10$ and $y = -10$, but there are many possibilities. What if $x = 1$ and $y = -100$? Then $x + y$ is not greater than 10. But if $x = 100$ and $y = -1$, then $x + y$ is greater than 10. It all depends. Eliminate choices B and D.

What about using both statements together? The answer still depends on the values you plug in; there are not sufficient data even with both statements.

30. **D.** The range of values depends on how you align the three men. If Cottam is between Pellaton and Roberts, then there are only 20 miles between Cottam and Roberts: Pellaton (15) Cottam (20) Roberts. But if you put Roberts on the other side of Pellaton, such that Pellaton is between Roberts and Cottam, the distance is like this: Roberts (35) Pellaton (15) Cottam. Now the distance between Roberts and Cottam is 35 + 15 = 50.

31. **D.** Number the angles as shown in the following figure. All odd-numbered angles are equal; all even-numbered angles are equal. Because x is an odd-numbered angle, it is equal to 110, also an odd-numbered angle.

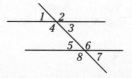

32. **B.** There are two ways to approach this problem: Forwards (create and solve an equation) or backwards (plug in the answer choices and see which one fits). Let's go forwards first.

    Set up the equation:

    $3a - 4 = 2 - 5a$. (You are told $x = y$.)

    Move the variables to one side, and the non-variables to the other side (be very careful to remember to change the signs as you do so):

    $5a + 3a = 2 + 4$

    $8a = 6$

    $a = \frac{6}{8}$ which reduces to $a = \frac{3}{4}$.

    But what if you were so confused you didn't know where to start, how to set up the equation? You always have the answer choices available to you and can plug them in. Doing so will take more work and more time, but you do have the option.

    Start with choice C, right in the middle. If $a = \frac{4}{5}$, then $x = 3\left(\frac{4}{5}\right) - 4$ and $y = 2 - 5\left(\frac{4}{5}\right)$.

    $x = \frac{12}{5} - 4$ or $\frac{12}{5} - \frac{20}{5} = -\frac{8}{5}$.

    $y = 2 - \frac{20}{5}$ or $\frac{10}{5} - \frac{20}{5} = -\frac{10}{5}$.

    Because x does not equal y, choice C doesn't work. Try choice B.

    $X = 3\left(\frac{3}{4}\right) - 4$ or $x = \frac{9}{4} - \frac{16}{4} = -\frac{7}{4}$.

    $Y = 2 - 5a$ or $2 - 5\left(\frac{3}{4}\right) = 2 - \frac{15}{4} = \frac{8}{4} - \frac{15}{4} = -\frac{7}{4}$.

    Hooray! $x = y$ so choice B is the correct answer.

33. **E.** Statement 1 alone is not sufficient to answer the question. How many terms are in the series? Maybe the series is 2, 4, 6, 8, 10, 2, 4, 6, 8, 10, ... Maybe the series is 10, 20, 10, 20, 10, 20, ... You can't figure out the hundredth term without knowing how many terms are in the series. Eliminate choices A and D.

    Statement 2 alone is not sufficient to answer the question. You need to know how many terms are in the series and how far apart they are. Maybe the series is achieved by adding 12 to each number (because $4 + 12 = 16$). Maybe you get the series by squaring each term (because $4^2 = 16$). The statement doesn't give you enough information; eliminate choices B and D.

    Putting the two statements together still doesn't tell you how many terms there are in the series or how the terms in the series are spaced. They could be 4, 16, 28, adding 12 each time, making the fifth term in the series even. Or they could be 4, 16, 256, . . . squaring the terms, still making the fifth term in the series even. All these numbers . . . and none of them work (kinda like getting phone numbers at a party, eh?).

34. **D.** If the school has 40% females, it has 60% males. That means that 84 (the number of males) $= 60\%$ of the total students at the school. $84 = 6T$; $T(\text{total}) = 140$. Now you can figure out how many students are female ($0.4 \times 140 = 56$). Given that 50% of the females are blondes, there are 28 blond females. Note that you don't want to do all this work, just realize that the data are sufficient to do the work. Narrow your answer choices down to A or D.

    Is statement two alone sufficient? If there are 140 students in the school, and 40% are females, there are $0.4 \times 140 = 56$ females. Half the females, or 28, are blondes. Yes, statement two alone is sufficient.

    Either statement one alone or statement two alone is sufficient, for answer D.

35. **C.** A percent increase (or decrease) is the number increase (or decrease) over the original whole. You don't have to find the actual percentages in this case; a look at the basic fractions will be enough.

Amanda: $^{15}\!/_{75}$

Bret: $^{10}\!/_{90}$

Carlyse: $^{30}\!/_{60}$

Denzil: $^{20}\!/_{100}$

Edmund: $^{20}\!/_{70}$

Because Carlyse is ½, significantly more than the fractions for the others, she had the greatest increase. (And speaking of fractions, did you ever hear this joke: What's the Least Common Denominator? Answer: King of Denominatorland!)

36. **E.** Statement 1 alone is not sufficient to answer the question. To find a probability, you need two pieces of information: the total number of items and how many items there are of the type you want. Statement 1 tells you how many total items there are but not how many yellow marbles there are. Eliminate choices A and D.

Statement 2 alone is not sufficient. You have information about eight of the marbles, but how many total marbles are in the jar? Eliminate choices B and D.

If you chose C, you walked right into the trap I carefully baited for you (so nice to know my work is appreciated). Try reading the question again: It asks for the probability of choosing a *yellow* marble, not a black one. Statement 2 tells you how many black marbles there are but not how many yellow. Ah, if you thought "$15 - 8 = 7$; there must be 7 yellow marbles," you made an unwarranted assumption. Don't assume that the only marbles in the jar are yellow and black. The jar may be a veritable rainbow for all you know.

37. **D.** The perimeter of a figure is the sum of the lengths of all the sides. In a rectangle, that's $l + w + l + w$, or $2l + 2w$. Statement one tells you that $l = 2w$. Substitute: $2(2w) + 2w = 36$; $4w + 2w = 36$. $6w = 36$. $w = 6$. Twice that is 12. Statement one alone is sufficient to answer the question. Narrow your choices down to A and D.

Statement two lets you make the equation: $l + w + l + w = 6w$. Because you know from the question stem that the perimeter (which is $l + w + l + w$ is 36), you have $36 = 6w$; $w = 6$. Statement two alone is sufficient to answer the question as well. If either statement one alone or statement two alone is sufficient to answer the question, the answer is D.

Sections 3 and 4

Note: There are no "right" or "wrong" answers to these essay questions. Go back to the Analytical Writing Assessment section and review the portion on how the essays are scored.

Make copies of your essays. Give a copy of them to four evaluators (choose people who know something about writing, like a professor or a journalist friend, not just your buddy down the hall) and ask each one to rate the essays on a 0–6 scale. Average the scores.

Ask each evaluator to focus on one different part of your writing. For example, ask one evaluator to read the passage for content and organization. Ask another evaluator to pay attention to grammar and usage and diction. Ask the next evaluator to concern himself with spelling, punctuation, and neatness. The final evaluator can do the "holistic" grading, giving you an overall score. The feedback from each person will help you work on your strengths and weaknesses.

When you have collated the comments, criticism, and carping from your evaluators, rewrite the essay. *Don't* time yourself; take all the time you want and do the job right. You'll need to go slowly to integrate the feedback. Speed can come later.

Part VIII
The Part of Tens

Sorry. I just find rotating my head helps me to relax during the test.

In this part . . .

This unit is your reward for surviving the preceding 21 chapters. No brain power is required for these next few chapters. You don't have to work through math problems; you don't have to stimulate the synapses at all. These chapters are just for fun, but they do provide invaluable information. For example, where else but in *The GMAT For Dummies,* 4th Edition, can you find ways to use math to get out of doing your share of work around the house? Read on.

Chapter 22

Ten Ways to Use GMAT Math in the Real World

*Y*ou have to learn this stuff, so why not get some use out of it? Your parents have dished out a lot of money for you to get a college education; here's your chance to show them what you've learned.

Getting Out of Paying for Gas

Promise your roommate that if he lets you borrow his new car to impress your date tonight, you'll fill up the gas tank if you increase the car's mileage by one percent or more. The amount sounds so small to your roommate, he'll probably agree . . . and you'll be getting away with your wallet intact. Let's say your friend's car has 60,000 miles on it. You can do this one in your head: 10 percent (or $\frac{1}{10}$) of 60,000 is 6,000; 1 percent is $\frac{1}{10}$ of that, or 600 miles. You'd need to have a heck of a date to put 600 miles on the car in one evening; chances are good you won't have to dish out a penny. So who says percentages are useless?

Saving Money Dining Out at Fine Establishments

Tell the waiter at your favorite pizza parlor that you want a (circular) pizza with the longest chord of 10 inches — but if he'll give you a discount, you'll settle for a pizza with a circumference of 10 (pizza?) π. Laugh at him behind his back as he struggles to figure out which one would cost you more. *You,* of course, know that the two pizzas would be the same. (The longest chord of a circle, in case you've forgotten, is the diameter. The circumference of a circle is $\pi \times diameter$, making the two pizzas identical.)

Making Your Roommates Clean Up Your Mess

Strike a bargain with your roommates over who must shovel out the living room after last night's party. Persuade them to agree that whoever is first in getting the right answer to a Pythagorean theorem problem can go watch TV while the others have to wade into no man's land. Act as though you're doing them a favor by reminding them that the Pythagorean theorem is $a^2 + b^2 = c^2$, where a, b, and c are the sides of a right triangle. Bluster and say they can use a calculator, but *you'll* do the problem in your head to give them an advantage. Then make up a problem in which the sides are 14: 48: x. While they're punching in numbers, you know that these figures are simply a variation on the ratio 7:24:25, with each number being doubled. You'll know in a flash, therefore, that $x = 50$ (double the 25). Hand your roommates the hip boots and go turn on the TV.

Getting Out of Your Share of the Work

Annoy your roommates by finding the area and perimeter (circumference) of objects around the house as you're cleaning. Announce your findings in a loud voice. "Hey, dude, did you know that the total surface area of our refrigerator is *xxx* square units?" "Roomie, you'll be delighted to know that the volume of your top desk drawer is *xxx* cubic units." If you get on your roommates' nerves enough, they'll kick you out of the place and finish the cleaning themselves.

Annoying the Elderly

Whenever your Great Aunt Tootsie — the one who always forgets your name at the family reunion — asks you how old you are, you can blithely answer, "Letting x equal my father's age at the time he married my mother, in $x + 42$ years from now I will have evinced a 200 percent increase in my age — although, of course, my father will have increased his age by only 184 percent." Step back and watch Great Aunt Tootsie self-destruct as she tries to figure out the numbers. . . .

Talking Your Way Out of a Speeding Ticket

Suppose that a cop pulls you over and asks you, "Listen, hot shot, do you have any idea how fast you were going?" You can look at the cop innocently and say, "Well, sir, let's see. I left Point A at 3:00 driving west and drove for 30 minutes. My friend Shandra left point B at 4:15 driving east and going 30 miles in 45 minutes. If we are now 75 miles apart, I guess that makes my speed — well, officer, what do *you* think? I'd value your opinion. . . ." Either you'll frustrate the poor cop and get out of the ticket — or you'll be in even bigger trouble for being a smart aleck. Are you willing to take the risk to have the fun?

Making Your Parents Think that Your Grades Are Better Than They Are

Unless your parents are math whizzes, they probably still solve an average problem by dividing the sum of the numbers they see by how many numbers there appear to be. Not having had the benefit that you have of being burned repeatedly by this book, they aren't paranoid enough to look for a weighted average problem. If you tell your folks that on your tests, you scored six 70 percents, three 90 percents, a 98, and a 100, they'll probably add $70 + 90 + 98 + 100$, divide by 4, and get 89.5 and think they've got a real A student in the family. Only you will know that you had to add the 70 six times, the 90 three times, and the 98 and 100 only once, for a total of 888 and an average of 80.7.

Rejecting a Date without Destroying an Ego

Suppose that someone asks you to go to a dance. You smile gently and say, "The probability of my attending this function with you is the same as the difference between the probability of tossing a 3, 4, 5 on consecutive tosses of a die and the probability of tossing 1, 1, 1 on consecutive tosses of a die." Only you know that the probabilities are the same, making the difference between them exactly zero, the same as the chances you're actually going to go out on a date with someone who can't even figure that much out. Now that you've mastered the math in this book, you're too good for that person anyway.

Confusing Your Parents about Where the Money Went

If your parents are paying for your college education, they probably want an accounting of how you spend their money. When your request for another hundred dollars to see you through to the end of the month meets with an exasperated, "What are you doing with all this money?" you can reply, "In September, my housing costs went up 20 percent; in October, they went down 25 percent and in November, they went up 11 percent." Your parents will think your costs rose 6 percent (because $20 - 25 + 11 = 6$). From having gone through the percentage problems in this book, you know that your costs remained the same. If you have real class, you'll use the extra 6 percent to help those less fortunate than you — buy copies of this book for students who can't afford it because their parents aren't as mathematically challenged as yours.

Stiffing a Waiter on a Tip

Tell the waiter he can have either a 15 percent tip or get x^0 times 100 percent as a tip, where x equals the value of your meal. Because most poor fools who haven't had the joy of going through this book will naturally think that any number to the zero power equals zero, he'll be thrilled to get a 15 percent tip. He'll never know that $x^0 = 1$ and that he could have gotten the entire amount of the bill (100 percent!) as a tip. The next time you go to that restaurant, why don't you give the waiter a copy of this book?

Chapter 23

Ten Wrong Rumors about the GMAT

● ●

In This Chapter (Remember: These statements are WRONG!)

▶ You can't study for the GMAT

▶ Your GMAT score will be about the same as your SAT score from high school

▶ The GMAT tests IQ

▶ You must pass certain classes to take the GMAT

▶ Your score won't improve if you keep retaking the GMAT

▶ The GMAT has a passing score

▶ You can take the GMAT on your own computer at home

▶ You can bring your own laptop to the testing center

▶ Missing the first few questions gives you an easier test and better score

▶ Computer geniuses have an unfair advantage on the GMAT

● ●

Sure, you've heard them: the horror stories about the GMAT. Rumors abound, growing more wild with each telling: "You have to know calculus!" (Absolutely not.) "It's an open book test this year!" (You *wish!*)

As a test preparation tutor, I get calls all the time from students trying to check out the latest scuttlebutt. Here are ten of the most common stories that make the rounds every year — as dependable as oversleeping the morning of your most important final.

You Can't Study for the GMAT

Why would I be writing this book if that were so? Studying can be done in two ways, each advantageous in its own right. First is the last-minute cram, a review in a few weeks of the types of questions, the approach to each question, the tricks and traps involved in the questions. (Sound familiar? This method is what you've been working on throughout this book.) Second is the long-range study program, in which you work on math questions from your freshman year in college on. Obviously, if you've got a year or two to put into this, you should get a dynamite score. Most people, however, benefit greatly from even a few weeks or months of intense study.

Your GMAT Score Will Be about the Same as Your SAT Score from High School

Are you the same person you were in high school? You have matured, learned better study habits, suddenly come to the shocking realization that no one is going to spoon-feed you anymore. You may not have studied much for the SAT, figuring that you could always get into *some* college, somewhere, no matter what your score. You were probably right. But getting into graduate school is not as easy. There aren't as many graduate programs as undergraduate programs, making the competition more cutthroat. Because you realize this, you study harder and study smarter.

The GMAT Tests IQ

Nope. The GMAT supposedly tests your ability to do well in graduate business school. Some cynics say that all the GMAT tests is your ability to take the GMAT. Getting into a debate over that point is rather futile because you're stuck with taking the GMAT, and worrying about it just wastes brain power you can use for other things. But be reassured that the GMAT is not an IQ test. You can learn to improve your GMAT score with all sorts of tricks, traps, and techniques; that's *much* harder to do on IQ tests.

 Have you ever heard of Mensa, the national high IQ society? Although the GMAT is not a measure of IQ *per se,* if you do well on the GMAT, you can sometimes get automatic membership in Mensa (something that looks great on resumes and impresses the socks off dates' parents). Call the local Mensa chapter to find out what the qualifying score is. Hey, you put the effort into getting the score; scarf up all the benefits from the score that you can get.

You Must Pass Certain Classes to Take the GMAT

Although taking classes such as advanced logic or linguistics is useful, let's get real here: Not many people take those courses today. If you are reading this book as a freshman or sophomore and have the option of taking logic classes, excellent. Doing so will help you with the Critical Reasoning portion of the GMAT. But you certainly don't *have* to have a class like that to do well on the GMAT. (That's a relief; who has room for that class in an already over-crowded curriculum?) As far as math goes, the GMAT tests basic algebra, geometry, and arithmetic. A year of algebra and a year of geometry are sufficient. In short, there are no "required courses" or "prerequisites" for the GMAT.

Your Score Won't Improve If You Keep Retaking the GMAT

Although having your score jump hundreds of points is uncommon, it has happened. Your score's improvement depends on the reason your score was low in the first place and on how much you study before retaking the exam. If your score was low because you didn't understand the format of the exam (for example, you looked at a Data Sufficiency question and wondered where the answer choices were!), you can certainly improve that score by taking a few practice exams and becoming more comfortable with the question styles. If your score was low because you fell for all the traps set in the GMAT, you can improve your score by going through this book, learning to recognize those traps, and studying the tips and tricks for avoiding those traps. But it is unrealistic for a slow reader to think that a few weeks of study is going to double her reading speed, or for someone who doesn't understand algebra at all to think she can get a year's worth of algebra instruction in an afternoon. You do need *some* basics under your belt.

The study time you put into preparing for the second exam is also important. If you take the exam, get back your scores, register for another exam, and then just a few days before the second exam begin studying again, you may as well forget it. Although experience helps, your score won't soar simply because you've done this before. You have to study for the second test, or you'll repeat the mistakes of the first.

The GMAT Has a Passing Score

You can't pass or fail the GMAT, but a particular graduate school may have a cutoff score that you must get to be considered for admission. This score is often based on your GPA. A school may decree, for example, that if your GPA is in the 3.0 to 3.5 range, you can get a total score of 550, but if your GPA is in the 2.5 to 3.0 range, your GMAT must be at least a 600. You will want to find out the GMAT ranges considered acceptable by the schools in which you are interested.

You Can Take the GMAT on Your Own Computer at Home

Oh sure, suuuuuuuuure. You can take the test at home, with your computer, your dictionary, your grammar reference books, and your cousin Morty the Math Genius all standing by, ready to help you! And while we're at it, I'll be glad to come by and stand at your shoulder, pointing out all the traps as well. Sorry. You cannot take the GMAT anywhere but at a recognized testing center, usually a Sylvan Learning Center (see discussion in Chapter 1 about testing sites).

You Can Bring Your Own Laptop to the Testing Center

Wouldn't taking your laptop be nice? You could load all sorts of programs into your computer, such as a spell-checker (not available during the GMAT), or math formulas and algorithms, and taking the GMAT would be a snap. Unfortunately, the GMAT people are way ahead of you on this one. Not only do you have to take the exam at a special testing center, but you also have to take it on their computers. The only thing you supply is the brainpower.

Missing the First Few Questions Gives You an Easier Test and Better Score

Right and wrong. The first five questions do indeed determine the difficulty level of the whole exam. For all practical purposes, you start off with a score of 500, right in the middle of the score range (your score can go from 200 to 800). If you get the first question right, you get about +100 and have a 600-level exam going. If you miss the first question, you get about −100 and have a 400-level exam going. The second question is worth about 70 points. If you get it right and you got the first question right, the computer thinks you're smart enough to be working at a 670+ level, and you get a nice hard test. If you miss the second question and you missed the first question, you're working down in the 300s. You'll get an easy test, but you have almost no way to bring your score back up into the 600s. The moral of the story is: The first few questions are that "first impression" the computer gets about you. You never have a second chance to make a first impression.

Computer Geniuses Have an Unfair Advantage on the GMAT

Computer geniuses have an unfair advantage over all of the rest of us in this age of high-tech; why should the GMAT be any different? Let's get real here: Sure, students who are very comfortable with a computer may have a little advantage because they have one less stress factor going into the test, but that's where the advantage ends. The computer skills required for taking the GMAT CAT are so minimal that they're almost irrelevant. Hey, if it makes you feel any better, computer geniuses tell me they feel at a disadvantage on the CAT because of the "annoyingly simplistic technology."

Chapter 24

Ten Dumb Things You Can Do to Mess Up Your GMAT

● ●

In This Chapter

▶ Losing concentration

▶ Panicking over time

▶ Cheating

▶ Worrying about the previous sections

▶ Worrying about the hard problems

▶ Rushing through the Confirm step

▶ Stressing out over your computer skills (or lack thereof)

▶ Trying to keep track of the question breakdown

▶ Ignoring the five-minute breaks offered

▶ Scheduling the test at the same time as your best friend

● ●

Throughout this book you've learned techniques for doing your best on the GMAT. I'm sorry to say, however, that there are just as many techniques for messing up big time on this test. Take a few minutes to read through them now, to see what dumb things people do to blow the exam totally. By being aware of these catastrophes, you may prevent their happening to you.

And no — no Booby Prize is awarded to the student who makes the greatest number of these mistakes.

Losing Concentration

When you're in the middle of an excruciatingly boring Reading Comprehension passage, the worst thing you can do is let your mind drift off to a more pleasant time (last night's date, last weekend's soccer game, or the time you stole your rival school's mascot and set it on the john in the dean's private bathroom). Although visualization (picturing yourself doing something relaxing or fun) is a good stress-reduction technique, it stinks when it comes to helping your GMAT score. Even if you have to pinch yourself to keep from falling asleep or flaking out, stay focused. The GMAT is just a few hours of your life. You've probably had horrible blind dates that lasted longer than that, and you managed to survive them. This, too, shall pass.

Panicking over Time

You know going into the test exactly how much time you have per section. The verbal exam is 75 minutes; the math exam is 75 minutes; the analytical writing assessment — the essay portion of the test — is 1 hour (30 minutes per essay). (This breakdown is covered in much more detail in Chapter 1.) It's not as if timing is some big mystery. You even have a clock that you can keep on-screen to remind you of Time's winged passage; you do have the option of turning the clock off for most of the test, if you'd like.

Cheating

Dumb, dumb, *dumb!* Cheating on the GMAT is a loser's game — it's just plain stupid. Apart from the legal, moral, and ethical questions, let's talk practicality: You can't predict what types of grammatical mistakes will show up in the questions; what are you going to do, copy an entire textbook on the palm of your hand? All the math formulas you need can't fit onto the bottom of your shoe. Copying everything that you *think* you may need would take more time than just learning it. Besides, the GMAT tries very hard to test critical reasoning skills, not just rote memorization. The test never asks a question as straightforward as, "How many degrees in a triangle?" The questions require thinking and reasoning, not just copying down a formula. Short of having a brain transplant, cheating is impractical.

Worrying about the Previous Sections

Think of the GMAT as four separate lifetimes. You are reborn three times and so get three more chances to "do it right." Every time the computer prompts you to go to a new section, you get a fresh start. You have two 30-minute essays, one 75-minute verbal section, and one 75-minute math section. (I discuss the breakdown in much more detail in Chapter 1.) The computer is inexorable. You cannot go back to a previous section if you suddenly recall a grammar rule that eluded you. You can't tweak your essay if your mind comes up with a brilliant insight while you're doing your math questions. (And what are you doing thinking about your essay when your mind should be on nonagons, anyway? Pay attention.) Forget one section as soon as you enter the next. Think of this as you would a new boyfriend or girlfriend in your life: out with the old, in with the new.

Worrying about the Hard Problems

The GMAT contains some incredibly hard problems. If you got the first few questions on the exam correct, the computer assumes that you're a genius and confidently offers you real mind-bogglers later on. If you miss the first few questions, the computer takes it easy on you and gives you a kinder, gentler exam (and, alas, a lower, wimpier score). Suppose that you ace the first few questions and then get some super-hard questions. Of course, you have to answer them, because the computer doesn't let you go on until you punch in an answer. But if the question is just way, way beyond you, make a quick guess (emphasis on quick!), go on, and don't fret. A ridiculously few students get total 800s every year. If you get into the 700s or even the 600s, you are in a super-elite club of only a few of the thousands and thousands of students who take the GMAT annually. Just accept the fact that you can't be sure of your answer on some of the questions and learn to live with your imperfections.

Rushing through the Confirm Step

When you answer a question, the computer gives you a second chance. Your screen offers you a Confirm button, which you have to click on before your answer becomes permanent. Life has so few second chances; take advantage of this one. Sure, you may feel rushed, everyone does, but take those few extra seconds. Keep reminding yourself that the CAT is not like a paper-and-pencil test in which you can come back at the end and double-check for careless mistakes. You make a choice, confirm that choice, and that's all she wrote. Take the few extra seconds before clicking on Confirm.

Stressing Out over Your Computer Skills (or Lack Thereof)

The GMAT in and of itself is stressful enough. The last thing you need to do is add more anxiety to the whole nerve-racking experience of taking the test by worrying about your computer expertise. Can you type, even a little bit, even in a one-finger style? If so, you have mastered all the computer skills the CAT requires of you. Before you begin taking the test, you complete a very brief tutorial (no, the time spent on that does not count as actual testing time) that refreshes your computer abilities, and you have the Help key available to you at all times during the actual test.

Trying to Keep Track of the Question Breakdown

Keeping track of your own (mental, emotional, and psychological) breakdown is a good idea. Keeping track of the question breakdown is not. By "the question breakdown," I mean the number of each type of question. You know that in the verbal portion, for example, you have questions in three formats: Sentence Correction, Critical Reasoning, and Reading Comprehension. These questions can be in any order, and the GMAT gives no guarantees that you will have exactly the same number of each. In other words, don't say to yourself, "Well, I've finished three Sentence Correction questions; I know it's time for a Critical Reasoning." The computer makes those decisions, not you. Worrying about which type of question comes next is the high-tech equivalent of flipping forward to see how many pages you have left to read of a novel. All you do is waste your time; you don't shorten the number of pages.

Ignoring the Five-Minute Breaks Offered

The CAT begins with two 30-minute increments for the Analytical Writing. Then you have an optional 5-minute rest break. Next comes the 75-minute Quantitative (math) section. A second optional 5-minute rest break is offered. Then finally you have the 75-minute Verbal section. If you don't take those rest breaks between the sections, you'll be sitting still for 210 minutes. I see students often pass on the breaks, especially the first one, wanting to get this whole ordeal over with as soon as possible. Although I sympathize with the desire, I strongly, strongly suggest that you take all the rest breaks that are offered. Even just standing up, swinging your arms, and grumbling a little bit will make you feel better.

Scheduling the Test at the Same Time as Your Best Friend

Depending on the size and availability of the test center, you and your buddy may be able to take the test at the same time. Big mistake. It's only human to try to compare your progress with your friend's. Unfortunately, you and your friend will not be getting the exact same exam. Your questions will be different. If you see your buddy zooming through the material, a big smile on her face, you may depress yourself unnecessarily. (Maybe she missed the first few questions and now is getting a much easier exam than yours. You never know.) The GMAT CAT is one place where the buddy system just doesn't work.

Chapter 25

Ten Relaxation Techniques You Can Try Before and During the GMAT

● ●

In This Chapter
▶ Breathe deeply
▶ Rotate your head
▶ Hunch and roll your shoulders
▶ Cross and roll your eyes
▶ Shake out your hands
▶ Extend and push out your legs
▶ Cup your eyes
▶ Rotate your scalp
▶ Curtail negative thoughts
▶ Before the test or during the break, visualize

● ●

Question: What sits at the bottom of the sea and shivers?

Answer: A nervous wreck!

*I*f you're too hyper and anxious to laugh at my lame jokes, you *really* need this section. Most people are tense before the test, with butterflies dancing in their stomachs. The key is to use relaxation techniques that keep your mind on your test and not on your tummy.

Breathe Deeply

Breathing is grossly underrated. Breathing is good. Take a deep breath until your belly expands, hold your breath for a few counts, and then expel the air through your nose. Don't take short, shallow breaths; they could cause you to become even more anxious, because they deprive your body of oxygen.

Rotate Your Head

Try to see behind your head. Move your head as far as possible to the right until you feel a tug on the skin on the left side of your neck. Then reverse it and move your head all the way to the left until you feel a tug on the skin on the right. Move your head back, as if you're looking at the ceiling, and then down, as if looking at your feet. It may surprise you how much tension drains out of you as you do this a few times.

Hunch and Roll Your Shoulders

While breathing in, scrunch up your shoulders as if you're trying to touch them to your ears. Then roll your shoulders back and down, breathing out. Arch your back, sitting up super-straight, as if a string is attached to the top of your head and is being pulled towards the ceiling. Then slump and round out your lower back, pushing it out toward the back of your chair. These exercises relax your upper and lower back. They are especially useful if you develop a kink in your spine.

Cross and Roll Your Eyes

Look down at your desk as you're doing this so that people won't think you're even stranger than you already know you are. Cross your eyes and then look down as far as you can into your lower eyelids. Look to the right and then up into your eyelids and then look to the left. After you repeat this sequence a few times, your eyes should be refreshed.

Shake Out Your Hands

You probably do this automatically to try to uncramp your fingers that have been flying over the keyboard during your Analytical Writing Assessment or curved over the keyboard during the questions, ready to strike a key as inspiration strikes you. Do it more consciously and more frequently. Put your hands down at your sides, let them hang below your chair seat, shake them vigorously, and imagine all the tension and stress going out through your fingers and dropping onto the floor.

Extend and Push Out Your Legs

While you're sitting at your desk, straighten your legs out in front of you; think of pushing something away with your heels. Point the toes back towards your knees. You feel a stretch on the backs of your legs. Hold for a count of three and then relax.

Cup Your Eyes

Cup your hands, fingers together. Put them over your closed eyes, blocking out all the light. You're now in a world of velvety-smooth darkness, which is very soothing. Try not to let your hands actually touch your eyes. (If you see stars or flashes of light, your hands are pushing down on your eyes.)

Rotate Your Scalp

Put your open hand palm-down on your scalp. Move your hand in small circles. You feel your scalp rotate. Lift your hand and put it down somewhere else on your scalp. Repeat the circular motions. You're giving yourself a very relaxing scalp massage.

Curtail Negative Thoughts

Any time you feel yourself either starting to panic or thinking negative thoughts, make a conscious effort to say to yourself, *"Stop!"* Don't dwell on anything negative; switch over to a positive track. Suppose that you catch yourself thinking, "Why didn't I study this math more? I saw that formula a hundred times but can't remember it now!" Change the script to, "I got most of this math right; if I let my subconscious work on that formula, maybe I'll get it, too. There's no sense in worrying now. Overall, I think I'm doing great."

Before the Test or During a Break, Visualize

Don't visualize *during* the test; you just waste time and lose concentration. Before the exam, or at the break, however, practice visualization. Close your eyes and imagine yourself in the exam room, seeing questions that you know the answers to, cheerfully punching the keys on your keyboard, happily finishing early and giving the time clock on your screen a raspberry. Picture yourself getting your immediate score back from the computer, jumping around in celebration, and then rushing out of the room to go tell your friends. Think of how proud your parents will be of you. Imagine the acceptance letter you get from the graduate school of your dreams. Picture yourself driving a fire-engine red Ferrari ten years from now, telling the *Time* magazine reporter in the passenger seat that your success started with your excellent GMAT scores. The goal is to associate the GMAT with good thoughts.

Chapter 26

Ten Questions You've Got a Real Shot At

- -

In This Chapter

▶ Sentence Correction questions

▶ Reading Comprehension's main idea or best title questions

▶ Reading Comprehension's attitude or tone questions

▶ Exponents questions

▶ Symbolism problems

▶ Formula problems

▶ Problems with drawn figures

▶ Data Sufficiency questions

▶ Linear algebra problems

▶ Critical Reasoning weakening questions

- -

*I*f you saw a $10 bill just lying on the sidewalk, you'd bend over and pick it up, right? Some GMAT questions put 10 points in your pocket as easily as you'd stuff in that 10 bucks. Your job is to keep your eyes open and recognize an opportunity when you see it. (***Remember:*** You can't skip any questions on the CAT because the computer demands a response before it allows you to go on to the next question. However, you can make quick, wild guesses on the "impossible" questions and thus free up more time to think carefully about these "sure shot" topics.)

Sentence Correction Questions

I've said repeatedly that I think the Sentence Correction questions are the best place to pile up points for your verbal score. After you've memorized the basic grammar rules, you can find the errors in the sentences relatively quickly and painlessly. Of course, *some* of the questions will seem impossible; that's a given. But for the most part, this is the only type of question on the whole GMAT that you have the best chance of getting right "by ear." If an answer sounds right, it probably is. You can trust your senses here, as not as many traps are built into this type of question as into the other portions of the GMAT.

Reading Comprehension's Main Idea or Best Title Question

In Chapter 5, you learned how to answer a main idea or best title question (usually by looking at the first paragraph of the passage). You also learned that this is one of the easier types of questions to get correct. Even if you are so flustered by an impossible reading passage that you have decided just to make random guesses at most of the questions, at least make an effort with this question.

Reading Comprehension's Attitude or Tone Questions

In Chapter 5, you learned that the attitude or tone of a reading passage is usually either positive or neutral, not negative. Knowing this tip usually enables you to eliminate a few answers and at least make a good guess.

Exponents Questions

Most questions featuring exponents ask you to add, subtract, multiply, or divide numbers to various powers. You learned how to do these operations in the math review section on exponents. After you master these four basic operations, working with exponents is simple.

Symbolism Questions

Symbolism questions in math look intimidating and demanding, but they are very easy after you learn the tricks described in the math review. These questions also take little work or time, especially any questions that merely require you to substitute numbers for symbols.

Formula Problems

Many geometry problems simply require you to write down a formula on your scratch paper and plug in the numbers, such as finding the interior angles of a figure or the total surface area of a figure (see Chapter 11 for the geometry portion of the math review).

Problems with Drawn Figures

Although occasionally you may get a complicated figure that looks like a wiring diagram with lines running every which way, in general, geometry problems with figures are pretty straightforward. Some of my students tell me the figures on the CAT are even easier than the figures in the paper and pencil exam, given the constraints of the format.

Data Sufficiency Questions

You can usually narrow your answer choices down to either A or D (statement one alone is sufficient or either statement alone is sufficient) or to B, C, or E immediately. Because you can put the odds in your favor by reading only one statement, this style of question gives you the best odds of any on the entire GMAT. If you're running short of time toward the end of the section and you get a DS question down to two choices, you may decide to make a random guess just to free up time to get on to another question.

Linear Algebra Problems

A linear algebraic equation such as $\frac{1}{5}x - 13 = \frac{5}{3}x - 10$ is a gift for you — something that you can do in just a few seconds.

Of course, don't get cocky. Because the problem is so easy to do, the test makers are sure to include answer choices that you could get by making careless mistakes. If you move a number from one side of the equal sign to the other and forget to change its sign (making a positive into a negative or vice versa), the resulting answer is almost certainly one of the answer choices. Easy questions should be carefully double-checked for stupid or careless mistakes.

Critical Reasoning Weakening Questions

This question is a "gimme" because you have so many ways to get it correct. To find a statement that weakens an argument, you can destroy its premise, show an incorrect cause and effect, overgeneralize, argue in a circle, or cite inappropriate authority. Sorry, "This argument is just plain lame" will not be one of the answer choices . . . although I have often thought it should be.

Chapter 27

Ten Points You Should Always Double-Check

My father's favorite thing to say to me before I take a test is, "Always double-check! If your mother and I had double-checked before we left the hospital with you, we might have brought home a *normal* child."

Mental and emotional child abuse aside, Dad has a point. Double-checking is integral to getting what you want. The test makers know what types of careless mistakes students make and build those mistakes into the exam. The following are some areas where people get sloppy.

Exponents

Make sure that as you multiply like bases, you also add the exponents ($x^5 \cdot x^5 = x^{10}$) and that as you divide like bases, you also subtract exponents ($x^9 \div x^3 = x^6$). Forgetting this and just multiplying ($x^5 \cdot x^5 = x^{25}$) or dividing ($x^9 \div x^3 = x^3$) instead of adding or subtracting is all too easy to do.

All Answer Choices for Critical Reasoning Questions

Critical Reasoning questions have answers that are not so much right or wrong as good, better, or best. All five answer choices can seem to make sense. If you are going to answer a Critical Reasoning question, be prepared to invest a little time. Go through *every* answer choice. Sometimes all of them seem right; your job is to choose the *best* one.

Commonsense Connections

Think about what a math question is asking. If you are asked to find the weight of a (human) baby and your answer is 400 pounds, something went haywire somewhere. If McCaela is bicycling and you deduce that she bikes at a rate of 220 mph, sign that woman up for the Olympics!

Decimal Places

If a question has two or more answers with the same digits, you know that the decimal point is being tested. If the choices are .05, .5, 5, 50, and 500, double-check that your decimal point is in the right place.

Political Correctness

The Reading Comprehension portion of the GMAT contains very few correct negative answers. If a passage talks about people, especially those in a minority group, it never says nasty things about them. The entire GMAT is sweetness and light; if your answer is petty and mean-spirited, it is probably wrong.

Subject-Verb Agreement

The most common mistake in many GMAT grammar sections is subject-verb agreement. If you think that the sentence is correct, double-check that the subject and verb agree in number and tense. If you are absolutely sure that something is wrong with the sentence but you can't quite identify what, guess that the error lies in the subject-verb agreement.

Pronoun Agreement

A pronoun should be like a red flag to you. As soon as you see any pronoun in a sentence, check that it has a clear antecedent (the word it is replacing). Check also that it agrees with the antecedent in number (singular or plural) and gender (feminine or masculine).

Diction Errors

Diction errors are mistakes in two words that are commonly confused, such as *lie* and *lay*. Know what these words are (you have a list of them in Chapter 2) and keep an eye open for them.

Don't outsmart yourself by immediately assuming that one of these diction traps is automatically wrong. A word may be one that's commonly confused, yet used correctly in this particular instance.

Sentence Structure

If you chose an alternate answer (any answer other than choice A, which means that the original sentence is fine as it is), reread the entire sentence with the new answer choice inserted. If the new sentence doesn't make sense or doesn't seem to flow logically, you were *this close* to falling for a trap. Check also that you haven't corrected one mistake (such as changing *lie* to *lay,* for example) only to introduce a new one (changing *who* to *whom,* for example).

Choice C in Data Sufficiency Questions

In Data Sufficiency questions, choice C means that you *must* have both statement one and statement two to answer the question. Many times one of the statements provides additional information that is nice to know but is not essential to solving the problem. Choosing choice C when both pieces are not absolutely *mandatory* is the most common Data Sufficiency error I have seen students make throughout the years that I have been tutoring.

Chapter 28

Ten Math Concepts You Absolutely Must Know

If you got the news that the world would end in two hours, what would you do? Order a pizza? Go surfing or play hoops with your friends?

Life has its priorities. If you were told your GMAT math study time was to end in two hours, what would be your priorities? Here are my suggestions (although pizza doesn't sound half bad).

Everything mentioned in this chapter is covered in the math review in Part V. If you can't do quickly (with a minimum of brain cramps) what each portion here tells you to do, go back to reread the appropriate section of the math review.

Ratios

The total possible is a multiple of the sum of the numbers in the ratio. A ratio is written as OF/TO or OF:TO.

Common Pythagorean Ratios

In a right triangle, sides may be in the following ratios:

3:4:5 $s{:}s{:}s\sqrt{2}$ $\left(\text{or } \frac{s}{\sqrt{2}}{:}\frac{s}{\sqrt{2}}{:}s\right)$

5:12:13 $s{:}s\sqrt{3}{:}2s$

7:24:25

FOIL Method of Algebra

To multiply algebraic expressions, use FOIL: *First - Outer - Inner - Last*. To reduce algebraic equations, use FOIL backwards.

Linear Algebraic Equations

Isolate the variable; get the variables on one side of the equal sign and the nonvariables on the other side (remembering to change from a positive to a negative or vice versa when crossing over the equal sign). Add like terms. Divide both sides by what is next to the variable.

Symbolism

The GMAT tests two basic types of symbolism: Plugging the numbers into the expression, and talking through the symbolism explanation in English.

Exponents

Know how to add, subtract, multiply, and divide like bases. Remember that a number to the zero power equals one and that a number to a negative power is the *reciprocal* (upside-down version) of that number.

Square Roots

Know how to multiply and divide like radicals and how to simplify radicals.

Plotting Points on a Graph

Know how to find a point on a graph given its (x,y) coordinates. Remember that the point of origin is (0,0) and that points along a line with the same (x,y) coordinates form a 45-degree angle.

Angles

Understand the various types of angles, especially how to identify exterior angles and how to solve for the sum of interior angles of any polygon.

Circles

Be able to find circumference, area, sectors, and arcs of circles, and degree measures of central and inscribed angles.

Index

• Q •

Notes

Notes

Notes

Notes

Notes

Notes

IDG BOOKS WORLDWIDE BOOK REGISTRATION

Register This Book and Win!

We want to hear from you!

Visit **http://my2cents.dummies.com** to register this book and tell us how you liked it!

✔ Get entered in our monthly prize giveaway.

✔ Give us feedback about this book — tell us what you like best, what you like least, or maybe what you'd like to ask the author and us to change!

✔ Let us know any other *For Dummies*® topics that interest you.

Your feedback helps us determine what books to publish, tells us what coverage to add as we revise our books, and lets us know whether we're meeting your needs as a *For Dummies* reader. You're our most valuable resource, and what you have to say is important to us!

Not on the Web yet? It's easy to get started with *Dummies 101*®: *The Internet For Windows*® *98* or *The Internet For Dummies*® at local retailers everywhere.

Or let us know what you think by sending us a letter at the following address:

For Dummies Book Registration
Dummies Press
10475 Crosspoint Blvd.
Indianapolis, IN 46256

™

...FOR DUMMIES

BESTSELLING
BOOK SERIES